African-American Workers in the Stockyards Area, 1904. (Chicago *Daily News*, Chicago Historical Society, IChi-24548)

SEEING WITH THEIR HEARTS

CHICAGO WOMEN AND
THE VISION OF THE GOOD CITY,
1871–1933

Maureen A. Flanagan

PRINCETON UNIVERSITY PRESS   PRINCETON AND OXFORD

Copyright © 2002 by Princeton University Press
Published by Princeton University Press, 41 William Street,
Princeton, New Jersey 08540
In the United Kingdom: Princeton University Press,
3 Market Place, Woodstock, Oxfordshire OX20 1SY
All Rights Reserved

Library of Congress Cataloging-in-Publication Data

Flanagan, Maureen A., 1948–
Seeing with their hearts : Chicago women and the vision of the good
city, 1871–1933 / Maureen A. Flanagan.
p. cm.
Includes bibliographical references (p.) and index.

ISBN 0-691-09539-6 (alk. paper)

1. Women—Illinois—Chicago—History. 2. Women civic leaders—
Illinois—Chicago—History. 3. Women in politics—Illinois—
Chicago—History. 4. Women social reformers—Illinois—Chicago—
History. 5. Chicago (Ill.)—History. I. Title.

HQ1439.C47 F53 2002

305.4'09773'11—dc21   2001058005

This book has been composed in Galliard

Printed on acid-free paper.∞

www.pupress.princeton.edu

Printed in the United States of America

10 9 8 7 6 5 4 3 2 1

For Jonah and The Flanagans

Contents

Figures

Acronyms

ASC	Alpha Suffrage Club
CCSA	Cook County Suffrage Association
CESA	Chicago Equal Suffrage Association
CFCWC	Chicago Federation of Colored Women's Clubs
CFL	Chicago Federation of Labor
CLU	Central Labor Union
CPEL	Chicago Political Equality League
CTF	Chicago Teachers' Federation
CWA	Chicago Woman's Aid
CWC	Chicago Woman's Club
CWTUL	Chicago Women's Trade Union League
IESA	Illinois Equal Suffrage Association
IFCWC	Illinois Federation of Colored Women's Clubs
IFRCWC	Illinois Federation of Republican Colored Women's Clubs
IFWC	Illinois Federation of Women's Clubs
ILWV / LWV	Illinois League of Women Voters/League of Women Voters
IPL	Immigrants' Protective League
IWA	Illinois Women's Alliance
IWDC	Illinois Women's Democratic Club (sometimes called League)
IWRL	Illinois Women's Republican League (sometimes called Club)
JPA	Juvenile Protective Agency
LFLU	Ladies' Federal Labor Union
MOL	Municipal Order League
PAWC	Protective Agency for Women and Children
WCC	Woman's City Club
WESL	Wage-Earners' Suffrage League
WRRC	Woman's Roosevelt Republican Club

Acknowledgments

THIS book had its genesis years ago in my dissertation research when I was investigating an urban political reform movement, the campaign to secure a new municipal charter for Chicago. At that time, I found in Jane Addams's *Twenty Years at Hull House* a passing mention that the immigrant women in her neighborhood were working with an organization of about one hundred women's groups to secure women's municipal suffrage in a new charter. This fact caught my attention. Current work on the politics of the early twentieth-century U.S. cities generally did not investigate women's participation in such municipal reform movements. And so women entered my dissertation. But the relatively small contribution that my dissertation and subsequent book made to increasing Chicago women's visibility in history by uncovering their participation in the charter campaign made me determined to find out more about women's relationship to their city in the crucial decades surrounding the turn of the last century. Years later, *Seeing with Their Hearts* is the result.

Across those years, my research and writing were aided immeasurably by colleagues and friends who helped me refine my ideas, think about the broad ramifications of my work, and keep my spirits from flagging as I struggled to break through the artificial boundaries erected between urban history and women's history. Harold Platt and Ann Durkin Keating read every chapter. Kristi Andersen, Robert Johnston, Robyn Muncy, and Maryann Gialanella Valiulis read parts of the manuscript, as did Erik Monkkonen, who may not even remember the comments he gave me on my first efforts to start writing this book several years ago. Suellen Hoy's careful reading of my introduction gave it much needed focus. She also suggested the title of the book; for which I thank her enormously. Suellen, Walter Nugent, and Harold Platt made a crucial connection for me. Innumerable conversations over the years with Jan Reiff have sharpened my understanding of Chicago history. My colleagues in U.S. history at Michigan State University—Tom Summerhill, Susan Sleeper-Smith, and Sayuri Shimizu—and graduate students Mike Czaplicki, Dan Lerner, Karen Madden, Jayne Morris-Crowther, and Ted Moore, helped sustain my belief that what we do is important. Archivists Archie Motley and Ralph Pugh in the manuscript room at the Chicago Historical Society were unfailingly generous of their time and expertise in helping me to locate the often-elusive evidence of women's activities, suggesting any possible collection in which I might find anything on women. Dennis McClendon of Chicago CartoGraphics created the original maps for the book. An NEH summer travel-to-collections grant helped finance research trips to archival collections in Chicago and to the Schlesinger Library at Radcliffe. Thomas Le-Bien and Maura Roessner were wonderful to work with at Princeton University Press, as was my copyeditor Tim Sullivan. No author could ask for better, more intelligent, editors.

Thanking an inanimate object may seem strange, but the city of Rome, where I lived for two years and several summers while writing, provided a wonderful atmosphere in which to contemplate urban history, even though of a dramatically different city. In the realm of the animate, my family has both kept me rooted in reality and prodded me to aim higher. My son, Jonah, and this book grew up together. He has always supported my work and proudly bragged about it to his friends. Dedicating it to him is to tell him how proud I am of him. The Flanagans—Chicagoans bred in the bone—have supported me even when they were not entirely sure what I, their daughter and sister, was doing. This one is also for them. Last, but never least, to Chip—*grazie tante carissimo*, for Rome, for Gothic cathedrals, and for living with this book.

SEEING WITH THEIR HEARTS

Introduction

City of Big Shoulders or City of Homes?
Re-envisioning Urban History

CARL SANDBURG's famous 1916 poem "Chicago" imagines the city as a striving, laboring male. Chicago is "Stormy, husky, brawling, City of the Big Shoulders . . . a tall, bold slugger . . . under the smoke, dust all over his mouth, laughing with white teeth . . . Laughing the stormy, husky, brawling laughter of Youth." It is "Hog Butcher for the World, Tool Maker, Stacker of Wheat." Just a few years before Sandburg published his poem, a Chicago banker declared that he used to dislike the noxious odors coming from the city's stockyards, then had changed his mind: "Do you know what it means to me now? Dollars."[1] Writing eight decades after Sandburg, a historian described Chicago as the " 'world-conquering spirit of the age' . . . scene of boiling economic activity and technological ingenuity." It was the country's "most explosively alive metropolis," overflowing with opportunity, and peopled by men, some honest and some corrupt, but all of whom were building the "City of the Century." A few years after that book appeared, another historian even published a history of Chicago entitled *City of Big Shoulders: A History of Chicago*.[2] Sandburg's vision of muscular enterprise was celebrated in both popular lore and scholarly work as the real Chicago.

Chicago did have temptations and victims, Sandburg admitted, but he depicted these as female. "I have seen the painted women under the gas lamps luring the farm boys." The faces of women and children bore the "marks of wanton poverty." Working-class "women adrift" threatened proper order and stability.[3] Yet all the problems would be conquered by hard-working men, or so the poem implied. And, according to later historians, these men did just that.

In 1913 settlement house resident Anna Nicholes envisioned a different city that came "from the hearts of women." Hers was a vision of the city as "not alone a business corporation" but "as a city of homes, as a place in which to rear children." This city would "care because babies die from preventable diseases," a city that would "open to all greater industrial and social opportunities within its borders," would make the "personal welfare" of all its residents first priority.[4] The Chicago banker may have elevated dollars over clean air, but the neighborhood women who formed an Anti-Smoke League in 1908 looked around their neighborhood and saw

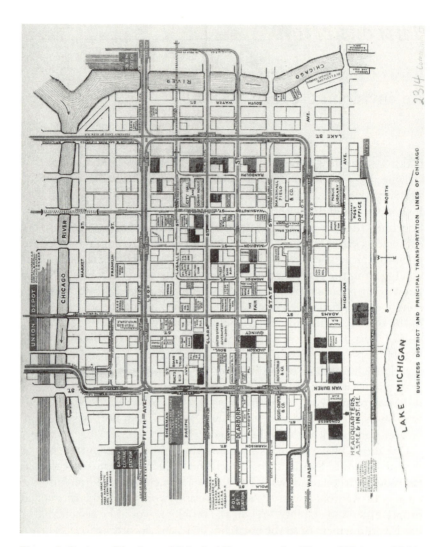

Figure 1. Business District and Principal Transportation Lines of Chicago, 1904. Showing sites of male activity: train stations, railroad lines, major department stores, banks, newspaper buildings, principal skyscrapers, and headquarters of men's clubs. (Drawn by American Society of Mechanical Engineers, Chicago Historical Society, ICHi-34342)

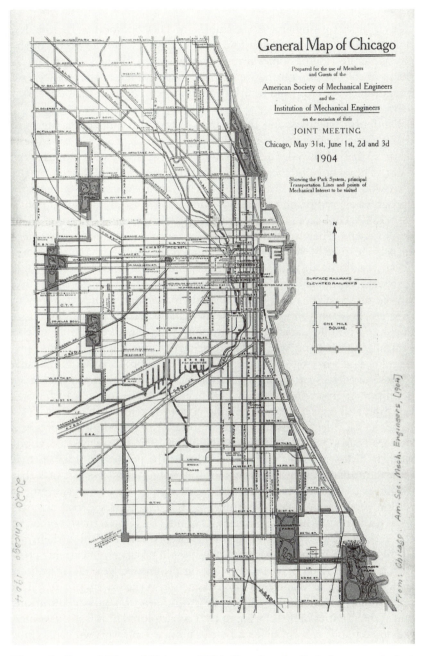

Figure 2. General Map of Chicago, 1904. Showing the Park System, principal Transportation Lines and points of Mechanical Interest. (Drawn by American Society of Mechanical Engineers, Chicago Historical Society, ICHi-34343)

clean laundry turning gray in the smoky air. They put food on their tables, only to find it covered with a fine layer of dirt.[5] Nicholes's vision of the city as a collection of homes inverted the vision embodied in Sandburg's poem of the city as a business enterprise. The women of the Anti-Smoke League declared clean and healthy homes more important than unbridled private enterprise.

Sandburg, Nicholes, and the women of the Anti-Smoke League were living through an era of municipal reform in which groups of urban residents struggled to redefine the powers and the scope of urban government. The history of these reform movements was first written by the men who participated in them, men who saw themselves as pursuing a "progressive" campaign to take government away from immigrant political bosses whom they blamed for inefficient, disorderly, and corrupt urban development. They wanted cities run by professionals and businessmen, such as themselves, whose business acumen and fiscal expertise, they believed, would produce orderly, efficient, and stable cities.[6] Because these men were so publicly visible and their writing so prolific, historians at first viewed progressive-era reform as a single movement, mainly disagreeing over precisely what motivated these men and whether to classify them as upper- or middle-class.[7] After historians John Buenker and J. Joseph Huthmacher challenged this interpretation by contending that ethnic, immigrant, and working-class men also engaged in progressive reform campaigns, historians of ethnic and labor movements developed a broader definition of urban progressivism that includes these groups.[8] Much work, however, still concentrates on middle-class male reformers.[9]

But just as Buenker insists on the importance of the ethnics for progressive-era reform, he is sure that nothing of interest can be said about women. "Most women," he asserts, "shared the political culture of their fathers, husbands, brothers, and sons." Another recent essay insists that its aim is to explore "how Dallas' developing planning and government reform movements reflect a significant shift in the way urban activists viewed their city," but one searches in vain to find any activist women in the account, even though women's historians have identified them for us.[10] Few other historians writing today would take such an extreme position as does Buenker. Yet much work on progressive-era reform still, at best, centers on men and only adds women into the existing story.[11] The exception of course is a growing body of work on women's organizations and their activities in this era. Sarah Deutsch explored how Boston women redefined public space; Gayle Gullett examined California women's clubs and the woman suffrage movement; Sandra Haarsager has written about the club movement in the Pacific northwest; Judith McArthur looked at Texas women's clubs; and Anne Meis Knupfer and Priscilla Murolo examined African American and working-girls' clubs.[12] What we don't generally see in these works, however, is how urban women and their organizations were contesting for political power in the city and seeking to reshape both the city and its government.[13]

A few other historians have opened new paths for examining women in the Progressive Era. Paula Baker saw two different reference points: "the business corporation created the model for the new liberalism [for men]" while politically active women "took the family and small community as an ideal." William Chafe pushed this observation further to theorize that the "two kinds of progressivism might coexist and in some ways even be complementary. They were, after all, both using the state to intervene. *In emphasis and values, however, they were dramatically different.*" Sara Evans locates women's voluntary organizations as "free spaces" between the public world of male politics and the private world of the home. In this space, women learned to debate public problems, but by doing so free from male interference, they brought their own experiences to bear on these problems. As a result, they formulated ideas and solutions that conflicted with prevailing male ideas about a good society.[14]

This book examines the development in Chicago of a women's vision of the city that promoted a concept of urban life and good government rooted in social justice, social welfare, and responsiveness to the everyday needs of all the city's residents. According to this vision, decisions on urban problems were to be made not on the basis of what was most profitable but for "human betterment." One group of Chicago women summed up this vision: "It is the first duty of Chicago to protect the health of its citizens."[15] Yet even to state this purpose is to pose the question: How can we speak of a "women's vision," or study women as a group, when we know that social factors of class, ethnicity, race, religion always separate women? We know that not all women always agreed on any issue. Some practitioners of gender analysis argue that we cannot study women as women because "woman" is a discourse-created category for which we can assume no shared interests, ideas, or experiences.[16] Historian Louise Tilly, on the other hand, has persuasively argued that knowing the history of women—their experiences as well as their interests and ideas—will provide a better understanding of how conceptions of gender have shaped human experience across time. And in 1994, the Organization for Economic Cooperation and Development held a conference in Paris on the subject of "Women in the City: Housing, Services and the Urban Environment." The proposal for the conference made this bold statement: "A major aim of this Conference is to accord higher visibility to women's 'vision of the city' . . . In order to take more into account their views and contributions to urban society." The conference's sessions and presentations all highlighted the idea that women have a particular *vision* of the city.[17]

Rather than attempt theoretical formulation, as a historian I have looked at the evidence to see what it reveals. I found that between 1871 and 1933, a large number of Chicago activist women made common cause in politics despite differences of class, race, and ethnicity.[18] By "activist," I mean, first, those women identified by name as active members, often leaders, of multiple women's organizations and who can be found actively pursuing a broad range of women's causes. A group of well-known club-women, whom I often characterize as "longtime activists," appears time and again in this book (see appendix A). I also extend the term to women whose efforts may have been less extensive or more anonymous, but who nonetheless do appear engaged in specific causes. These women appear to have belonged to fewer organizations, or their participation in politics was measured in years rather than decades (see appendix B). What is especially significant about the political activities of both groups of women is how they frequently took public stances that diverged from those of men of their class or race. Thus we see elite women willfully violate the dictates of the elite male Chicago Relief and Aid Society regarding aid collected after the disastrous fire of 1871, African American women support a black aldermanic challenger instead of the official white candidate preferred by African American men in 1914, and ethnic women vote differently from the male members of their communities that same year. These are just a few examples of the evidence presented here that support the existence of a female "ethic of solidarity" described by philosopher Nancy Love, which has allowed women to forge common identities even while they acknowledged their social differences.[19]

Yet it would not be enough to talk only about the most visible and identifiable women and their organizations. Thousands of Chicago women participated in the movements discussed here through their membership in a range of female organizations. They are names on a list about whom we know little more, and often not even that. But, clearly, without their work and adherence to the principles espoused by the leadership, women's mobilization and participation in Chicago's municipal affairs could not have taken place on the grand scale that it did. These are the women who circulated throughout the city in the 1890s petitions demanding the appointment of women to the board of education, and the public school teachers who took their crusade door-to-door in city neighborhoods at the turn of the century to force corporations to pay their taxes. Immigrant women of the Hull House neighborhood joined a hundred other women's organizations to oppose passage of a new municipal charter in 1907, and other immigrant women registered to vote despite their husbands' wishes. Ten thousand women showed up at an outdoor suffrage rally in the middle of winter in 1914, and five thousand women marched through the streets of downtown to support the mayoral candidacy of William Dever in 1927. The members of the Alpha Suffrage Club forced the election of the city's first African American alderman in 1915, and Catholic, Jewish, and Protestant women worked together to gain suffrage, to elect women to offices responsible for public welfare, and to make health care for mothers and children a government responsibility.

The public world that activist Chicago women confronted in the years covered by this book was growing steadily more complicated and chaotic. Industrialization, technological development, and massive immigration brought dramatic changes to the city.[20] The Hog Butcher of the World was also the site of thousands of deadly industrial and street accidents every year.[21] The city was dirty and polluted and ugly. In many neighborhoods the streets were unpaved, unlit, and reeking of uncollected garbage. There were far too few public schools. Tens of thousands of Chicago's residents had little access to decent housing, indoor plumbing, clean water, or fresh air. Infant mortality was high; tuberculosis and typhoid outbreaks were all too common.[22] These conditions existed because the municipal government's provision and regulation of municipal services was still limited at the end of the nineteenth century. Many Chicago men opposed the expansion of government power because if government provided such services, property taxes would surely increase. But they also opposed expanded government provision of public services because they favored giving private business the opportunity to make money from such services.[23]

Along with such lack of municipal services, periodic economic downturns, an oversupply of cheap labor that kept wages low and unemployment a constant threat, and a virtually unregulated and unprotected workplace produced severe and often violent labor strikes. Socialist and anarchist movements suggested the imminent arrival of class warfare. By the 1890s, Chicagoans viewed their city with a mixture of awe for its progress, trepidation for its future, and disgust for the inhumane living and working conditions suffered by too many of their fellow citizens. The tool-making and wheat-stacking city was, for Jane Addams when she founded the Hull House Settlement in 1889, a city as much characterized by the wanton hunger of children as by brawny male enterprise. It was a city, she wrote a decade later, where the "well-to-do men of the community . . . are almost wholly occupied in the correction of political machinery and with a concern for the better method of administration, rather than with the ultimate purpose of securing the welfare of the people."[24] By the time Addams wrote these words, many Chicagoans could no longer disregard the threats to health and safety in their city. To remedy the problems, however, they had not only to consider which remedies to adopt for specific problems, but also to rethink ideas about the scope and purposes of municipal government. As a result, much progressive reform was a struggle over who would control the city, what powers government would have, and what ends it would seek to achieve.[25]

As Chicago matured into a major metropolis, thousands of Chicago women turned their attention from the private world of the home to the public world of the state, and, as this book details, they saw this public world differently than did many men. Truly, as Sarah Deutsch shows so well in her recent book, a significant change took place in cities in this era as women not only moved into the public sphere but also sought to rearrange the appropriate meanings, uses, and inhabitants of public spaces. Daphne Spain elegantly argues in her recent book that women's organizations at the turn of the last century founded "redemptive spaces" in the city, within which they attempted both "to balance the city's exaggerated emphasis on growth and profits" and "to save the city from the tremendous strains resulting from shifting population dynamics." Both books significantly contribute to bringing women more fully into the history of cities, but this public world comprised more than public spaces or redemptive spaces, and Chicago women's vision of the city encompassed more than these spaces.[26] As an urban historian, my attention focuses on how activist Chicago women sought to rearrange the institutions of municipal power in the city, not just its spaces, to create a city that worked for all of its residents. One example here illustrates both the difference between men's and women's visions of the city, and in perceiving women's activities as attempts to refashion the institutions of power more than rearrange the city's spaces. In the 1880s, men tried to bar the women of the Protective Agency for Women and Children from appearing in court, by arguing that it was not a place for respectable women. When the women defied this ban, they did of course open this public space for women, but their purpose was far broader: they appeared in court because they wanted to eliminate court practices that discriminated against women being charged with prostitution, to help women obtain divorces, and to stop the appointment of incompetent judges.[27] Men were accustomed to uncontested power over women in court; when they objected to women's presence, they were fighting to maintain male power to order and dispense justice.

This book examines the development across six decades of Chicago activist women's vision for urban development and how and why they developed a vision of the city different from that of most activist Chicago men. To understand both how Chicago women were part of this struggle as well as their actions and ideas, we must situate them inside their city and see their development across several decades. To capture the ways activist Chicago women developed their ideas and actions in stages that related to events within the city itself, the book is divided into three chronological parts. Part 1 considers the development of women's voluntary organizations beginning with the fire relief groups of 1871, when Chicago women for the first time publicly challenged the prerogatives of the men of their own social standing (including their husbands) to reorganize Chicago as they saw fit. Desiring to bring relief to more people than the men intended, the women came to realize that because they lacked a public voice and public power, men could easily thwart their plans. As the numbers of activist women and their clubs multiplied through the 1880s, these women increasingly demanded that municipal government solve the city's problems and that women be given official, direct participation in municipal affairs. These activist women formed coalitions of their organizations—the membership of which often crossed race and class lines—to increase their visibility and power, and to learn from each other.

Part 2 examines Chicago women's activism from the late nineteenth century into the second decade of the twentieth century. During this time, the number of Chicago women's organizations grew steadily, and many of them were specifically dedicated to direct involvement in municipal affairs. The chapters in this section explore the development of progressive activism among Chicago women and how they formulated a vision of the city that brought them into direct conflict with many men. Chicago residents fiercely contested how to solve complex problems of public education, such environmental questions as beach building, garbage disposal, and air pollution, housing, charter reform, municipal ownership of public utilities, electoral reform, and the city's institutional structure, among others.[28] In this period, activist women also organized a powerful movement to gain the municipal vote as a means to help secure their desired policies. This part thus also explores the intersection of women's vision for a good city and their municipal suffrage campaign.

Part 3 examines the effect of suffrage on women's participation in public life. From late 1913, when the Illinois legislature gave women the vote in municipal and federal elections, until the early 1930s, activist women gradually shifted toward working within the established political institutions. But having developed their own ideas and urban agenda within their female organizations, activist women resisted abandoning either their organizations or their agenda by fully integrating into male organizations and the political parties. Moreover, Chicago men shut the door on women asking for an equal role in developing urban policy: the political parties refused to nominate women for municipal office, and when women did run in the party primaries, male voters generally refused to vote for them.

The book ends in 1933 as the Democratic party, which had been hostile to women's ideas for the city, virtually consolidated its hold over the city and the Republican party was moribund. Activist women thereafter could either abandon municipal politics or fit themselves into the party structures, doing what men allowed them to do.[29] Then, as the Depression deepened and the Democrats won the presidency, attention for policy decisions to relieve the impact of the economic depression on the city began decisively shifting toward Washington, D.C. As the city grew more dependent on the federal government, women were even more excluded from municipal decision-making.

The struggle over reform priorities in Chicago exposes deep gender conflicts as activist women challenged male politicians, and civic, business, and labor leaders. To appreciate these conflicts and how activist women developed their vision of the city from women's experiences, throughout this book I compare the ideas, actions, and agendas of activist Chicago women and men. Few historians have yet made such comparisons, but those who have identify gender differences toward the means and ends of reform.[30] The women examined in this book wanted an activist municipal government whose top priority was to secure a common welfare for all Chicago residents. Most Chicago men preferred a government whose first priority was to protect the economic desires of men. That all Chicago men did not have the same economic desires was, of course, another source of urban conflict. But, as this book details, most activist Chicago men rejected most of the activist women's ideas and demands for the city because they held a different vision of the city.[31]

Activist Chicago women won some battles, but they lost many more. This book, however, is not a story of failure. It is the story of a vision of what a good city ought to be and of a struggle to change the nature and purposes of Chicago's government to make it work for the general welfare of all its people. There are many reasons why these women did not achieve much of their vision, and this book explores these failures and their reasons. Yet this book also seeks to bring women squarely into the struggle to reform municipal government, to explore their ideas and interactions across social boundaries, and to uncover the alternative vision of a good city that motivated them. Understanding these elements of Chicago history changes our understanding of its development, allows us to view women as an integral part of the city's growth, and brings thousands of these women to life. Pushing the "shoulders" metaphor in a different direction, we see how Chicago women heeded Louise de Koven Bowen's call for them to become "third-class passengers" on the train of life—"women who will get out and push; who will put their shoulders to the wheel and their whole hearts into the work."[32]

Part One

CRAFTING THE VISION

One

"The Whole Work Has Been Committed to the Hands of Women": Women Respond to the Fire of 1871

ON THE evening of October 8, 1871, a wind-driven fire blazed a destructive path across Chicago, ravaging a three and a half square mile area by the time it spent itself the following evening. The city's entire commercial and governmental district had burned to the ground along with the bulk of the city's housing. The Great Chicago Fire caused almost two hundred million dollars worth of property damage and destroyed fifteen thousand buildings, leaving one hundred thousand people—one-third of the population—homeless. It was the worst fire in a major U.S. city in the country's history.[1] Providing relief for thousands of homeless, injured, and hungry city residents became the city's top priority, but the municipal government doubted that it had the authority to undertake such a massive relief effort. At that time, city governments still were generally confined to deciding on public works projects and questions of tax revenues; conducting a major relief effort was beyond anything Chicago's government had ever before done.[2] Rather than direct fire relief himself, Mayor Roswell Mason turned to the Chicago Relief and Aid Society, a private organization founded in 1857 run by a collection of Chicago's most eminent professional and business men.[3] In doing so, Mason surrendered to the Society all control of the relief monies, which would total nearly five million dollars. This money began pouring into the city from across the country and around the world even as the fire still blazed.[4]

The mayor's decision was not uncontested, and the fire of 1871 and the questions of who should and how to provide fire relief gave prominent Chicago women a totally new urban experience. It produced their first significant encounter with a massive municipal problem and connected them in ways they had never before known to the larger arena of their city and its problems. In the coming months they would organize, direct their own activities, learn to forge alliances with one another, and work more openly in public view than ever before. The fire experience would also force women to articulate the principles upon which they based their actions. In doing so, they would espouse principles of public actions that brought them into public conflict with men of their same status.

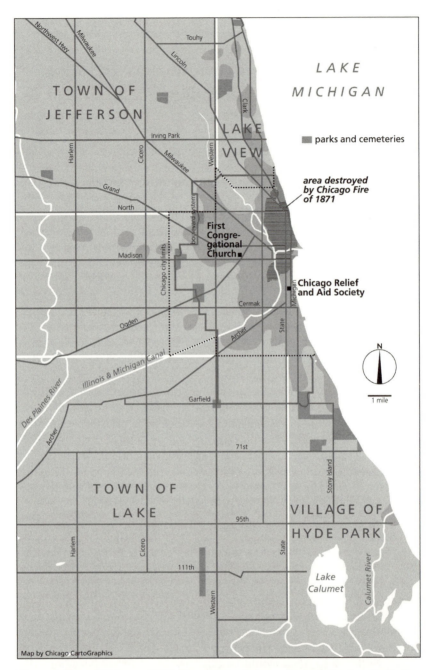

Figure 3. Map of Chicago, 1871. Showing settled area, burned district, city limits, and Chicago Relief and Aid Society Headquarters and First Congregational Church (Drawn by Dennis McClendon, Chicago CartoGraphics)

When the directors of the Relief and Aid Society had petitioned the mayor to give them the responsibility for fire relief, they were following a course traditional to nineteenth-century charitable endeavors in which private citizens, not public government, managed such affairs. But the Society's leaders had more at stake than a desire to manage charity. They believed that the fire relief effort had to be carefully directed to facilitate the rebuilding of the city in ways most useful to businessmen such as themselves, and also to keep control of the thousands of now homeless and jobless workers in the city.[5] The Society's initial actions, which placed stringent requirements on receiving relief, bear out their intentions. The day after Mayor Mason turned over the relief funds to the Society, it quickly stopped issuing "able bodied men" free railroad passes to leave the city. The rule was enforced by a Society committee, headed by railroad entrepreneur George Pullman, that routinely rejected applications from these so-called "able bodied men" and even boys, sending them instead to a Society employment committee where they would be assigned a job.[6]

The Society followed these measures with a decree that "not a single dollar [was to] be expended for persons able to provide for themselves. . . . [A]ny man, single woman, or boy, able to work, and unemployed at this time, is so from choice and not necessity." It also prepared application forms to be completed in writing and accompanied by the testimony of "well-known" citizens that the applicant was totally destitute and thus worthy to receive outdoor relief, or that the applicant had suffered a tangible loss of property that entitled him or her to shelter.[7] These principles were strictly enforced. By mid-January, the Society's shelter committee had received 9,272 requests for housing, of which it rejected 2,853. Among the surviving applications is one from a woman with an injured husband and five children, all of whom had been burned out of their previous dwelling and were now being evicted from their current dwelling by her landlord. She petitioned the Society for lumber to build a shanty—the approximate cost of which was $115. The Society rejected her application for lumber because "this family had two months rent paid [previously by the Society]—had one stove, one [unreadable], one table, four chairs, and some bedding."[8] Until it declared the relief effort closed in early 1874, the Relief and Aid Society never budged from its strict position that only those residents who could prove themselves utterly destitute, or who had lost tangible property, were qualified to receive relief.

As the men of the Relief and Aid Society went about their work, so too did many Chicago women, who, after taking care of their own families, turned to relieve suffering throughout the city. At first, women responded as individuals, providing whatever aid they could to others in need. Harriet Hubbard Ayer (who lost her own baby in the fire) recalled "sewing for the destitute" in the days immediately following the fire while her mother-in-law "was in charge of a center that provided clothes for the penniless; each day she handed out not only warm clothing but soup and milk."[9] Mrs. Hudlun, an African American woman whose house had survived the blaze, dispatched family members out into the streets to bring the homeless and injured they encountered back to her home.[10]

Other women joined the Ladies' Relief and Aid Society, organized as an auxiliary to the men's group, to help with fire relief. Four of the six officers of the Ladies' group were married to directors of the men's Society. Some women volunteered to help at Society headquarters. Katharine Medill, wife of the part-owner of the *Chicago Tribune*, the man who would be elected mayor in early November 1871, joined this group.[11] In very short time, however, Chicago women dramatically expanded their relief efforts and removed themselves from the control of the Relief and Aid Society. Two weeks after the fire, for example, Aurelia King, who was married to Society director Henry W. King, wrote privately to her friends that if they wished to make their contributions directly to the general relief fund they could of course do so, but that if they would instead send them "directly to me, I will distribute to the needy that I know personally." She told her correspondents that she had "already received money and other things from different places which I divide and apportion exactly as I see most pressing need."[12]

Katharine Medill quickly grew disenchanted with her work at the Relief and Aid Society and quit. But rather than quit relief work altogether, she readily accepted her friend Annie McClure Hitchcock's offer to solicit donations so that she could direct a relief effort out of her own home. Hitchcock wrote to a friend in Boston explaining the desperate needs of Chicago's fire victims and the way that she and Medill wanted to help. Medill, wrote Hitchcock, had tried working with the Relief and Aid Society but had chafed under the regulations that made it difficult for many people to secure any relief. Rather than continue to follow the Society's dictates, Hitchcock continued, Medill had told her [Hitchcock] that "it would be a great satisfaction to be able to supply the wants I hear of every day of people who are in every way worthy and get beyond the Aid Society's Rules." After explaining the situation, Hitchcock then asked her friend if she and other Boston women could send donations of clothing directly to her. "These general rules [of the Relief and Aid Society] are so hard to follow," she wrote. "It would be such a comfort if some Boston ladies felt like sending some boxes of clothing to be distributed in violation of all general rules."[13]

The two rules that Hitchcock and Medill proposed to violate were essential to the Society's control over the dispersal of relief. After receiving its mandate from Mayor Mason, the Society divided the city into districts and ordered that all locations supplying relief would henceforth "be subject to the control of the [Relief and Aid Society] Superintendent of the district and those in charge of the same will give out no more supplies except on his order."[14] To control further the distribution of relief, the Society also decreed that any donations sent into the city had to be distributed within the district of the city to which they were sent, and distributed only by the Society's appointed representative in that district. By setting up a distribution center in her home, Katharine Medill was violating the first decree. Annie Hitchcock not only conspired with Medill but also intended to violate the second decree. Hitchcock lived on the south side of the city, in the Hyde Park area that was not burned in the fire. According to the Society's rules, anything sent to her had to be distributed in Hyde Park. But Hitchcock wanted to distribute clothing in the desperately needy areas of the city's burned-out west side, and she had no intention of obeying the Society's rule. By contrast, those Chicago men who were engaged in relief activities seemed inclined to let the Society take over directing the work of relief. In an open letter to the Relief and Aid Society that appeared in Chicago's newpapers, Mr. C. T. Hitchcock assured the Society that his ad hoc relief group, which had been distributing relief since immediately after the fire, would comply with the Society's order and no longer distribute relief except under the Society's supervision.[15]

Medill and Hitchcock were not the only women running relief efforts in violation of the Society's orders. A number of women's groups headed by prominent Chicago women also began relief work soon after the fire. Historians have missed the significance of their work, both for the women themselves and for their place in Chicago history, because they rely too heavily on male sources to describe the relief work of women. The most important primary source for studying Chicago's fire relief—the records of the Relief and Aid Society—details an organization run by men who always regarded women as under their control. They spoke of women in this way in the reports and thereby conveyed the message that women were subservient to men in fire relief.[16] Most other primary sources—all of which were written by men—concentrate on the work of men: Newspapers heralded the activities of the Relief and Aid Society but relegated those of women to small paragraphs on inside pages; contemporary accounts of fire relief paid scant attention to women's activities; and the collections of biographies of leading men of the city—and there are many for Chicago—include little mention of their wives and none at all on these women's fire relief activities.[17] That women did not explicitly publicize their actions, rarely talked about themselves (except to one another), and formed organizations without paid staff to compile accounts of their actions, contributes to the relative paucity of primary material. When the Society's explanations are accepted at face value, and because, as a legacy of the earlier nineteenth century, many women's organizations were still headed by boards of male advisors, historians assume that the Society's organizational framework controlled women's response to relief.[18] But if instead of seeing women and their work through the eyes of men, one looks at what women's organizations actually did and how they presented themselves, their work and their activities assume quite a different character.[19]

In the manuscript collection of the United Charities of Chicago—the successor organization to the Relief and Aid Society—survive some circulars and letters that testify to the work of various women's relief groups. According to these documents, the Ladies' Christian Union, the Ladies of the First Congregational Church of Chicago (located at the corner of Washington and Ann streets), and the Ladies' Industrial Aid Society of St. John's church, for example, distributed circulars throughout the city and contacted women's organization in other cities asking for contributions of money, household utensils, crockery, and hospital supplies— specifically soliciting supplies donated directly to themselves and not the Society.[20] Even the Ladies' Relief and Aid Society, which was supposedly controlled by the male Relief and Aid Society, and the Ladies' Christian Union, which had a board of male advisors, went around the Society to get the supplies that they wanted.[21] Ten days after the fire, the Ladies' Christian Union held a public meeting for the purpose of organizing its own "system of relief for the multitudes of women and children rendered destitute" by the fire.[22] Although several of these groups were organized from churches, these women do not speak of religious motivations for their activities. While we can be certain that they were religious, so too were the men of the Relief and Aid Society, and both genders were undoubtedly influenced by their religion. Yet men's and women's differing responses to the suffering after the fire seem much more in line with Barbara Berg's observations that a developing sense of women's shared common experiences and needs drove urban women to see the problems of the city differently, especially as those problems concerned women.[23]

After the fire, Chicago women seized the opportunity presented by the need for relief to found two new organizations, the Good Samaritan Society and the Woman's Industrial Aid Society, both of which publicly rejected any control by the Relief and Aid Society, or men in general, over their actions. At its organizational meeting, the Woman's Industrial Aid Society declared itself independent of all other relief organizations. One of its vice presidents was Katharine Medill. The Good Samaritan Society said that it would cooperate with the Relief and Aid Society, but that its purpose was to "afford immediate relief to deserving women who are unable to make known their wants before the committees" of that organization. Its president in 1871–72 was Mrs. John C. Haines, the wife of a former mayor.[24] The Woman's Industrial Aid Society seems to have strictly kept its vow of independence. Available sources reveal that from November 1871 to the end of 1872 it received only $386.92 from the relief funds distributed by the Relief and Aid Society. The Good Samaritan Society accepted one disbursement from the Society of $1,000.[25] Whether these two organizations rejected money offered by the Society, or whether the Society refused to give official relief funds to them as a way of trying to thwart their relief work, is impossible to know.

Women's organizations evaded the Society's dictates in a variety of ways. They disregarded the Society's rules about who would distribute relief and where; they appealed outside the city for donations of usable goods rather than money, which was the Society's preferred method of relief contribution; and they expressed outrage at the Society's definition of worth and neediness. Their relationship to a relief group from Cincinnati is particularly enlightening. Shortly after the fire people from Cincinnati arrived in Chicago with a load of relief supplies and thousands of dollars that they had collected in their city; they used the money to set up a free soup kitchen that they continued to operate as the bleak Midwestern winter closed in on the city.[26] The longer they operated this soup kitchen, though, the more vigorously the directors of the Society fought to close it down. Wirt Dexter, chair of the Society's executive committee, claimed that the soup kitchen was unnecessary because the Society was itself distributing "abundant and satisfactory provisions" to everyone in need in the city. But when he complained that the soup kitchen doled out soup "without either visitation or record," and that such aid would produce an "evil influence" on the character and habits of those receiving it, he revealed the Society's truer motive: the soup kitchen violated the Society's control to decide who was worthy to receive relief and of what kind.[27] The Society pressured the Cincinnati people incessantly until, in the dead of winter, they closed the kitchen and returned home.[28]

The Relief and Aid Society was unrelentingly hostile toward the soup kitchen, while many women's organizations wholeheartedly supported it. Women located a room in which to house the kitchen, made their own investigation into how the kitchen was run, and reported "favorably upon it." Women also publicly rejected Dexter's claims that the soup was unnecessary and unworthily bestowed, and the Good Samaritan Society rebuked the Relief and Aid Society for implying that those receiving soup simply wanted something for nothing, contending that the "very fact that thousands come daily, many of them from long distances, for this soup, is in itself, in our opinion, a sufficient refutation, of [these] disgraceful charges."[29]

When the Cincinnati group ceased its active relief operations, it returned to Cincinnati with around sixty thousand dollars that its fellow citizens had donated to the relief effort. The Society had rejected the plan that the Cincinnati group use these monies to purchase supplies to donate to the Society and instead had insisted that the Cincinnati relief people give the money directly to the Society so that it could purchase the supplies itself. One of the returning Cincinnati relief workers explained that they had felt that they had no choice in the matter.

> [Dexter] insisted that we should turn our money, in money, over to his committee, and we refused, holding that our instructions were to furnish supplies, which we were willing to buy and send from Cincinnati to Chicago. That Society refused to receive anything further from us except money, and we refused to furnish money, but were willing to furnish what was required in the way of food or clothing.[30]

When the Relief and Aid Society refused to accommodate the Cincinnati group's wishes, the group withdrew from the city with its money.

Women, on the other hand, readily sought donations from the Cincinnati people. Unable to obtain enough supplies from the Relief and Aid Society to meet the need they saw, the Ladies' Christian Union and Ladies' Relief and Aid appealed for donations to the Cincinnati committee.[31] During other episodes women also violated the Society's dictates that donations from beyond the city be made in cash rather than goods. For one example, several Chicago women wrote to women's groups in Pittsburgh thanking them for sending "well-chosen goods instead of money, as relief has been more immediate." One of the signatories of this letter was Mrs. J. V. Farwell, the wife of a director of the Relief and Aid Society.[32]

Why did many prominent Chicago women refuse to follow the rules of the Relief and Aid Society? Women's decisions were often privately made, and unrecorded—in contrast to the myriad public declarations of men's intentions. Thus it would be difficult to make a definitive statement about women's motivations. But their activities and the fragments of their public statements left to us suggest three primary reasons. First, and it becomes obvious once one delves into the Society's financial accounts, women refused to follow the Society's dictates out of necessity: their work received only limited support from the Relief and Aid Society. In the most crucial relief period, immediately following the disaster, from October 1871 to the beginning of January 1872, the Society spent $1.5 million in relief funds; of this, it gave exactly $4,809.87 (.3 percent) to the relief efforts of women's organizations. The next year's contributions fell slightly to .287 percent as the Society gave $6,535.41 to women's relief groups from a total of $2,276,255.31 expended.[33] Rather than give women money to purchase relief supplies and direct their own relief efforts, the Society had expected to put women to work making supplies and dispensing them under male direction.[34] In this regard, the male-run Relief and Aid Society followed a pattern for dispensing relief that historians have found elsewhere during the nineteenth century. Nancy Hewitt has demonstrated in

her study of women's public activism in Rochester, New York, during the
early to mid-nineteenth-century how the male leadership rarely gave
money directly to female-run and dominated enterprises, and Kathleen
McCarthy's study of philanthropic endeavors in Chicago found this same
pattern.[35] After Chicago's fire, the men of the Relief and Aid Society
viewed women's groups as volunteer labor that they could put to work
doing some of the actual good deeds while men remained firmly in charge
of all the legal, fiscal, and administrative decisions. The result was that
women and their organizations indeed received little money from the relief funds.

Second, women defied the Society because it did not provide nearly
enough help to women harmed by the fire. Other historians have contended that certain categories of women (widows, deserted women, the
self-employed) were of special concern to the Society.[36] But the evidence
from Annie Hitchcock suggests that by seeking to explain fire relief as
solely a class issue, historians have too heavily relied on statements of the
Society's men. Even by its own account, the Relief and Aid Society was
miserly in its dealings with women. One of its main activities was to give
them sewing machines, but in fact it had distributed only 132 machines
by December 1871. Distribution was further limited because a woman
applying for a machine had to bring a statement from her "Pastor, Priest
or some other prominent person" testifying that she was worthy of receiving a machine. These sewing machines, moreover, were not free; to receive
one, a woman usually had to pay half its cost.[37] Since few women could
afford to make this payment, many more had to settle for employment in
sewing rooms set up by the Society, where they were paid a daily wage to
sew blankets and garments for the needy. Although the Ladies' Relief and
Aid Society and the Ladies' Christian Union directed the sewing rooms,
the Relief and Aid Society set the policy and controlled the wages and
conditions of work. The Society's contributions to helping destitute
women were so negligible that the women's groups had to appeal on the
sewing women's behalf for donations of "material for bedding and for
clothing of all descriptions especially for winter wear" so that "employment may be given to needy women and girls in [the Ladies' Christian
Union's] sewing department."[38] Even historians who see class as binding
men and women together on fire relief admit that the Society's principal
concern was with men and controlling and reordering the male relationship to property and work in the city.[39]

Women engaged in fire relief believed that the Society's perspective ad-
versely affected the city's women and children. For example, the Society
had dictated that outdoor relief could be given only to replace something
tangible lost by the fire or to prevent imminent starvation or freezing.
Using these criteria, the Society's shelter committee rejected the request

of a homeless widowed washerwoman with five children for lumber to build a small shanty because she had not owned her own home before the fire.[40] The Society's concern to ensure that men not receive relief if they had any means to support themselves also ensured that many women and children suffered. Annie Hitchcock saw no relief coming for "music teachers, teachers of languages, dressmakers, young women who have been clerks and bookkeepers who ask only employment." Because such women had lost no tangible property, they would receive no tangible relief from the Society.[41] In another case, a widow's petition for winter clothing for her three children had been rejected because she possessed an insurance policy and therefore had property. But to immediately receive any money from the policy she would have to redeem it at a large discount. If, on the other hand, she could keep the policy until the national insurance crisis provoked by the fire had subsided, she would receive enough compensation to build new lodgings in which to run a boarding house—her pre-fire occupation and source of income. What little money she still possessed went for food and to keep up payments on a sewing machine, her only current source of income. Thus, as Annie Hitchcock observed, "her children are suffering for warm clothing" because of the Society's rules.[42]

The third reason why women responded differently to fire relief stemmed from differences in gender experiences. A contemporary account of fire relief provides two drawings that capture perfectly the male ideal of men's and women's relationship to fire relief. The first sketch shows the directors of the Society meeting around a large table in a comfortably appointed room, with a cozy fire blazing in the background. They are poring over figures and reports, obviously making decisions about how to dispense relief. The second sketch presents a completely different portrait. Here, well-dressed young women mingle in rough quarters with the poor and homeless, slicing bread and dispensing food while poorly clad children sit at their feet.[43] Men envisioned themselves as decision-makers; women were the ministering angels. The vision of "ministering angels" aside, women in fact had more direct and personal empathy and contact with the fire's victims. They were touched by the suffering of people without homes, food, clothing, and employment, which, together with women's ability to identify particularly with the needs of women and children—a logical consequence of the fact that the world of women of all classes was tightly bound to home and children—left many of them unwilling to accept male stewardship in relief when that stewardship left them without the means to relieve the suffering as they wanted.[44]

Prominent Chicago women, therefore, identified with other women's losses and their children's needs. They surveyed the terrible aftermath of the conflagration through their own eyes and those of other women, and saw, as Annie McClure Hitchcock's letter indicates, people without decent

Figure 4. The Relief Committee in Session. (From Rev. E. J. Goodspeed, *History of the Great Fires in Chicago and the West*. Chicago, 1871)

places to live, children without enough food and warm clothing, and women without schools, boarding houses, or dress shops to which to return and support themselves and their families. They believed that alleviating the distress of people suffering dreadful losses in the face of the cold Chicago winter months should take clear precedence over any concern about the rights of property. This fundamental difference in perspective about the nature and purposes of fire relief caused women to turn to their own resources and to ignore the Relief and Aid Society. The Woman's Industrial Aid Society, for example, established its own sewing rooms to employ women to sew clothing that was then distributed for free. This group declared emphatically that "the whole work has been committed to the hands of women because it is believed that they are more competent to ascertain and relieve the distress of their own sex than men." From this same belief that women had to help other women, the Ladies' Christian Union formulated its own relief system directed toward women and children, as mentioned above.[45]

On the other hand, the men of the Relief and Aid Society—businessmen—looked at the ruins of their city and saw the lost property of burned department stores, manufactories, banks, and warehouses. They also saw

Figure 5. Young Ladies Ministering to the Homeless. (From Rev. E. J. Goodspeed, *History of the Great Fires in Chicago and the West*. Chicago, 1871)

and feared the potential for mob violence against the private property of the city's wealthier classes, and against themselves personally as the representatives of that wealth.[46] They regarded the funds they controlled as providing an opportunity to direct business toward vendors they chose, including themselves (or their own businesses). This was their rationale for rejecting the goods that the Cincinnati relief group proposed to provide. These men steadfastly maintained that fire relief had to be structured to protect and rebuild private property and to guard and maintain their own positions within the city.

It is not that prominent Chicago men did not see or were not moved by the suffering of their fellow citizens. But the concern of the Society's directors to restructure and rebuild the city led them to their own conclusions about the nature of that suffering and how it should best be handled. In the Society's *First Special Report* after the fire, these men asserted that one of their chief priorities was to distribute relief in a way that would protect the city's "fair" name in the minds of the rest of the country. They claimed, without any evidence, that people donating to fire relief demanded the very rules that the Society designed. On the basis of this claim, the Society summarily rejected any criticism of the "red tape" that petitioners had to cut through to receive relief, roundly condemned any critics of their methods as those people whose applications most needed thorough investigation, and turned aside all suggestions for loosening relief requirements as "pressure upon us toward irresponsible and promiscuous disbursement." Finally, the directors of the Relief and Aid Society defended their system as unassailable because it was the only one that would guarantee the "accurate, systematic accounting" to protect "our beloved city" against the "darker disgrace" it would suffer through "the waste and spoilation of this fund."[47] No statement better reveals the linkage these men felt between themselves and the city than the report's conclusion that "it were almost better for those of us who are left to have perished in the flames on that memorable night, than that so indelible a stain [of waste] should be fixed upon our hitherto fair name."[48]

As the cold Chicago winter deepened, the women of the Good Samaritan Society, in an open letter to the city, castigated the Relief and Aid Society for its priorities, especially for assuming that discovering the "worthiness" of those applying for relief ought to be the highest priority. The group declared it quite as important "to afford immediate relief to suffering wherever found, as to institute searching inquiries in relation to the antecedents of the sufferer."[49] The term "worthy" is a red flag in the study of late nineteenth century urban charitable endeavors, and the "worthiness" of potential aid recipients was discussed by both men and women engaged in providing charity at that time. Women's relief groups did make judgments about who should receive fire relief and in what form, as is clear from the Woman's Industrial Aid's practice of visiting the homes of the women it employed to learn of their situation and necessities to induce "those who can elsewhere find suitable work with fair compensation to give their places at the [sewing] room to those who are less fortunate."[50] Yet important distinctions have been missed because of a tendency almost solely to interpret Chicago's fire relief efforts as adhering to earlier nineteenth-century ideas about urban charity that were presumed the same for both men and women: to preserve urban order, the poor had to be at least minimally cared for, but always at the discretion of the more well-off members of the city, whose money was being spent.[51]

Primarily viewing fire relief within this framework creates two problems. First, it misses how this episode was directly connected to ideas about city building; second, it prolongs the assumption that women merely followed men of their same socio-economic status. Seeing fire relief as charity, historians most often depict it as an episode of class conflict, the contours of which can be explained by examining prevailing notions of charity, such as the idea of worthiness. In this interpretation, prominent Chicago men treated fire relief as they would have any other charitable endeavor, using it to implement a class agenda aimed at keeping men of lower classes in their place, and using prominent Chicago women as adjuncts to their work.[52] Since prominent women had always played an integral role in delivering charity in their cities, especially for any endeavor including women and children, and since earlier in the nineteenth century they had done so under the control and direction of men who founded, funded, and directed these institutions and women's work within them, it is easy to see why historians might continue to think of Chicago women's fire relief activities as merely including a "more compassionate form of women's benevolence."[53] According to such interpretations, the only political content of Chicago's fire relief was its "debates over the very meaning of community"—whether the urban community was defined by the existence of tight class stratifications or by a more inclusive middle class.[54] This analysis for Chicago stems from the idea that the middle-class women who had engaged in sanitary work during the Civil War thereafter "severed their own benevolent work from its traditional moorings in the ideology of gender differences" and turned instead to developing new formal ties to the state that demonstrated "a newly explicit loyalty to their class."[55]

While this assessment may pertain to particular women and events, it is not readily applicable to Chicago's situation after the fire. Most women engaged in Civil War relief were from well-established social and women's groups in the East responding to the horror of a national struggle that rallied both men and women to a common cause with a definable external enemy. It would seem logical that undertaking this national crusade transformed some women's ideas about the nature of women's benevolent work, but it is wrong to presume that Chicago women responded to their city's post–Civil War disaster with the same motives as perhaps was the case elsewhere. The four leading Chicago women in the Sanitary Commission—Eliza Porter, Mary Livermore, Jane Hoge, and Myra Bradwell—were not among those women responding to fire relief, nor, as the following chapters demonstrate, were they responsible for forming women's municipal organizations by the late 1870s.[56] Rather, the pivotal aspect of fire relief is its local context.

Chicago was a city barely three decades into incorporation with only two generations of leadership behind it when the fire struck. The magnitude of the fire inspired real fear that the city itself might vanish, or at best that heroic efforts would be necessary to restore Chicago's economic vigor. In this context, the men of the Society understood perfectly well that whoever controlled relief would also direct the rebuilding of the city. Despite their exterior bravado—George Pullman, for instance, "ordered" Mayor Mason to provide armed guards at Society headquarters "tomorrow . . . at 6 am"—these men were not certain of their ability to control the city.[57] They were still entrepreneurs on the make, eager to use the fire to reestablish themselves financially, and they believed it imperative to control every aspect of fire relief to direct the city's rebuilding and thereby their own prosperity. Their agenda did not include sharing the effort with the broader citizenry or the municipal government. The earlier nineteenth-century idea that the wealthier members of a city were entitled to decide why and how relief was to be dispersed allowed them to apply fire relief to achieve their own public and private ends.

Women drew a different conclusion from the magnitude of the disaster, seeing it as a great public tragedy that mandated a public, not a private, response. They deemed the old rules on worthiness inappropriate when so many had been rendered destitute by circumstances for which they were not personally responsible. Moreover, the Society was administering not money donated principally by the directors themselves but funds that flowed from outside the city, from the American public at large. The Good Samaritan Society articulated both ideas in an open letter addressed to the city, acknowledging that they too discriminated in how and to whom they distributed available supplies, but that they rejected the Relief and Aid Society's definition and means of determining worthiness as far too narrow and inappropriate to the need. They rejected its regulation, enacted in February 1872, that "special relief"—that is, distribution of such items as stoves, furniture, bedding, or clothing to those not totally destitute—could only be obtained by applying in writing including the names of two "well-known citizens" as reference.[58] In the women's view, the crisis was not over; Chicagoans still needed and were entitled to relief. "All that such people ask for, and all that they need, is that to which they are *justly entitled—immediate assistance*," these women proclaimed.[59] This last statement is a most interesting and novel argument about fire relief. Even when the Relief and Aid Society had organized its Bureau of Special Relief, it never considered people as entitled to assistance, only that "public opinion, as well as private feeling, made it necessary to devise some way" of dealing with them.[60] The Good Samaritan Society in this letter, furthermore, rejected the Relief and Aid Society's presumption that it possessed any automatic entitlement to decide on fire relief, contending that "[w]hen dispensers of the *world's* generosity . . . subject [petitioners] to an ordeal of impertinent questioning, they presume too far upon the little brief authority with which they are invested."[61]

In one succinct letter the women of the Good Samaritan Society dismissed the old rules about charity and recast fire relief as a broader public endeavor. Implying quite correctly that the men controlling fire relief had personally donated *none* of the five million dollars in relief funds, these women informed the men that while they might possess the power to decide how to distribute their *own* money, they possessed no such inherent right over relief monies that were theirs neither in fact nor in principle.[62] Prominent Chicago women engaged in fire relief rejected both the mayor's assumption that he could give this private organization authorization to carry out all fire relief without any public accountability, and the assumption of the Society's directors that their status entitled them to such power and authority.

This conflict between men and women of the same class over fire relief raises the question of what role gender may have played in decisions about public events. We can gain some perspective on this question by looking at it from an angle different from that commonly used: instead of looking only for solidarity among women, we can consider the actions of the male Cincinnati relief committee for evidence of solidarity among men. The directors of the Chicago Relief and Aid Society had no coercive power over the relief people from Cincinnati. The Chicago men were unpleasant and obstructive, but they could have evicted the Cincinnati people neither from the city nor from premises that they had legally rented for their soup kitchen. Yet when the Society insisted, these men withdrew their money and supplies from Chicago and closed their soup kitchen, despite the active help and encouragement of some Chicago women.

Two probable reasons might explain the withdrawal of the Cincinnati men from Chicago, and both are rooted in gendered ideas about the city. They responded in outrage to the attitudes of the Society, castigating it for opposing the soup kitchen because it could not "measure out red tape at the soup-houses," but they did as they were asked first because they likely agreed that the Chicago men were entitled to decide everything on fire relief.[63] If it had been Cincinnati, they would undoubtedly have acted the same way.[64] Because it was not their city, they had the best of both worlds: they argued the high moral ground while acting in accordance with prevailing notions of male entitlement. Second, the struggle over purchasing relief supplies was a contest between the businessmen of these two cities over which would profit through the furnishing of relief supplies. Chicago men wanted to funnel as much of the money back into Chicago enterprises, businesses, and, not coincidentally, their own firms. In total, the businesses of the directors earned at least $343,287 from selling supplies to the Society (or slightly over 10 percent of the total expended for that purpose). A scandal even erupted in the city in February 1872 over charges that the businessmen of the city were trying to keep lumber prices high by urging Congress not to remove the tariff on imported lumber. Among the pro-tariff leaders were Relief and Aid Society directors Wirt Dexter and T. W. Harvey, both of whom had considerable money in the lumber trade.[65] Not coincidentally, massive amounts of lumber were still needed to rebuild the city.

For their parts, the Cincinnati relief men wanted to purchase supplies from Cincinnati firms. In a letter to Chicago newspapers, Mr. J. L. Keck described the disagreement between his group and the Chicago men in just these terms.[66] In all their actions and decisions the directors of the

Relief and Aid Society viewed the fire, however tragic its immediate consequences, as an opportunity to assert their control over rebuilding the city
and turn their own personal tragedies—that is, business losses—into economic opportunity. One prominent supporter of the Relief and Aid Society declared, "There has not been, for the last twenty years so good a time
for men of capital to start business in Chicago as now."[67]

Prominent Chicago women, on the other hand, believed that the fire
was a great tragedy for the entire urban community, a tragedy that entitled
its victims, the people of their city, to immediate relief. They sometimes
resented the presence and actions of women relief workers from outside
Chicago, but they never seem to have rejected anyone's help, money, or
supplies.[68] When these women refused to follow the dictates of the Relief
and Aid Society, they challenged male control over every aspect of urban
development, from the municipal government to private municipal organizations, which men simply assumed was unquestionably theirs.[69] In cities
in the 1870s, businessmen assumed an absolute conjunction between business and municipal interests.[70]

Admittedly, women's challenge to male power in 1871 and 1872 was
small. Their resistance had only limited consequences, and the emergency
that provoked it was so extraordinary that it might seem to have few implications for the more routine business of government. Yet this challenge
would have ramifications for Chicago's development.[71] It raised to public
view the questions and issues that would frame the political debates in
Chicago for decades to come: from where did authority to exercise public
power come, what constituted the public good, and how was power in
civil society to be "conceptualized, organized, and exercised."[72] No other
group in Chicago so early asked what constituted a broad public good, or
to what the people of a city were entitled or how these ends should be
achieved. In mid-March 1872 the Common Council began to debate re-
trieving the money from the Relief and Aid Society, but as late as December 1873 the Council only discussed this in terms of what they could
legally require of the Relief and Aid Society. That month, at a mass meeting of workers suffering from the spreading national economic depression,
Chicago's working-class leadership publicly articulated the concept that
"as members of the body politic the needy had a right to demand assistance
from their government." But their argument excluded women, who as
non-voters were not members of the "body politic." These men clearly
claimed this right on the basis of their position as productive workers in
the capitalist system—again excluding the masses of women.[73]

The fire of 1871 and its aftermath gave middle-class women a new experience on which to build women's relationship to their city. As chapter 2
shows, within five years of the fire Chicago women were building volun-

tary organizations free from all male control, proposing to expose and solve municipal problems rather than to dispense charity. By the early 1890s, these women's organizations were articulating and promoting a conception of democratic government rooted in the arguments women had advanced during fire relief, arguments that varied considerably from those held by most Chicago men.

Two

"Thoughtful Women Are Needed": Forming Groups and Forging Alliances

FEW WOMEN-ONLY organizations had existed in Chicago before the fire of 1871. When prominent women had wanted to contribute to their city, they did so through charitable work in such institutions as the Chicago Nursery and Half-Orphan Asylum, the Erring Woman's Refuge, the Chicago Orphan Asylum, and the Chicago Home for the Friendless. Women sometimes oversaw the daily operations of these institutions, and in this capacity they could wield significant power. When the lawyer for a man who had abandoned his children attempted to reclaim the children from the Home for the Friendless after they had received a small inheritance, Director Jane Hoge stifled his impertinent complaints about the lack of male authority: "Women are in authority in this house, sir," she told him, "and they will excuse your presence, now and forever." Nevertheless, men administered these institutions, controlled their finances, and made the crucial policy decisions.[1] Even the Good Samaritan Society fell under male stewardship when it was officially incorporated in 1874, and men thereafter served as its directors, treasurer, and secretary.[2]

The first female-run organization in the city was the Chicago Sorosis, founded in 1868 by Mary Livermore, lawyer Myra Bradwell, and Kate Doggett, each of whom had worked for the Northwestern Sanitary Commission during the Civil War. The Sorosis did not insert itself into municipal affairs. The Chicago Sorosis, modeled after a New York club, described its purpose as "to increase the social relations of women and mankind, and to advocate anything that will, in any way, tend to promote the welfare of both sexes—the female sex especially." Thus, its primary focus in its early years was suffrage.[3] Another female-run organization, the literary and cultural Fortnightly Club, organized in 1873 by Kate Doggett, "deliberately rejected the policy of involving itself in public work . . . club policy forbade the exploration of grittier social issues."[4] Despite subsequently founding and supporting the Illinois Training School for Nurses, the Club worked mainly in the pre-1871 tradition of women's benevolent and cultural organizations.

Caroline M. Brown founded the Chicago Woman's Club (CWC) in 1876 when she invited other Chicago women to join her in organizing a new women's group. What Brown had in mind, as she later recounted, went beyond traditional women's work. She wanted "a club of women in Chicago, not so much for mental culture, excellent as that was, but to take up the live issues of this world we live in. . . . Questions were coming up every day in regard to the city, the country, the general interests of the community, upon which I wanted more light."[5] Twenty-one women met at Brown's house in February 1876. The CWC grew slowly at first: to 64 in 1880, increasing tenfold by 1893 to 620, and twenty years later almost doubling to 1,200.[6] The CWC grew slowly in the beginning because it structured its work in ways new to women's groups. Sorosis and Fortnightly had each met as a whole to discuss a designated topic or to hear a speaker. The founders of the CWC designed a more activist, participatory structure for their group, dividing CWC activities into major areas of interest, with committees on Home, Education, Philanthropy, and Reform to take charge of investigating issues appropriate to each area. Philosophy and Science and Art and Literature were added later. The CWC by-laws furthermore mandated that each member had to participate in the work of at least one committee.[7] It took time for these women to learn how to manage this novel club structure and to integrate more members into its working style.

Although the CWC only gradually defined the full scope of its work, from its inception Club members were clear on two issues: they intended theirs to be a woman's club unfettered by male direction, and they intended to go beyond the bounds of women's previous work in charitable and cultural endeavors. The CWC's motto, *Humani nihil a me alienum puto* (Nothing human is alien to me), a classical, human-centered motto that would take these women beyond then-acceptable "womanly" activities, gave the CWC justification for expanding its endeavors as far and as wide into municipal affairs as it desired. It is virtually impossible to believe that these women had not been influenced by women's actions and ideas after the fire. The topics reported on in the CWC's first years reflected its determination to become involved in their larger society: the protective tariff and its relationship to workers, the feasibility of temperance legislation, the role of the state in general education, organized labor and the eight hour day.[8] Four years after its founding, the "prevailing opinion" of the members spurned the suggestion that women could best serve as the moral voice behind men in politics rather than participating directly in politics, and rejected a proposal to form an anti-suffrage group within the CWC. President Lucretia Heywood declared "such a society out of keeping with the character of the Club."[9] By 1883, after exploring several avenues that their work might follow, the women of the CWC answered affirmatively the question "Shall the Club Do Practical Work?"[10]

Once they had made this commitment, Club members undertook their first sustained encounter with men of the city on the issue of public education.[11] As early as April 1877, the CWC had sought women appointees to the board of education. Then they had compiled a list of names of suitable women, sought the backing of some prominent Chicago men for this effort, and sent a committee from the CWC to meet with Mayor Monroe Heath to present the list and lobby for women's appointments.[12] In Chicago, the school board was an independent governing agency whose members were appointed by the mayor, usually in consultation with the city's businessmen; the school board then controlled all appointments within the system. Modifying the membership of the board or giving women teachers new positions within the administration would have stripped men of their sole prerogative on decision-making for the schools, which was exactly what women had in mind. A decade later, the CWC was still requesting that women be appointed to the board and that women educators be appointed to supervisory positions within the system.

Having had no success, in 1888 the CWC shifted its tactics from private lobbying to the public and political tactics of petitioning, canvassing, and demanding municipal offices for women. Early that year the CWC engaged the city's Central Music Hall on the corner of State and Randolph streets in the heart of downtown for a public meeting during which they demanded women on the board of education. Over the next three years the CWC escalated its public crusade, soliciting the written support from people throughout the city to "publish the opinions of leading citizens in regard to placing women on the City Board of Education,"[13] and petitioning the mayor and city council to appoint two more women. The CWC argued its case, saying that women were as much concerned with public education as were men, and not just as mothers: "The interest of the women of Chicago in all that pertains to education, whether as mothers, teachers or citizens, being as great as that of men, entitles them to a voice in all that concerns the public schools of our city." The women's demand for women on the board also reflected their opposition to letting men decide the fortunes of working women, an opposition similar to that which had motivated women after the fire to found new organizations dedicated to helping the female victims of that tragedy. "There are 1,680 women to 70 men teachers in the public schools of Chicago," declared the CWC. "The interests of these women should not be confided entirely to men."[14]

These more public efforts produced results: In 1889 Ellen Mitchell became the first female appointee to the Board, and Ella Flagg Young and Lizzie Hartney were named as the first women assistant superintendents. In July 1891, Mayor Washburne appointed CWC member Lucy Flower to the board of education. But Chicago men continued to oppose women on this issue, so in 1892 the CWC named a committee of sixteen to lobby for more women on the board and publicized its efforts in the press. The mayor refused to meet with this committee and by letter rejected the CWC's demands for more women saying that "with the present Council it was impossible to place another woman on the School Board—the fight is against *women*—not *a* woman."[15] Thereafter the CWC escalated its activities by circulating public petitions demanding that more women be appointed to the board on a regular basis. [16]

In 1897, the CWC formed a committee expressly dedicated to forging alliances with other women's organizations throughout the city on the issue of public education.[17] Such alliances were possible in 1897 because the number of women's organizations had multiplied significantly in the two decades since the CWC's founding. Some of these new organizations, such as the Woodlawn Presbyterian Ladies Aid, the South End Flower Mission, the Jewish Young Ladies' Aid, the Union of Bohemian Women, the Masonic Order of the Eastern Star, and the Ida B. Wells Club, were local and specialized, and appealed to middle-class women on the basis of either their neighborhood or their ethnic or religious affiliation. These groups pursued a variety of social and charitable activities. The Young Ladies' Aid helped hospital patients and distributed blankets to the poor; the Union of Bohemian Women provided protection and programs for self-improvement for its members; the Ida B. Wells Club opened nurseries and kindergartens.[18]

Chicago women also founded new citywide organizations, most notably the Protective Agency for Women and Children (1887), the Cook County Suffrage Association (1888), and the Chicago Ladies' Federal Labor Union (1888). These organizations worked to transcend neighborhood, local, and class barriers that had kept women from working together. All of them recognized not only that they needed to work together as women but also that the individual ills against which their organizations fought were all part of a larger network of urban problems. The Woman's Christian Temperance Union is one organization omitted from this list. Although the Illinois branch of the WCTU had a strong presence in the Chicago area from the mid-1870s through the 1880s, from the 1890s onward I found little evidence that it played a part in Chicago politics. (Some of the activist women discussed in the book belonged to the organization, but they as individuals never tied their activities to the WCTU, nor did the organization appear in the lists of women's allied organizations.) [19]

The connections that activist women made among themselves and their causes can be seen in the Protective Agency for Women and Children (PAWC), whose organizers included CWC founder Caroline Brown. The declared purpose of the PAWC was to attack the unequal treatment of women before the law.[20] Members of the PAWC appeared at court hearings to support women, especially to protest the courts' practice of dismissing criminal assaults on young girls "with a trifling fine for 'disorderly conduct.' " The PAWC also helped women obtain divorces and demanded the appointment of more competent and worthy men as justices of the peace. Men complained that it was not women's place to appear amid the sordid doings of court proceedings, to which the president of the PAWC retorted: "We stand for justice rather than policy." Furthermore, she argued, the women of the PAWC wanted to educate public opinion "to considering the virtue of poor women as well worthy of the protection of the law as the purse of a rich man."[21] The PAWC raised funds for its activities through subscriptions that seem overwhelmingly to have come from women.[22] We do not have the complete subscription lists to tell us how far this group's work spread through the community of women, but in 1887 avowed socialist and the Ladies' Federal Labor Union (LFLU) leader Corinne S. Brown, CWC members Ellen Henrotin, Julia Holmes Smith, Ada Sweet, Lucy Flower, Celia Parker Woolley, and Leila Bedell, and Mary Ahrens (who the following year helped organize the Cook County Suffrage Association), sat on the agency's board. In the next few years, women from chapters of the Bohemian Women's groups, and Dr. Sarah Hackett Stevenson and Frances Crane (later Frances Crane Lillie), joined the PAWC's governing board.[23]

The Cook County Suffrage Association, for its part, sought to bring together women of all classes to pursue the vote to ensure that all children had education, protection, responsibility, and opportunity.[24] The CCSA itself was founded by a working woman, newspaper writer Caroline Huling, who published the newspaper *Justitia: A Court for the Unrepresented* to record the Association's activities, to follow the activities of suffrage groups around the country, and to give women a public forum that they otherwise lacked.[25] Trade unionists Elizabeth Morgan, Lizzie Swank Holmes, and Corinne Brown organized the LFLU to advance women's positions in trade unions. Within four years, the LFLU had organized working women into twenty-three craft unions. But the LFLU also connected working women's concerns to urban development, as its connections to the PAWC as well as the Illinois Women's Alliance would show.[26]

It is difficult precisely to know what generated this new municipal activism, but the increased activity did come as the city was experiencing extensive labor problems. The Haymarket "Massacre" of 1886 in which policemen and bystanders were killed at the end of a labor protest meeting, the subsequent hysteria that resulted in death sentences for several of Chicago's anarchists despite no evidence of any direct responsibility for the deed, and angry controversy over the actions of the police department in this and other municipal disturbances, brought many Chicago residents face-to-face with the frightening consequences of urban growth. Added to this image of urban chaos were the escalating municipal problems caused by massive immigration. The abilities of either government or private enterprise to provide schools, housing, or such sanitation services as garbage removal, sewers, and clean water were failing dramatically.[27]

Whatever its exact causes, the heightened concern about the direction of urban growth led activist women in 1888 to create two umbrella organizations—the Woman's League and the Illinois Women's Alliance—for the specific purpose of coordinating the activities of women's groups. The Woman's League was the idea of Dr. Leila Bedell, immediate past president of the CWC. She envisioned an organization in which women could work together to bring "the women of leisure in the city into closer communion with the working women." Such an organization, she wrote, "will be a great thing if it does no more than teach the women of leisure in the city that there are other women who see the sun rise every morning."[28] Representatives from fifty-six women's organizations answered Bedell's call and organized the Woman's League in late May, 1888. These women mostly came from middle-class groups, but their number also included Elizabeth Ro[d]gers, a former member of both Local Assembly No. 1789, which was the female local of the Knights of Labor, and its predecessor, the Working Women's Union. Rodgers had also headed the Knights of Labor Chicago District in 1886 and belonged to the Chicago Trades and Labor Assembly.[29]

Little evidence survives of the Woman's League's activities beyond its founding and sketchy accounts of its first few meetings. In early October 1888 the League did formulate an agenda to investigate the problems of child labor and the incarceration of children in the adult jails.[30] We also know that the League was acutely concerned with the situation of women and children who were not being supported by their husbands and fathers. The League believed that the only solution to this problem lay in government responsibility. To this end, it prepared a bill asking the state legislature to mandate that in the event of a man's failure in this regard caused by habitual drunkenness "the State, city or county shall put him at compulsory work, and meanwhile maintain his wife and children at public expense."[31] By contrast, the one male-dominated Chicago organization directly concerned with this problem, the Bureau of Justice, preferred to solve this problem in the old-fashioned way outside the structures of the state. In the case of wives petitioning for support from their husbands, the bureau of justice proposed that the "community" through its charitable organizations run workhouses where such men "would be put to work and their earnings turned over to their families."[32] The *Tribune* dismissed the Woman's League's proposal as uninformed about the nature of government: "The excellence of their intentions is matched in some cases by the profundity of their ignorance of the ways and means [of government]. It may be doubted whether it would be public policy to make the family of habitual drunkards direct pensioners on the public."[33] Despite this male derision, the League had introduced into public discussion the idea that it was government's responsibility to provide directly for its people. The League would soon disappear, but the idea did not.[34]

The second umbrella organization founded in 1888, the Illinois Women's Alliance (IWA), endured until 1894.[35] Trade unionists Elizabeth Morgan and Corinne Brown of the newly formed LFLU drew up a plan for the IWA and invited women's groups throughout the city to join it. In early October Caroline Huling and women from several middle-class groups, including Annie H. White of the Woodlawn Reading Club, Frances M. Owens of the Woodlawn Presbyterian Ladies' Aid, Alvah Perry of the South End Flower Mission, and Dr. Harriet M. Fox, joined Morgan and Brown to form the IWA and organize its first coordinating committee.[36] Although a few of the member organizations were church affiliated, the vast majority were secular. This membership list, and the fact that from 1877 to 1903 none of the leaders of the Women's Home Baptist Mission Society, one of the city's largest church-affiliated women's organizations, appears in the ranks of any other important women's municipal organization, suggests that religious motives were definitely not the spark that ignited Chicago women's municipal activities in the late 1880s.[37]

The prominent role of working women in the IWA has meant that it has been studied mainly as a working-class organization. But the majority of its member clubs were middle-class, and many objectives proposed by the IWA had been at least considered by earlier women's groups and would later be taken up by women's groups that were largely middle-class. Before examining its actions, it is important to consider how the IWA's initiatives squarely stood in a women's, rather than a class-specific, milieu of urban activity because labor historians have written so much about the organization as a prolabor, class-based organization.[38] But being prolabor was only one part of these women's agenda: they were pro-women and pro-children in ways that male union members were not. The IWA's engagement with women's issues emerges most vividly when its ideas and activities are juxtaposed with prevailing male conceptions about the proper role of municipal government in the United States. Before 1888, urban government confined itself to "passive regulation" of property by levying property taxes to raise money necessary for building an urban infrastructure, facilitating business needs, furnishing a minimum of municipal services, and protecting property rights. It constructed sewer systems, furnished clean water, and laid out and maintained streets. It passed and enforced laws to safeguard the business and private property of a city's middle-class residents. It did not provide "active service" to its residents.[39]

In the 1860s, after the great fire, and during the depression of 1873, working-class men had occasionally departed from the ideal of passive regulation to argue that government ought to protect the labor of working men by regulating the length of the working day and providing jobs on public works projects for unemployed men during economic downturns.[40] On the other hand, these arguments—as well as those made by male Chicago socialists in the 1870s and 1880s—to define the role of government more broadly (for example, by advocating government operation of transportation and communication networks)[41] still conceived of the role of urban government as protection of property. Male workers' organizations wanted to expand government to protect *their* property, too, rather than just businessmen's property.[42] In the depths of the depression of 1893 and 1894, the radical Central Labor Union (CLU), led by Thomas Morgan (husband of Elizabeth Morgan), petitioned the city council to substitute a system of public relief for the existing system of private relief. The CLU justified this appeal by declaring that private relief "is so degrading to the recipients . . . un-American and disgraceful in the light of the declaration of independence . . . [and] the fundamental principles upon which our government rests—that is, the right of every individual to life and liberty."[43] It is clear from the petition that Morgan's primary objective was public works employment for unemployed *male* laborers. He did not declare it the duty of government systematically to intervene "to change the conditions that caused individual impoverishment," an idea that Eric Monkkonen has shown was actually being discussed in some cities by the end of the century.[44]

Of course middle-class Chicago men remained even more firm in their advocacy of minimalist, business-property-protecting government. Twenty years before, in 1874, the *Tribune* had editorialized against public employment:

> The doctrine of the right to employment is the negation of property. . . . Governments were instituted to defend the individual against the many. The advocates of the right of employment set the many over the individual and make of government an institution to pillage the individual for the benefit of the mass.[45]

Then in 1884, the men of the Citizens' Association had rejected the idea that supplying housing for the city's poor residents should be a public enterprise. The Association declared, "Our system of business needs no governmental aid or advice" on this issue.[46] In 1894, city council member Mann responded to the CLU petition declaring that "the law and government under which we are organized does not impose upon city officials the obligation nor allow them the power to lay out and prosecute great public improvements for the purpose of furnishing employment to its citizens."[47]

From its beginning, then, the IWA pronouncements, activities, and agenda challenged both the minimalist, passive, property-protecting idea of government advocated by middle-class and business men, and the call of working men's organizations for government protection of their labor. The IWA picked up the threads of the Woman's League's idea about government responsibility and wove them into a comprehensive argument that it was the *duty* of government to provide for the general welfare. The IWA declared that it was "manifestly the function and duty of the State to care for its dependent children and not leave any important matter of public welfare to private charity."[48] It asserted that "the fundamental principles of the American Constitution are violated whenever the State neglects to provide State Institutes for its wards and dependents, and . . . is false to itself when it delegates its functions to a private sectarian institution."[49] And, in contrast to the limited appeal of the CLU, the IWA proclaimed that government had the "duty . . . to provide at the expense of the city, immediate relief for all cases of destitution. . . . [W]e consider it the duty of the city to furnish employment for all men and women out of work. . . [W]e consider it the duty of the city to provide lodging-houses for temporary relief of the unemployed and homeless persons." The IWA emphasized and repeated the word *duty* throughout its declarations.[50]

In one other way, the IWA was far ahead of male leaders in the city: it attempted to breach the race barrier as well as class barriers. One of its original twenty-six organizations was the Prudence Crandall Club, founded by socially elite African Americans in late 1887.[51] Details of the connection are hard to come by, but the IWA's *First Annual Report* lists the Crandall Club among its members, and Fannie Barrier Williams, Lottie McCary, and Viola Bentley as the Club's representatives to the IWA.[52] Williams became an IWA vice-president in late 1889 and subsequently played an important role in the IWA's committee to have the city provide free public baths.[53] The IWA left few documents of its own, apart from the *First Annual Report* preserved in the Caroline Huling Manuscript Collection, so the only other sources of information on the IWA are newspaper accounts that never directly refer to the Crandall Club itself although they mention the participation of Williams.

Believing that women and children were not being protected by the state and municipal government, the IWA invited existing women's groups in the city to send three delegates to work directly with it. "Thoughtful women are needed," said the IWA, "to amend the trying conditions under which their less fortunate sisters are earning their bread, and to secure children the requisite training for a life of usefulness." The delegates, in turn, would be liaisons, keeping the members of their respective groups informed of the IWA's actions. The IWA set its first tasks as securing the enforcement of existing factory ordinances and of the 1883 compulsory education law, which required all children between eight and fourteen years old to attend school for a minimum of twelve weeks annually. The IWA also sought more strict factory ordinances and more extensive school laws, as well as appointments of women inspectors everywhere that women and children were employed.[54] In early December 1888, it demanded that the mayor and city council appoint women in each ward as school inspectors to investigate school conditions and student attendance, and grant those inspectors police power to enforce the laws. Two women, one from the CWC and one from the LFLU were appointed school inspectors as a result. The IWA then requested that the city council both issue the organization five badges for women to act as factory inspectors, and appoint additional women as unpaid volunteer inspectors in factories. When the council ignored its requests, the IWA sent thirteen women to a meeting of the city council health committee to submit a list of women acceptable to the IWA from which the committee could choose these inspectors. Ultimately, only one woman listed by the IWA was appointed a factory inspector. The IWA's effort pointed to the problems that middle-class and working-class women faced as they tried to develop cross-class links. The question of whether women should be paid or unpaid inspectors caused serious problems for the IWA. Middle-class women saw paid positions as opportunities for women, but the men of the Chicago Trades and Labor Assembly pressured the working-class women of the IWA to reject paid inspectors as potential political appointees.[55]

The IWA next stepped into the realm of school finance and expenditures, where men did not expect women to venture. Even when men grudgingly acknowledged any legitimacy to women's request for a place on the board of education, they misunderstood the reasons for women's desire for involvement in the schools. A *Tribune* editorial, for instance, suggested that a token female appointee to the board of education would satisfy women's demands, and assured its readers that the city might benefit from such an appointment because "it certainly will be in [women's] power to introduce a great deal of 'sweetness and light' into the immediate management [of the schools]." The same editorial reassured Chicagoans that "it is not likely that they will trouble their heads about routine matters of finance and building unless they are invited to do so." The *Tribune* finished its editorial by advising the city that it would be better to give women something now before they got really angry because when they feel mistreated, women "scratch like cats."[56]

By the time this editorial appeared, the IWA was already probing the school board's operations and publicizing its financially suspect methods. The women presented a list of pertinent questions to the city council that they wanted answered:

> Why does the Board delay paying teachers a week beyond the end of the month?
> Where is the money for teacher pay deposited, does it draw interest, and if so
> who gets the interest? Why does the Board withhold until April twenty-five

percent of the teachers' pay for the months of January, February, and March? And why are none of these fiscal machinations mentioned in the Board's annual report?[57]

After much prodding from the IWA, the city council suggested to the Board that it change some of its procedures for paying teachers, but board president Graeme Stewart responded angrily to the IWA's interference in school affairs by declaring that the board was free to conduct school business as it wanted, independent of the wishes of either the council or the citizenry.[58] The city, at least, responded to the IWA's pressure and agreed to terminate its practice of a three-month delinquency on paying city employees, if only for its lower paid employees.[59]

Then the IWA, in the type of legal maneuver that the Teachers' Federation would adopt in the next decade, countered the school board's intransigence by investigating the municipal laws. What it found was that Section 371 of the Municipal Code mandated that the board provide the city council "such information within their possession as may be required" of it by the council.[60] But Stewart resisted turning over any information, the council backed away from pressuring the board, and in 1889 the mayor refused to appoint more women to the board. In response, the IWA called for the restructuring of the school board by replacing the politically appointed board with a popularly elected one of thirty members, of which at least half were women.[61] Although they did not succeed in this attempt, activist Chicago women pursued the possibility of an elected board of education over the next three decades.

At the same time that it was making these demands on the public schools, the IWA joined the CWC and PAWC in attacking festering problems within the justice system. The IWA formed a police committee, headed by Fanny Kavanaugh—who belonged to both the LFLU and the male-dominated Chicago Trades and Labor Assembly—to investigate the plight of women in the city's justice of the peace courts. Kavanaugh adopted the PAWC's method of direct investigation and frequented the courts and police stations to learn how the courts dealt with crimes, especially prostitution, involving women and how they generally treated women. She found that working-class women were arrested as prostitutes merely for walking alone at night, and that they were often denied the right of habeas corpus. When these women were arrested for solicitation, the men who supposedly patronized them or who openly solicited them were not even required to testify in court because the testimony of the arresting officer was enough to convict the woman.[62] Kavanaugh and the IWA so extensively publicized her findings on the system's mistreatment of women in the courts and stations that the police barred her from visiting the women's section of the jail at the city's main station on Harrison

Street. When attempts were made to bar the IWA from the courts, IWA president Caroline Huling declared that because the courts were in the public interest, women had a right to free access, and she vowed that the IWA would continue "to test this matter."[63]

In 1889 and 1890, the IWA expanded its attack on the police and courts into a critique of the city's entire justice system, charging that the system bred corruption because its elected justices and politically appointed bail bondsmen depended for their income on revenue garnered from fines and bail fees. The court personnel's search for this income, according to the IWA, made women the pawns of personal greed. Women, Kavanaugh charged, were "arrested in droves and fined only according to their ability to earn, so that the bailer is sure of his fees, the shyster of his, and even the judge received a small fee for signing the bond."[64] When its findings did not persuade the men controlling the courts to make appropriate changes, the IWA prepared a bill for the state legislature to create a new municipal court to replace the existing system. As with several of activist women's earlier initiatives, the IWA's plan to reform Chicago's justice system failed at the time, but such efforts did later find success, including establishment of the Municipal Court in 1905.[65]

The IWA also launched a third major initiative: to have the city build and maintain public baths. No free public baths existed in the United States at the time; even the male trade unions, which had debated the question of public baths, had remained unconvinced that this was the appropriate work of government. A significant minority of the leadership of the Trades and Labor Assembly had even objected that such a notion was "socialistic."[66] Despite lack of precedent, in 1889 the IWA organized a committee on free baths chaired by Elizabeth Morgan and Mrs. J. H. Randall, head of the Woman's Refuge and member of the LFLU; Fannie Barrier Williams became a member of this committee. The IWA took its crusade for public baths directly to the people, circulating petitions throughout the city's wards demanding that public baths be built, especially for women and children. The crusade to obtain public baths revealed how the IWA was learning to calculate the location of power in the city. In its first attempt, the IWA called for building public baths on park lands. Here it encountered the barriers of the decentralized governing system that characterized late nineteenth-century cities. In Chicago, park lands were administered through a system of three park boards—the West, South, and Lincoln Park boards—whose members, like those of the school board, were appointed rather than elected, and thus (as the women learned) even further insulated from popular pressure. But when the men controlling all three boards ignored the IWA petitions, the IWA circulated new petitions beginning in late 1889 demanding that the city council fund and build free public baths. As part of this effort, Elizabeth Morgan went to the Trades and Labor Assembly and asked the leadership to sign a circular letter to request that the city council establish free public baths.[67]

Although the council also tried to ignore the IWA, the women continued their campaign. They found support for the public bath movement in early 1892 from the newly formed Municipal Order League (MOL), an organization of middle-class women among whose founders was future CWC president Ada C. Sweet. The MOL acted after it heard a presentation by Dr. Gertrude G. Wellington, a physician newly arrived in Chicago, who expressed her concern with the multitudes who had no facilities for bathing themselves or their children, and suggested to the MOL that they begin work on this issue. The MOL promptly divided the city into three sections, each of whose needs for baths would be investigated by a committee. It appointed three woman physicians to head the committees—Wellington, Dr. Sarah Hackett Stevenson (the incoming president of the CWC), and Dr. Julia R. Lowe.

The MOL, like the IWA, saw public baths as a municipal problem that necessitated a municipal solution. One contemporary account credits Wellington for realizing that women would have to go directly to the source of power and money—the municipal government. Although the MOL did not immediately support her suggestion that they directly appeal to the city council, by the end of 1892 Ada Sweet had declared that the remedies for sanitation and health problems were indeed "to be found in legislation and the City Council."[68] Activist Chicago women were learning that petitions were not enough to convince men to change their thinking about either public baths or creating more activist government, especially if the signatures came mainly from women, who could not vote. Thus, the MOL also lobbied Mayor Washburne and then Mayor Carter Harrison, both of whom declared themselves in favor of the baths, and who in turn persuaded several prominent Chicago men and the newspapers to support public baths. At this point, the council's resistance to public baths crumbled, and it appropriated the money to build the first one. One of the alderman attested that the city owed this achievement to women

> I have been importuned both night and day for I don't know how long. . . . The persuasive manner in which these ladies came upon the council at all times and hours is what led that body to finally conclude that there was plenty of money in the treasury to be used for the purpose they desired.[69]

The first free municipal public bath in the country opened in Chicago in January 1894, just north of Hull House on land that the settlement had donated for that purpose. By 1908 twelve free baths had been established around the city. Most existing sources at least tacitly acknowledge that

Chicago women had conceived of the public need and the public good served by public baths and had decided it an appropriate task of the municipal government to provide for this need.[70]

When the MOL divided the city into specific and manageable sections for investigation, it was following the practice of the IWA of spreading responsibility for investigating municipal conditions among women throughout the city. Frances Dickinson had led the IWA in doing its investigatory work. At the precinct level, in every ward, two women were charged to investigate conditions therein and then to report their findings back to the IWA on a weekly basis.[71] The Ward and Precinct Committee of the IWA had justified its methods in this manner:

> In order to secure good public services, it is not only necessary to pay taxes, elect representatives to levy, collect and spend these taxes . . . but there needs to be in every precinct a self-appointed body of resident men and women who fearlessly act as a vigilante committee, and report to a central body of women who have no "bread and butter" to lose when agitating for a common right to all humanity.[72]

The IWA's activities greatly increased the public presence of women. They attended meetings of the city council and board of education and went into the courts and other public arenas, demanding that more public functions be opened to women and recognized as their suitable province. In effect, the IWA refused to concede that any public issue or venue was beyond the scope of women's presence, interests, or actions.

The Hull House settlement is generally credited with initiating personalized investigation among Chicago women, and Hull House would subsequently play an important and ongoing role in organizing women's municipal activities. From 1892 to 1894, Hull House residents Florence Kelley, Ellen Gates Starr, and Alzina Stevens (a former textile mill worker who had migrated to Chicago to become the first woman admitted to Typographical Union No. 16 and who had subsequently joined the Working Women's Union and the Knights of Labor Local Assembly 1789) had worked with the IWA to secure factory legislation for women and children. But the IWA, with its working-class and middle-class women working on equal footing, initiated women's personalized style of municipal investigation in Chicago.[73] Moreover, the IWA's attack on the structures of the court and public education systems represented Chicago women's first organized efforts to reshape municipal governing structures. They thrust women squarely into the kinds of public affairs that Chicago men had heretofore reserved for themselves, and Chicago men did not accept this intrusion gracefully. According to Caroline Huling, school board president Stewart, in a meeting to discuss compulsory education, said he "couldn't imagine who we were anyway, he had never heard of us before;

[and] he considered us very impertinent in going to the Council." At the end of his remarks, Huling wrote, "he whipped out a cigar and lighted it with gentlemanly vigor."[74]

As it pursued its investigations and crusades, the IWA came more fully to recognize that a principal obstacle to its desires was the weakness of the municipal government. Children could not be assured a decent public education because the priorities of the board of education lay elsewhere and the government had neither the will nor in some cases, the authority to enforce changes. The city had a shortage of school buildings, many of which were decrepit. But the problem was not lack of money. The board had two million dollars in unspent building funds that it simply refused to use to build new schools in poor areas in the city. The root of this refusal, the IWA believed, was an alliance between the city's Real Estate Board and the businessmen on the board of education in which they colluded to steer new school building into "new subdivisions for the purpose of increasing the value and sale of lots," thereby increasing economic profits for businessmen. "Are there not enough money making industries," demanded the IWA, "without using the educational needs of the children as one?" Elizabeth Morgan indignantly proclaimed the refusal to build schools for poor children "a most disgraceful state of affairs in a wealthy community like this, that calmly contemplates the expenditure of from $30,000,00 to $50,000,000 for a drainage system, $10,000,00 for a World's Fair, and hundred[s] of thousands of dollars for a Grand Opera."[75]

Under the existing political structure, however, the city council had no power to compel the school board to build the thirty-nine new schools that the IWA calculated necessary, at minimum, to accommodate school-age immigrant children. Nor could the council facilitate a new compulsory education law that the IWA wanted.[76] School board president Stewart had dismissed the IWA as "impertinent," while other men proclaimed that women ought to stay out of the whole matter because they lacked a "practical and business appreciation of the situation and facts."[77] The IWA responded by attacking the prevailing priorities of municipal government, suggesting that "it would be better to stop at once for a short period all such improvements as paving, lighting, etc., and turn the whole attention to providing schools for our children."[78] Faced with a combination of official impotence and male intransigence, the IWA then attacked male claims that the schools were not open to public discussion and issued a six-point declaration arguing that because the State had the power to determine educational policy, "the school question has entered the political arena. We welcome it as a political issue." The IWA demanded stricter enforcement of compulsory education laws, the employment of the "best" teachers, methods, and textbooks, and the appointment of school board members who believed in the "necessity of the state to perfect and to maintain the public school system." The IWA insisted that it was the job of the government to provide adequate public educational facilities, set and enforce educational standards and compulsory education laws, and see to it that all school boards complied with these standards and laws. It also argued, in an idea later adopted by other women's groups, that no child should be allowed to leave school without being able to read, write, and speak English because any child without these skills would be severely disadvantaged in American society.[79]

In 1881 the Citizens' Association Committee on Education had declared that the "object of our whole educational system" was "to produce good citizens who shall in every way promote the welfare of the state" and complained about a lack of "practical training" in the schools to prepare children to become "useful and productive" workers.[80] The IWA had turned this idea completely around, declaring that the purpose of public education should be to prepare the individual child to succeed in society. No matter how hard Chicago men tried to ignore women, the IWA's activities on the public school system guaranteed that the discussion of educational priorities would never again be confined to men—those on the board of education, in their own groups, or in the editorial pages of the *Tribune*.[81] Furthermore, in its emphasis on the duty of government, the IWA forced a broadening of the discourse on the role of government in directing and managing urban growth. Among the arguments made available for subsequent women's actions was one that asserted that government had the duty to provide for human needs as a matter of right, not as a matter of either individual need or protection of property. As one example, the IWA argued that the city had to furnish free school books to all children not based on their need for free books but so that there "may be no stigma of pauperism on any child. For all children are, or ought to be dependent; it is their right."[82] In this and other arguments, the IWA had begun both to articulate a women's conception of democratic government and to establish a women's municipal agenda that differed in theory and practice from that espoused by most men.[83]

Race and Class Relations in Women's Alliances

The IWA disintegrated in 1894 primarily because its middle-class and working-class membership could not entirely agree on the direction of the organization's work. Differences on whether to support Labor candidates for the board of education and how strongly to support eight-hour day legislation, along with internal struggles over who should control and direct the organization, led to its demise late that year. But this first attempt by women to work across class divisions was more than the misalliance that it has been judged by some scholars.[84] Precisely because it could mobilize support from across class lines, the IWA gave women a more prominent place in public affairs; Caroline Huling even gave a speech before the Trades and Labor Assembly, certainly one of the few occasions on which a female non-member did so.[85] The shared gender concerns of the women who worked together within the IWA sometimes led them to take positions that were unheard of for men of their class. In 1894 activist Ellen Henrotin—a woman almost as prominent as the queen of Chicago society, Bertha Palmer—addressed a 1894 rally, described as "one of the greatest socialistic meetings ever held in Chicago," to give her support to the eight-hour work day.[86] The enduring impact of the IWA, finally, is attested to by continuing cross-class cooperation after 1894, as we shall see when we trace the efforts to reform the public schools in the 1890s and 1900s and the fight for municipal suffrage in the first decade of the twentieth century.

The IWA also initiated activist women's attempts to form cross-race alliances. If the evidence of white women's municipal work in the late nineteenth century is scarce compared to that for white men, the existing primary evidence for the work of black women is even scarcer. While we have lists of clubs, and the names of some women members, we often have little more. The available evidence does suggest that African American women in Chicago approached their municipal work by organizing as "race" women but also by making alliances with white women.[87] Some white women were also open to projects involving cross-race cooperation, although there were too few of them to produce a lasting breach of racial barriers.[88] It is nonetheless essential to notice that on some occasions similarities of gender experience and gender treatment, notwithstanding racism, drove white and black women to develop similar concerns and ideas about the city and political reform even when working separately.

The first African American club open to women was the Prudence Crandall Club, an organization described in 1888 as seeking to promote the "mental culture" of the city's African Americans. The first all women's club, founded in 1893 in the wake of the World's Columbian Exposition, was the Ida B. Wells Club, which one historian has described as "dedicated to 'civic and social betterment,' " but which a more recent historian describes as pursuing the idea that social uplift was "a collective responsibility."[89] Unfortunately, we know little more about its early work, beyond its founding of nurseries, kindergartens, and homes for working girls. By the end of the decade, however, Chicago African American women had at least seven different clubs and had allied themselves with the Woman's Civic League of Chicago.[90]

Fannie Barrier Williams, an early leader of the city's African American community, who with her husband, S. Laing Williams, helped found Provident Hospital, the city's first African American hospital, provides a glimpse of the kind of cooperation possible in this period between African American and white women. As a member of the IWA Williams served both as a vice-president of the organization and as a member of its committee on public baths.[91] Her experience with the IWA appears to have helped shape her ideas about women's work in two ways. First, it imbued her with the idea that women's organizations had to function as advocates for municipal reform. For example, in 1889 the IWA had attacked the problem of homeless children by declaring that women had "organized not for charitable purposes but to secure the enforcement of the laws and the proper exercise of the governmental functions of society for the protection of its weaker members."[92] Writing five years later for *Women's Era*, Williams advocated such direct activism when she supported calling a "Convention of Colored Women's Clubs, Leagues, and Societies," but only if women could avoid "repeating the mistakes of black men whose conventions and councils tended to be talk and more talk."[93] Throughout her public career, Williams kept her attention focused on the problems of women and children. When she wrote her account of the early years of the black women's club movement, Williams stressed the interest of these clubs in the conditions of women, especially young women, and children.[94]

The motto of the IWA, adopted in 1888, and that of the Illinois Federation of Colored Women's Clubs (IFCWC), adopted in 1899—nearly identical but for a few words—most clearly expressed the mutual interest of white and black women in the welfare of Chicago's women and children. For the former, the motto read: "Justice to Children, Loyalty to Women"; for the latter, "Loyalty to Women and Justice to Children."[95] According to Wanda Hendricks, the members of the IFCWC worked to "support education, the integrity of the home, and the interests of women of every community."[96]

In late 1894, activist Celia Parker Woolley—supported by Ellen Henrotin—recommended Williams for membership in the CWC, which took this occasion to discuss the issue of race and membership.[97] The discussion within the membership committee reveals little opposition to admitting African American women; by a vote of 9 to 4 it approved a resolution "that it is the Sentiment of the Chicago Woman's Club that no one can be excluded from membership on race or color lines." The CWC as a whole passed this motion by a vote of 194 to 33, and Williams became a member.[98] Within a year of admitting Williams, the CWC again amended its membership criteria to read without regard to race, color, religion, or politics.[99]

Admitting Williams, of course, did not indicate that all of these middle-class white women firmly believed in racial equality, nor did it mean that African American women flocked to join the CWC. It admittedly helped Williams that she was very wealthy and light skinned. Yet the CWC did indeed take this step, and African American women would continue to look to the CWC for support on racial issues. Moreover, neither in the 1890s nor later did white Chicago men's organizations admit black members or seriously address the problem of racism. I did not, for example, identify any African American men in the City Club for 1903, 1904, 1909, or 1916; in the Citizens' Association in the 1880s; or in the Commercial and Merchants' Clubs in the 1880s, 1890s, or early twentieth century.[100] In her annual report of May 1895, CWC president Ada Sweet declared that passage of the resolution to disregard race or color was an event that "stands out conspicuously, and is remarkable." But this was not mere self-congratulation, for she placed the resolution in the context that it was necessary for women to face squarely the problem of race in their city. "It was right and proper," concluded Sweet, "for the Club to clearly enunciate its opinion upon the subject of race and color prejudice, and to refuse to aid its continuance or growth."[101] Moreover, over the next five years, the CWC continued to confront the issue of race in a way that no white male organization in Chicago did. In 1900 the CWC officially protested the exclusion of the delegates from the African American Woman's New Era Club of Massachusetts from the biennial meeting of the General Federation of Women's Clubs. The CWC approved by a vote of 175 to 53 the motion "that the Chicago Woman's Club regrets the exclusion from membership in the General Federation of Women's Clubs of the Woman's Era Club of Boston and reaffirms its unwavering belief in equal opportunity to all without regard to race, color, religion, or politics."[102]

Clearly, the CWC remained an exclusive organization—with a membership of just over six hundred at the turn of the century—but its formal acknowledgment that women had to confront racism as both a municipal and a membership issue surely helped broaden the public activities of Chicago women during the following decades. Although Ida B. Wells-Barnett seems never to have joined the CWC, she actively sought the organization's support on issues of concern to African American women. She and Jane Addams together led a protest against discussions in Chicago to segregate the public schools.[103] At Wells-Barnett's request, the CWC adopted a resolution protesting such school segregation in Alton, Illinois, stating "it to be illegal and un-American to make distinctions in educational matters as to race or color; and greatly depreciate any division of school children or school funds on these grounds.[104]

The CWC's openness to the principle of opposing racial discrimination was reflected in the actions of Chicago women toward the National Association of Colored Women when it met in Chicago in the summer of 1899. On that occasion, Jane Addams invited delegates to lunch at Hull House, an invitation that one activist African American woman called "the breaking of the color line." Ellen Henrotin, settlement house resident Mary

McDowell, and former IWA leader Corinne Brown addressed the meeting. Brown deplored "the differences which were being made between colored and white women and admonished that the only remedy was for these two groups to work together for the common purpose of abolishing distinctions."[105] Since Henrotin, McDowell, and Brown represented three different strands of the white women's movement—the women's clubs, settlement houses, and working-class and more radical women reformers—they present to us a broad picture of activist women confronting the problem of racial division among Chicago women.

None of this discussion intends to suggest either that the mass of white Chicago women advocated racial equality or that African American women such as Williams did not realize that racial prejudice gave their gender concerns an urgency distinctly different from that of white women. As Deborah Gray White and other scholars have shown, gender was a primary issue for African American club women because white society specifically degraded them in contrast to white women. When black men complied with this degradation by remaining silent in the face of white attacks on black womanhood, black women charged that neither they nor the race as a whole could hope for equality. Thus in their club work, African American women faced the double bind of having to promote both gender issues and racial equality, often in the face of both white and black male hostility. "[G]ender tension was the price black women paid for their feminism," according to White. "There would also be," for African American women, "the competing notion that patriarchal norms, not feminist principles were the foundation on which race progress would be built."[106]

On the other hand, a comprehensive picture of women's municipal activism must include African American women in a "women's" movement even while realizing the inequalities and prejudices that restricted their participation. It is important to look beyond the South as the representative norm of U.S. race relations in the late nineteenth century and to avoid characterizing the Progressive Era as a period of total "disenfranchisement of all women and black men" and of legalized segregation, as some historians have suggested.[107] African American men in Chicago voted and held political offices from the ratification of the Fifteenth Amendment in 1870, and African American women voted when women received the partial vote in 1913.[108] Chicago African American women's activism was not shaped solely by concerns within the African American community itself, nor was "motherhood" the singular underpinning of their activism. At times black and white women in Chicago were concerned to resolve the same municipal problems so that they did collaborate in their work. But even when working separately, both groups of women pursued many of the same goals of making the city work better for women, children, and homes.[109]

None of the women working in the IWA, the Woman's League, the CWC, or the Ida B. Wells Club, or at Hull House knew in the early 1890s how extensive women's municipal activism would become in the near future. They did not have a unified vision of how they would proceed in confronting the urban problems they had already identified as most pressing. They did not know that they would construct an entirely new municipal agenda. Even as the IWA was disbanding in 1894, however, Chicago was seized by the new reform fervor beginning to sweep through American cities. In this progressive movement, a broad range of Chicago residents created new ideas and formulated new strategies for the city's development. The progressive reform movement then furnished the context in which activist women could promote their ideas about government responsibility for all the people of the city, ideas that they had begun to develop in their earlier endeavors.

Part Two

EXPANDING THE VISION

Three

"The First Thing Is to Create Public Sentiment and Then Express It at Every Opportunity": The Growth of Progressive Activism

The Columbian Exposition and the Pullman Strike

The world's Columbian Exposition held in Chicago in 1893–94 and the Pullman strike of 1894 brought Chicago directly into the country's growing progressive reform movement. These two events, combined with the ongoing crisis within the Chicago school system, pushed activist women into forming more alliances and finding more aggressive ways to present to the public their ideas for the city's development. By 1905, women were acting through mass meetings, founding new voluntary organizations, further developing the IWA's method of direct, personal investigation of municipal problems, and conducting sophisticated political lobbying campaigns.

Chicago had desperately wanted the fair to exhibit the city's industrial accomplishments to the world; in fact, it was the city's relentless, verbose lobbying for the fair that first earned it the enduring sobriquet of the "Windy City." Easterners had initially resisted this request, predicting that any fair in the Midwest would present to the world "a vulgar, materialistic display worthy of a state agricultural fair."[1] These sectional sourgrapes were muted as national and international visitors praised the fair's "White City," which displayed all the wonders of modern achievements in manufacturing, agriculture, machinery, transportation, and other technological advancements inside enormous white neoclassical buildings. One fairgoer praised the fair as an "ethereal emanation of pure and uneconomic beauty." Another congratulated the city for the picture it conveyed "of so many ways open to human industry; the sight of so many natural resources."[2]

But if Eastern fears of agricultural vulgarity had not materialized, visitors to the Exposition did notice the dark side of the industrial city. Giuseppe Giacosce, the same Italian playwright who had marveled at the city's industry and resources, also found Chicago an appalling place. "I would not want to live there for anything," he declared. "I did not see anything in Chicago but darkness: smoke, clouds, dirt and an extraordinary number

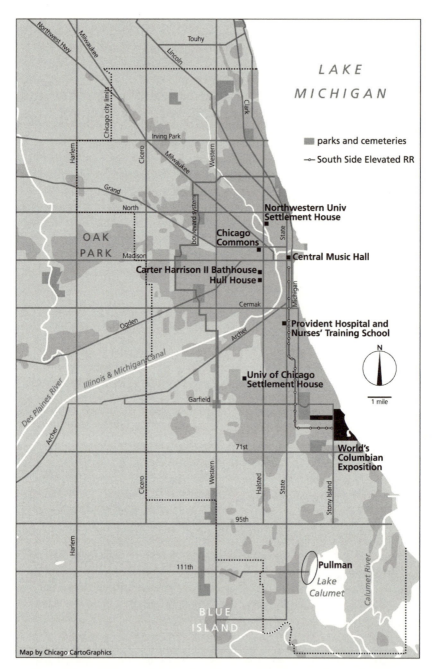

Figure 6. Map of Chicago, 1893. Showing city limits, settled area, and sites of women's activities up to 1894. (Drawn by Dennis McClendon, Chicago Carto-Graphics)

of sad and grieved persons."[3] The English visitor William T. Stead prowled the city's streets and alleys and noted the striking difference between the monumental "White City" and the mean tenement housing of the city's immigrants. In a public speech in November 1893 at the Central Music Hall, Stead excoriated Chicagoans for the social, moral, and political corruption of their city. A group of middle-class Chicagoans who had been justifiably proud of the city's efforts in the Exposition were now stung by Stead's accusations that they had turned a blind eye to Chicago's defects. Led mainly by male activists, they organized the Civic Federation, open both to men and women, and vowed to work through this organization to address the urban problems identified by Stead. Hull House, of course, had already been open for five years, attempting to address these and other problems, but Addams and other women welcomed any new reform impulse.[4]

For activist women, however, their participation in the Exposition itself was as important as Stead's critique. First, the fair gave women new opportunities to engage in public work. Chicago socialite and clubmember Bertha Palmer headed the national board of lady managers, which supervised the gathering and organizing of displays of women's work from around the world for the fair's exhibits. Individual Chicago clubwomen such as Mary Wilmarth, Ellen Henrotin, and Fannie Barrier Williams contributed to this work, as did the CWC and other women's organizations. New women's organizations such as the Catholic Women's League and the Ida B. Wells Club were formed out of the experiences of working on the Exposition.[5] Second, the fair afforded activist women another opportunity to engage in municipal decision-making when prohibition and religious groups demanded that the fair be closed on Sundays. Many of Chicago's activist women publicly opposed the proposal because Sunday was the only day on which workers and many women could attend. The CWC even sent two members to speak in favor of the Exposition's remaining open on Sunday before a national public hearing in Washington, D.C., in January 1893, an enormous step for women whose only experience in public participation had been municipal. While many Chicago men saw the fair primarily as a showcase for the city's economic progress, many activist women defined it as a public event to be enjoyed by all the people of the city.[6]

Third, public participation in the Columbian Exposition raised for women the issue of race, even while the CWC confronted the same issue. Organized African American women demanded to be included on the board of lady managers and in the fair's activities. The board generally agreed that African American women ought to be included but split about the extent of their participation both on the board and at the Exposition. Moreover, African American women were not united, arguing about who would represent them and about what issues to raise as part of their contribution to the fair. This internal debate, the undoubted racism of many white women, and the prominent role of some Southern women on the board of lady managers ensured that African American women would be slighted at the fair.[7] But the debate among white women and the disagreements among black women presaged a dilemma with which activist women would struggle in the future: could a woman's vision of a democratic city truly exist if it did not include all women?

The Exposition's effect of fostering women's activism was reinforced in mid-1894 by the contentious strike against a major Chicago industry, the Pullman Palace Car Company. Few middle-class women had publicly reacted to the Haymarket Massacre of 1886, or expressed any solidarity with the working-class women who had participated in the labor demonstrations leading up to Haymarket.[8] Ellen Henrotin had written privately to support commuting the death sentences of the Haymarket figures, but the CWC seems not to have officially discussed the tragedy.[9] By 1894, however, the relationship of middle-class women to labor problems in the city had changed, doubtless as a result of their experiences in the IWA. Now middle-class women—often to the annoyance of middle-class men—attempted to mediate the strike and provided relief to striking workers and their families. One of the women engaged in seeking financial contributions for the families of striking Pullman workers was Fanny Kavanaugh— a leading activist in the IWA.[10] Moreover, the unsatisfactory resolution of the strike gave pause to such activists as Jane Addams to rethink the nature of their city and its problems, and the relationship of all groups within the city to the citizenry as a whole. Addams gave a talk to the CWC, musing in retrospect on the failure of all those involved in the strike to realize their shared interest in resolving the strike in ways that would achieve a common good.[11]

At the time of their fire relief efforts, Chicago women had little experience acting in public. Then they either had disagreed with male policy only in private correspondence or did what they wanted without making much public display of their objection. Their open letter denouncing the closing of the Cincinnati-run soup kitchen after the 1871 fire had been one of women's few public denouncements of male-directed fire relief. Two decades later, their experiences during the 1880s in the CWC, the IWA, and other women's organizations had produced a culture of political activism among women. When banker Lyman Gage turned away Fanny Kavanaugh when she sought his financial help for the Pullman strikers and their families, it is doubtful that she left "in tears" as the *Tribune* reported .[12] And if she had been in tears, far more likely they were tears of rage and frustration than of chastisement and hurt female feelings. In the aftermath of the Pullman strike, and as the economic depression of 1893 deepened misery in the city, activist Chicago women were primed to confront the array and depth of the social, economic, and political problems facing the city. From 1895 to 1910, Chicago women created a new public sentiment and a new women's politics through which they reconceptualized the primary role of the municipal government as directly providing for the welfare of its people.

Schools

Although activist Chicago women would address a range of municipal issues between 1895 and 1910, their engagement with the public schools provides a focused example for understanding both the ideas behind and the methods of their activism. Following the demise of the IWA in 1894, the CWC, the Chicago Association of Collegiate Alumnae, the Chicago Teachers' Federation (CTF), and settlement house residents took up the struggle to reform the schools. These women had a vision of public education that conflicted with that of the board of education and many Chicago men. Women's views of public education, in Chicago and in cities across the country, do not comfortably fit into the categories devised by men during debates over public school reform. Women are not consistently centralizers or decentralizers, and still less can they be said to regard schools either as sources of patronage jobs or as bureaucracies to be administered with business-like, nonpartisan efficiency. Chicago women, including teachers, considered supporting an elected board of education, while San Francisco women, among them the city's teachers, wanted to change from an elected to an appointed board. Memphis women fought for the right to stand for election to the school board. In Boston, where the board was elected and women could vote, Irish Catholic women supported the male "Yankee" David Ellis against the female "Irish" candidate Julia Harrington Duff, whom Irish men supported.[13] In each case women were introducing their voices into the realm of municipal politics, which tells us much about the growth of women's activism. That different women in different cities took different stands on the same issues bedeviling their schools indicates that they were responding to the context of specific patterns of growth in their cities and how these specific circumstances thwarted what they wanted from their city.

In Chicago, school reform involved a number of complex, interlocking issues: finances were not easily separated from taxation, on the one hand, and curriculum and teachers salaries, on the other. For clarity of exposition, I discuss first the teachers and their efforts to unionize and protect their labor, and then the struggle after 1902 to set the school system on a sound fiscal foundation. But, as I show, those issues were not separable from each other. Teachers' salaries depended on finances and taxation, while the taxes citizens were prepared to pay depended to some extent on their ambitions for the public schools. In all these issues, although activist women did not always agree among themselves, they nonetheless tended toward policy objectives distinct from those of the men who still controlled Chicago's municipal institutions.

Teachers and Their Union

In the 1890s, public school teachers constituted the only large group of female public employees. The men on the board of education set criteria for their hiring, retention, and pay that significantly differed from those applied to other municipal public employees. Historian Marjorie Murphy has shown that when hiring teachers, nineteenth-century school boards valued the supposedly feminine character traits of "deportment, moral character, social obedience, domestic virtue, and firm habits" over such supposedly masculine traits as intellectual prowess and analytical ability, and that a teacher's status was dictated by how well she met this ideal of femininity.[14] Using such criteria gave the men running the schools justification to declare teachers incapable of participating in such institutional and financial decisions as curriculum, testing, or classroom size. School boards also expected women teachers to be cheap labor—neither needing nor deserving of pay or pensions equal with those of male public employees—and quiescent, docile employees.[15]

The Chicago teachers had not received a pay raise since 1877; the pension fund that they had won in 1895 was underfinanced, and, by state law, voluntary. But middle-class men in the city had little regard for the teachers' finances. A special committee appointed by Mayor Harrison to study revising the school system released a report in January 1899 that recommended a pay raise for male employees of the schools; ninety-eight percent of the teachers were female, but they were to be given no raise. Moreover, this "Harper Report" complained of the paucity of male teachers and called for the recruitment of more male teachers, who would be paid more than the women and promoted more rapidly through the system. No female teachers or women had sat on this committee.[16] Two months later the teachers went unpaid when the city's comptroller, who paid teacher salaries, died suddenly. No one thought there was any hurry to appoint a replacement for him or find another mechanism through which to pay teachers, despite their frantic pleas.[17] In 1899, 1900, and again in 1901, the board cut teacher salaries to save money, while in 1902 it granted a pay raise for the (male) employees of the board architect's building staff and refused to rescind teacher salary cuts.[18]

Female teachers were systematically treated differently from other public employees in a variety of ways. They were not protected by the provisions of an 1895 civil service law that protected such male employees as police and firemen from arbitrary work changes and provided them pensions. Chicago men constantly attacked the credibility of any woman holding power within the system. School board member Alexander Revell declared, "I yield to no one in my admiration for woman and her marvelous work in her own behalf and for the world, but I am not willing to see her take entire charge of the education of the children of Chicago." Revell was unhappy that there were only ninety-two male elementary school teachers, and that as a result too many women were being promoted to positions of authority as school principals. He was seemingly in agreement with Cornell University Professor Charles DeGarmo that "women teachers are a menace to the public school system of America."[19] In June 1899 such unrelenting male hostility drove Ella Flagg Young, one of the few woman administrators in the system, to resign her post as District Superintendent. Teachers charged that a concerted effort was underway to replace all women in positions of authority with men. Based on the available evidence their fears were credible.[20]

The hostile attitude of the board of education and many male politicians and businessmen convinced teachers to form their own professional clubs and then in 1897 to organize the Chicago Teachers' Federation. The treatment of female teachers also angered the middle-class women's clubs, who in 1895 began a movement to elevate the teachers' status within the system. In that year and again in 1902, women's organizations fought efforts of the board of education and the state legislature to prohibit married women from working in the schools as "unconstitutional because it legislates against a class of working women, as a class, without reference to merit."[21] In 1896 the CWC and the Collegiate Alumnae Association opposed the board's attempts to reduce teacher salaries, saying that only "sufficient and secure" salaries could attract and retain the best quality teachers.[22] Female principals, teachers, and representatives from women's clubs met in June 1899 to plot strategy to stop Ella Flagg Young's resignation; Mrs. Frake, a former school board member told the *Tribune* that she believed nine out of ten women's club members backed Young.[23]

Marjorie Murphy has argued that middle-class clubwomen often supported policy proposals for performance reviews, retention, and promotion that differed from those sought by the teachers themselves. Noting that according to the *Tribune*, CWC member Lucy Flower submitted an anti-pension report to the general meeting of the Illinois Federation of Women's Clubs (IFWC) in 1900, Murphy inferred that CWC, or middle-class women generally, opposed teachers' pensions.[24] But other evidence does not support this conclusion. To begin with, newspaper coverage of women's activities must be weighed against evidence from the women's records themselves. This is especially true of the CWC, which refused to allow the press to attend its meetings, complaining that when allowed to attend, newspapers chronically misrepresented the CWC's affairs and ideas.[25] Moreover, the CWC regularly invited speakers whose point of view the majority of women did not necessarily endorse. The *Club and Board Minutes* of the CWC indicate neither support for Flower's position nor a general disinclination to support teacher pensions. The CWC accepted the IFWC report supporting teacher pensions, repudiating Flower's position without even discussing it.[26]

A more useful way to understand activist women's school ideas and what such ideas might reveal about their municipal vision is to investigate the points on which they agreed. From 1895, teachers and women's clubs shared four basic ideas: Teachers were better judges of educational quality than businessmen; education was a public good that must be supported by the state; school reform must be a public endeavor and not left to a small group within the city, nor men generally; and, the goal of education reform was to provide a democratic education for all children. Activist women often mixed these ideas in their responses to individual school issues. The CWC opposed state laws barring married women from teaching because it thought such measures discriminated against women. But it also opposed these kinds of state law because they would enhance the power of the all-male state legislature at the expense of a municipal body— the school board. Working so hard to place women on the school board to increase their influence over educational policy, and facing much opposition in the city as Mayor Hopkins refused in 1892 to appoint more women to the board, emphasizing that the council would refuse to name *any* women, Chicago's activist women could not countenance laws that removed women even further from the process.[27] Such proposals were complicated: women wanted to protect female teachers and the right of married women to work, but they were also alert to institutional initiatives that might limit their ability to make decisions on the development of their public school system.

Although this desire to gain power over school decisions sometimes conflicted with what teachers wanted, teachers and activist women consistently cooperated in the effort both to involve a wider public in decisions on schools and to find common ground among themselves. CWC leader Ellen Henrotin emphasized this search for a common ground in a talk before a gathering of teachers. "Women are teachers" and "women's clubs are educational," she said; the popular education movement, she continued, and the woman movement are the two great movements of the latter nineteenth century through which teachers and clubwomen would find strength to work together to achieve their goals.[28] Clubwomen such as

Henrotin and Mary Wilmarth and settlement house residents Jane Addams and Florence Kelley addressed meetings of teachers; in return, teachers such as Ella Flagg Young addressed gatherings of middle-class women, and teacher Frances Temple was a member of the CWC education department.[29] Female alliances on education reform were a practical necessity— "a strategy of coordinated reform encompassing labor, teachers, and women, representing the factory, the school, and the home for the pursuit of social reform"—dictated both by an internal logic that sprang from women's sense that they had a common outlook on education, and by the external necessity of men's hostility and determination to retain control over the schools.[30] The Teachers' Federation signaled that it understood this situation for women teachers: in 1902, it officially joined both the Chicago Federation of Labor and the IFWC.

Pursuing education reform forced activist Chicago women even further in challenging prevailing male ideas about municipal development. As they contested with men over the purposes of the public schools, they developed a clearer understanding of how municipal institutions functioned, of how intimately related were all municipal problems, and of how these problems necessitated political solutions.[31] The next step was to translate their understanding and experience into direct political action, which they did by confronting the financial situation of the schools.

The Financial Structures of the Schools

By the late 1890s, the question of school financing had attracted the attention of many Chicagoans, and activist women picked up where the IWA had left off. They set out to investigate in detail both the revenues and expenditures of the school system, even though such inquiries risked provoking severe opposition from certain quarters in the city. School funding depended heavily on property tax revenues, so examining property tax assessment and collection procedures could well uncover property owners paying less than they should, and elected officials would not welcome being put in the position of raising their constituents' taxes. School financing was further complicated by the legacy of federal government policy ceding property to localities to use for school purposes. In Chicago, the board of education and leading political and business leaders had a long record of disposing of this property through private deals. When a school fund was established with proceeds from the sale of these properties in 1833, for example, the commissioner of schools lent local businessmen money from sale of federally ceded lands; when several of those borrowers defaulted following the economic panic of 1837, it was discovered that, rather than having been made from interest produced by the fund revenues (which would have been legal), the loans had been made illegally from the principal. To make matters worse, in trying to recover the loans the commissioner had spent more than one half of the interest revenues on legal fees. As would become the recurring pattern during the rest of the century, the teachers always paid the price for this shortfall in school revenues by having their salaries delayed, frozen, or even cut.[32] When the IWA declared that the school board decided where to build new schools based on real estate interests, this charge had behind it the weight of several decades of shady dealings between the board and businessmen.

For many Chicago men, educational decisions were business decisions: the economic profitability that business (or, as we shall see in later chapters, union labor) could derive from the decisions was a priority similar to that which had driven decisions on buying provisions for fire relief in 1871. Many, however, felt that even the generous scope permitted by such a conception had been violated when it came to light in 1895 that the board had given long-term leases at very low rents to some of the city's big businesses. The board, for instance, had modified a *Tribune* lease to waive the original ten-year reevaluation clause, instead giving the paper a ninety-year lease at $31,000 until 1985.[33] One of the members of the board at the time was A. S. Trude, the attorney for the *Tribune* company. The public outcry against this transaction charged a conspiracy between the Board and the "newspaper trust" not only to manipulate school monies but also to censor the news on school decisions. The public felt, reasonably enough, that any newspaper executive sitting on the board would ensure that his paper printed only information favorable to his decisions.[34] With suspicions of a conspiracy between business and the school board already aroused, the board only fanned the flames of public outrage when it divided school finances into two accounts: the building fund and the instructional fund. The building fund was only for new school construction, and its revenues were drawn from a separate tax fund; the instructional fund had to finance all other school expenses, including all repairs and maintenance to existing buildings, instructional supplies, and teacher raises and salaries. Revenues could not be transferred between the two funds. While the building fund gathered a surplus, the instructional fund was insufficient to meet its goals.[35]

When the board ended the 1899–1900 school year early to save money, the teachers took the occasion both to appeal to Mayor Carter Harrison and the board president, Graham H. Harris, to restore their lost wages and to protest ongoing violation of teacher pay schedules. The CTF alleged that even when lost school days were factored in, the board consistently underpaid teachers. In 1899 a second-year teacher was to earn $550 annually; even when the $12.50 from lost school days was computed, she was in fact being paid only at the rate of $500 per year.[36] Harris suggested that if the teachers wanted their wages restored, then they should challenge the state law on taxation, the Juul law of 1898 that had set the allowable property tax rate for any taxing body at 5 percent of the assessed valuation of the property within its jurisdiction. This approach was guaranteed to fail. Not only did no evidence exist that the legislature could be persuaded to raise the allowable rate of taxation, the leaders of the newly organized CTF understood perfectly well that the problem was not getting individual small property owners to pay more but taxing the assets of corporations that currently paid very little.[37] When teachers' leader Margaret Haley, the CTF, and activist Chicago women initiated a sustained investigation, they discovered that the elected state board of equalization chronically under assessed corporate properties by failing to include such "intangibles" as the value of a corporation's capital stock together with tangible, physical property. Because the franchises held by major public utilities in Chicago enjoyed similar exclusions, Haley, operating from the CTF's downtown headquarters in the Unity Building, shrewdly followed a lawyer's advice to challenge the tax records of public utilities rather than private corporations because public utilities could not threaten to leave the city.[38] The CTF first asked the city council not to enact any further franchise extensions for the utilities until they paid their property taxes.[39] When the Council ignored this request, the CTF filed suit to compel the revaluation of the properties of several public utility corporations to recover lost revenues. In 1901 the Illinois courts decided in favor of the teachers' suit and the corporations were compelled to pay millions in back taxes. The enormity of the revenue that had been lost to the city can be seen in the increased franchise worth for tax purposes of two utilities: the value of Chicago Edison (the electric company) was ultimately increased from $1.725 million to $9 million, while that for Peoples' Gas increased from $2.25 to $46 million.[40]

Throughout the battle between the board and the CTF over teachers' wages, the board tried to split the union from its supporters in the women's clubs by presenting budgeting issues as choices between additional money for the teachers or the educational innovations sought by women's groups such as kindergartens, night schools, and vacation schools. In 1900 the board had responded to the protests against cut-backs in kindergartens by cutting teachers' salaries. In any financial crisis the board threatened to cut educational innovations such as kindergartens thereby forcing women's groups to plead for continued financing, at which point the board could justify cutting teacher salaries.[41] When the board found itself in July 1902 with an additional $264,000 as a result of the successful teachers' tax suit, it allocated only $20,000 to the teachers, restoring their sick benefits but not their paycuts, and used the rest to fund kindergartens and night schools, general repairs, and fuel and heat, and to give the (male) janitors a raise.[42] The teachers secured a legal injunction to prevent the board from allocating the back tax money without restoring teacher pay cuts, and the board again dismissed teacher demands for pay raises as "self-seeking and detrimental to the entire school program." It defied the injunction and told the teachers that they could "apply for a hearing" before the board's finance committee after all other allocations were finished. The board attorney publicly labeled the teachers "disturbers and insubordinates."[43] In its actions, the board, undoubtedly with the support of many other Chicago men, was trying to force activist women into a position of having to choose between educational programs and teacher salaries. The newspapers, especially the *Tribune*, presented the issue in such a light as to make the teachers look bad—one headline read "Teachers Strike at Kindergarten."[44]

But no one could report that middle-class women's organizations opposed pay raises for teachers because no evidence supported this conclusion. The board's handling of the recaptured back taxes was such a blatant attack on female public employees, and its ploy of playing kindergartens against teacher salaries so transparent, that middle-class women could hardly have failed to appreciate what was going on, especially when the board at the same time approved pay raises for its architect's male staff. Mayor Harrison ignored the teachers' plea for help, although he did urge the city council to use some of the recaptured tax revenues to rescind the pay cuts of male municipal employees. On this issue as well as others the mayor and city council hid behind the argument that they had no power to force the school board to do anything. While technically true, the mayor applied no political pressure to his appointees to reach a better accommodation with the teachers, even as he championed the wages of male public employees. In contrast, from the late 1890s the CWC held meeting after meeting to "bring together the teachers and the members of the Education Department [of the CWC]" to seek common ground and make common effort on school reform. [45]

The demands both of the newly formed League of Cook County Clubs—the third body formed by white women to place their voluntary groups under an umbrella organization that could coordinate and publicize women's activities—and of the CWC that the board not reduce expenses by cutting kindergartens were made several months before the board made it clear that kindergartens were to be traded against teacher pay.[46] Moreover, one of the CWC's leaders in this protest against cutting kindergartens was a teacher, Frances Temple. With no control over the decisions on schools, and no power to vote on municipal concerns, activist women were constantly forced into difficult positions. In such circumstances, the records of the CWC indicate that activist women tried to advocate the policy that they believed would most benefit the community as a whole while trying their best to bring all women's voices into the decision-making process. The debate over the institutional structure of the school system is a further example of how this process functioned.

The Institutional Structure of the School System

At the turn of the century, Chicago's schools were run by an administrative structure established when Chicago was a much smaller city. Thus, the schools were in desperate need of restructuring. Here, too, women's organizations and the teachers had definite ideas about such reforms. The 1898–99 Harper Committee to study school reform recommended reducing the number of board members, and giving the superintendent extensive power to decide all instructional issues, including the power to hire, fire, and transfer teachers without appeal. This was a typical "progressive" reform proposal aimed at rationalizing decision-making by concentrating it in the hands of a small number of people. Because state statutes would have to be changed to enact these proposals, the recommendations took the form of a bill submitted to the state legislature. It was clear almost immediately that the so-called Harper Bill lacked support in the city. The Chicago teachers vehemently opposed the bill, especially for increasing the power of the superintendent: as the workers who would be most directly affected by this institutional restructuring, the teachers objected to the reduced control they would have over their own labor. They immediately called a mass meeting of teachers to draw up an alternate public education bill.[47]

Other scholars maintain that middle-class women split with the teachers to support the Harper recommendations and dismissed teacher demands for higher pay because their middle-class sensibilities made them support centralized and rationalized efficiency.[48] The Collegiate Alumnae had supported the recommendations of the all-male Harper committee in 1899, and the CWC had hosted a talk by Dr. Emil Hirsch in which he roundly condemned the teachers for opposing a report compiled by "men competent to handle such subjects."[49] The *Tribune* printed the statement of an anonymous woman excoriating teachers for "being nothing more than labor unions seeking to advance their wages and to protect themselves against discharge."[50]

But as with teacher pensions, there is no evidence of a split between the two groups, despite the board's obvious effort to divide women against one another. Hirsch, for example, was only one of many education "experts," including teachers, that the CWC invited to address the club on the issue of public school restructuring. Indeed, although the education department of the CWC originally declared approval of the Harper Bill's provision to increase the powers of the superintendent, within a month it had reversed itself and called for renewed discussion within the CWC because "some of our ablest members [oppose] certain features of the bill" and "so many teachers objected to this plan."[51] The CWC held discussion sessions on school reform throughout 1899, and along with other women's clubs called for the formation of a new citizens' committee to look into school reform. In March 1899, CWC and CTF members met with the Civic Federation and decided to replace the appointed Harper committee with a broader citizens' committee to write a new education bill.[52] The Committee of 100 that resulted from this meeting included teachers' leaders Margaret Haley and Gertrude Bratten, and CWC education committee members Gertrude Blackwelder, Clara Kretzinger, Mrs. Duncanson, Mrs. Bolte, Sadie American, and Frances Temple, who was also a teacher.

Since no women had sat on the Harper Committee, the composition of the Committee of 100 itself indicates that activist women were playing a growing role in municipal affairs.[53] Furthermore, this strategy and other events on school reform indicate that teachers and middle-class women were working together and also that teachers, who had to protect their labor, were able to sway clubwomen to their side even though they could never see school reform in exactly the same way. When Margaret Haley addressed the IFWC in 1901, she turned aside doubts about supporting teacher pensions because it might be class legislation, pointing out that so too were pensions for policemen, firemen, and soldiers. "Why," she asked these women, do you then "criticize pensions for women and not for men?" This was the meeting that resolved to support teacher pensions, a resolution the CWC absolutely accepted.[54]

As they debated the Harper Report, a coalition of teachers and clubwomen prevented the resignation of Ella Flagg Young when she threatened to leave her position as district superintendent because of her frustration and disillusionment with the school board.[55] In 1900 and 1901, while Haley and other teachers dug through tax records to expose corporate tax-dodging, middle-class women held public meetings and raised money, at a "Tax Fund" benefit in early 1901, to sustain the legal costs of the teachers' fight.[56] The CWC was pleased that the proposed school legislation written by the Committee of 100 "recognizes the legal right of teachers to form Councils for the discussion of all educational subjects . . . and to make recommendations to the Board of Education and to the Superintendent." While this was possibly not the ringing endorsement of teachers' unions that the teachers desired, it reflected the clubwomen's support of the right to organize. The CWC concluded that the new proposed legislation "is not perfect . . . but recognizing the many factions and difficulties besetting the [Committee], and the general merit of its intent, the [CWC education committee] voted unanimously to approve the Bill as a whole."[57] The records of the CWC and its actions make it clear that it sought compromise and consensus on school measures that had the best interests of the children at heart, while acknowledging the professional expertise and need for protection of the teachers.

This spirit of compromise toward a common welfare was perhaps best expressed by Jane Addams in her remarks to a mass meeting at the Central Music Hall called by the CTF in late 1900 to protest the corporate evasion of property taxes. Addams rejected the corporations' defense that they had done nothing technically illegal in not paying taxes on their intangible property because it had not been assessed. She acknowledged that when businessmen "act in their corporate capacity especially and think only of the legal side, I suppose it seems to them quite right to evade taxation." She nonetheless refused to allow that this was sufficient. Addams argued instead that business had a public responsibility to pay these taxes and that businessmen could no longer be allowed to think that their needs came before those of the community as a whole.

> We will have to bring to bear the whole pressure of the community . . . until it shall be a great disgrace that any great corporation does not pay its adequate taxes; until any share holder shall be ashamed to receive a dividend if out of that dividend has not first been paid that which is legitimately owed to the city. And that, I take it, is simply a matter of public opinion, and the public opinion can only be manufactured by all of the people and for all of the people.

Addams viewed as interconnected all citizens of the municipal community and had come to believe that every individual—and corporation—owed something to the whole. For corporations to act within the letter of the law was insufficient if by doing so they harmed the good of the whole. The meeting adopted a resolution declaring complete support for the teachers' campaign, stating in addition that it was imperative that "no class of property shall escape its just portion of the public burden at the expense of the owners of other property."[58]

The remarks at this same meeting of Dr. Rufus White provide a useful contrast to Addams's idea. White argued that the corporations should pay taxes on their intangible property because their interests were so largely represented in the state legislature that they were guilty of "representation without taxation, and [this] also is un-American." In other words, they should be compelled to pay these taxes because not doing so violated the accepted procedures of government; taxation and representation went hand in hand, and no one deserved one without the other. White's argument resembles that made by the Central Labor Union six years earlier, that it was "unAmerican" for the municipal government not to meet the needs of working men. And White's argument came perilously close to saying that those who did not pay taxes (who in 1900 included non-property owners) did not deserve representation. Neither White in 1900 nor the CLU in

1894 elevated the good of the whole over the good of the individual or of individual classes within the city, as Addams had suggested.[59]

Addams developed her point in her 1902 book, *Democracy and Social Ethics*, when she further argued that businessmen limited the scope of municipal reform movements by occupying themselves with "a concern for the better method of administration, rather than with the ultimate purpose of securing the welfare of the people . . . [and] fail to consider the final aims of city government."[60] While Addams sought to focus on final aims, White emphasized methods. A few years earlier, the IWA and CLU had exhibited a similar difference between ends and means. When the CWC called retention of bad teachers "a crime against children," it too focused on final aims.[61] When groups of activist women such as the CWC made "the common good" the aim of their school activities, they and teachers could disagree over the means to that end but not over the ultimate end of education reform itself. Both groups of women put the common good, which could be realized through a well-educated population, above the needs of the individuals in that population. The teachers rejected business-driven proposals for the institutional restructuring of the system, believing that power centralized into the hands of the superintendent would bring undemocratic education that would harm the common welfare. In 1903 Margaret Haley told the Civic Federation that under business-like restructuring, teachers, "who are in fact the real educators of the children, have no security of tenure or office or salary, except that which the will of one man assures, and no more voice in the educational system of which they are a part than the children they teach."[62] This split in reform thinking, between achieving administrative efficiency in municipal institutions and reform that would promote a common good, continued to divide activist Chicago women and men during the coming decades. As their engagement with school reform made activist women recognize the nature of this split, they became even more determined to involve themselves in a broader range of municipal decisions.

Women's Municipal Activism

Without the vote and with no direct representation in the political parties, activist women continued to be frustrated in their efforts to effect municipal reforms. In early 1902, in a speech to the Lake View Woman's Club, settlement house resident Julia Lathrop urged women to proceed along two lines: "[T]he first thing is to create public sentiment and then express it at every opportunity." "When the present indifference has disappeared," she continued, "then go to the Legislature."[63] In her strategy, Lathrop envisioned women constructing strong alliances, working through these alliances to capture the attention of the city, and making their ideas into public causes that the political system would have to acknowledge. Among the tactics that activist women were using within such a strategy was the mass meeting that in public drew together as many people as possible. One may note the irony in women's turning to mass politics at the same moment when male political leaders and parties were abandoning such methods in favor of expert leadership and administrative functions.[64] But without the vote, women had few other options, and this strategy had yielded some initial success in stopping the Harper Committee school re-organization plan and in suing over corporate taxes. As Marjorie Murphy described it from the perspective of the teachers, "They developed a work style that allowed them to function in public affairs where they had neither legal rights nor traditional positions of authority."[65]

Chicago women bolstered the tactic of the mass meeting with a more aggressive version of personal investigation that had originated with the IWA. In 1893 and 1894 the CWC adopted this tactic by circulating peti-tions throughout the city to support appointment of women to the school board. The teachers used this strategy, and expanded upon it, in their crusade against the non–tax paying corporations. CTF members held mass meetings and fanned out into the neighborhoods to bring the campaign directly to the people, a tactic that was made all the more necessary by the newspapers' reluctance to publicize this campaign. As Margaret Haley described it, the teachers went armed with graphs and charts, printed sheets and leaflets, and explained how the nonpayment of taxes by corpora-tions hurt the rest of the citizenry. "They passed out pamphlets at church doors, tacked signs on telegraph poles, and left our so-called literature in barber shops, drug stores, meat markets, and saloons."[66] Then the CTF established "Citizens' Precinct Co-operative Committees" in every city precinct to circulate petitions to all residents asking for their support in the suit against the corporations. Margaret Haley told the teachers that no organized group in the city was as close to the general public as teachers and thus it was their "duty to assume some of the most important func-tions of citizenship" and lead the tax campaign.[67]

Without this grassroots political work, women could hardly have suc-ceeded in getting anything that they had wanted for school reform. One of their leading opponents, for example, was Chicago real estate executive and legislator David Shanahan, who led the legislative fight to further eviscerate what little pension protection the teachers had. Haley recounted a conversation in which he implied that his bills were retaliation for the teachers' suit. "When you teachers stayed in your schoolrooms we men took care of you: but when you go out of your schoolrooms, as you have done, and attack these great, powerful corporations, you must expect that they will hit back."[68] Even if Haley embellished the story, women knew that without actual political power they were prey to this kind of retaliation from businessmen, politicians, and political bodies.

Without the vote and without actual representation, the mass meeting and grassroots, precinct-level organizing were activist women's most effective tactics for securing a public voice. But even as they perfected these tactics, they began to work for municipal suffrage, recognizing it as the only means that would ensure that their voice would be listened to and that would give them the ultimate weapon in a democratic system toward securing what they wanted for their city.

Four

"The Welfare of the Community Requires the Admission of Women to Full Citizenship": The Campaign for Municipal Suffrage, 1896–1912

As THE suffrage movement gained momentum in the early twentieth century, the Chicago Woman Suffrage Party, headed by Antoinette Funk, communicated with the national movement over issues of national policy. But the suffrage movement in Chicago owed as much to municipal activism as it did to national suffrage efforts. The reasons for this situation lay in both the state and local contexts. In the mid-1880s ties between the national suffrage movement (NWSA) and the Illinois Woman Suffrage Association (IWSA) were weak, and the national organization was frustrated by what it perceived as the state organization's lack of activity. Then in 1884 the IWSA, which the next year changed its name to the Illinois Equal Suffrage Association (IESA), decided to focus its efforts on gaining the municipal suffrage, thereby enhancing the role of local organizations in the suffrage effort.[1] This shift enhanced both the potential power of local suffrage organizations and their ability to shift their emphasis to local organization and local criteria. Earlier, in the 1860s, the Chicago Sorosis had promoted suffrage as a right of political equality. But when the Cook County Suffrage Association (CCSA) and then the CWC took up the issue in the 1880s, these groups began shifting the argument from suffrage as equal rights to suffrage as a woman's political need in the city. Caroline Huling, one of the CCSA's founders, declared that its members wanted suffrage "to insure children education, protection, responsibility, and opportunity." The organization's newspaper, *Justitia: A Court for the Unrepresented*, proclaimed its goal as rooted in municipal conditions, as did the broad interests and activities of some of its founding members. Most of the information we have about the CCSA is contained in Caroline Huling's small manuscript collection. Huling herself was also a founding member of the IWA . Among the other CCSA founding members, Mary Ahrens was on the governing board of the PAWC in the late 1880s; and physician Julia Holmes Smith was on the first governing board of the PAWC, was the first woman on the board of directors of the bureau of justice in 1894, and was an active member of the CWC, including serving both as its second president and on its education committee.[2]

Until women gained the vote, much suffrage activity in Chicago was thus the work of women's clubs, settlement houses, and working women, who were not only already engaged in a variety of municipal causes but also focused the suffrage movement on the specific aim of using women's votes to better urban development.[3] This element of the Chicago suffrage movement made it different from the urban suffrage movements explored by Gayle Gullett and Sarah Deutsch, for example. Rather than seeing suffrage as a means to "good government" as defined primarily by middle-class male reformers, woman suffrage was a priority in Chicago across class, race, and ethnicity because it was a necessary step toward restructuring the institutions of municipal government to provide for the common welfare.[4]

Municipal Suffrage

At its meeting of May 23, 1894, the CWC adopted the resolution offered by Celia Parker Woolley (who had also nominated Fannie Barrier Williams for membership in the CWC) to organize a committee "for the study of the principles of political equality." Joining Woolley on this organizing committee were one of the city's leading suffrage figures, Catharine Waugh McCulloch, and clubwomen Mary Wilmarth and Ellen Henrotin. That fall, the full Club agreed to adopt Woolley's suggestion and founded the Chicago Political Equality League (CPEL).[5] Celia Parker Woolley became the CPEL's first president, and its first board of directors included McCulloch, Henrotin, and Dr. Julia Holmes Smith. Members of the CWC who wished to join were automatically eligible for membership; non-members of the CWC could be proposed for membership by women belonging either to the CWC or the CPEL. The only limiting qualification to this membership—and it signaled the CPEL's distinctly municipal character—was that all members either had to be residents of Chicago or someone "whose daily business place is in Chicago," a measure that indicates that these activist women thought of themselves as members of a community of women that extended beyond the city's boundaries. Nonetheless, during its existence most of the leaders and members of the CPEL lived in Chicago. In 1895, five of six officers and fifteen of twenty-one directors were Chicago residents; in 1900, 148 of the 162 members lived in the city; and in 1913–14, 1,203 of its 1,398 members lived in the city. The vast majority of members who did not live in Chicago lived in the nearby western suburb of Oak Park.[6]

The CPEL's "By-Laws" articulated a double purpose: to "promote the study of political science and government" and to "foster and extend the political rights and privileges of women." To perform these functions, the CPEL constituted two standing committees. The Public Meetings and Study Class was charged to hold monthly public meetings for discussion of a specified political topic. During its first year of work, the CPEL cast issues in the form of a proposition, inviting one speaker to argue in favor and another in opposition. Among the propositions debated the first year were "That Partisanship in Politics is Destructive of Patriotism and Women are Injured by Participation Therein," and "That Women's Direct Influence is not Needed in Legislative Reform." The next year's program shifted to presentation and discussion on specific topics, including possible legislation for women and children, and village improvements and city government. This latter topic led the CPEL to make "The Government of Cities" the subject of its entire 1897–98 season of study meetings.[7] In November and December 1900, the CPEL hosted Jane Addams in a series of lectures that would form the basis of her subsequent book, *Democracy and Social Ethics*. The CPEL's second standing committee, the Ward and Precinct Work, Suffrage Literature and Petitions, was charged with circulating suffrage petitions and literature within the city's wards and precincts, thus continuing the women's practice of grassroots activity.[8]

The CPEL, however, was not the only center of suffrage activity in Chicago at the turn of the century. In 1902 a group professional women and clubwomen, many of whom belonged to the CPEL, began a separate campaign to secure the vote for taxpaying women of the city; such partial suffrage, they hoped, could appeal even to those who did not believe in full suffrage for women but who might "admit the justice of the principle that those citizens whose property is taxed to support the government should have a voice in the levy and expenditure of taxes." Activists Henrotin, Lucy Flower, Ada Sweet, Sarah Hackett Stevenson, and Kate Tuley, among others, had been pursuing suffrage using this strategy for several years. Now this group asked sympathetic women to present the idea in their clubs, canvass their neighborhoods, and pressure state legislators to consider such legislation.[9] The question of whether to secure a limited suffrage as a "foot in the door" toward full suffrage was a constant theme running through the debates of national suffrage organizing, so it is not surprising to see it appear in Chicago. But these women quickly dropped the idea of limited suffrage when a movement in 1902 to draft a new municipal charter offered an opportunity to secure full municipal suffrage. From 1902 until the failure of the charter reform movement in 1910, activist women used the issue as a means to organize and sustain a cross-class engagement with municipal affairs.

Municipal Suffrage and Charter Reform

In the United States, all municipalities receive their authority to govern and their specific powers from their state legislature, either in the form of a charter—a legal document—written for a specific city or through a general incorporation act that applies to all municipal corporations in the state. In the late nineteenth century, Chicago fell into this latter category: since 1875 its government had functioned within the restrictions of a statewide general incorporation act that applied to all cities and towns with populations over two thousand. The legal restrictions imposed by this law had led to a steadily worsening political situation for Chicago by the end of the century.[10] State law seriously limited the municipal government's power; for instance, the city exercised no control over the board of education or the three park boards. In total, seven distinct governing bodies administered various public services within the city's boundaries.[11] State law also set the percentage of tax revenues for each governing body so that the city could not legally redistribute funds from one body to another according to need. Furthermore, under then-current state legislation, Chicago had reached its legal limit of bonded indebtedness and could not issue more municipal bonds to finance services.[12] With a population of 1.8 million at the turn of the century, the city was desperately short of funds to finance critical public services. Finally, because the state retained the right to decide crucial issues of urban development, organized groups, such as the real estate board, regularly turned to Springfield to circumvent any Chicago City Council opposition to their plans.

When the Civic Federation announced plans in 1902 to study the feasibility of writing a new charter for Chicago, activist women already understood that one critical obstacle toward implementing their demands on, for instance, public education and public baths was that the municipal government lacked both the power and the revenues to make changes even if it had wanted to. A new charter could consolidate the overlapping governing bodies into a system more manageable and accountable to the citizenry; it could be a strong home-rule charter to free the city from the dictates of the state legislature and the machinations of such groups as the realtors. Best of all, a new charter could grant women municipal suffrage. As Chicago formalized the process of securing a new charter, women grew more determined to play a role in the movement. The men controlling the process, however, refused to invite women to participate in preliminary discussions for writing a new charter. They did not permit women to serve as delegates to the official Charter Convention that met from 1906 until 1907 and refused them permission to address that body.[13] As it turned out, the Charter Convention's decision to exclude women from the process, which it then followed with a refusal to provide municipal suffrage in the proposed charter, would have serious ramifications for the charter's fate. The episode as a whole exposes the strong connections that activist women and men made between woman suffrage and a municipal agenda; how Chicago women bridged social distinctions through the suffrage movement; and how Chicago's male progressives gave lip service to middle-class women's activities but by the turn of the century either recognized that they and activist women wanted different things for the city or deliberately misunderstood the women. Either way, the result was the same: men excluded women from the charter movement and refused to support municipal suffrage.[14]

The CWC acted first by appointing a committee in April 1902 to study the charter question and its importance for city government, especially the idea of consolidating the municipality's governing bodies.[15] When a new charter committee met in October that year to write the enabling legislation needed to allow the city to write a new charter, it included no women members, and women's correspondence and written recollections are too sporadic and at times undated to permit us to trace their activities before the charter debates became public. Once the state legislature and the voters had approved the enabling legislation in late 1904, a seventy-member charter convention was appointed to meet in 1906 to write a new charter. At this point, activist women, originally unaware of one another's actions, set out to influence the convention's work. In January 1906, Catharine Waugh McCulloch, in her capacity as the legislative superintendent for the IESA, moved to arrange a meeting between her group and the charter convention. In the meantime, Ellen Henrotin and Jane Addams were about to do the same, as Henrotin indicated in a letter to McCulloch, and then suggested that they all cooperate in the endeavor.[16] A few months later, the Chicago Women's Trade Union League (CWTUL) sent a resolution drafted by waitress union leader Elizabeth Maloney to the Chicago Federation of Labor (CFL), asking it to work on behalf of woman suffrage in the new charter.[17] Then in May, Henrotin's name appears listed as head of the IESA committee on municipal suffrage.[18]

In her dual capacity as legislative superintendent of the IESA and a leader in the CPEL, McCulloch directed much of the women's efforts throughout the summer of 1906, especially those promoting municipal suffrage. The charter convention was not officially to meet until October, but the delegates held preliminary meetings during the summer to discuss how they wanted to proceed. McCulloch took advantage of this interlude to circulate a letter among convention delegates and other men in the city listing the reasons the new charter should grant women the vote. This letter provides a direct link between woman suffrage and municipal development. Chicago women, McCulloch wrote, wanted the vote to participate not just in the election of municipal officials but also in deciding upon such vital municipal issues as police and fire protection, construction of tenements, water, light, heat, and telephone service, food inspection, and sewage and garbage disposal.[19] McCulloch's manuscript collection contains two letters of response that reveal the gulf between male and female activism on charter reform. Richard T. Crane, one of the city's leading

businessmen, wrote that he would rather see suffrage restricted than expanded because only limited suffrage would make it possible to conduct
municipal government "on the same general principles that prevail in the
management of business enterprises." In the other letter, A. C. Bartlett
replied to McCulloch that he completely opposed the municipal suffrage.
Women did not, he assured her, need municipal suffrage because they were
not interested in such pressing municipal issues as water, light, phone, and
so on.[20] Unlike what some women's historians have described as the case
in other cities, activist men and women in Chicago often failed to cooperate on suffrage. Moreover, women's activism was motivated neither solely
by maternalist impulses that men could accept nor by a sense of good
government that resembled that of Chicago men.[21] When activist Chicago
women wanted to redirect municipal development in ways that differed
from those of men, Crane, Bartlett, and other men saw them as interfering
in male prerogatives and were determined to prevent this from happening.

Women were not encouraged by this response to their initiatives on
municipal suffrage, but they intensified their campaign as the convention
prepared to open in late 1906. The CWC urged its members to do whatever they could to secure municipal suffrage in any new charter.[22] McCulloch wrote to CWTUL leader Margaret Dreier Robins' husband, Raymond Robins—one of the few convention delegates who expressed
support for the suffrage initiative—asking him to lead the fight to include
suffrage in the charter.[23] The convention committee on elections actually
granted women a hearing on the subject but then voted five to four against
recommending woman suffrage in the charter. The women's plea to take
their case to the whole convention—voiced by delegate Louis Post—was
denied.[24] Those delegates supporting woman suffrage then raised the issue
before the convention, but the majority refused to reconsider. Opponents
of woman suffrage argued, predictably, that voting would pollute wom-
en's "tenderness . . . those feminine qualities which particularly appeal to
men," and that women did not want to be dragged "down from the pedes-
tal to mix in ward politics." But the convention delegates also argued that
it would be injudicious of these middle-class men to grant women suffrage
because it risked giving a voice in municipal affairs to the wrong women.
The problem, they said, was "that the influence of the ladies that we seek
to obtain will not be obtained."[25]

When it became clear that the charter convention would refuse to provide municipal suffrage in the new charter, Chicago women put together
a broad-based coalition to defeat it. McCulloch asked Margaret Dreier
Robins, who was helping lead the CWTUL's fight for suffrage, to address
the CWC on the issue.[26] Activist clubwomen compiled a list of speakers
available to address anti-charter gatherings, a list that included settlement

house figures Jane Addams and Mary McDowell, clubwoman Henrotin, and labor leaders Robins and Corinne Brown.[27] A "Committee for Extension of Municipal Suffrage" to coordinate the anti-charter efforts appointed Henrotin as honorary chair and Addams as vice-chair.[28] Addams claimed that a cross-class organization of one hundred women's groups was working against the charter. Their campaign, she recounted, was composed of

> organizations of working women who had keenly felt the need of the municipal franchise in order to secure for their workshops the most rudimentary sanitation . . . by federations of mothers' meetings, who were interested in clean milk and the extension of kindergartens . . . by property-owning women, who had been powerless to protest against unjust taxation; by organizations of professional women, of university students, and of collegiate alumnae; by women's clubs interested in municipal reforms.

Addams also claimed that the immigrant women of the Hull House neighborhood had come to her asking what they could do to secure the municipal suffrage in the charter.

> [S]ome Russian women waited upon me to ask whether under the new charter they could vote for covered markets and so get rid of the shocking Chicago grime upon all their food; and . . . some neighboring Italian women sent me word that they would certainly vote for public washhouses. . . . It was all so human, so spontaneous, and so direct.

In March, 1906 Addams urged the members of the Lake View Woman's Club to support municipal suffrage because a city's problems resembled the chores women were doing already in their homes, such as educating children and inspecting food.[29]

The CTF and other working women's organizations joined the women's anti-charter forces. The CTF had attacked the charter convention for its lack of popular representation and for its attempts to give businessmen even more control over the public schools.[30] In late 1906, the organization resolved to accept only a charter that both freed the city from the state legislature and dramatically increased political democracy in the city: "We reiterate our demands for a home rule charter for Chicago, to be framed by the elective representatives of the people of Chicago, subject to referendum vote of the people and with power in the people to amend said charter on their own initiative."[31] The finished charter contained none of these provisions, so the CTF was receptive to the appeal of Elizabeth Maloney, representing the Self-Supporting Women's Equal Suffrage Association, and Alice Henry, of the CWTUL and the West Side Equal Suffrage Association, that the CTF work against the charter.[32] In mid-June, the CTF

Figure 7. Milk Sterilization Center at Northwestern University Settlement, 1903. (Chicago *Daily News*, Chicago Historical Society, DN-0000806)

asked the CFL to oppose the charter. At that time, the CTF constituted a committee of 250 teachers authorized to work with other women's groups to defeat the charter.[33]

In various venues, the women's anti-charter forces made known their opposition to the charter because they wanted more of a voice for women in municipal affairs. Jane Addams wrote, "[It] seemed as if the time must be ripe for political expression of that public concern on the part of women which had so long been forced to seek indirection . . . [to] seek an opportunity to cooperate directly in civic life through the use of the ballot in regard to their own civic affairs."[34] An unnamed female activist was quoted as saying: "The women of Chicago are not indifferent to Chicago's welfare. By painful round-about efforts they have initiated much public improvement. . . . We have patiently used our antiquated, clumsy, labor-wasting methods of meeting our needs. We now demand a modern implement—the ballot."[35] Speaking before the CWTUL, Elizabeth Maloney observed that if the charter passed, working women would "lose the opportunity of securing suffrage for twenty years."[36] The CPEL made municipal suffrage the main topic of its discussions from October 1906 through January 1907, with Henrotin, Addams, McCulloch, and teachers' leader Margaret Haley among the main speakers, and Ida B. Wells-

Figure 8. Italian Mothers' Club, Chicago Commons Settlement. (Photographer unknown, Chicago Historical Society, ICHi-30452)

Barnett in charge of the "question box" into which members were to submit their queries at the December meeting.[37] Despite this obviously well-organized and far-reaching campaign, the media gave little coverage to women's anti-charter efforts, and men's groups in their publications and public pronouncements on the charter generally ignored women. The city's three largest circulation dailies, the *Tribune*, the *Record Herald*, and the *Daily News*, supported the proposed charter and conspicuously ignored women. Only the two papers opposing the charter—the *American* and the *Inter-Ocean*—covered women's activities.[38]

Municipal Suffrage and Women's Coalition-Building

Chicago voters defeated the charter by referendum vote in September 1907. How much women's opposition contributed to the charter's failure is difficult to assess, but women believed that their actions had contributed to the charter's defeat, which in turn helped galvanize more coalition-building.[39] The legislative department of the IESA extolled the anti-charter work done by a "women's committee from ninety-seven women's organizations" and declared that women had worked against the charter because it omitted municipal suffrage, discriminated against women in civil service laws, kept women from voting for school officers, and in-

Figure 9. Three Chicago Women at Entrance to 1908 Republican Convention, Chicago Coliseum. (Chicago *Daily News*, Chicago Historical Society, DN-0006265)

creased women's taxes. In short, it blocked women's right to equal access to the political realm of decision-making and office-holding.[40]

Clearly, the anti-charter campaign had consequences for developing women's activism, for example, by drawing more women into the cause of both suffrage and municipal reform. The municipal suffrage campaign helped convert clubwoman Madeleine Wallin Sikes to suffrage. Sikes, who was married to Chicago progressive reformer George Sikes, had told him in 1893 that the highest calling of womanhood was to "live a fuller and more complete life right where she always has—in the home as the unit of society."[41] But her engagement with activist women, including serving as education legislative chair for the national Association of Collegiate Alumnae, pushed her to see the necessity and the justice of "full public participation" for women.[42] Thus, in 1909 Sikes wrote to her father:

> I am more interested in this proposal [municipal suffrage] than I have ever been in any suffrage movement, for it seems to me that the women of Chicago have earned the right to share in civic affairs. . . . Moreover, many persons who are not moved by the theoretical application of democratic principles, are yielding

to the pressure of expediency, and are beginning to demand the ballot as the most effective means of bringing about what they wish to accomplish. I confess this is the argument that appeals to me.

Sikes further observed that she had been won over to suffrage by the fact that "so many women who I admire are now counted among the suffragists."[43]

The charter campaign also intensified women's efforts to pursue their aims across the bounds of class and ethnicity, even if their preferred methods at times differed. Hull House began to hold suffrage meetings, which drew neighborhood women into the effort. Russian-Jewish immigrant Hilda Satt Polacheck later recalled distributing leaflets at the corner of Halsted and Taylor Streets announcing one such meeting. Polacheck, who was a Socialist and later joined the Woman's Party, did think the Hull House suffrage activities rather tame. "The group that met at Hull House was rather polite in asking for the vote," she commented. "It was considered best to be a 'lady' and not offend the men, who had the power to give the vote to women."[44]

When activist men began a second charter reform effort in 1908–9, women again brought up municipal suffrage. This time, more men appeared ready to listen to women and perhaps to write municipal suffrage into a proposed charter. The delegates even reversed their previous stand and invited women to address the convention as a whole. But the result was much the same: while influential progressive Charles Merriam actively supported municipal suffrage, Walter L. Fisher, another leading progressive reformer, said that no law on women voting should be enacted before polling the sentiment of the entire female population.[45] In the end, this charter convention, too, refused to place municipal suffrage in a new charter and ducked the issue by declaring it a matter for the state, drafting a separate bill on municipal suffrage for the legislature.[46] The convention members hoped that this tactic would keep Chicago women from opposing new charter legislation. Chicago women accepted the compromise and traveled to Springfield in 1909 to lobby for municipal suffrage. Joining familiar suffrage figures Addams, McCulloch, and Henrotin on this trip were Agnes Nestor of the glovemakers' union, Elizabeth Maloney of the waitresses, and Mrs. James Witkowsky, president of the Jewish Chicago Woman's Aid (CWA). All of these women heavily stressed the desire and need of working and ethnic women for the vote. During this phase of the municipal suffrage campaign, Nestor spoke to the CWC on the subject of how "the ballot could help the girls in the Industrial World," and unionized Chicago women increased their campaign for the suffrage among their ranks.[47]

Not only did the municipal suffrage bill fail to pass the state legislature in 1909, this time the legislature refused even to pass the new charter.[48] Chicago women intensified their suffrage efforts. In 1912 the CPEL succeeded in placing an advisory ballot on woman suffrage before Chicago voters. Although most accounts of the Illinois suffrage campaign focus on middle-class women, ethnic and working-class women were also working hard for municipal suffrage.[49] The immigrant women of the University of Chicago Settlement Woman's Club, located at 4630 South Gross Avenue in the stockyards neighborhood, promoted the suffrage ballot by selling buttons marked "Votes for Women" on one side and "CWTUL" on the other. Volunteers stood outside polling places urging men to vote for suffrage.[50] The CWTUL appealed to the men of the Chicago labor movement to support the proposition: "We vote with you men in the union meetings; we want to vote with you at the ballot box. . . . Woman Suffrage will help emancipate half of the working class and makes for the highest democracy."[51] To spread their message as broadly as possible, the CWTUL distributed sample ballots in Yiddish, Italian, Polish, and Lithuanian, as well as English.[52]

The 1912 advisory ballot failed, 135,410 against and 71,354 in favor. But the campaign for it, along with the earlier support that activist middle-class women had given to working women's causes (discussed in more detail in chapter 5), had helped to forge broader women's coalitions. The anti-charter campaign had catalyzed women to reach out to one another in new and far-ranging ways. By the second decade of the century, white middle-class women's clubs, suffrage organizations, the CWTUL, the CTF, and individual women's unions had formed a coalition representing tens of thousands of women.[53] In the second and third decades of the new century, African American and other ethnic women's organizations would join this coalition. In late 1913 the municipal suffrage campaign succeeded. The state legislature gave all Illinois women the vote in federal and municipal (but not state) elections. Municipal suffrage had crystallized the coalition, but once the coalition was in place and municipal suffrage gained, women's activism was such an integral part of Chicago politics that it could be put to work to bring women's voices and ideas into virtually every area of the city's development.

Chapter 5 examines activist women's work from 1910 to 1916 on a broad range of municipal problems. Housing, public health and safety, recreation and lakefront development, strikes and the use of police power, and public education all became focal points of women's activism. During this second decade of the century, progressive reform was in full swing as Chicagoans of almost every kind discovered that they could not ignore these problems. The great amount of activism during these years makes it possible to present in some detail the differences between activist men's and women's agendas for urban growth and reform.

Five

"To Bring Together Women Interested in Promoting the Welfare of the City": The Expansion of Women's Municipal Work, 1910–16

In 1910 activist Chicago women founded the Woman's City Club (WCC) and began a new stage in women's municipal work. With a membership that grew from 1,250 in 1910 to over 5,000 a decade later, the WCC led the activist women's coalition that had formed in the anti-charter and municipal suffrage crusades.[1] A high percentage of those married women serving as officers and directors of the WCC during its first decade were married to members of the male City Club.[2] In composition, size, membership policies, and ideas about municipal development, however, the two clubs differed, and these factors make it useful to compare the two clubs throughout the chapter.[3] Both clubs constituted internal committees dedicated to investigating municipal issues, but the men used and paid outside experts to investigate municipal problems and then to advise the CC of appropriate solutions. The WCC practiced the personal grassroots activism that can be traced directly back through the CTF tax campaigns to the IWA of the late 1880s and to women's response to fire relief in 1871. It organized members according to the political ward in which they resided and instructed these ward-based committees to investigate the local conditions of streets and alleys, housing, schools and churches, smoke pollution, infant mortality rates, numbers of children and juvenile delinquency, parks, playgrounds, beaches, dance halls, saloons, hotels, jails and courts, and garbage collection and disposal.[4] The personalized style of municipal activism that these women had been forging across the decades stands in marked contrast to the habits of the progressive members of the City Club, who would gather to debate municipal issues and listen to experts present their opinions.[5]

These contrasting approaches cannot, I believe, be attributed solely or even primarily to financial considerations. Louise de Koven Bowen, for example, a founding mother of the WCC, was a fabulously wealthy widow who gave more than five hundred thousand dollars to Hull House between 1895 and 1928.[6] The WCC's first president, Mary Wilmarth, was also a quite wealthy widow who generously gave away money. But underwriting professional investigators was not activist women's style. Jane Addams later recalled how as a member of the Legal Aid Society, Wilmarth had responded to the plight of women strikers arrested while picketing. "I can see her now standing in the dingy police station at DesPlaines Street bailing out people," Addams recounted.[7] Wilmarth was then well into her seventies and could simply have provided the money, but she chose to do the work herself. Nor can it be argued that women necessarily had more time at their disposal to undertake their personal, activist approach to municipal problems. Many of the activists were working women: doctors, lawyers, teachers, university professors, gloveworkers, waitresses, and journalists who juggled careers, homes, and municipal work, often giving as much attention to their municipal work as did the widows, the middle-class women, who did not need to work to support themselves, and the social workers, whose professional sphere overlapped with their municipal activism.

As this chapter shows, activist Chicago women continued to define the appropriate ends of municipal work differently from activist men during this decade. In her 1913 essay, Anna Nicholes, who served as superintendent of the WCC in its early years, described the women's perspective on municipal work. She began by asking the question that the WCC used to recruit new members: "Madam, Who Keeps Your House?"[8] Framing the discussion in these terms, Nicholes appealed to all women to transform their personal housekeeping experiences into a broader municipal housekeeping. Although scholars have generally viewed women's municipal work in this era as women cleaning the city as they cleaned their homes, imagining the city as a shared home gave women a metaphor through which to articulate and establish a different and rather more comprehensive set of priorities for city government than the men of the time were prepared to imagine.[9] Nicholes theorized that men saw the city as a "business corporation . . . a center for business representing big municipal contracts" in which men weighed every municipal issue in terms of money. She recounted the story of a prominent Chicago banker who told her that he used to dislike the putrid odors coming from the city's stockyards, then had changed his mind: "[B]ut do you know what it means to me now?" he asked. "Dollars." Nicholes insisted that women instead were developing a "city sense."

> [A] conception which might almost be said to come from the hearts of the women, a sense that the city is not alone a business corporation . . . but that the city is becoming conscious of itself as a city of homes, as a place in which to rear children. . . . We are building now a new city—a spiritual city, where the watchword is "personal welfare." . . . This new city will care because babies die from preventable diseases . . . will work to decrease the procession of little chil-

dren going through the Juvenile Court; will open to all greater industrial and social opportunities within its borders.[10]

Nicholes linked the personal realm of housekeeping to the public realm of municipal work, in much the same way that political theorist Anne Phillips has described late-twentieth-century feminist politics as making the practical matters of everyday life into the primary purpose of government.[11] "The relation between a woman and her city is real and tangible," Nicholes told her readers, urging them not to remain aloof from municipal problems, because women could reshape the city into a more livable and truly democratic space. Moreover, Nicholes exhorted women to immerse themselves in the practical details of municipal government so as to understand all of its political and financial aspects and then to translate their new sense of the city into practical political work that would result not in "a vision of a purified city" but a city that worked "for human betterment."[12] Nicholes used a "traditional" woman's concern for sick children as a concrete example of the linkage. She agreed that activist women's support for visiting nurses was "noble work . . . for the poor babies of the congested city neighborhoods," work that had surely saved many lives. But social work, however efficacious, missed the larger point that municipal government had to be made to assume the responsibility for providing for the common welfare. If government, for instance, enacted ordinances strictly to regulate the processing, sale, and distribution of fresh milk, it could safeguard the health of all the city's children by preventing illness in the first place.[13] But, Nicholes warned, even new ordinances were not sufficient; effective action meant understanding the organization of the municipal governing structures. It mattered *who* headed such administrative departments as the department of health or such independent boards as its school and park boards; *how* those administrators were chosen; *what* specific powers state and local government gave these bodies; and what share of the tax revenues they received. Nicholes urged women to take an active part in investigating all municipal politics and decision-making as the only way to achieve a municipal government that worked for the common good rather than the needs of business. Eight years earlier, Harriet Fulmer of the City Visiting Nurses Association had told the West End Women's Club that they should work to create a municipal office of baby commissioner inside the city government.[14]

Now, in the 1910s, activist Chicago women were working along the lines suggested by Nicholes and Fulmer, proposing solutions to municipal problems that reflected an active vision of a municipal democracy and citizenship that worked for the common welfare. This vision is reflected in the variety of municipal problems they set out to solve, the reasons they

Figure 10. Harriet Fulmer, Head of Visiting Nurses Association, 1906.
(Chicago *Daily News*, Chicago Historical Society, DN-0004470)

articulated for their solutions, and the stark contrast that emerged between women's and men's political agendas. Housing, public health and
safety, recreation, strikes and police power, and public education were
among the most pressing and challenging municipal problems that activist
women addressed—pressing because the city had reached a crisis point on
each problem, and challenging because women's solutions often directly
conflicted with those of Chicago men. This chapter examines each issue
and concludes by reassessing men's and women's activism in Chicago in
the 1910s.

Figure 11. Activist Jewish, Catholic, and Protestant Women Engaged in Social Welfare Work, August 1913. Seated from left: Minnie Low, Dr. Clara Seippel, Florence Vosbrink, Gertrude Howe Britton, Leonora Meder, Mrs. McMahon, and Dr. Anna Dwyer. (Chicago *Daily News*, Chicago Historical Society, DN-080956)

Municipal Problems

Housing

In *Moralism and the Model Home*, Gwendolyn Wright noted the male and female approaches to housing reform at the housing exhibit held in spring of 1913 in Chicago.

> [The] Woman's City Club section emphasized the value of community participation in matters of health, garbage collection, child welfare, and control of advertising. The City Club, on the other hand, stressed the need for expert guidance in these complicated matters . . . [and] encouraged architects, sanitarians, engineers, and social scientists to suggest improvements for inner city and suburban housing.

For men, Wright concluded, "[h]ousing had become an abstract problem to be solved with scientific research." Wright drew few other conclusions from her observation and mistakenly concluded that the WCC thereafter concentrated on educating women in government procedures rather than pursuing housing reform.[15] In his examination of progressive-era housing movements in Chicago, Thomas Philpott was chiefly concerned with revealing the limits of middle-class sensibilities when it came to dealing with housing for the poor, especially for African Americans.[16] He declared that in "1917 the housing movement in Chicago was in tatters," shattered by a combination of the ignorance of middle-class white housing reformers both about how to solve the problem and about the slums of the city's segregated "Black Belt."[17] Philpott's evidence is strong for men, but he never considers the housing proposals offered by women. In fact, activist women remained firmly engaged in housing reform; if the men's movement was in tatters, the women's was not.

As noted in chapter 2, differences between activist Chicago men and women on housing appeared as early as the 1880s. The tone and context for much male activism on housing was set by the Citizens' Association 1884 report on Tenement Housing, a report that presented new housing as an opportunity for ameliorating labor tensions—better housing would "refine [workers'] political and moral tastes and habits" and make them "better workmen, more contented and reliable." But the Citizens' Association also saw constructing housing for workers as a profitable business enterprise for which business needed "no governmental aid or advice."[18] This was a "business" perspective—private enterprise and not government determined and satisfied housing needs—that thereafter underlay almost all activist middle-class male perspectives on housing. Working-class organizations showed not even this much interest in housing during the 1880s and 1890s: the Trades and Labor Assembly, and even the more radical CLU active during the depression of 1893–1894, kept their sights focused on economic gains for working men.

By contrast, the IWA had contemporaneously declared it the "duty of the city to provide lodging-houses for temporary relief of the unemployed and homeless persons."[19] In this instance, the IWA thought in terms of temporary lodging houses and not permanent housing, but simply raising the issue pushed women's housing concerns into public discussion and demonstrated the differences in men's and women's ideas on the problem. After the IWA folded, Hull House residents began the first systematic survey of the city's housing stock. In 1895, they published their extraordinarily detailed survey of housing in their neighborhood in *Hull House Maps and Papers*, the first publication to expose the depth and human cost of the housing crisis. Shortly thereafter, male and female housing activists organized the City Homes Association, an independent housing agency financially supported by Anita McCormick Blaine, the daughter of one of the city's leading industrialists, that in 1901 published another comprehensive report on the city's housing. Sanitarian Charles Ball, settlement house residents Jane Addams and George Hooker, and social workers Sophonisba Breckinridge and Graham Taylor inspected the city's housing stock and gathered information to support their demand that the city undertake systematic and rigorous sanitary inspections of all housing and more strictly enforce all existing building regulations. Although their activities resulted in city council passage of a "new housing" ordinance in 1902, this and other regulations had little effect. A corrupt and inept building department failed to perform the necessary inspections, while owners of tenement buildings strenuously resisted implementation and enforcement of even the most meager municipal regulations, arguing that these interventions of government violated property rights, and the 1902 law applied only to newly built housing.[20] Philpott argued that corruption was the primary cause of housing reform failure at this juncture, and urban environmental historian Harold Platt bolsters this argument. He details the use of a "stay book," a list of health department suits that were never prosecuted out of "courtesy" to various politicians, including aldermen, judges, and congressmen.[21] Yet even honest men opposed housing reform that would have in any way restricted the rights of property.[22]

Although men and women activists shared the work on housing reform at the turn of the century, their efforts thereafter often diverged. Women discovered that ordinances were inadequate if the government had neither sufficient power nor the will to enforce them, but activist men rejected giving municipal government enhanced power to solve the housing crisis. The 1909 Chicago Plan unveiled by the businessmen of the Commercial Club contained no provision for new housing because, as Philpott writes, businessmen believed that "the building of houses, unlike the widening of streets and boulevards, was business in the *strict* sense and therefore not a proper matter for public endeavor." The City Club objected in 1912 to the proposed transfer of building inspectors from the sanitary bureau to the city's building department, declaring that building inspectors should not be part of municipal government.[23]

Activist women, however, turned decisively toward government as the primary means to solve the housing problem. In late 1905 Chicago juvenile court worker Sadie T. Wald reported to the convention of the Council of Jewish Women, which met in Chicago, that in visiting the wards of the juvenile court she found the majority "to come from the most miserable houses—three of them from the worst sort of hovels."[24] This experience convinced her that the city's 1902 "new" housing ordinance had done little to improve housing conditions in the city. The ordinance itself remained largely unenforced and applying it mainly to new construction did nothing to alleviate the appalling conditions of existing buildings.[25] Wald believed that the housing problem reflected lack of cooperation or actual hostility between the city's building and health departments, which shared jurisdictions over tenements, and urged the city to establish a separate tenement-house department. Furthermore, Wald reported that she did not see that private efforts could solve the problem and argued that housing was a public responsibility.

> Private enterprise, praiseworthy as it may be, may build model tenements, but only a few are benefitted. We have a right to demand of the municipality that, for the good of all, only suitable new tenements be erected, and that every old tenement either be made habitable or be torn down. . . . [W]e are tampering with the fundamental principles of the nation when we deny the child the privilege of a home—not a shelter, if you please, but a home.[26]

Bad housing was inextricably intertwined with "poverty, disease and crime," Wald declared. This being the case, "no one can safeguard himself against the evils that affect the body politic."[27]

Wald's plea for municipal attention to the connection between good housing and a good city found receptive audiences in Chicago. In the 1910s, the men of the Chicago Association of Commerce, the City Club, and the Commercial Club, and the women of the WCC and the CWC, all formed housing committees, thus providing the means to undertake a sustained comparison of men's and women's views of housing. Each organization adopted a more municipal focus by shifting emphasis of its work from improving the sanitation of existing housing to building sufficient housing for the city's population.[28] But there the agreement ended. In late 1912 Chicago delegates to the Second National Conference on Housing gave presentations to the City Club. Each of the men identified himself as representative of a profession and stressed the role of private enterprise and professional expertise in solving the housing problem. George Hooker, a settlement house resident and civic secretary of the City Club, extolled the financial possibilities for private enterprise in building garden cities. Lawyer Edward T. Lee wanted public officials (preferably lawyers) trained in administration to solve housing. Realtor Fred J. Pischel declared that housing problems would cease when the real estate man was shown "that in providing [workers' housing] he could get a reasonable return on his investment." John C. Kennedy, secretary of the Association of Commerce committee on housing, favored laws guaranteeing property owners control over their land, not municipal ordinances and regulation, to solve the housing problem. These concerns well reflected a discussion that had taken place earlier in the year at the City Club, where it was argued that property owners be educated to understand that "just as much money can be made on better and more sanitary tenements."[29]

Only one woman made a presentation at the conference, Mrs. Edward T. Lee, who chaired the civics committee of the CWC (and wife of the above-mentioned Edward). Mrs. Lee declared that she represented at the conference "this great, heterogenous Chicago family." Then she proposed that the interests of private property had to be reined in by law and strict regulation, possibly even on the state level if that was the only means to keep local property owners and businessmen from subordinating to their own interests the people's need for equal, uniform access to decent housing.[30]

The gender differences remained when delegates to the Third National Conference on Housing reported to the City Club in early 1914. The men again emphasized professionalism and business methods.[31] Herbert Friedman from the Association of Commerce proposed more urban zoning. Architect Robert Spencer regretted that the conference had not sufficiently discussed "subdivision and neighborhood planning . . . floor plans for economical houses and flats . . . large scale operations for housing people," and how cities (or states) could provide the best possible financial climate for private builders and investors through controlling the costs of labor. Professor Howard Woodhead of the Chicago School of Civics and Philanthropy said that rail lines to the city periphery would "make it possible for us to bring in an outlying area upon which we can build our cheap houses and to which the people can go to live." Finally, George Hooker called again for "Garden Cities" that would give "profit on the investment."[32]

On this occasion, professors Sophonisba Breckinridge and Edith Abbott, both of whom were colleagues of Woodhead at the School of Civics and Philanthropy, addressed the City Club. Breckinridge was a director of the WCC; each woman held a Ph.D. Together they were investigating Chicago's housing problems, applying the scientific research methods they had learned in the University of Chicago graduate school.[33] Despite sharing professional training with men, both women addressed the housing problem differently from the men. Rather than cost-efficient labor, Abbott proposed a minimum wage for workers to give them the means to afford decent houses. Breckinridge pointed out that constructing new transportation networks, garden cities, or model housing would take time to implement when immediate relief and remedy was required. Both women also stressed that citizen action, not that of "experts," and enhanced powers for the municipal government were needed to solve the housing problem. Breckinridge acknowledged the problems, shortcomings, and corruptions of municipal government, but she believed profoundly both in the efficacy of democratic government and policy-making and that once Chicagoans were sufficiently aware of the housing problem they would force government to enact and enforce laws to raise public standards for housing to levels "below which no living in the community will be allowed to continue."[34]

> Can we not . . . take hold of this outworn and awkward tool, the city government, and extract all the service possible. . . . Can we not here and now notify the Council that we will have no more improper exemptions [from the housing

code]; let the Building Committee of the Council know that the eyes of influential men are upon them to resist exemptions, not to seek them; make known to the corporation counsel that we are not children to play a game of make-believe; and [obtain] from [city government] not in a remote future but here and now, in the year 1914, all the benefit it has for the dwellers in the poorer quarters of our city?[35]

Male civic organizations always deferred to the rights of property owners. The City Club committee on housing conditions promoted zoning, planning, and street layout rather than what it termed "paternalistic ideas in government." This desire to protect property rights was so deeply ingrained that the City Club even wanted professional experts to be employed by businessmen rather than by government.[36] The Club housing committee worked with the Association of Commerce to frame legislation that would allow corporations "the privilege of owning and operating real estate for housing."[37] By 1916 the City Club had apparently concluded that because housing "is bound up with land and land capitalization, with the organization of industry and commerce and their profits, processes and wages," it could do no more than study land use and development; its main activity thereafter was to map the city by lots, building types, and industrial land use.[38] Anything else was to be left to the experts who were equipped to study technical details.

When the City Club in 1916 sponsored a competition for plans for a model subdivision, not surprisingly, the winning entry of architect Wilhelm Bernhard reflected the Club's ideas that separating business from residences, regulating traffic flow, and creating community centers to serve as a focus for business and civic life were the important features of housing reform. The new concept of creating separate residential and commercial zones was, moreover, an opportunity for businessmen to make profits and for experts to practice their professions. During a 1919 City Club conference on the subject, one participant declared, "Zoning will increase Chicago's wealth $1,000,000,000 in twenty years." Government "interference" in the form of zoning laws was acceptable to businessmen only if it fostered their economic aims.[39]

Activist women followed the ideas of Abbott and Breckinridge: housing was crucial for securing the decency and welfare of the city's residents. The WCC's first venture into housing had occurred with its participation in the spring 1913 City Housing Exhibit. In spring 1914, linking insufficient housing to a variety of health and social problems, the CWC declared it "wasteful and inefficient to spend large sums for the tuberculosis institution, the children's welfare, and visiting nurses associations and free dispensaries when scarcely a beginning has been made at the root of the evils requiring these remedial agencies—adequate housing."[40] Shortly thereafter the CWC formed a separate housing committee, one of whose first resolutions was that no further surveying of conditions was needed to take "concentrated and vigorous action." For the 1915 mayoral election, the CWC housing committee interviewed mayoral candidates on their views about housing, and publicized these views for the new women voters. In its annual report of late 1915, the WCC declared that a citizens' housing committee could "correlate all the forces of our city, [who] could see to it, not only that the laws were enforced, but that even the humblest citizen had a clean, comfortable, sanitary dwelling."[41] By the time that the WCC organized its housing committee, women were finally able to vote in municipal elections.

The only entry submitted to the City Club's 1916 competition by a female architect, Anna Schenck of New York, stressed the plans she and other women were developing for low-cost housing for Washington, D.C. In Schenck's plan, the key element was family needs. Her designs focused on the *content* of the buildings themselves, attending to such details as providing various sized apartments to accommodate different sized families, incorporating laundry, library, and hospital facilities into the buildings, and providing neighborhood nurseries and playgrounds. Schenck's entry was the sole design that deviated from the City Club's emphasis on building "model communities," rather than planning model buildings as homes. Her plan reflected many women's idea that satisfying family and household needs had to be an integral feature of any housing reform.[42]

Scholarly investigations of housing reform movements almost never see women's housing activities in this way. They either focus on discovering the class bias of the housing movement, or they look only at men in this time period. A recent book on the growth of public housing in Boston combines these two approaches in a unique way. According to Lawrence Vale, only female settlement house residents worried about housing—thereby ignoring the possibility that other women's organizations may have been working on this problem—and that their "central intellectual spokesperson was Robert A. Woods," who Vale says, "had a palpable nostalgia for the New England villages . . . [and] so many other housing activists, at the time and in the decades that followed, seem to have shared his sentiments."[43] There is no evidence of this nostalgia among Chicago women activists, nor would any of them have accepted any man being appointed as their "intellectual spokesperson."

In the debates over housing reform, activist men and women also differed in their views about the role of racial discrimination in creating the city's housing crisis. Middle-class men's organizations rarely addressed the connection between race and housing, but when they did they either advocated more racial segregation or debated how to make money from building housing in African American neighborhoods.[44] For these men, the social reality of racial segregation and its inherent injustice had nothing to do with decisions about zoning, profitability, and regulating traffic flow. Middle-class white women consistently argued that the problems of racism and racial segregation were integral to the city's housing problems. Breckinridge had included African American neighborhoods in her professional housing survey "even when the Health Department told her the areas weren't worth canvassing."[45] Her investigations convinced her that "a decent home . . . in a respectable neighborhood and at a reasonable rental" was one of three indisputable rights of African American citizens (the other two being equal chances for employment and education), rights that should have been protected by law and the city.[46] The CWC sponsored a symposium on housing discrimination at the interracial Frederick Douglass Center in late 1913. Breckinridge and WCC leader Louise de Koven Bowen both addressed the meeting. The following month, the CWC considered the problem at its regular monthly meeting; Breckinridge and Bowen were joined as speakers by Mary Wilmarth, Mary McDowell, and Fannie Barrier Williams.[47] One could not on such slender evidence conclude that such comparative openness on the subject of race was typical of women generally. But it does show that the experience of cooperation between white and black women since the days of the IWA, however fragile, had prepared them to face issues that white men preferred not to discuss.

Far from losing their interest in housing after securing the vote, activist women made housing reform a political issue. By 1920, despairing of action at the municipal level, the WCC turned its attention to the national government and called for a federal bureau of housing within which, in addition to the male "experts," women would work. In 1921 activist Harriet Vittum expressed women's exasperation with the situation when she called upon concerned citizens to "build and work as well as think and talk about the problem." In contrast, the City Club housing committee appears moribund by 1918.[48]

Public Health and Safety

Activist Chicago women also promoted public health and safety as a right of citizenship, one that transcended business concerns and was to be safeguarded and promoted by government with the help of an active, participatory citizenry.

GARBAGE COLLECTION AND DISPOSAL

Until the early twentieth century, cities mainly used the franchise system for garbage collection and disposal. The government awarded a contract (called a franchise) to a private company that paid a fee to the municipal government in return for the right to provide the service.[49] The franchise holder then charged fees for service and kept the profits. When the garbage-removal franchise of the Chicago Reduction Company was due to expire in 1914, the city council had already debated for two years whether to renew the franchise, award it to another company, or cancel the franchise altogether and have the city assume responsibility for garbage collection. Led by the WCC, activist women favored the last option, saying that only municipal ownership of garbage collection and disposal could maximize urban health. Mary McDowell bluntly told the City Club that businessmen supported the franchise system and one particular means of garbage disposal—the reduction method—"because you can extract money out of the garbage."[50]

Activist women's decision to support municipal ownership of garbage removal had its roots in the late nineteenth century when Jane Addams had organized the women of the Hull House neighborhood to attack the accumulations of garbage and debris in their ward, the result of building owners' failures to pay for the service or to provide trash bins. Having collected the franchise payment, the city council expressed little interest in the problem on the neighborhood level.[51] Addams and other activist women began working to convince Chicagoans to investigate the problem at the local level and to force the city to take responsibility for garbage removal rather than leaving it to business. When initial efforts failed to move the city council, landlords, or the Reduction Company, women escalated their efforts. In 1908 the CWC organized a ward-based garbage clean-up campaign. Shortly after its founding, the WCC formed ward committees to study neighborhood needs, give public lectures on the subject, erect neighborhood exhibits showing people the extent of the garbage problem and how it could be solved, and distribute printed leaflets throughout the city urging support for a municipal solution.[52]

Without a centralized authority responsible for ensuring the removal of garbage, private garbage collectors easily ignored areas of the city where it was not profitable. The city could revoke a franchise for slipshod service, but municipal officials rarely felt pressured enough by the urban poor to do so, especially when the holders of franchises were prepared to reward the government for ignoring some deficiencies in service. Moreover, the council had a long record of rewarding its own members when doling out franchises. An investigation during the franchise renewal debates revealed that alderman Charles Martin had owned stock in the Chicago Reduction Company when the original franchise had been granted in 1907. He had temporarily transferred the stock to another person, who transferred it back to him when he lost his re-election bid that year.[53]

In 1911 the WCC and other women's organizations—including the CWTUL—asked Mayor Harrison to appoint a municipal commission to study the garbage problem and design a citywide solution. The WCC declared that the essential point of garbage removal was "not the financial returns to be received, but the character of the service given." The house-keepers of Chicago, declared the WCC, "have learned that it must be first a sanitary problem and second an economic one." Only a citywide system of garbage removal could protect the public health, and only the municipal government could effectively and efficiently undertake such a citywide effort.[54] As the WCC poetically stated it in one of its leaflets:

> Any number of departments
>   Caring for our waste;
> Woman's City Club wants one,
>   And wants that one in haste.[55]

The men of the City Club adamantly opposed municipal ownership and fought to keep all municipal services for private enterprise and profit.[56] When the city council decided in 1914 not to extend the municipal garbage franchises and began planning municipal ownership and operation for garbage collection and disposal, the victory on garbage disposal went to the women. Coming as it did shortly after Illinois law gave women the right to vote in municipal and federal elections, women attributed their victory here to their new power as voters (a subject addressed in chapter 6).

FIRE PREVENTION, THEATER VENTILATION, AND CLEAN AIR

Activist Chicago women also worked to have the government safeguard daily life in the city through fire prevention, building ventilation, and clean air standards. Women's concern with fire prevention originated with the horrendous 1911 Triangle Shirtwaist fire in New York City, in which 141 women workers died for lack of adequate fire safety precautions in their fifth floor factory. Chicago women feared that their city risked a similar catastrophe because of the poor conditions of many existing buildings, so in 1911 the WTUL and the WCC began urging the city to establish a fire prevention bureau within the city fire department.[57] A fire department responsible for citywide fire prevention followed from women's vision that a combination of increased government responsibility with citizen vigilance and action would secure a good city. The fire department was located in every neighborhood, so department personnel could bring fire prevention information directly to all Chicagoans and easily inspect neighborhood residential and industrial properties for adherence to regulations; all citizens, in turn, could have direct access to their local fire company, thereby facilitating citizen participation in fire safety. Assigning responsibility for fire safety to the fire department would also centralize all aspects of fire safety into one government department, enabling citizens to know who to hold accountable.

This last idea was a key element of activist women's municipal agenda. Women never underestimated the possibilities for corruption in government, and they were as keen as activist men to install good government in Chicago. But activist Chicago women believed that an educated citizenry would make government accountable at election time,[58] while activist male progressives often advocated reforms that further removed government from popular participation by placing professional "experts" rather than politicians in important municipal posts.[59] For example, a group of Chicago architects vigorously countered the WCC and CWTUL demands for municipal fire inspections. These men wanted to reserve all decisions and actions on fire safety and prevention to the "professional" building safety experts (i.e., architects) within the city's building department, the same "experts" who planned buildings and issued permits. But these "experts" were few in number, and in only irregular contact with the public; they were not positioned to educate people about fire safety, to make on-site safety inspections, or to confer with citizens in the neighborhoods, which was what activist women envisioned. In the summer of 1912, the city council created a Bureau of Fire Prevention and Public Safety inside the fire department, so here too activist women's emphasis on government and citizen responsibility for public safety triumphed over the male concern for limited government and professional responsibility.[60]

Women also demanded that the city enact municipal ordinances requiring factory owners and other businessmen to hold compulsory fire drills in their establishments. They believed not only that the common enterprise of living in the city was sufficient reason to justify compulsory fire drills and other safety measures, but that municipal ordinances compelling fire drills would compel the city council to appropriate the money to enforce its own laws, further acknowledging the government's responsibility for public safety and fostering a closer cooperation between city authorities and citizens on issues of fire prevention and safety.[61] The New York Federation of Women's Clubs had faced similar opposition as it unsuccessfully lobbied the New York City Council to institute fire drills in factories in both 1908 and 1910; only the tragic Triangle Fire, with its 141 fatalities, moved lawmakers to reconsider fire safety, but there the state took responsibility for the problem. Although the Chicago city council passed a fire drill ordinance, factory owners successfully appealed to the State supreme court, arguing that the city government did not have the power to pass such laws. Activist women refused to concede the point when they were blocked this way; rather, they turned to the state legislature and helped draft legislation to give the city council such power.[62]

Businessmen also resisted any proposal regulating conditions inside factories. While many of them agreed with governmental regulation of building materials (e.g., using brick rather than wood) or to provide a citywide water supply system (the lesson of 1871 was that fire did not respect property boundaries so there was both a public and a business interest in such regulation[63]), businessmen contended that the public interest stopped at the door of their factories. So activist women had mixed success with a crusade to compel adequate ventilation. The WCC convinced the city council to pass an ordinance that required a certain level of ventilation in public theaters and created a Bureau of Ventilation inside the Department of Health to ensure compliance. Businessmen opposed this ordinance as government intrusion against property and convinced the council to suspend the ordinance. When Mayor Harrison vetoed this suspension, the council building committee deliberated and reduced the ventilation requirements. Women throughout the city then deluged the council with protests. According to the WCC, forty-nine women's organization responded to its request to write the council demanding that it not lower the ordinance's requirements, and women's clubs sent delegations to public hearings on this issue. Such pressure convinced the council to instruct the Bureau of Ventilation to begin enforcing the original ordinance. By 1914, the WCC reported, of the city's six hundred theaters, the number with proper ventilating equipment had increased from 225 to 583. When the ventilation ordinance was ruled constitutional, women had secured another victory.[64]

Activist women had less success on the issue of air quality. Chicago was a coal-heated city, and coal was a dirty fuel. Activist men and women were both outraged by Chicago's poor air, and although they worked together at times, the men's stress on professionalism and expertise clashed with women's emphasis on government responsibility and citizen participation. The quality of the city's air became an increasingly public issue from 1907, when a new city ordinance required the chief smoke investigator be a trained engineer. John Schubert, who had actually made a great deal of headway in attacking smoke pollution in the city, was replaced with Paul Bird, a steam "expert" from the Illinois Steel Company. A three-member advisory board was then named, one of whom was an officer of the Illinois Coal Operators Association, and another a steam engineer from the Corn Products Company, a company that Schubert had attacked for air pollution the year before. According to environmental historian David Stradling, "[T]he reorganization of the smoke department had greatly increased the influence of industry within the municipal regulatory body."[65] Women were not impressed by this emphasis on "expertise." The next year, a group of Chicago women formed the Anti-Smoke League, led by Annie (Mrs. Charles) Sergel, who later became a director of the WCC as well as the ward leader for the WCC's activities in her home ward, the sixth. The Anti-Smoke League declared that women were tired of hanging clean laundry outside only to have it soon covered with black grit, and of

Figure 12. Smoky Chimney, 1908. Virtually obscures the VIM Company Building. (Chicago *Daily News*, Chicago Historical Society, DN-0005614)

finding a layer of dirt on their food and all the surfaces of their homes. In conjunction with the CWC, Sergel and the Anti-Smoke League held community meetings in field houses in a number of the city's parks to inform the residents of smoke problems in their neighborhoods.[66] Although this initial campaign against smoke pollution was short-lived, a few years later the WCC declared the elimination of smoke pollution a high municipal priority. Activist women demanded that the city government immediately enact strict smoke abatement ordinances and dispatch smoke inspectors throughout the city to enforce such regulations; they called upon all citizens to monitor air conditions in their own neighborhoods, report polluters, and immediately switch from using high-sulfur bituminous, or semi-bituminous, coal to the virtually smokeless anthracite variety. To facilitate "individual responsibility towards the smoke problem," the WCC distributed posters throughout the city and to children in the public schools.[67]

The City Club declared that clean air could be achieved only "professionally and scientifically" by experts gathering facts and figures to determine the extent of the problem.[68] This task fell to the Committee on Electrification and Smoke Abatement of the Association of Commerce. Four railway officials, four former city officials, and eight members of the association composed this committee, which spent $300,000 "determining . . . the amount of smoke pollution in the city's atmosphere and the amount attributable to each [sector of the city's coal-burning services]." Even then, the committee did not recommend specific policies. Chairman W.F.M. Goss reported to the City Club in September 1913 that the committee still needed to determine the environmental hazards posed by burning coal, how much pollution might be attributable to each type of source, and what, if any, recommendations should be made to eradicate air pollution.[69]

Women looked around their homes, neighborhoods, and the city, and saw children breathing dirty air, laundry yellowing on the line, and grit on the food they were feeding their families. Smoke traveled; it could not be confined to one neighborhood. Nor did women want it confined, because it would damage the health of the people in that neighborhood. The solution to the problem could not be left to businessmen. As Anna Nicholes had observed, businessmen would always decide on allowable levels of smoke based on economic considerations. Indeed, the men of the City Club and the Association of Commerce were doing just that. On this issue, which so profoundly affected the city's businesses, Chicago men prevailed. The municipal government enacted no substantial regulation of smoke emissions in this decade.[70]

CLEAN CITY CAMPAIGN

For activist women, public health also included municipal cleanliness. In 1914 a group of African American women organized the Chicago Women's Street Cleaning Bureau to monitor the conditions of streets and alleys in their neighborhoods. In this work, they joined other activist Chicago women already engaged in a campaign to "clean up" accumulating dirt, litter, and general paper waste and to educate Chicagoans not to litter. In spring 1913 the WCC had sponsored a weeklong citywide clean-up campaign. It printed and distributed throughout the city leaflets in seven languages, publicized the campaign on the public transit lines, and sought the cooperation of the city's department of health. Chicago, the WCC said, "is certainly old enough by this time to pick up after itself. . . . [I]t is high time that the citizens of this city should also learn order and through the enforcement of order learn to have a city-wide pride in cleanliness."[71] This campaign was not simply a desire to make a more aesthetically pleasing city, or to make people more orderly.[72] It was part of the broader conception that government and citizens had to work together to provide a common welfare. If they exaggerated in 1913 the health hazards posed by dirt and litter, as our contemporary understanding of germs and disease makes apparent, women nonetheless introduced into the public realm of politics the idea that keeping the city clean was a public responsibility. One aim of the Chicago Women's Street Cleaning Bureau, for instance, was to ensure that sufficient amounts of ward appropriations were spent to achieve an acceptable level of health and cleanliness in the ward.[73] The WCC declared it a legitimate government responsibility and expenditure to purchase and furnish waste receptacles around the city, and stressed that the government must do this work because "private contractors could not be trusted."[74]

Contemporary observers usually failed to appreciate the women's purpose. The editor of the *Defender* loftily praised the efforts of African American women, saying "[T]he dear ladies will have the hearty support and earnest co-operation of all" but went on to explain that he thought this work laudable primarily because it would harass ward bosses.[75] Men's reform groups rarely showed any enthusiasm for city cleanliness beyond emphasizing individual action and property rights. The City Club urged property owners to beautify the areas surrounding their property, particularly by planting shrubbery.[76] That activist women were promoting a different vision of public health, or the joint responsibility of government and the citizens to maintain it, did not register with most men, who continued to speak of women as housekeepers.[77] But clean-up campaigns were not mere housework. Mary McDowell's explanation of the importance of the garbage collection and disposal crusade could aptly be applied to the clean-up campaign: "[It] became to us more than simply getting rid of an unpleasant and unsightly matter; it became a symbol of the standard of living of a whole city."[78]

Recreation and Lakefront Development

That middle-class urban women wanted to create more and better recreational facilities in their cities is well-known historical fact. But by emphasizing as the women's main social motivation concern for child welfare, as historians generally do, they miss the point that here too activist Chicago women challenged the position of most activist Chicago men that government action was acceptable only when it satisfied the economic demands of private enterprise.[79] In the 1910s businessmen saw Chicago's more than twenty-five miles of lakefront property as a vast economic opportunity. To this end, they proposed developing the lakefront as a tourist attraction with new municipal harbors and grand, profit-making beaches through cooperative efforts of private enterprise and government. Private enterprise would hire professional experts to draw the plans, and the city council would finance the recommended projects. The Commercial Club gave

architect Daniel Burnham one hundred thousand dollars for staff and expenses toward designing a "Chicago Plan" for the lakefront and city center.[80] The city council subcommittee on harbors, wharves, and bridges
consulted an array of "professional" experts—engineers, shippers, and
members of the city's Association of Commerce—and recommended that
the city construct a "substantial harbor immediately north of the mouth
of the Chicago River," with "docks, wharves and piers . . . so arranged in
units of construction that additional units may be added . . . as the increasing lake traffic makes more harbor space and dock room desirable," and
plan for additional harbors stretching south between Grant Park and
Thirty-fifth Street. The subcommittee argued that harbor development
could "be arranged and developed to dovetail perfectly with the [privately
developed Chicago Plan], so that the harbor construction work can be
made to form an important step in the development of the lake front
plan."[81] The City Club expressed "unanimity of opinion" with ex-chief
engineer of the sanitary district Lyman E. Cooley's declaration that "for
the industries of Chicago you want water front by the mile, for the industrial element is the largest element in the population. The next is the commercial element."[82] Recreational facilities along the lakeshore were also
conceived as grand projects, with potential profitability used as the bench-
mark for development. In 1916 the aldermen and businessmen of the Special Parks Commission, appointed by the city council, encouraged the city
to issue a $1.2 million bond to build a grand beach on the city's south
side at 75th Street, with a restaurant pavilion, a boardwalk, automobile
parking spaces, a playground, and a bath house containing fifteen thousand lockers.[83]

Activist women rejected these grand plans. First, they wanted free and
easy access to all recreational facilities. As discussed earlier in the book,
women had raised this issue in the 1890s in the Free Bath and Sanitary
League. The "Souvenir" they printed and distributed in 1897 to record
both the opening of a free bathhouse and women's work in securing it,
countered the belief of the city council and the park boards that the lake,
its shoreline, and the bordering parklands were property to which they
could restrict access. The League, according to the "Souvenir," had
fought to overturn the ban on bathing in the lake to give "the children
of Chicago, as well as its citizens, their undeniable *right*, i.e., access to the
waters of Lake Michigan."[84] In 1905 the CWC had made a similar argument when it protested the South Park board's plan to erect iron fences
around the parks under its jurisdiction. "Our parks belong to the people,
and should serve their uses in the most convenient way," the CWC had
declared. Parks should be "as free of [*sic*] access as possible to the sick
and feeble, the old and infirm, to tired mothers with little children. The
management of these public pleasure grounds should be in a broad and

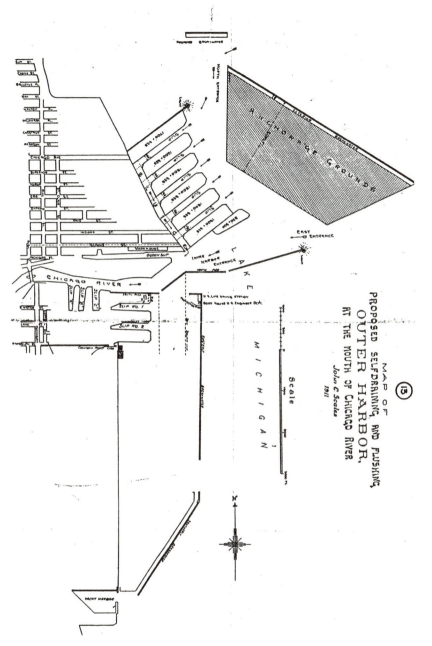

Figure 13. Line Drawing of Proposed Selfdraining and Flushing Outer Harbor at the Mouth of Chicago River, 1911. (From City Council of Chicago, "Proceedings of the Subcommittee on Harbor Development of the Committee on Harbors, Wharves and Bridges of the City Council of Chicago," *Journal of the Proceedings of the City Council.* Chicago, 1911)

democratic spirit."[85] In 1907 Jane Addams had encouraged Daniel Burnham to plan the lakefront and other city parks for the public benefit of the city's poor. While he expressed agreement with the idea of designing the lakefront "to draw out the working classes," his plan ultimately reflected other priorities.

> In his own words, he expressed this priority. The "plan frankly takes into consideration the fact that the American city, and Chicago pre-eminently, is a center of industry and traffic. Therefore attention is given to the betterment of commercial facilities; to methods of transportation for persons and for goods; to removing the obstacles which prevent or obstruct circulation; and to the increase of convenience."[86]

This desire for free and easy access to the lake led the WCC to reject the men's vision of the place of the automobile in lakefront development and to recommend instead the extension of public transit lines to the lakefront. The WCC's Committee on Bathing Beaches directed all club members to demand of the city council that "all east and west street car lines . . . carry people to the lakefront directly. Say that you want to see the lake accessible to EVERYBODY."[87] Paul Barrett's study of urban transit in Chicago emphasized the class basis of such arguments. Settlement house workers and aldermen from working-class wards, he argued, fought to extend mass transit to the lake, while middle-class residents of lakefront neighborhoods resisted such proposals.[88] But the activist middle-class women of the WCC demanded streetcar extension so that the city's greatest natural resource could be a true public resource. They wanted the lakefront developed as a long line of free and accessible beaches for the people. Most businessmen and activist middle-class men continued to think of the industrial and commercial elements as the city's largest and most important population, and thereby justified new harbors and commercial beaches. In this regard, note that as far back as the 1880s even Chicago's male union organizations had conceded that "the Lake Park must be eventually absorbed by the commercial development of the commercial interests of the city."[89] Moreover, activist men had even proposed to extend transit lines to their envisioned harbor areas, but not to recreational beaches.[90] Transit lines were never extended to the beaches of Chicago. In the 1930s, construction of a major north-south lakefront artery, Lake Shore Drive, made even pedestrian access to beaches much more difficult.

Activist women's second major concern was to secure more and smaller beaches along the lakefront. With this as its purpose, the WCC attacked the City Club's proposed grand beach at 75th Street. "We wonder whether the interests of the citizens of Chicago would be better served if more beaches of less expensive type were located at frequent intervals along our lakefront?" The Club declared the proposed 75th Street beach a "Coney Island."

> We do not need a $50,000 restaurant pavilion at a bathing beach. Nor do we need a beach which will attract 45,000 people on one day. . . . What Chicago wants is smaller beaches located at more frequent intervals along the lake front, where people can more easily reach them.[91]

Grand, expensive beaches, the WCC feared, could ultimately only be paid for by charging user fees, making beaches exclusive enclaves for the more well-to-do. These fears were not unfounded. Even as women proposed their scheme for smaller, more numerous beaches, the city council was being urged to charge people for using all beaches within the city limits. The council did experiment with this idea at a north-side beach.[92]

Activist women's struggle over lakefront development increased their understanding of municipal politics and the need for government responsibility. This was made clear to them beginning in 1911 when the WCC, led by its Bathing Beach Committee, headed by Jennie Purvin, worked to reclaim a stretch of lakefront south of the downtown area that had become a dumping ground for cinders from the Illinois Central Railroad. Initially, the WCC thought that this could be done through volunteerism: women would solicit the funds and volunteers needed to turn this insalubrious patch into a summertime bathing area, especially for children. Women from the Juvenile Protective Association helped the WCC clear the cinders, set-up changing rooms, hire two matrons, a police officer, and a lifeguard, and install lights. But the process illuminated the shortcomings of volunteerism within the prevailing context of municipal government. At every turn, the women discovered how decentralized municipal authority, combined with a lack of municipal policy on lakefront development, limited what even active citizens could do on a voluntary basis. They found the independent Small Parks Commission, the municipal authority responsible for overseeing such small scale development, "hopeless" and unwilling to provide any financial support.[93] The volunteers had to pry the funds and necessary permits from the city council Reclamation Committee, the mayor, aldermen, the city law department, the police chief, and the president of the sanitary district. The WCC reported needing to convince "half a dozen Aldermen and the Mayor" to see the "possibilities for a neighborhood beach" as they made the rounds from one official's office to the next.[94]

This experience proved invaluable for focusing activist women's attention on the need to have municipal government take charge of beach development. In late summer 1916 the WCC denounced the endless delays in

Figure 14. Children's Bathing Beach, Lincoln Park, 1905. (Library of Congress Prints and Photographs Division, Detroit Publishing Company Collection, LC-D4-18850)

beach development brought on by activist men's insistence that any such project wait until the existing three city park districts were consolidated into a single district with centralized authority. The WCC encouraged members to write to the city council demanding "before another season comes we may have sufficient beaches to take care of all our citizens."[95] Activist women did not reject a statistical analysis of urban problems— another of the City Club's demands—but they believed statistics unnecessary to understand that people without other means wanted to use the lakefront for recreation during the city's hot summers, and they rejected the need for park consolidation before more parks could be built.[96] The need to construct a series of beaches "at frequent intervals along our lakefront" seemed obvious to these women. Such a vision allowed activist women to separate as two distinct issues beach development and park consolidation. In fact, many of them supported consolidation as the only way to secure "justice for the city as a whole."[97] But activist women's patience with the "professional" approach to lakefront development was sorely tried as city officials rejected women's persistent demands that women be named to the various park boards and as these same park boards refused

Figure 15. State Street during a Snowstorm, Winter 1903. (Chicago *Daily News*, Chicago Historical Society, DN-0000276)

to supply social workers at each playground "to cooperate with the committees of the CWC, the WCC, and the CPEL in the social work which they are undertaking in the parks." These women were particularly annoyed with these refusals because they believed that women and children used the city's parks more frequently than did men. The CWC was also demanding the organization of neighborhood civic leagues to work at every playground.[98] By mid-decade, activist women were convinced that middle-class male organizations and politicians would do nothing that women wanted about recreation if their proposals conflicted with what men wanted. Such experiences increased these women's awareness that citizen activism could only work if accompanied by more centralized government with more direct responsibility over municipal development.[99]

Police Authority and Strikes

Between 1910 and 1915 three bitter labor strikes involving significant numbers of working women caused activist Chicago women to reassess the authority of the police department and its relationship to government and the citizenry. In October 1910, forty thousand garment workers, half

Figure 16. Parading Garment Worker Strikers, Winter 1910–11. (Chicago *Daily News*, Chicago Historical Society, DN-56268)

of whom were women, struck Chicago's leading clothing manufactories.[100] Activist women and men were concerned to end this strike before it stretched into the winter, leaving thousands of workers unemployed. Yet the women who organized a citizens' committee that worked with the CWTUL also believed that a just solution to the strike was not only important for the striking employees but "also most important for the welfare of the city." Activist women on this committee included Henrotin, Anna Nicholes, Addams, Grace Abbott, Bowen, Breckinridge, Harriet Van der Vaart, Vittum, and Mary Wilmarth. Clergymen, male professors, and settlement residents belonged to the committee, but women's leadership was unmistakable. Under Robins's organization, women's club members went door-to-door in the city's wealthier neighborhoods to raise money for the strikers.[101] The CPEL appointed a committee, chaired by Grace W. Smith, to investigate the arrest of women strikers, and Smith and members of the Woodlawn Woman's Club walked the picket line at Lamm and Company, one of the manufacturers located on Jackson near

Figure 17. Middle-Class Women on Picket Lines. (Chicago *Daily News*, Chicago Historical Society, DN-31812)

Green Street, as replacements for striking women workers who had been arrested there. Unlike prominent Boston women, who, as Sarah Deutsch put it, could not imagine working alongside working-class women and hired substitutes for even the innocuous activity of canvassing, Chicago middle-class activists threw themselves into this kind of activity.[102]

The strike stretched on, and the manufacturers remained completely intransigent with one leading employer declaring that "[a]s . . . there were no grievances," he saw "no reason for taking measures to correct them."[103] The manufacturers refused to consider collective bargaining or union organizing, and reserved the right to blacklist any strikers they identified as having committed acts of violence.[104] A coalition of women representing the CWTUL, the Citizens' Committee, and other women's organizations supported the workers' reluctance to accept settlement under these terms. Louise Bowen declared, "Undoubtedly my sympathy is on the side of the workers who are now striking."[105] The newly formed Woman Suffrage Party directed its members to ride the streetcars to solicit funds for striking workers.[106] The CWTUL, settlement house resident Ellen Gates Starr, and Louise Bowen jointly castigated the city's "well-to-do" citizens' opposition to the garment workers' cause as "criminally selfish and short-sighted." A just and speedy settlement of the strike on behalf of the workers, these women declared, would show the city's workers "that justice and democracy and human brotherhood lie at the foundation of our civilization."[107] The CWC contributed to the strike fund; individual Chicago women such as Katherine (Mrs. Walter) Fisher—whose husband generally sided with businessmen in such disputes and had opposed municipal suffrage in the charter conventions—made personal contributions, and Fisher attended a CWTUL meeting to discuss aiding the strikers. Seventy-five clergymen, on the other hand, agreed to a CWTUL request that they ask their congregations to aid suffering strikers, but they themselves refused to endorse the strike.[108] Even though preoccupied with its own labor and wage problems, the CTF supported the strikers both financially and with speakers.[109] Activist women appealed to all Chicagoans who "believe[d] in fair play and the right of wage-earners to organize for mutual betterment, to face your responsibility in this grave crisis in our city's history." The CPEL appointed a committee to investigate the arrest of women strikers.[110]

The Association of Commerce concluded that no external arbitration or municipal help was needed to resolve the situation. The men of the association also asserted that the employers would surely show good will in listening to grievances and would reinstate "non-violent" strikers. The CWTUL retorted, "The conclusion of the association is so at variance with well-known facts as to appear ridiculous. . . . [They have] ignored the evidence submitted by us as well as the conclusions reached a month ago by the Citizens Committee."[111]

The strike was settled soon thereafter, but neither the workers' grievances nor activist women's ideas had been adequately addressed. In 1914, after the police arrested peaceful waitresses picketing Henrici's, the popular downtown restaurant on Randolph Street, activist women demanded that the city take an active role in resolving labor disputes. Under existing municipal codes—and accepted practice—the police department regularly sided with business in strikes, and the police chief appointed businesses' private guards to act as special police.[112] The WCC deplored "the practice of permitting firms . . . to hire and arm men to act as special police who are not directly controlled by the police department," and middle-class women joined the waitresses' picket lines. Clubwomen Ruth Hanna McCormick, Bowen, Mary Wilmarth and her daughter Anna Wilmarth Ickes, and Elizabeth Bass (president of the CWC); teachers Margaret Haley and Mrs. Ben Page; university professors Breckinridge and Edith Abbott; and settlement house leaders Starr, Addams, and McDowell, joined this labor action, which was led by waitress Elizabeth Maloney, their co-worker in suffrage campaigns. The middle-class women, among them Anna Wilmarth Ickes, also bailed out arrested strikers and testified in court that police actions against peaceful pickets were violent and had incited crowd disturbances outside the restaurant. This last point was important because the restaurant's owners had used the excuse of the crowd's action to justify securing a legal injunction against the waitresses.[113]

Activist women's concern with police violence against strikers was further inflamed when the city's garment workers struck in late 1915. Middle-class women again joined the picket lines. CWC president Helen Webster Cooley led a Club contingent on the picket lines where they were joined by women from the CPEL, the WCC, Ellen Gates Starr (who had been arrested in 1914 picketing in support of the waitresses), and women from two prominent Chicago families, Frances Crane Lillie and Ruth Hanna McCormick.[114] Lillie, who was arrested along with a number of women garment workers, excoriated Mayor Thompson for allowing the use of "the police forces to crush the desire of liberty" and for giving private police free reign to "beat up strikers while the city police look on and take no action."[115] At a meeting of the CWC attended by representatives from numerous women's organizations, Grace Abbott read a list of affidavits gathered by the Immigrants' Protective League (IPL) attesting to police brutality against strikers.[116] Complicity between the police and businessmen seemed confirmed when Police Chief Charles Healy told a national newspaper "that he had been waited upon by representatives of the clothing manufacturers before the strike was called," and a police officer testified that "he had been transferred from strike duty . . . because he refused to allow a slugger to beat up pickets."[117] The city council committee investigating police conduct during the strike found these reports credible enough to recommend that "the police be not permitted to do any work for either side in an industrial controversy" and that a strike bureau be created within the police department to ensure a fairer response from the police in future labor actions.[118]

Not surprisingly, businessmen's groups rejected the council's conclusions. The City Club committee constituted to investigate these matters concluded that the police department "did not take sides," despite acknowledging that M. J. Isaacs, the attorney for the Associated Garment Manufacturers, attended police organizational meetings. The City Club's report instead attributed police brutality against strikers to ethnic hatred between Irish police and East European Jewish strikers. The committee conceded that manufacturers had misused their private guards and ignored some municipal ordinances in that regard,[119] but the City Club nonetheless insisted that employers be allowed to continue to hire private guards with authority to act as police during strikes.[120]

The WCC, in contrast, pounced on the proposal for a strike bureau and expanded it into a demand for a municipal strike bureau.[121] Such a municipal office, the women proposed, would both make government responsible for resolving strikes equitably and give citizens closer involvement in settling economic disputes. The Chicago *Post* saw the women's attitude toward labor actions as a strike against middle-class male control of the city:

> [It] shows again that the women of Chicago who have intellectual background and wealth, the women who might easily become the equivalent of the intellectual reform class among the men, are not entering upon their newly won right of citizenship from this avenue. They are entering upon their part in our public life by the democratic approach. . . . [T]hrough all [women's] protest runs a thread of revolt not against economic abstractions but against nondemocratic realities.[122]

This article compared middle-class women and men, but working women and men also differed in their views of labor issues. The CFL and individual male-run unions continued to focus on the rights of labor to strike and organize rather than on a municipal solution to labor problems, while Agnes Nestor, a gloveworker, union organizer, and leader of the CWTUL, publicly backed the idea of a municipal strike bureau.[123]

Education

As earlier chapters have detailed, public schools were always a priority for activist women. By the 1910s, many of these women agreed that schools were an invaluable institution for promoting urban welfare and that specific municipal policies on schools were needed to make them better function as such. Activist women's ideas on the role of public education were reflected in their ideas about vocational education, support for teachers and the CTF, budget and resource allocation, and more democratic participation in running the schools. In each area, activist women's desires for the school system differed from those of many men.[124]

For years activist men had tried to pretend that women were only interested in children's welfare in schools and were neither interested in, nor capable of, participating in bureaucratic and administrative affairs. These men claimed that men, especially businessmen, were best suited to decide all educational matters. But activist Chicago women for years had been "intruding" upon this alleged male prerogative. Chicagoan Madeleine Wallin Sikes—chair of the education legislative committee of the Association of Collegiate Alumnae—had urged all women to increase their voice in schools by monitoring the decisions and work of state legislatures, city councils, and school boards.[125] Since 1907, when republican Mayor Fred Busse had forced the resignation of school board members sympathetic to the CTF,[126] the ongoing conflict between teachers and male organizations, politicians, and board members (described in earlier chapters) had become a chronic problem for the city. Simmering tensions erupted into a public controversy in the summer of 1913 when Superintendent of Schools Ella Flagg Young resigned her position amid curriculum and financial disputes with the school board. A delegation of Chicago women marched into Mayor Harrison's office and demanded that he use his influence with his board appointees to bring back Young. Harrison persuaded the board not to accept Young's resignation, but several months later the board failed by one vote to reappoint Young to her position. Jane Addams and Elizabeth Bass led another women's delegation to Harrison to protest the board's actions; then Addams and the CWC called a mass protest meeting at the Auditorium Theater and, again with Harrison's help, forced Young's reappointment.[127] The board was hostile to Young because she was a teacher not a professional administrator, and the men of the board felt that she sympathized too much with teachers, who had finally received pay raises after Young had assumed her office.

Young's predecessor, Edwin Cooley, had had strong ties to business organizations, and for years Chicago men had been able to cut teacher pay and spend school monies to benefit themselves.[128] In 1913, to fight Young, Chicago realtors secured state legislation that cut school taxes but left the school construction budget intact and gave additional tax exemptions for buildings constructed on school lands.[129] With less tax revenue, the only way to finance education would be to cut the instructional fund, which meant cutting teacher salaries because the board never touched the salaries of male school engineers and janitors who were also paid from the instructional budget. In early 1915 the teachers attempted to fight back by suggesting that these payroll expenses more logically belonged to the building fund, but they did not succeed in having them removed from the ledger of the instructional budget.[130] At the same time, the board sought a new state law giving it control over the teacher pension fund and specifically barring teachers or their chosen representatives from serving on the board administering the pensions. In 1912 the board president, Alfred Urion, was corporation counsel for one of the city's biggest meat packing companies, Armour and Co. He wanted Ella Flagg Young to persuade teachers to accept more board members on the teachers' pension fund board. At the same time, Urion was defending Armour and nineteen other corporations against another CTF tax suit. According to one historian of the Chicago public school system, "[T]here could be little doubt that Urion . . . wished to use the pension board as a means of controlling the activities of the CTF or to use it as a source of investment funds."[131] The teachers managed to thwart such legislation with the support of the CFL, and the women participating in the December 1913 mass meeting passed a resolution calling for the removal of those board members who had opposed teacher representatives on the pension board.[132]

But the fight was far from over. In May 1915 the board again proposed teacher pay cuts and then passed the infamous "Loeb" rule, barring teachers from joining any organization affiliated with any association of trade unions, or that had officers, business agents, or representatives who were not members of the teaching force. The rule further required every teacher to sign a pledge that she (the overwhelming majority were female) did not belong to any such union.[133] The namesake of this rule was board president Jacob Loeb, a real estate and insurance agent, who enjoyed the support of the newly elected Mayor William Thompson as well as many of the city's businessmen. Three of the five women on the twenty-one-member school board—Helen Gallagher, Gertrude Howe Britton, and Tena MacMahon—spoke strongly against the rule. Gallagher claimed that "we are American citizens, and as such each one has a right to join any body that he or she chooses."[134] Then-current head of the CWTUL, Agnes Nestor, wrote to Alderman Robert M. Buck protesting that "to maintain a democracy we must have free citizenship, and free citizens cannot be developed in schools taught by subservient teachers." She demanded that the city council refuse to confirm anyone to the school board who would infringe the teachers' constitutional rights to belong to any organization they might choose.[135] At a women's mass meeting of March 1916, middle-class clubwoman Helen Hefferan called the rule an interference "with the private rights of the teachers as citizens . . . designating to what organization a teacher should or should not belong." To the cheers of the audience she declared it "undemocratic, autocratic, and intolerable, and I insist as a citizen of the city of Chicago that some force get to work by which the teachers may be allowed to exercise their rights as private citizens, together with the freedom of organization and political action." The schools committee of the WCC sent a letter to the school board strongly protesting the "immorality in the school system" that would result from the board's activities.[136]

The CFL sustained the teachers' struggle against the Loeb rule, viewing the rule as "part of a scheme to strike a blow at organized labor," Loeb having proclaimed that he intended to keep unions "from taking over the schools."[137] But the WCC, Nestor, and the women's mass meeting understood the rule as an attack against women and their struggle as teachers to have their educational expertise recognized. Even though board member John Sonsteby had noted that the Loeb rule singled out the board's female employees while not opposing unionization among male employees, he was no friend of the teachers, having previously opposed teacher representation on their own pension board.[138] Board member Ralph C. Otis voted for the Loeb rule, but was attacked for having shown himself willing to meet with and talk to women who were supporting the teachers. Loeb's own declarations showed that his rule was not merely an attack on worker rights to organize but was very much directed at women. "In unionism the teacher forgets the nobility and sacredness of her profession in salary-grabbing activities." Union activities for teachers were a "lasting detriment of the most sacred charge God has given us, the mind of the child."[139] For Loeb, female teachers had overstepped their gender boundaries and he felt no compunction against telling the city, "We'll cut their [teachers] professional throats if we have to."[140]

Passage of the Loeb rule further convinced activist women that under the existing system, the board would always represent the interests of businessmen and politicians. The WCC concluded that short of an elected board (a remote political possibility), the city needed to make two important changes to the school system. There ought to be a citizens' public school league that would resist all attempts to lower school standards and "insure a democratic organization of the schools," and the teachers ought to be made central to the educational process. The city had to give "Chicago's real intelligence on school problems . . . its teaching force" a strong voice in "the shaping of its educational policies." To implement such changes, activist women organized a Joint Committee on Education to which about forty women's organizations, determined to keep school issues in the public eye, sent representatives.[141] After 1916, activist women's and men's organizations would engaged in a constant struggle over who should control the school system and to what ends.

Male and Female Urban Activism in the 1910s

Because evidence from women's sources shows a stark contrast between activist Chicago men and women in their ideas about municipal development and policy to solve housing, recreation, schools, pollution, sanitation and garbage removal, and labor problems, one must ask why historians have resisted seeing this. That scholars researching the city and its residents take male ideas as the norm is largely responsible. Activist Chicago men consistently sought to fashion a city that would function to promote male economic concerns, whether the specific concerns of middle-class businessmen or workers. According to historian Georg Leidenberger, Chicago trade union activists promoted municipal ownership of public utilities, believing that such political innovation would enhance the political voice of male workers and make state power support workers rather than employers.[142] This contrasts with the economic concerns of many Chicago businessmen, but it remains a male perspective. In the work of other historians, women are reduced to being the promoters of a more womanly ideal of civilization and never viewed as "real" political actors in an urban struggle.[143] Women scholars, for their part, have often devalued the work of white, middle-class women, chastising them for presuming to speak for all women and for projecting their middle-class bias toward family and respectable motherhood into the realm of social welfare policy development.[144] Class, race, and ethnic differences surely strained the possibilities of women's solidarity in Chicago and elsewhere. But, as Dorothy Sue Cobble has revealed, Chicago waitresses—whose leader, Elizabeth Maloney, worked closely with middle-class activists—organized white and black women into the same locals, something that male locals did not do. In 1904 Mary McDowell and Irish and southern European working women had organized twelve hundred women into a stockyards workers union that included African American women.[145]

To view activist women's municipal work only in terms of class or race further overlooks the originality of their thinking and the extent to which so many women rejected the male framework of urban politics. In the words of Florence Kelley's recent biographer, Kelley and her sisters in activism were "reaching beyond the betterment of their own class to shape a new social compact for the society as a whole."[146] The ties between working and middle-class women that had been forged in common causes for suffrage, against the charter, for working women's rights, and other such issues, significantly aided the women's trade union movement in Chicago. According to Elizabeth Payne, the CWTUL had a "democratic" vision reflected in Margaret Dreier Robins' call for all women "to 'mother' the world by entering the arena of the larger society through suffrage, politics, and the professions." But Robins' "conception of motherhood" had broad implications for society, implying that "women more fully embodied the public because they alone understood the social consequences of private acts."[147] For instance, unwanted pregnancies produced social consequences. The CWTUL's demand for readily available birth control information reflected both this understanding and a belief that it was a "democratic right" of women to control these social consequences. By contrast, male urban working-class politics never linked this type of "private" act to democratic rights or to public consequence because these were not men's concern.[148]

Chicago activist Dr. Rachelle Yarros, who led the CWTUL health committee, crossed the boundaries of class and ethnicity. She was a Russian immigrant who after being forced to flee Russia for subversive political activities worked in a New York sweatshop. She then began practicing medicine among the poor, but she also belonged to the WCC. She persuaded that most middle-class of women's organizations, the CWC, to work with the CWTUL on birth control, helping the CWC organize its own birth control committee that evolved into the Illinois Birth Control League. The CWTUL and CWC worked together on birth control and other issues despite the CWC's having rejected Robins application for membership in 1908 because of her "radical" theories.[149]

The evidence for Chicago indicates that in the early twentieth century neither were activist women solely motivated by female concerns with motherhood, nor did middle-class white women simply impose an agenda on other women. Theirs is more properly understood as a shared urban vision, not an identical one, that emanated from women's similar private experiences. Philosopher Nancy Love argues that we must recognize how women have often functioned from an "ethic of solidarity" that can represent *feminist* commitments women share and communicate to one another but that does not represent *women* as being and thinking exactly alike. According to Love, women have often united in common cause while acknowledging differences and tensions among themselves. Working to reorganize the city and its institutions to provide a common welfare distinguished many activist Chicago women from the men of their class and even race. As a recent biographer of Ida B. Wells-Barnett has argued, Wells-Barnett firmly believed in woman suffrage and "government responsibility in social welfare." In these beliefs and in much of her activism in Chicago she acted in concert with activist white women. But in her methods and ultimate aims she often disagreed with these women, as she often disagreed with black men about social welfare and government responsibility. Nonetheless, her overall vision of a just city clearly resembled that of white activist women.[150] This is neither to argue that activist middle-class Chicago women had best defined this common welfare nor to say that we cannot ask that if some groups of women had been more attentive and open to other women's perceptions, whether this common welfare would have been defined somewhat differently. But by seeking to embed into Chicago's political structures the idea of a common welfare best promoted by government, activist Chicago women in the early twentieth century tried to change the institutions and the purposes of urban government in ways inimical to what most men wanted from urban government.

Anna Nicholes believed this in 1913 when she wrote about the bankers' sense of the city as an economic venue versus a women's sense of a city of homes. Even when men did talk about the homes of the city, they did so from their own perspective. Two years before Nicholes's essay appeared, Chicago architect Jens Jensen— a member of the City Club Planning Committee—wrote that a "city should be based not on commercial benefits but on ideal homes." But Jensen meant something far different than did Nicholes. For Jensen, the goal was expertly planned homes. He wanted a municipal department of civics that

> would see to utilitarian planning matters, such as the width and layout of streets . . . organize neighborhoods, first by its power to approve new subdivisions, and even more tellingly by its commitment to create neighborhood centers based

around schools, churches, settlement houses, clubs, and . . . workplaces . . . in order to make life more pleasant and home life more wholesome for all classes in the ideal society.[151]

This vision of expert planned model neighborhoods containing ideal homes for the ideal society is a fundamentally different perspective from that which Nicholes and other activist women had when they thought of Chicago as a city of homes. For one thing, when these women talked about homes they talked about the people in them and of homes as "a place in which to rear children to live a joyous life." Jensen and other male experts talked about the physical structures. And as for a municipal department of civics stuffed with expert planners, Nicholes believed that civic sense came from the people, not from the experts, and without it "city reforms are impossible."[152]

Nicholes wrote her essay in the year that Chicago women entered almost full political citizenship. The next chapters examine activist Chicago women as voters, potential officeholders, and political party members. They explore how women pursued their idea of using government to promote the common welfare and changing the political system, including the ways that the political parties functioned. As they became voters, activist Chicago women hoped, as Grace Abbott expressed it, that they would "hold definitely to those principles in regard to public affairs that are really different from the men's point of view."[153]

Part Three

CAMPAIGNING FOR THE VISION

Six

"I Do Not Think the Husband Will Influence the Wife's Vote in Municipal Affairs": Women as Voters and Potential Officeholders, 1913–19

IN HER memoirs, activist Louise de Koven Bowen recalled a disturbing incident that took place while she was seeking a state bill to create and fund probation officers for the juvenile court. After encountering one stumbling block after another, she turned to a state legislator of her acquaintance, whom she hoped would be sympathetic. He agreed to help her and excused himself to make a phone call to another legislator. Bowen recounts the offhand manner in which her friend told his colleague to pass the bill because it contained nothing of interest to either of them but a woman he knew wanted it. The unspoken message was that neither man would have supported the bill if it interfered with the desires of the party or its male supporters. Not long afterward, Bowen became an ardent suffragist, determined to use the vote to effect the policies she and other activist women were fighting for and to prevent "bad" bills from passing the legislature in the same way.[1]

Contemporary observers and later scholars have puzzled over American women's voting behavior immediately after suffrage. Suffragists had promised that with the vote women would change the political process and enact strong social reforms, but when neither happened scholars concluded that suffrage did not make much difference in U.S. politics. Indeed, because no rebalancing of party politics took place after woman suffrage, many concluded that women voted just as their husbands did. Kristi Andersen's recent examination of state-level data demonstrates that women neither voted "just as their husbands did" nor failed to make a difference. In an earlier essay, Nancy Cott suggested that rather than focus on women's votes per se, it is more significant to explore how, once women could vote, they may have tried to implement the programs they had promised to pursue.[2]

The almost daily struggle over issues of municipal development in which activist Chicago women engaged can answer Cott's question because the struggle left behind documents, unlike national-level politics in which few women were yet engaged in the 1920s. Evidence from Chicago also supports and amplifies Andersen's work because we have ballots separated by gender for every primary and general election from 1914 through 1920. At the time, the city held an annual spring primary and general election for half of the seventy aldermanic seats. In addition, we have the data for both critical mayoral elections in 1915 and 1919, and additional primary and general elections in the falls of 1914, 1916, and 1919. Thus, we have several sets of statistics through which to track activist women's voting behavior. But the Chicago evidence also allows us to ask questions that connect women, ideas about gender, and urban development. This chapter, therefore, examines how Chicago politics worked immediately following suffrage: the political campaigns themselves, the activities women pursued in these campaigns, how the parties and male activists treated new women voters, and how activist women worked both inside and outside of the party system. Investigating these issues leads to three conclusions. First, activist Chicago men and women had many different and often conflicting municipal priorities that they sought to institutionalize into government. Second, these different priorities were rooted in differing gender perceptions and experiences of the city. Third, male control of the political system made it virtually certain that activist women's comprehensive vision of the good city would never prevail.

Registering Women Voters

It was an important victory for activist Chicago women when Illinois became the first state east of the Mississippi to give women the suffrage for local and federal elections, even though local politicians immediately secured court rulings limiting women's voting rights, preventing women from voting for county offices, which included the important post of Cook County commissioners, and barring them from serving as election judges.[3] Given these restrictions, Chicago activists continued to disagree about whether to work for a state constitutional amendment for full suffrage, but they all welcomed the suffrage law. Many activist men said they welcomed women's new political power, and even party politicians, although initially wary of women's potential power, seemed disposed to listen to what women wanted. Some city council members expressed support for such women's aims as municipal government ownership of garbage collection and disposal. In this atmosphere, activist women were optimistic that they were entering a new era of municipal politics in which women could change the city's political process and use government to enact their vision of a common welfare.

This optimism would soon be tempered as women realized that having the vote did not mean that there were candidates for whom they wanted to vote. By early 1915 the WCC lamented the lack of real alternatives in the mayoral primary: "The voters are often told that they ought to support principles, not men. But here were four men promulgating practically the same platform."[4] Activist women would quickly discover that without access to political offices and the party structures, women would have little actual political power. Since the doors to the key political institutions did not swing open for women as they had in the past for most newly enfranchised male citizens, women would not experience an increase in their political influence commensurate to their absolute numbers.[5]

Nevertheless, activist Chicago women plunged into political work, registering voters, running for municipal office, and casting their ballots. The CPEL, CWC, and WCC mounted a massive women voter registration campaign for the municipal primary of February 1914. Newspapers published photos of prominent Chicago women registering at their local polling place.[6] But interest in voting had long extended far beyond white middle-class women. The CWTUL, CTF, and ethnic women's groups also had actively campaigned for municipal suffrage. In addition to the women discussed in earlier chapters, Chicago socialist Josephine C. Kaneko and CWTUL members Gertrude Barnum and Mary McEnerny had worked with the mainstream suffrage movement. In 1908 Kaneko had urged the national socialist meeting in New York City to participate in the movement. Barnum had attended the 1906 national woman suffrage convention, and McEnerny had spoken at its 1913 meeting in St. Louis. At the September 1908 Midwestern interstate meeting, CWTUL delegates—among them, Chicago activists Emma Steghagen, Mary Anderson, Elizabeth Maloney, Mary McEnerny, and Agnes Nestor—overwhelmingly approved closer cooperation with the national suffrage movement.[7]

In mid-1913, Steghagen, a CWTUL delegate to the 1908 meeting, organized the Wage Earners' Suffrage League (WESL) to coordinate the locals of the CWTUL to work for passage of the new state suffrage law.[8] When that succeeded, the WESL mobilized to register working women to vote. Steghagen's reported goal in 1913 was for the WESL to register 110,000 working women by election time.[9] I have never located any figures that indicate how far she progressed toward that goal, but at least one newspaper story indicates that the WESL was quite busy. By October, Maloney and Nestor had led waitresses and gloveworkers, respectively, into the WESL. They were joined by Mae Nihil and the suspenders' workers; Helen Phillips and the felt hat workers; Mary McEnerny and five hundred foundry workers; Isabel McAlpine and typographical workers; Kitty Murphy and the horse nail workers; Katherine Frett and the cigar box makers; Anna Harris and the laundry workers; Mary Anderson and the shoe workers; Bessie Abramowitz and three thousand garment workers; and Katherine Wagner and Dora Levin with contingents of household and necktie workers, respectively.[10] Many of these women had long been involved with the suffrage movement, and the WESL generally heeded the spirit of cooperation recommended by the 1908 resolution to work with other women's organizations to register working women. The WESL, for example, hosted lawyer and CPEL leader Marion Drake. McEnerny exhorted working women to register and vote, and urged them to elect women to the city council.[11]

African American and ethnic women and their organizations had worked hard for suffrage and now participated in the voter registration drive. African American women had alternated between working in their own organizations and mainstream suffrage groups. Between 1900 and 1907, Ida B. Wells-Barnett belonged to the CPEL, and Fannie Barrier Williams had spoken to the 1907 NAWSA convention meeting in Chicago. In early 1910 women at the Mt. Olivet Baptist Church hosted the president of the African American branch of the New York PEL, who had urged them to join the suffrage movement. In early 1914, Wells-Barnett and the Alpha Suffrage Club (ASC) (founded in January 1913) led a registration drive among African American women, organizing a block system to canvass every ward where African Americans lived to urge these women to register and vote. It held weekly meetings at the Negro Fellowship League during which members instructed women in the procedures for registering and voting. Although many white suffragists in the movement did not willingly work with black suffragists, Ruth Hanna McCormick marched with Chicagoan Irene McCoy Gaines at her side in a 1914 suffrage parade in Chicago. Chicagoan Mary C. Byron was working for NAWSA in 1914.[12]

In her study of black women's politics in Illinois, Wanda Hendricks found that by 1913 activist African American women in Chicago had come to regard full suffrage as an absolute necessity for their municipal agenda, which included securing "the proper care for dependent and delinquent children, reform of jail conditions, and attacking discrimination." Chicago activists Adela Hunt Logan and Elizabeth Lindsay Davis had expressed virtually the same concerns in two woman suffrage symposia printed in the *Crisis*. Logan asserted, "Colored women feel keenly that they may help in civic betterment," and that where an African American woman already had the vote "she is reported as using it for the uplift of society and for the advancement of the State." "Good women," she said, "try always to do good housekeeping." Davis, a national organizer for the National Association of Colored Women's Clubs, believed African American women would use the vote to benefit "the abandoned wife, the wage earning girl, the dependent and delinquent child, or the countless hordes of the unemployed." The Chicago *Defender* claimed in early 1914 that African American women's politics were motivated by concerns over municipal garbage collection, transportation services, and child welfare.[13]

Figure 18. Suffrage Parade, May 2, 1914. (Chicago *Daily News*, Chicago Historical Society, DN-62620)

In late January 1914 more than thirty thousand women representing over 130 ethnic women's organizations attended a rally to urge ethnic women to attend a women's mass registration meeting scheduled for February 1 and to vote.[14] Norwegian women later recounted that they had used the enthusiasm generated by the registration drive to organize the Federation of Norwegian Women's Societies.[15] Suffrage leaders addressed the Bohemian Women's Citizens' Club. Mary McDowell spoke to the Socialist Women's League of Chicago. The WCC scheduled voter registration and information sessions at settlement house women's clubs.[16] Voter registration was complicated for ethnic women by the federal act of 1907 that made women ineligible for citizenship if their husbands were not citizens.[17] The leaders of ethnic women's organizations now instructed women as to their rights, reminding them that to register, a married woman had to prove her husband's citizenship.[18] Despite the obstacles, ethnic women were ready to vote, as they had shown since their participation in the anti-charter campaign in 1907. Russian Jewish immigrant Hilda Satt Polacheck, who had distributed suffrage leaflets from Hull House a few years earlier, recalled that on her wedding day she realized that by marrying a citizen, she had automatically become a citizen. "It is curious that I should have thought of this at such an auspicious moment," she later recalled, "but I did."[19] Harriet Vittum told of a woman in her

neighborhood who was determined to register despite her husband's refusal to give her his naturalization papers. She went to her local place of
registration where the workers told her that because they knew who she
was, if her husband registered then she could, too. The husband delayed
his registration until late on registration day, but when he finally told her
that he had registered, as she told Vittum: "I did not say anything to him,
but I put my shawl over my head and I did not dress up. I took the milk
bottle. He thinks I go for milk. After a while I come back and I pretty
proud, I say 'Humph, I registered.' " Her husband was not pleased, she
told Vittum, "But I don't care, I vote."[20]

The women's mass outdoor meeting for registration on February 1
drew more than ten thousand women who stood in the winter cold to
hear speeches by Addams, Bowen, teachers' leaders Margaret Haley and
Ella Flagg Young, CWC leader Elizabeth Bass, and others. Foreign-lan-
guage translators were on hand for non-English-speaking women. The
following day, even the conservative *Tribune* paid tribute to women's new
political potential in a cartoon showing women bashing the city council's
notoriously corrupt aldermen with a club marked "the vote." Middle-class
women's organizations took advantage of the interest in suffrage among
women throughout the city and held meetings in ethnic and working-
class areas during the following week. The CPEL scheduled Sunday meetings so that working and business women could attend. The leaders of the
WESL vowed that all of its members would register and vote.[21]

This collaborative effort to register women paid off handsomely, with
one hundred fifty thousand women registered before the primary. Female
registration in Chicago's working-class, heavily foreign-born wards generally lagged behind that in middle-class, native-born wards, but that dispar-
ity should not be overstated, especially given the additional impediments
facing foreign-born women. In McDowell's 29th ward three thousand
women, or 23.3 percent of the adult female population, registered for the
spring 1914 election, while in the affluent 6th and 7th wards 37.5 and
44.9 percent of adult women registered, respectively. By spring 1915,
however, 31.7 percent of the women in the 29th ward were registered.[22]
Similarly impressive results were seen in the city's 1st ward, the preserve
of "notorious" politicians Hinky-Dink Kenna and Bathhouse John
Coughlin, where women claimed to have registered "about one thousand
more women than the [aldermen] would admit live[d] in the ward." They
were pleased with the "keen interest" African American women showed
in registering. Wells-Barnett declared that her 2nd ward produced the
sixth highest total of women registered by ward in the city, even while
enduring male mockery in the streets and in the press.[23]

Activist Chicago women were neither afraid of ethnic women's having
the vote nor that they, or any women, would vote as their husbands did

or as their husbands told them to. When Bowen stated flatly that "I do not think the husband will influence the wife's vote in municipal affairs," she meant this for all women.[24] Anna Allen, the resident nurse at the University of Chicago Settlement Club, urged the women of that club to register and to vote and wondered aloud "if the very rigid laws we have pertaining to undue influence, intimidating, or in any way interfering with the rights of franchise would apply to this entirely new situation [e.g., husbands' influencing wives]."[25] In the decade before securing the vote, middle-class and working women had frequently worked together and spoken before each other's organizations, urging all Chicago women to support municipal suffrage. After gaining the vote, the WCC continued to urge working-class, immigrant women to register and to vote.[26] Finding women still alive who voted early in the century is almost impossible, and few working class, ethnic women left memoirs for us to consult regarding their attitudes toward whether they would allow their husbands to influence their vote. I did interview one such woman, Anne Hagerty Kennedy, born into a working-class Irish family in Chicago in 1897. Mrs. Kennedy was emphatic that she registered to vote and voted without consulting her husband. If anything, only another woman had influenced her, for she recalled that the first time she registered, one of her female neighbors was doing the registration. The neighbor asked Mrs. Kennedy with which party she was registering, and when Mrs. Kennedy replied that she did not know, her helpful neighbor told her she was a Democrat just like the rest of them![27]

Partisanship or Non-partisanship in 1914

Activist Republican women may have been unhappy with Mrs. Kennedy's choice of party, but they would have understood the partisan politics involved. And activist middle-class Democratic women would not have seen this as an example of ethnic women being an impediment to good government. Chicago's activist women understood that with the vote came the decision on whether to pursue political work and their municipal agenda through a non-partisan strategy or by declaring allegiance to a party. Activist women across the country faced this same dilemma. They had come to politics through their voluntary organizations, and these organizations had often dedicated themselves to ending corrupt municipal party politics. Activist Chicago women's first municipal votes, however, cannot be understood within the partisan / nonpartisan dichotomy that has been used by political historians to describe both male political behavior generally and progressive-era urban reform particularly. A more complex and logical progression of women's political development was at work that had come from within their own organizations rather than from within the party structures.[28] Nor had activist Chicago women ever securely hitched themselves to male reform organizations. Almost no Chicago women's organization had ever put good government into its title, as was the case with the Boston Equal Suffrage Association for Good Government, or had made "good government" its rallying cry, as had California women. The only exception that I have found is one mention of the forming of a "Woman's Democratic Council for Good Government" in 1915, whose leaders included Elizabeth Bass and Hannah Solomon, neither of whom would have embraced the types of good government activism pursued by the Boston and California women, as subsequent details of Bass and Solomon's political partisanship reveal.[29] The experience of working to secure a general welfare for the city's people would enable activist Chicago women to seek realistic compromises with traditional partisan politics, even as they sought to change the nature of politics.

In reality, maintaining strict non-partisanship was hardly possible in Chicago, where even to cast a ballot in the municipal primary a voter had to declare a party affiliation, after which she or he could not vote for another party for a year. Nor had activist women completely eschewed partisan politics before. As early as 1896 the Cornelia Club had abandoned its social agenda for a political one, and renamed itself the Democratic Woman's Club of Chicago to gain more credibility to lobby for women candidates for the board of trustees for the state university.[30] Such individual activists as Nestor and McCormick had affiliated with a political party, and women's ward party organizations existed before the suffrage law. In 1914 Addams and Bowen urged women to declare a party affiliation and to vote in the primary. Only the more conservative activists such as Grace Wilbur Trout, who had willingly settled for the Illinois partial suffrage, suggested that women shun the partisan primary.[31] Yet activist women's belief in a political mission to end "politics as usual" led them to temper their partisan message. Bowen declared that women should by all means vote in primaries when one candidate was clearly better; Bass, a professed Democrat, declared that women need not vote in wards where the best candidate was already certainly the primary winner. Still, women in the 7th ward rejected the call of Charles Merriam and his male nonpartisan organization to shun the ward's primary because the organization was going to run an independent in the general election. Instead, a group of women in the ward—none of whom can be identified as leading activists—advised women "to lose no time in exercising their right of franchise."[32]

Because activist women were determined to seek out the candidates who promised to back their municipal agenda, it was also difficult for them to be strictly partisan. Their prepared list of questions for aldermanic candidates, which all women were urged to ask of their own candidates, indicates the differences between male and female politics at this stage.

What have you done, and what do you propose to do for the welfare of the city and of your ward? What is your attitude toward the segregation of vice? Ventilation? Fire Protection? Censorship of moving pictures? Schools as social centers? What is your attitude toward the complete enfranchisement of women in Illinois? On the subways? On bond issues? On protection of girls from the dance hall and saloon evils? On the permanent solution to the garbage question?[33]

Men almost always either backed the party choice or focused on a candidate's stance on economic or "clean government" issues. It is noteworthy that "clean government" was not listed among the activist women's concerns.[34]

So activist women did not just rush to join the parties. Existing women's organizations dramatically increased their political organizing after passage of the Illinois partial suffrage statute and pursued political activities through grassroots education and investigation, strategies that they had pioneered. The CWC, led by Elizabeth Bass, who later became an important figure in women's Democratic Party circles, formed a new Committee on Public Affairs, dedicated to increasing the members' knowledge of municipal affairs and to bring them more fully into the political system. This committee's three subcommittees were to monitor the affairs of the city council, the Cook County Board of Commissioners, and the board of education. Bass and Harriet Vittum co-chaired the committee of the whole, the vice-chair was Grace Temple, and the secretary was Marion Drake. Other women organized branches of the CPEL, called women's civic leagues, to work on the ward, neighborhood, and even precinct level. McDowell chaired the league in the 29th ward, and vice chairs represented each nationality in the ward.[35]

On the other hand, ample evidence demonstrates that activist women neither shunned political work nor failed to understand how to work within the existing political system.[36] Existing ward branches of women's Democratic and Republican clubs stepped up their activities, while women organized new political groups, several of which were ethnic organizations. Goldie Young and Bessie Pine led the Northwest Side Jewish Woman's Democracy; Clara Piucinski organized the Women's Democratic Club of Irving Park and Mayfair to add to those she had already organized in the Avondale and Jefferson neighborhoods.[37] When anti-suffrage forces tried to block women from serving as poll judges in late 1913, the CWC, the CPEL, the Non-Partisan Club of Polish Women from the 29th Ward, the Woman's Republican Club of the 13th Ward, and other groups petitioned the court to safeguard this right for women. The court ruled in women's favor, and women's groups urged women to undertake this work.[38] Women in the 21st ward canvassed house-to-house, carrying registration cards; women in ward-based party organizations publicly supported specific candidates; and women participated in the local Progressive Party nominating convention, this time as voting members.[39] For the April 1914 general election, women accelerated their political organizing. The WESL divided the city into four districts and then assigned members to organize political activities within each district; it scheduled election rallies for every ward.[40] Republican women of the largely middle-class, native-born 7th ward who had resisted "progressive" men's calls to refrain from voting in the primary now campaigned vigorously for Independent Republican John Kimball, whose ideas they believed were closer to the women's political agenda than those of the regular Republican nominee.

> [They] formed a flying squadron in groups of two, for making house-to house canvasses. They sent out a circular letter. . . . Pledge-blanks promising support to their [candidates] were presented to every woman . . . of their ward for signing. . . . A card catalogue was made of all the voters, men and women, who had pledged their support . . . and a large number of automobiles were enlisted on election day to get these voters to the polls.[41]

When registered Chicago women went to the polls for their first municipal election in the February 1914 primary, they voted in percentages equal to male registered voters: 29.9 percent for women and 30.5 percent for men. Forty-one percent of registered women voted in the heavily African American 2nd ward against 33.9 percent of registered men. In the 10th, 17th, and 25th wards, each with a high foreign-born population, registered women's participation equaled that of registered men's.[42] Women's voting behavior in the primary and then the April general election also demonstrates their determination to use political power to promote a particular vision of the city while navigating the tricky currents of political partisanship. In the 29th ward, Mary McDowell supported the regular Republican nominee despite wishing she had a better choice. In an open letter to the voters of her ward she explained,

> I have decided to give my vote to Mr. Frank B. Buszin. . . . I wanted to give this my first municipal vote to an Independent Candidate but the 29th Ward offered none, therefore I had to consider the two men only who have any chance of election. . . . [Buszin] seems to realize that the ward and the city demand a new kind of politics that considers the city's welfare above the national party.

McDowell charged Buszin's opponent with having "voted against every measure for the welfare of the children of our ward and our city." She also based her support of Buszin on the fact that "the Republican Committee of the 29th Ward have agreed to the policy that will leave him, if elected, free to vote with all parties for the best interests of the city and the ward."[43]

As a longtime activist, McDowell's stance is perfectly logical. There are signs that this wish to support a women's agenda extended deep into the ranks of voting women. In the primary, women had voted for women candidates.[44] In the 1st ward Progressive primary, 49.5 percent of women voted for Marion Drake, but only 5 percent of men did so. In the 2nd ward Democratic primary, 45.2 percent of women voters chose Sara Hopkins against 15.6 percent of men. Since the majority of African Americans lived in the 2nd ward, where for the first time an African American candidate contended in the Republican primary, substantial support for Hopkins must have come from white women.[45] In the 23rd ward, the ratio was 37.3 percent of women to 11.7 percent of men for Marie Gerhardt in the Democratic primary.

In the April general election, the pattern of women voting for women continued with one notable exception. Five women candidates were listed on the April 1914 ballot: Progressives Marion Drake and Bernice Napie-ralski in the 1st and 12th wards[46]; Independent Harriet Vittum in the 17th ward; and Socialists Josephine Kaneko and Lida McDermut in the 6th and 7th wards, respectively. Vittum's platform called for better housing and sanitation, scientific garbage disposal, better street cleaning and lighting, and a city commission to provide work for the unemployed: all issues that women's organizations had been identifying as vital for the city to address and solve in certain ways.[47] Her campaign organized a 17th Ward Mothers' Independent Club, located at the Northwestern University Settlement at 1400 West Augusta Avenue, and issued campaign literature in various foreign languages, appealing to ethnic women in the same terms used to appeal to middle-class voters. An Italian-language flyer urged all eligible women to register for the sake of the ward and the city as a whole but also because they and their children deserved the same good schools, playgrounds, clean and well-lit streets, sanitary milk, and other measures that they as mothers knew were necessary for the health of their children, that were available to children in more privileged areas of the city.[48] Bowen, Addams, and Wilmarth contributed financially to Vittum's campaign even though they did not live in her ward and could not vote for her. Margaret Dreier Robins did live in the ward, and she sat on the campaign executive committee.[49] As middle-class activists, Addams, Bowen, Wilmarth, and Robins could be expected to support one of their own. But running as an Independent in the heavily Democratic and ethnic 17th ward (with a total foreign-born population of more than 35 percent), Vittum received 35 percent of women's votes against 20 percent of men's. Many of her votes must have come from ethnic, working-class women, who urban historians generally regard as voting as did their ethnic male counterparts and especially not for middle-class reformers with professed Republican Party sympathies.[50] Similarly, women in the heavily ethnic, working-class, Democratic 1st ward cast 32.1 percent of their ballots for Progressive Party reformer Marion Drake; men gave her

22.4 percent of their vote. The regular Democratic candidate—the notorious "Bathhouse John" Coughlin—received 48.8 percent of women's votes, but 67.7 percent of men's.

The pattern of women voting in greater numbers for women was ruptured, however, for women Socialists. Lida McDermut received 2.56 percent of women's votes to 3.6 percent of men's; for Kaneko, the votes were 2.66 percent to 2.69 percent.[51] On the one hand, such results might seem surprising because the socialist women's municipal agenda very closely resembled that of other activist women. Addressing the 6th ward women's civic league, Josephine Kaneko had outlined an agenda that was closer to those of the WCC and CWC than to that of the male-dominated Socialist Party.

> The Socialists stand for progress, the women stand for progress. . . . As a member of the city council from your ward it would be my duty and my pleasure to see that our streets are kept in good repair; that sanitary conditions exist throughout the ward; that the housing and other existing ordinances are enforced; that all new laws making for the betterment of the general comfort are enacted. . . . I would insist upon municipal ownership of public utilities . . . the inauguration of municipal markets . . . the erection of municipal lodging houses for working women and girls . . . extension of the playgrounds system to the public parks, and the opening of the schools for social centers. I would do what I could toward the alleviation and abolition of the white slave traffic by providing employment for working girls and by paying both men and women a living wage and opening respectable places of amusement for the city's great army of young people.

Kaneko spoke about the city as a home, telling her audience "there is one fundamental point upon which we can agree—that is we cannot expect much from a home in which children are hungry and ragged and dirty." Socialist candidate Lida McDermut expressed similar sentiments in her campaign. She noted that "the influence of women in government will be to emphasize the human side rather than the mere business side of public questions."[52] And activist middle-class women did believe that they and socialist women were largely working for similar ends. When socialist activist Corinne Brown died in 1914, Dr. Frances Dickinson (IWA) eulogized her as "a widely known Socialist, suffrage advocate, settlement worker, and club organizer." The CWTUL, Mary McDowell, and the Socialist Women's League sent memorials. But clubwoman Ellen Henrotin, suffragist Grace Wilbur Trout, and Margaret Haley also spoke at her service.[53]

On the other hand, it would have been difficult for middle-class activist women to embrace such Socialist candidates as Kaneko because the broader Socialist agenda was largely determined by male socialists and it violated too many of their class norms.[54] Of course, both Kaneko and McDermut also ran in solidly middle-class wards where they stood no chance of victory, but in all the aldermanic contests that year, fewer women voted for Socialist candidates than did men. Such results remind us that while women's political objectives may appear to modern historians to share similarities with those of the Socialists, or even those of the labor movement, activist middle-class women in fact saw themselves as pursuing an agenda different from those of both movements. Ida B. Wells-Barnett, according to her recent biographer, never shared "labor's demand for power sharing through 'industrial democracy'."[55] Moreover, working-class and working women in several instances seem to have preferred candidates who clearly articulated a women-and-children-oriented agenda, such as those of Vittum and Drake, when they were offered the chance, rather than that of a male politician preferred by the men of the ward or a socialist candidate, even if this were a woman.[56]

Although they failed to carry women into office in spring 1914, that fall and in subsequent years women participated with enthusiasm and in steadily increasing numbers in party primaries and general elections and formed more partisan political organizations. Mrs. William Severin of the Illinois Women's Republican League claimed that two thousand women in the 31st ward, one thousand in the 23rd, eight hundred in the 24th, and four hundred in the 26th, belonged to ward-based women's Republican clubs, and called upon these women to bring Progressive women back into the regular party. She also reported that her group "had a governing body that consisted of 150 delegates representing all the wards in Chicago." Johanna Downes, head of the Illinois Women's Democratic League, claimed that in November 1914 "more women voted the straight democratic ticket than men" and that its operations were "based upon ward organizations called 'branches.' "[57]

The WCC urged women to vote in the fall 1914 primary to select candidates for municipal sanitary district, municipal court judges, and Cook County commissioners. The club appealed to women voters to "help nominate the best candidates of their parties." It printed and distributed fifty thousand leaflets that urged women to register for this election and declared that their "ward leaders and all other members of the Woman's City Club feel personally responsible to get a large registration of women and an equally large vote" for the fall 1914 general election. Despite the WCC's profession of neutrality in all elections, it publicly supported Mary McDowell and Harriet Vittum for Cook County commissioner and two men running for sanitary district trustees in 1914. McDowell and Vittum's candidacies were doomed after the Illinois supreme court ruled women ineligible to vote for this office.[58]

Women's voting increased with each election. In the 1915 municipal primaries (which drew a much higher participation rate because it was a mayoral primary), voting by registered women ranged from 50 to 75 percent by ward. The turnout rate for registered women voters in the general elections of 1914, 1915, and 1916 (which included their first aldermanic, mayoral, and presidential ballots, respectively) was also high. In 1914 their turnout rate was lower than men's only in three wards.[59] In the 1915 general election, women's turnout rate was lower than men's in twenty-five wards but still generally exceeded 85 percent, barely lower than the male turnout rate.[60] Female registration also increased. It rose nearly 12 percent between the spring 1914 and the fall 1916 elections, during which time male registration fell almost 2 percent. Women's rate of registration increased in every ward accept the 10th, with an especially noticeable rise in working-class, foreign-born wards such as the 4th, where it went from 17.2 percent in spring 1914 to 34.7 percent in spring 1915. By the spring 1916 primary, total registration for women was 261,172; by spring 1918, 286,634.[61]

Elections of 1915 and 1916

Despite 1914's disappointments, activist Chicago women saw the 1915 mayoral election as a test of their political potential and hoped to nominate from each party the man who best understood their vision of a responsible municipal government dedicated to ensuring the general welfare and who would promise to move government in this direction as mayor. They urged women to register and to vote in the primary as "the only method of nominating good candidates. . . . [I]f poor candidates were nominated [in the primary] your vote on election day would be a choice between two evils." A list of activist women and their preferred candidates was published in the newspapers. The WCC dedicated its February 1915 calendar to the primary election, arranging political gatherings in many wards and inviting women to come hear about the aldermanic candidates, attend presentations by the mayoral candidates, and discuss general political problems. Other women's groups organized educational meetings within their wards.[62] What activist women found, however, was that the politics-as-usual approach of the parties paid scant attention to the women's agenda. In this election they discovered the strength of the party system, and its ability to adapt to changing circumstances such as women suffrage and to keep control of both the party machinery and electoral outcomes.

Two candidates sought the nomination of each party in the 1915 primaries: the "regular" Republican, William Hale Thompson, and the challenger, Judge Harry Olson; and the Democratic incumbent, Carter Harrison II, and his challenger, Robert Sweitzer. Of the four, Thompson had the most scandalous reputation. He had engaged openly for years in "boodling" (corrupt payoffs between businessmen and politicians). He had also recently angered women by failing to pay the IESA the money he owed it for political advertisements he had placed in a special suffrage publication. Few activist women supported him. Bowen, Wilmarth, Addams, McDowell, Vittum, Grace Nicholes, and Republican activist Mrs. William Severin, backed Olson. Since many activist women believed Thompson was a tool of the commercial interests, Olson at least offered women some hope that he was not beholden to the businessmen of the Republican Party. Wilmarth said that Olson was the clear choice because he was "familiar with women's point of view in government."[63] In a jibe against Thompson's ties to businessmen, the WCC appealed to women voters to ask themselves,

> Shall I vote for the man who listens to the commercial interests . . . or to the man who listens to that greatest interest which women naturally represent? . . . Do I represent in my voting the human welfare interest which is a municipality's chief function to preserve? Will I hold fast to this belief that the welfare of human beings is the chief business of a city government?

The WCC reminded women voters that "Chicago asks us to live for her welfare. She asks us to hold firm that city-wide patriotism that wants all the children of all the people to have the best conditions in which to grow."[64]

The choice for activist women seemed less clear in the Democratic race. Harrison had better suffrage credentials than Sweitzer; he had even occupied a place of honor and had led the grand march at the suffragists' annual ball that winter. Teachers' union leader Margaret Haley and school superintendent Ella Flagg Young backed Harrison, who had a good record in supporting teachers. But other Democratic women saw Sweitzer as being more in tune with their agenda; Johanna Downes, leader of the Illinois Women's Democratic League, and Elizabeth Bass both supported him.[65]

Activist women's conception of a good city would seem to account for the way women voted in the 1915 primary election, particularly in the Republican primary. Here Olson received 55.6 percent of women's votes, but only 44.2 percent of men's—a gap of 11.4 percent. In the Democratic primary, where both candidates were considered more or less acceptable to activist Democratic women, 38.4 percent of women voted for Harrison as compared to 34.9 percent of men (or, from the other vantage point, women voted 61.2 percent for Sweitzer and men voted 64.5 percent).[66] Since Olson lost the Republican primary, and Democratic women and men had voted almost alike for Democratic winner Sweitzer, scholars have assessed such results as a failure to "make a difference" and have concluded that women's politics were not strong. But the voting gap in the Republican primary, the reasons women gave for opposing Thompson, and the almost two-thirds of their votes that they cast for Sweitzer, who many activists declared more open to women's agenda, are specific political manifestations of activist women's dissatisfaction with the course of municipal development. These results again raise the issue of what we can tell from urban women's voting behavior, especially whether women voted as did their husbands. One structural problem with this question is that scholars ask it of general election results. By doing so, they do not take account of the rules of the party primary and the nomination process.

After the primary, the women's options were limited to supporting the party nominee, switching parties, or not voting. In 1915 many women already had partisan sympathies and they chose to stick with their party nominee. This was not especially difficult for Democratic women. Downes and the IWDL optimistically predicted that the "three solid Carter Harrison leagues will now join in our wonderful [Sweitzer] success and all will be harmonious in April." This prediction was largely correct.[67] For Republican women the situation was more problematic, as their behavior during the campaign indicates. Pro-Olson women seem to have refrained from giving Thompson their public support, but in the end most of them seem also to have stayed with their party. Marion Drake, on the other hand, who along with other Progressive Party leaders originally decided to back Thompson provided he adopt some progressive principles, ultimately refused to support him.[68]

A *Tribune* "straw poll" conducted in the weeks before the election, which included seventeen hundred women, recorded that among "club and society women" polled, 63 percent favored Thompson and 34 percent, Sweitzer. Of the several categories designed to describe women, only the group designated "housewives" gave Sweitzer a higher number of votes.[69] Thompson was the only name on the Republican ballot, and Republican women were determined to vote, so they went to the polls and cast their ballots according to the rules of the political game, just as male voters had been doing for decades.[70] But voting for Thompson did not mean that women were happy about their choice. Edith Abbott concluded, "It was the men's vote that created a situation in which the voters had to choose between Mr. Sweitzer and Mr. Thompson." Moreover, the 1915 aldermanic contests showed a gender gap. In twenty-six of the thirty-eight contests, women voted on average 3.57 percent higher for the candidate endorsed as a reformer. In several instances, women's votes contributed significantly to that candidate's success. In the 22nd, 23rd, and 33rd wards, women's vote for the reform candidates was nine points higher for the Democrat in the 22nd, six points higher for the Republican in the 23rd, and nine points higher for the Republican in the 33rd. Yet, overall, women could not overcome the superior number of men's votes to make much difference in most outcomes.[71]

The leaders of the WCC were obviously disappointed with the results of women's first mayoral election. But the organization advised women to continue to work hard in their wards for good candidates and hoped that in the future women could form a citywide organization to "unite forces for the common good and act together."[72] And activist Republican women did not stop trying to nominate and elect candidates more to their liking, as their relationship to their party over the succeeding years makes clear. Expressing a "general disgust at the turn in city politics" under Thompson, many of these women backed a slate of anti-Thompson aldermanic candidates in the February 1916 primary. Women gave Thompson candidates only 44 percent of their votes, down from 63 percent in 1915. In several wards, this carried the contest for the reform challenger, but the Thompson forces were still numerous enough to control the city council.[73]

A Woman's Municipal Platform

The 1916 municipal elections were a turning point for activist women. After three rounds of municipal elections, they more fully appreciated how difficult it was going to be, to use Jane Addams's words, to "translate human needs into political action."[74] Despite women's moderate successes on garbage collection, smoke ventilation, and lakefront development, municipal policies continued primarily to reflect the ideas and interests of men who tightly held to political power. In 1914, 1915, and 1916 neither party nominated any women for municipal offices. Once in the mayor's office, Thompson showed complete disdain for women's agenda[75]; the Democrats were little better in paying attention to women's wishes. In this context, in the interval between the 1916 primary and the municipal election, activist women returned to the old-style mass meeting, calling women together to formulate a single document that would promulgate "a civic ideal which Chicago women hope to attain," specifically, that elected officials had to be made to understand that their chief purpose was to safeguard "the interests of the entire community."[76] No account of this meeting at the Auditorium Theater gives a complete list of participating women's organizations, but they included the WCC, CWC, CPEL, CESA, CWA, Woman's Church Federation, Juvenile Protective Association, CWTUL, CTF, the Central Eleanor Council, the Federated High School teachers, the Women's Association of Commerce, and local women's organizations such as the University of Chicago Settlement Woman's Club and ward-based suffrage and women's clubs. Newspaper accounts reported that three thousand women attended the meeting.[77]

The participants ratified a Woman's Municipal Platform that gathered into one document the ideas activist women had been promoting for years. The Platform demanded a municipal Department of Recreation into which all authority over parks and recreation centers in the city would be consolidated and directed by the government. It advocated more stringent municipal controls over housing construction and demanded that the city council strictly enforce housing ordinances and immediately cease its decades-long practice of casually granting exemptions to builders and property owners. It demanded that teachers "be allowed to exercise all the rights of citizens . . . including the freedom of organization and political action," a demand that was greeted with "prolonged" applause. The Platform called for a municipal strike bureau, municipal ownership of garbage collection and disposal, a popular referendum on whether to municipalize telephone service, a reorganized department of public welfare, and more municipal attention (beyond simple prosecution after the fact) to preventing crime.[78]

In their speeches to the meeting, women denounced the current practice of party politics that sought to benefit its particular members rather than working to ensure the common welfare. They especially attacked the "politics" surrounding the board of education, accusing politicians of making appointments "to favor some political party, faction or affiliation; to represent some nationality . . . or to represent some religion—possibly the Catholic or the Protestant . . . or to represent some part of the city," rather than for the welfare of children. They advocated a citizens' "organization created for the public schools . . . so that that organization should keep track of what is going on and watch the votes of the members as they take place on every important question."[79] In a city with as many Catholic and Jewish immigrants as Chicago, the religious element to public education reform is always difficult to sort out. Other historians have seen a strong element of religious prejudice in urban school reform movements. There is evidence of collusion between Jacob Loeb and anti-Catholic groups in the contest over the "Loeb" rule. Yet three factors of activist Chicago women's approach to public education belie any strong religious dimension. First, these women attacked any religious-based appointment to the board of education. Second, no evidence of religious bias or concerns exists in the documents of women's organizations. Third, Ella Flagg Young wanted to promote her Catholic assistant, whom the board of education opposed, at same time that women's organizations were supporting the retention of Young.[80]

The women also attacked the ties between the police department and the political parties, which they believed made the police force "the tool of some political henchman" instead of the protector of the common welfare. They declared that the police "should be able to give protection to every citizen in the city, to rich and to poor, to every kind of person in every part of Chicago, on the streets and in their homes and in their places of amusement, wherever they may be."[81]

The women ended the meeting, pledging "our citizenship to the promotion of the welfare of all the citizens and to the securing of equality of opportunity for 'all the children of all the people.' "[82] They restated the principle of a common welfare beyond that of the individual, the attainment of which was the purpose of democratic government. No Chicago men or male organization, whether middle class or working class, ever conceived of the primary purpose of municipal government as promoting a common welfare or equality of opportunity for "all the children of all the people."[83] These differences were not just rhetorical; activist women did not just idealize the promotion of welfare through specific legislation. By writing and proclaiming their Platform, by labeling it a Municipal Platform, activist women were publicly advertising their wish to institutionalize within municipal government the power and obligation to promote the common welfare.

Accounting for the Lack of Women's Political Power

Between their failures in the official political arena and the resounding silence of Chicago men toward the Woman's Municipal Platform, activist Chicago women found themselves in a no-win situation. They were prepared to participate in organized politics and to utilize many of the same tactics and methods as did men. But having developed their political ideas and behavior outside the regular party system, they remained determined also to pursue their own political methods and to agitate for a specific municipal agenda that ran contrary to that of most men. Even if women had been prepared to practice politics-as-usual, clearly, Chicago men did not especially welcome women's political presence. As the remaining chapters show, Chicago men almost totally rejected women's ideas. The parties also worked to exclude women from the voting process whenever they could, until passage of the Nineteenth Amendment. In 1915 they managed to disqualify women from serving as poll judges. Then men in the town of Lake—incorporated into the city in 1889—successfully petitioned the Chicago corporation counsel (a political appointee) to disqualify women from voting on petitions to establish saloons inside the town boundaries, despite the clear right given to women to vote in such cases by the 1913 law. The following year Illinois women were ruled ineligible to vote for the crucial political posts of ward committeemen and delegates to the national party conventions.[84]

This resistance to accepting women into political parties contrasts markedly with the treatment accorded African American men after passage of the Fifteenth Amendment. The Chicago Republican Party did not treat African American men as equals but nevertheless slated them for the Cook County Board of Commissioners, state representatives, and minor municipal posts. Acceptance into the party structure, coupled with the district-based electoral system, enabled African American men to elect candidates and to wield a certain amount of decision-making power. Despite undeniable racist treatment, Chicago's African American men became members of the system, serving in political office and participating in candidate selection. White hostility, for instance, kept Wells-Barnett's husband, Ferdinand Barnett, from being elected to the municipal court in 1906, but African American men were appointed to county or municipal offices or nominated and elected to positions on the Cook County Board of Commissioners. R. R. Jackson was elected state representative in 1912.[85]

Women's experience in the 1910s was different. The regular parties categorically refused to slate any women for the thirty-five aldermanic positions up for annual election or for any other elective offices for years to come. The ten women who ran for city council in the 1914 primaries did so as Independents, Socialists, or Progressives, or as challengers. This was the high point of women's relationship to city council elections for over fifty years. In 1915 one woman ran for alderman; four tried in 1916; and two in 1919. When the city was redistricted into fifty wards in 1923, four women stood for city council with no success.[86] The parties' refusal to slate women as candidates for seats when there was a realistic possibility of winning meant that no woman was elected to the city council until the 1971 elections of Marylou Hedlund and Anna Langford.

Of course, the city's ward-based voting system was partially responsible for this situation. The Republican Party could accede to nominating African American candidates in the 2nd ward to help keep African Americans in the party by giving them a voice in "their" ward. Chicago Republicans' indifference to capturing women's allegiance, however, is particularly interesting because many activist middle-class women believed that it or the Progressive Party offered women their best hope for the future. Moreover, since Chicago was becoming increasingly a Democratic city, securing the allegiance of tens of thousands of new women voters might well have changed the fortunes of the Republican Party in municipal elections. Yet, as the final chapters shows, through the 1920s party leaders of all factions consistently rebuffed women's requests for equality and ignored women's call to dedicate the party to a true municipal reform agenda. Rather than cultivate the allegiance of activist Republican women, the party immediately alienated them by choosing William Hale Thompson as its mayoral candidate in 1915. Once elected, Thompson ostentatiously defied the wishes of activist women. He ignored their plea to appoint a competent person as commissioner of welfare, and instead appointed Louise Osborne Rowe, one of his campaign workers. In early 1916 women employees of the Department of Public Welfare accused Rowe of demanding financial kickbacks. McDowell complained that she and a large contingent of women had pleaded with Thompson to appoint "an able person" telling him that "the women voters of Chicago would not be satisfied with any 'second best' appointment," but that Thompson had only replied, "Ladies, I am sure that you will be satisfied with my appointment."[87] Then Thompson disbanded the Voluntary Advisory Board to the Department of Public Welfare, which had been staffed by many of these activist women.

Finally, in the wake of the Rowe uproar, he left the position of commissioner of welfare vacant from 1917 until he left office in 1923.[88] Thompson cultivated some of the worst elements of the Republican Party, so one might argue that he did not represent the party as a whole. Yet the public comments of more respectable elements within the party were not exhortations to make better appointments but discussions of how the Rowe scandal proved women unsuitable for public office. Furthermore, no evidence exists of protests against the fate of the welfare department.[89]

The Republican Party was not unique in its treatment of new women voters. The Democrats were out of the mayor's office from 1915 until 1923, so they had less opportunity to dismiss women. But other than the mayoral term of Edward Dunne (1905–1907), they likewise had made no significant gestures toward welcoming women's political presence. The grudging thanks that African American men gave to African American women for the important role they had played in securing the aldermanic nomination of Oscar DePriest as Chicago's first black city council member, was overshadowed by their reluctance to admit these women as political equals. After the 1914 primary, African American men denounced those women "who worked and voted against" the African American challenger Cowan, conveniently forgetting that a greater percentage of women than men had voted for Cowan. After the 1915 primary, men chastised women for loitering at the polls, saying they "made it look bad for the race"—again ignoring the ASC's work for DePriest, including its unanimous vote to expel any member who worked for a white candidate, and the fact that in the April general election women of the 2nd ward gave DePriest a slightly a higher percentage of their vote than did the men.[90] Deborah Gray White has observed that African American men saw women's intrusion into the public sphere as a challenge to their own prerogatives to race leadership.[91] I do not mean here to single out African American men, for men of every ethnic group and political party in the city treated women the same way. But considering the work that the ASC had done to secure a black aldermanic candidate, their hostility to women as political actors is a particular example of how men wanted women to "help" in politics but not be equal.[92]

A mix of political factors, history, and social attitudes shaped the experiences of activist women vis-à-vis those of almost all men upon entering the political system. The key features of the U.S. electoral system—two-party control, the absence of party slates, and a district-based, winner-take-all system of representation—all worked against activist women's participation in politics. But whenever women received the vote, they were additionally handicapped by entering the political system after almost a century of universal (free) male suffrage: between 1870 and 1920, women had been the only *citizens* constitutionally excluded from suffrage.[93] On the one hand, exclusion had given women the opportunity to develop ideas that distinguished them from men and the experience of calling upon other women as women to support specific initiatives and candidates.[94] On the other, women entered a political system in which men had already struck their political bargains in a way that determined the membership and objectives of the political parties themselves.[95] As scholars of politics have long known, once in place, institutions restrict actions: government structures circumscribe the policies adopted, while the political process itself limits the ways in which participants can function within the system.[96] In Chicago, the political process and the institutional structures of municipal government helped men exclude women from political power. The city's district-based, winner-take-all ward system made the two parties reluctant to slate any women for alderman. The city council was the source of power in the city, and each party sought to elect as many of its candidates as possible, so neither party wanted to slate a weak candidate in any ward that it thought it could win with a strong one. In 1919 the Democrats slated Laura Young in the 33rd Ward only after the regular Democrat (a man) withdrew after the primary. As the *Tribune* rather inelegantly but undoubtedly justly put it, Young was a "sacrifice" candidate in a largely Republican ward.[97]

But probabilities of winning aside, party leaders wanted successful candidates whom they believed would follow the party line. Independent action by an alderman could threaten a party's power in the city council. Women's idea of partisanship undoubtedly enhanced male suspicions of their trustworthiness. Moreover, programs most popular with women candidates and female voters risked arousing opposition from male voters. Finally, when women's first votes revealed them without enough overall voting strength to overwhelm male votes, politicians calculated that they did not have to court women voters.[98] Men were unwilling not only to accept women as political equals but also to support many of the municipal policies favored by activist women. If activist women had succeeded in implementing even part of their Municipal Platform, for example, Chicago's municipal development in the twentieth century might have been quite different. The absolute silence with which Chicago men greeted the Platform testifies to their implacable opposition.

Despite the relative bleakness of their situation, activist women refused to abandon their municipal agenda and kept working to promote women's voices into municipal affairs during the 1920s. As passage of the federal suffrage amendment loomed, the next test for Chicago's activist women was whether they could influence the course of municipal development during the 1920s by becoming more of a force in electoral politics and the legislative process.

Seven

"Looking Out for the Interests of the People": Municipal Activism through the 1920s

As Chicago approached the mayoral primary of early 1919, the WCC asked Chicago men and women what kind of mayor they wanted for the city. Regular (but progressive) Democratic alderman Ulysses S. Schwartz and progressive Republican George Sikes wanted strikingly similar things. Both men emphasized good administrative skills as their highest priority in a mayor. Schwartz wanted someone "to maintain control of administrative tasks and bureaucratic development; to build, grow, and maintain prosperity." Sikes wanted a mayor who would know how to appoint a "proper board of education" and who would "work in cooperation with the City Club." Two anonymous WCC women suggested different priorities for the mayor, favoring someone who would "be able to adjust the differences which are now acute between those who are appropriating an unjust share of this world's goods and the disinherited," someone "who sees clearly that a just government does not consist in the autocracy of a few who may be able to wield power through wealth, but who has at heart the common welfare of all." Sophonisba Breckinridge—a self-identified progressive Republican—agreed with this general sentiment but was even more specific. She wanted someone with

> the ability to examine all questions from the point of view of the general interest and the common good, and the habit of dealing with public affairs for the benefit of the public . . . a recognition of the rights of all children to air, light, clean streets, decent housing, places to play, and a chance of education, the right of young persons to decent recreation, the right of all to the protection of an efficient and honest police, and to common enjoyment of such natural advantages as the lake front and open spaces.

Breckinridge concluded that this agenda could only be executed by someone who understood "the hopes, aspirations, capacities, and limitations of the people," someone with "courage" because

> an administration based upon consideration of the public good would involve encounters with the gross and open privilege of entrenched vice and alcohol, with the more decent but no less hostile forces of greed so often in control of public utilities, and with the subtle forces of social prestige based on economic advantage.[1]

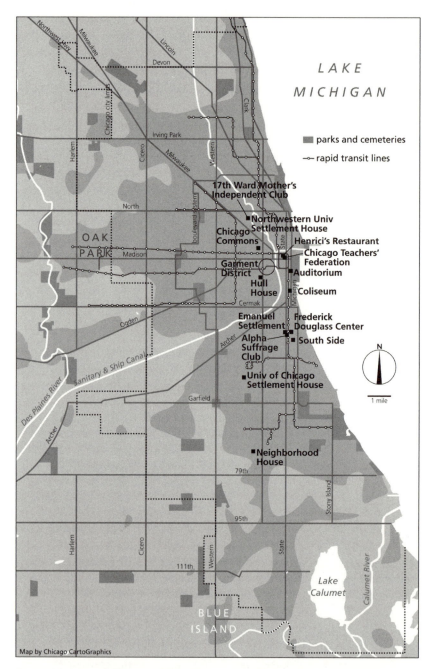

LAKE
MICHIGAN

■ parks and cemeteries
-o-- rapid transit lines

17th Ward Mother's
Independent Club

■ Northwestern Univ
Settlement House

Chicago
Commons

Henrici's Restaurant

Chicago Teachers'
Federation

Garment
District

Auditorium

Hull
House

Coliseum

Emanuel
Settlement

Frederick
Douglass Center

Alpha
Suffrage
Club

South Side

Univ of Chicago
Settlement House

N

1 mile

Neighborhood
House

OAK
PARK

Lake
Calumet

BLUE
ISLAND

Map by Chicago CartoGraphics

Figure 19. Map of Chicago, 1919. Showing rapid transit lines, and sites of wom-
en's activities during first two decades of the twentieth century. (Drawn by Dennis
McClendon, Chicago CartoGraphics)

Breckinridge's words are remarkably similar to those used by Harriet Vittum in her 1914 campaign for alderman of the ethnic, working-class 17th ward, when a much higher percentage of women voted for her than did men. During the 1920s, activist Chicago women continued to pursue a vision of the city based on these principles.

In its examination of the continuing struggles of activist Chicago women to influence municipal development during the 1920s, this chapter emphasizes the specific urban context. Activist Chicago women's limited success in that decade tells us much about women's position in Chicago and exposes how difficult it was for them, no matter how unified they might have been, to combat men's domination and the notions of the city and the purposes of government that men had embedded into urban life long before Chicago women learned how to exercise political power. But the chapter also suggests new ways to think about the relationship of all urban women to their cities after they gained suffrage.

Were Activist Chicago Women Unique?

To pursue their vision, activist women became increasingly involved in municipal politics. They campaigned especially in mayoral races, and identified and targeted other elected and appointed offices through which to influence municipal development. They continued to work through women's organizations and expanded upon their existing alliances in the process. They used the League of Women Voters (LWV), founded in Chicago in February 1920 at a convention held at the Congress Hotel (among those Chicago women in attendance were Jane Addams, Louise de Koven Bowen, Margaret Haley, Agnes Nestor, and Ida B. Wells-Barnett), as a vehicle for keeping women working together to foster their vision of a good city. In addition, the CWC and WCC remained important municipal organizations, the number of women's local and neighborhood organizations expanded, and women founded new partisan political organizations both inside and outside the official party structures. Housing, the health and welfare of women and children, public education, and the rights of working women continued to be paramount urban issues for activist women. Finding a way to foster racial justice also remained high on activist women's agenda as an absolute necessity for securing the common welfare.

It is difficult to address the question of how unique Chicago women's engagement with municipal development during the 1920s might have been because most work on woman suffrage or women and progressivism ends with 1920. For women's historians, urban women are important participants in the subsequent growth of state and national welfare programs, but the urban context is peripheral to these historians' themes.[2]

Furthermore, a good comparison for Chicago requires examining other large cities where the political and social contexts are far different from those of small cities. Sandra Haarsager's book on Seattle mayor Bertha Knight Landes, appropriately subtitled *Big City Mayor*, is one of the few of its type.[3] Current work on urban history and the expanding field of urban environmentalism usually includes women but still focuses overwhelmingly on men and their organizations.[4] Sarah Deutsch's and James Connolly's recent books on Boston provide significantly more detail on that city's women in the 1920s.[5]

A women's historian, Deutsch follows the approach pioneered by Mary Ryan, examining women manipulating urban space and expanding their appropriate place within it.[6] Boston women, according to Deutsch, "intruded" on geographic spaces previously regarded as reserved for men, challenged and ruptured gendered spatial boundaries, and then rearranged urban spaces within ideas about class and race. In her study of the 1920s, Deutsch focuses on women standing for office (a public space) to show the class and race conflicts embedded in such contests that divided women and kept them from sustaining cross-class or cross-race alliances. Her subjects are primarily the Boston League of Women Voters and those few women vying for a select number of appointed and elected offices.[7] Deutsch asks why "more Boston women went to the state legislature than to City Hall," and finds her answer in the class and race conflicts that erupted over which women would occupy public space.

Yet urban historians know that with rare exceptions, women had more success winning offices in small cities and state legislatures than in big cities where big business and party politicians successfully controlled entry into important municipal offices and where the stakes were too high to allow women control over fiscal and other municipal matters. In 1922, for example, there were fifteen women mayors serving towns ranging from 145 residents to 4,335. When surveyed about their experiences as candidates, they revealed how in the smaller towns men did not want to bother being mayor because it distracted them from their own businesses. In small towns at the time, municipal government rarely had much effect on business. An examination of their work as mayors reveals them as interested in improving their town's infrastructure, building roads, providing clean water, and building parks. But the author of this survey also theorized that these women differed from male mayors in two regards. First, they thought of these improvement in terms of "municipal housekeeping" rather than "engineering." Second, "she goes a step further—and here is where housekeeping is broader than engineering. She is deeply interested in educating children." Hence, Deutsch's question of "why not in Boston" is most readily answered by paying attention to women's vision for the city and how men felt their control threatened by that vision. [8]

James Connolly locates the actions of 1920s Boston women more squarely within the context of urban politics and institutions. Shrewd politicians and party leaders, such as James Michael Curley, manipulated the political system to their desired ends even after good government reformers had secured a new charter that they hoped would give elite business leaders control of the city and its finances. According to Connolly, ethnic and neighborhood politics prevailed in Boston; the Boston League of Women Voters and the pre-suffrage Women's Municipal League were linked to the elitist Good Government Association, and groups of women were divided against one another.[9] But Connolly also shows that women's urban politics in the 1920s was about more than office-holding and reorganizing public space. Organizations such as East Boston's Women's Improvement Association, the Leagues of Jewish Women and Catholic Women, and the Italian *Circoli Femminili* worked through the 1920s with a "continued emphasis on female solidarity that echoed the ideas of the Woman's Municipal League." For instance, the membership of the League of Catholic Women topped ten thousand during the decade, with more than eighty local affiliates.[10]

Connolly's assessment of Boston women's relationship to the political process supports Nancy Love's idea of an "ethic of solidarity" within which fluid individual and social identities can form and function around similarities of interest.[11] Even as Boston women failed to sustain the Boston League of Women Voters and Women's Municipal League as citywide female forces across the 1920s, "the rhetoric of unity that suffused women's activism in Progressive Era Boston persisted, but with multiple meanings." The presidents of the League of Catholic Women in the mid-1920s served on fourteen public commissions and committees and were "a force to be reckoned with on such legislative issues as child labor, health reform and prison policy."[12] As Connolly demonstrates, women's urban activism did not necessarily emanate from nor depend on any one class or group of women. The Boston League of Women Voters and the Women's Municipal League may not have forged sustainable alliances, but vast numbers of Boston women continued to work within a vision that made providing for the common welfare a municipal priority. The League of Catholic Women president claimed that the League was " 'doing public service for the people of the city and the state.' "[13]

The timing and nature of Chicago's white settlement created a particular climate for women's activism. As the commercial economy gave way to the industrial, Chicago's need for massive numbers of laborers helped create a more fluid social and political situation than was the case in an older city such as Boston. Older families may well have resented and feared the immigrants—as the response to Haymarket in 1886 showed—yet Chicago had no social equivalent to Boston Brahmins and many prominent

Chicagoans were themselves newcomers from the East. As the book's earlier chapters explained, since the 1880s Chicago women's activism had no equivalent to the elitism of older eastern cities, nor to that of the newer cities such as Los Angeles where upper-class women joined with men to control the city's growth and development. The IWA clearly differed in membership and purpose from both the Boston and the San Francisco Women's Education and Industrial Unions; the CWTUL seems to have maintained close relationships with middle-class women's groups, unlike such groups in Boston. Regarding the Boston WTUL, Deutsch notes one elite woman referring to arrested female strikers as "girls" to illustrate class attitudes. But Chicago gloveworker and union organizer Agnes Nestor often referred to female strikers as girls. In many cases, striking female workers at this time were in fact very young women, and using the word "girls" may signify nothing more than age difference. And Chicago women were not constrained by white racism and institutionalized segregation as were Southern urban women. Ethnic, neighborhood, and local politics was very strong in Chicago but did not, as this chapter shows, preclude a women's citywide movement toward a gendered urban vision as it may have done in Boston. But even for Boston we do not know this for certain because we have not made this type of investigation.[14]

Electoral Politics: 1919–1927

During the 1919 mayoral primary, Harry Olson again challenged Thompson, but progressive Republican Charles Merriam also declared his candidacy, forcing anti-Thompson women to choose between Olson and Merriam. Progressive Republicans, including Addams, Vittum, McDowell, Breckinridge, and Margaret Dreier Robins, were joined by Democratic women such as Helen Hefferan and Hannah Solomon (a founder of the National Council of Jewish Women) on a Committee of 100 that appealed to women to vote for Merriam. Other Committee of 100 members included Amelia Sears, civic director of the WCC since 1915; Jennie Purvin of the WCC and the IESA, a leader in Jewish women's organizations, and participant in the short-lived Advisory Board to the Department of Public Welfare; Mabel (Mrs. Bertram] Sippy, WCC member and former corresponding secretary of the CPEL; and Madeleine Wallin Sikes and Emily Napieralski, both of whom belonged to the WCC and other women's groups. Only Myrtle Tanner Blacklidge, who had earlier directed the Olson women's campaign, seems not to have been previously involved in women's organizations, but she had been president of the Illinois Women's Republican League (IWRL) in 1916.[15]

When Thompson won renomination, many activist Republican women refused to support the man they considered personally corrupt, and responsible for the infamous anti-teacher Loeb Rule, the 1916 scandal in the public welfare office, and the general failure of that office to carry out its duties.[16] Vittum was particularly vocal during a women's meeting held at the working women's Central Eleanor Club, where she denounced the Thompson administration's venality, corruption, and lack of regard for securing public health.[17] When the Democrats again chose Robert Sweitzer as their mayoral candidate, a number of Republican and some Democratic women, including Vittum, Julia Holmes Smith, Napieralski, and Wells-Barnett, chose to support Independent candidate Maclay Hoyne, believing that as mayor he would be more attentive to their demands.[18] New names began to appear in the ranks of public political activists in this election: Gertrude Howe Britton, a WCC member who had vigorously opposed the Loeb Rule as a member of the Board of Education and was subsequently not reappointed by Thompson, now campaigned for Hoyne, as did Nellie O'Connor (former president of the CWC), Kate Rutherford (a former Thompson supporter), and Mrs. Glenn Plumb. Rutherford and Plumb would later run for political office. The teachers of the Ella Flagg Young Club also supported Hoyne. Newspapers gave only perfunctory coverage to women's campaigning, making it difficult to ascertain the extent of their activities. For instance, the newspapers mention a women's political meeting scheduled for March 27 but provide no follow-up coverage.[19]

Wells-Barnett's support of Hoyne is interesting. Although she had supported Thompson early in the 1915 primary, she withdrew her support when Olson announced his candidacy. Wells-Barnett belonged to Olson's progressive Republican faction, and he had appointed her to a position as an adult probation officer. Now in 1919 she chose to back Hoyne, the man who two years before had prosecuted the city's first African American alderman, Oscar DePriest, on vice charges. DePriest had been acquitted, but the notoriety had prevented him from seeking re-election. Wells-Barnett never explained what motivated her choice in 1919. She clearly did not get along with DePriest because she believed that he and other African American men had told Thompson not to name her to a seat on the school board.[20] She also faulted him for forgetting that the loyalty of African American women had secured his initial political success in 1915, when the ASC early endorsed his campaign. Her decision to support Hoyne cannot have been easy because she was a fierce advocate for racial equality and had a strong "race" identification, while Hoyne injected racist appeals into his campaign. Later, in 1919, Wells-Barnett would be furious with Hoyne when as state's attorney he failed to prosecute any white rioters following that summer's racial rioting in the city. But she did support

Hoyne's mayoral bid, and the most reasonable explanation seems to be that this was a combination of her fierce political independence—she firmly believed that Thompson was a cynical exploiter of African American votes[21]—and her longtime, if always contentious, alliances with white women's organizations and their reform agendas. The relationship between activist white and black women in Chicago was more complicated than has been acknowledged. Following the racial rioting in the summer of 1919, the WCC Committee on Race Relations wrote to Mayor Thompson, the police chief, and State's Attorney Hoyne asking them to explain "why no arrests were made of those who were bombing the homes of colored people." A committee from the CWC visited the mayor and the police chief to discuss this same question.[22] Wells-Barnett never underestimated white racism, and she was never as accommodating to white women as were other upper-class black women in Chicago. But Wells-Barnett seems to have believed that black and white women had much in common as women. The ongoing contacts between Chicago black and white women is discussed in greater detail later in this chapter.

Nineteen nineteen clearly was not a good year for activist women's municipal aspirations. Hoyne received 16.8 percent of women's votes and 15.5 percent of men's, not nearly enough either to elect him or to cause Thompson to lose the election to the Democratic Sweitzer. Only two women had even tried for seats in the city council in 1919, a measure of activist women's pessimism about the possibilities of winning these seats. Newspapers said little about either woman, Labor Party candidate Ida Fursman, a high school teacher and head of the Teachers' Federation who ran in the 27th ward, and Laura Young, the Democratic "sacrifice" candidate from the 33rd ward. Young challenged her Republican opponent to a public debate, but he apparently declined, so no public record of her campaign exists. In this largely Republican ward, women did vote more heavily for her (38 percent) than did men (31 percent).[23] In the aftermath of Thompson's re-election, activist women's disappointment with the municipal situation was palpable. WCC President Bowen told the Club that "perhaps our city has never been so completely in the grip of a corrupt administration as at the present time."[24]

Passage of the federal suffrage amendment in 1920 finally opened every political office to Chicago women, and they looked forward to working to secure acceptable candidates for more important municipal positions while continuing to try to influence mayoral politics. Activist women especially prized the post of Cook County commissioner because the county board of commissioners administered the public hospital, the juvenile detention home, county jails, and the recreational areas of the county forest preserves. The citywide, non-district-based nature of this post also offered women some hope of electoral success. Of the fifteen county commissioners, ten came from the city, and five from the rest of Cook County. Each party ran a city slate and a county slate, and the top ten votegetters in the city and the top five for the county from each party advanced to the general election. Since the ten city seats almost always went to Democrats, a woman who made it through the Democratic primary was almost certain to be elected.

Democrat Annie Bemis and Republicans Helen Bennett, Emily Washburn Dean, and Myrtle Tanner Blacklidge won party nominations in 1922. Bemis had served as the first director of the Cook County Bureau of Public Welfare in 1914, chaired the WCC committees on the sanitary district and the social evil, and directed citizenship classes for the Club. Dean belonged to the WCC and women's Republican clubs. Blacklidge had headed the women's campaign for Thompson in 1915. Only Bennett was a newcomer to women's politics. During the primary campaign, women's clubs called on women to vote for these women. CWC president Grace Temple asserted that women wanted this office because "[f]or more than twenty years the organized women of Cook County have realized that almost every function of the county board has to do with the human interests in which women are specialists." WCC president Bowen maintained that the women running for these posts "will be valiant in the protection of . . . defenseless people." Mary (Mrs. B. F.) Langworthy, a ward leader in the WCC, second vice-president of the newly formed Woman's Roosevelt Republican Club, and future president of both the CWC and WCC, proclaimed that the board's welfare responsibilities "demand a woman's insight into the needs of children, the sick, and the very poor." When Mrs. Edward Gudeman, president of the CWA, asserted that "[t]he women nominated will not make their duties as commissioners side lines to private business," she expressed an opinion shared by many activist women that this office with its myriad welfare responsibilities was not being given enough attention by its male incumbents or current candidates.[25]

In a campaign speech to the Woman's Roosevelt Republican Club (WRRC), Dean pursued this theme. She stressed the fitness of female candidates for the job of county commissioners in language similar to that noted above. But her speech also revealed how thoroughly activist women had transformed a nineteenth-century social vision into a twentieth-century political agenda that envisioned municipal government responsibility for ensuring the common welfare. The board's "humanitarian duties," asserted Dean, cried out for women's participation, not because they had a "soft and understanding heart" but because the position required a "hard and understanding head for the wise and effective administration of the County's charity budget . . . in order to insure the best service to the greatest number of those requiring help and care." According to Dean, Chicago women had learned from

years of experience and varied service . . . many lessons and the one that has borne
in deepest upon our realization is that if we had better officials in public offices,
if our laws were more ju[s]tly enforced there would be much less necessary work
left for private organizations to perform. If the laws . . . were rightly enforced it
would just about put the Juvenile Protective Association out of business.[26]

Worth noting here is Dean's advocacy of putting the Juvenile Protective
Association, one of activist women's own organizations, "out of business"
and replacing it with direct government responsibility for social welfare.

When Democratic candidate Bemis was elected to the county board she
was activist women's first direct political success. Not only was that success
too limited to satisfy activist women, but they had also begun to notice
an another disturbing sign in municipal politics: as women's political possibilities expanded, the intransigence of male politicians of both parties to
women seemed to be hardening. During the campaign, a rally of Republican women presided over by Bowen opposed the re-election of a Thompson ally, Republican county judge Frank Righeimer, charging that he
helped foster "unfair, unjust, unpleasant treatment" of women at voting
places.[27] Activist women were accustomed to such treatment by the Thomp-
sonites in the party, but they had hoped for more support from progressive
Republican men. They discovered in the next mayoral election that they
held this hope in vain. In late 1922 activist women floated a possible mayoral candidacy for Louise de Koven Bowen. The WCC thought this "a
logical sequence that those who are seeking to re-establish in Chicago an
honest and constructive system of government, should have looked upon
Mrs. Bowen as a thoroughly equipped candidate for the office of Mayor."[28]
Progressive Republican men opposed her candidacy, arguing that a
woman could not handle such administrative tasks as dealing with the
police department—an absurd notion when applied to Bowen, who had
spent years dealing with the police department over juvenile justice and
care for women prisoners. Chicago newspapers reflected the male perspective on women as political candidates. The *Tribune* assured the city that a
woman, no matter how capable, could not manage a city administration
composed largely of men. "Even assuming that Mrs. Bowen has executive
and administrative qualities far exceeding those of any other candidate
possible," the paper declared itself unable to support her "because the
affairs of Chicago, from the Mayor's cabinet to the streetsweepers, are
now conducted by men, and no woman, however capable, could overcome
such a handicap." The *Evening Post* suggested that women's role in politics
was to help the party "discover the right man." The *Tribune* then com-
pounded its insult by editorializing that "unfortunately also the ladies are
not always guided by sober judgment, but rather by their emotions and
impulses." In the end, Bowen removed herself from consideration, though

not without identifying the real problem: "It was amusing to see how much the men resented the possibility of having a woman for mayor," she wryly observed. [29]

Thompson withdrew from the 1923 primary in the face of a "progressive" challenge from Arthur Lueder. The Democrats nominated their own "progressive," William Dever. Progressive Republican women were now faced with a choice because Lueder's progressivism was of the "expert administrator" type. Bowen, for instance, endorsed Lueder but refused to campaign actively for him. Other activists, such as Vittum and Napieralski, did work on the committee to elect Lueder, and women's Republican clubs supported his candidacy.[30] But Lueder's lukewarm support from activist Republican women who had long adhered to the progressive wing of the party resulted from their doubts that he would enact any of their desired municipal programs. Democratic women, on the other hand, felt that they finally had a good candidate on whom they could all agree. Activists McCulloch, Julia Holmes Smith, Janet Fairbank, and Anna L. Smith worked in the Illinois Women's Democratic Club for Dever campaign. Margaret Haley addressed large rallies of teachers, urging them to vote for Dever, while Julia Lathrop, who had only recently returned to Chicago after heading the Children's Bureau in Washington, also supported Dever.[31] When Dever won, Democratic women and "Independents" such as McDowell and Lathrop were pleased and regular Republican women were ready to give him the benefit of the doubt. Yet beyond banishing Thompson, women had little reason to feel empowered in the city in 1923. The four women who stood for alderman that year in the newly structured nonpartisan contests were politically unknown, lacked regular party support, and received few votes. A total of 1,531 votes cast were cast for these women, the bulk of them (1,260) going to Ella Waful, a member of the WCC who ran in the 5th ward.[32]

A lack of success in local elections was a chronic situation for women in big cities, where the economic stakes were too high for men to acquiesce in nominating or voting for them. Unsurprisingly, therefore, activist women in both Chicago and elsewhere looked for other political possibilities that might have given them a better chance to achieve their agendas. In April 1924 WCC members Katherine Hancock Goode and Rena Elrod, Republican activist Kathryn Rutherford, and Socialist Florence Hall ran for seats in the Illinois House. Hall had unsuccessfully tried for a city council seat the year before. Only Goode now made it through the primary. Chicago activists, Democrats Janet Fairbank and Anna Smith and Republicans Dean, Rose L. Murfey, and Grace Meeker, all members of the WCC, ran for national party convention delegate. African American activist Mary F. Waring, who headed the 2nd ward suffrage league and belonged to the National Association of Colored Women's Clubs and the

Illinois State Federation of Colored Women's Clubs (IFCWC), also sought a seat at the Republican convention.[33] Fairbank, Smith, Dean, and Meeker won convention seats; Smith actually polled more votes running as an at-large delegate than did former Chicago mayor and Illinois governor Edward F. Dunne, who ran in a district race.[34]

Activists were thrilled with these successes, but the successes were too few to have much effect on municipal conditions. Then, in 1927, an already difficult situation for activist women turned disastrous. Despite the opposition of thousands of Republican women, including the Polish Women's Republican Club, Big Bill Thompson returned to defeat the regular nominee, Edward Litsinger, in the party primary.[35] Progressive Republican women flocked to support the re-election of the Democrat, Dever. Addams, Flora Cheney, and Vittum joined Democrats Bass and Nestor on the People's Dever for Mayor Committee. Bowen, Cheney, and Sears were reported to be members of the Independent Republicans for Dever Committee. On March 31, five thousand female Dever supporters, including Vittum, McDowell, Nestor, Fairbank, Cheney, Sears, Langworthy, and Hefferan, marched through downtown Chicago, many carrying signs declaring themselves former Republicans or Independents for Dever. The WRRC sent representatives to the march.[36] The Democratic party leadership rallied around Dever, but even with the support of some progressive Republicans and Independents, Dever did not win. The mayor, unfortunately for these activist women, was burdened with some difficult baggage. He had angered many ethnic voters by enforcing Prohibition legislation and had alienated Margaret Haley and other CTF members with his support of school superintendent William McAndrew, whom the teachers opposed. African-African voters promised to turn out in force to support Thompson. And, despite the defection after the primary of some progressive Republican men such as Merriam, the Republican party in Chicago, led by Litsinger and Charles Deneen, steadfastly backed Thompson.[37]

Party Politics and Women during the 1920s

Thompson's victory in 1927 was a fatal blow to activist Republican women's already flagging hopes that they could reform municipal affairs by working through the party system. Republican women had always known theirs would be an uphill fight. In 1921 Bowen had led a delegation to the party leaders demanding that as representatives of one hundred thousand women, they be given a voice in candidate selection. The meeting was not a success, as Bowen recounted in a speech a year later: "What did these men do? They were extremely polite, even soothing—one patted me on the shoulder . . . [but] we were never called in." She and other activists thereafter organized the WRRC and returned the following year making the same demands. This time, she said, "they did not pat me on the shoulder. . . . [T]hey were not even quite as polite, but they did say, 'Well, who are your candidates?' "[38] Yet any gains made by that show of force were fleeting, as party rejection of a possible Bowen candidacy two years later demonstrated.[39] To many activist Republican women the message was clear: to have any success they would have to pressure the party by organizing strong women's political groups. Thus through the 1920s, three Republican women's organizations functioned inside Chicago: the Illinois Women's Republican League (or Club), the WRRC, and the Illinois Federation of Republican Colored Women's Clubs (IFRCWC).[40] Organized by Bowen, Dean, Ruth Hanna McCormick in the aftermath of Bowen's unproductive meeting with the party leaders, the WRRC was particularly strong.In terms of achieving political party equality and a municipal agenda, Bowen and women Republicans were caught in a bind that they shared with activist women elsewhere. In 1920 Republican National Chair William Hays told Midwestern Republican women that they were "not to be separated or segregated, but assimilated and amalgamated."[41] Chicago Republican women, however, had been forced to organize their own party clubs to demonstrate enough strength to force party leaders to listen to them. When they did, male politicians attacked women as not sufficiently partisan to deserve equal party representation.[42]

In addition, activist women were not willing to abandon years of work toward specific municipal ends that they believed the party leadership did not share. Assimilation and amalgamation, they feared, would subordinate them to Hays and the men running the party apparatus. If women did not take the lead in shaping their own political destinies, Bowen told a meeting of the ILWV, "the men . . . will choose for us women who are their tools."[43] The membership application of the WRRC clearly indicated activist women's desire to maintain some independence of action. The form explicitly acknowledged that "the new women citizens find it necessary to organize along party lines and to take an active part in the choice of candidates in the party primaries" and that the club's purpose was to organize the Republican women of Chicago and Cook County to work inside the party. Yet applicants were also informed that WRRC women refused to abandon a women's agenda. "Should it develop that it is deemed advisable to conduct a coalition campaign by a union of Democrats and Republicans," the form read, "the club will stand ready to throw its full strength and support into such a campaign."[44] Local politics also forced the women of the WRRC to adopt such a complex strategy in hopes of achieving any of their agenda. The Republican Party was badly split into hostile factions. Two reform groups in the party, one led by former Governor Charles Deneen and the other by Medill McCormick and

Charles Merriam, not only challenged Thompson but also each other for control of the party. The price of party politics is often complete allegiance; Republican women were unwilling to sacrifice their agenda to give complete allegiance to the party should it follow leaders and programs to which the women objected.[45]

Ida B. Wells-Barnett distanced herself from the Republican Party leadership in late 1927 when she founded the Third Ward Women's Political Club and deliberately chose not to give this new organization a party affiliation. Wells-Barnett gave the club motto as "For Women, of Women, by Women," and called for "women uniting politically and supporting women for office." Wells-Barnett also wanted this club to train women to run for office and to be a forum for presentations from female elected officials.[46]

Republican women were so demoralized by their party's hostility that some would even support the Democratic candidate Anton Cermak, a quintessential ethnic, machine politician, for mayor in 1931. Bowen gave her support to Cermak saying that "[he] has made such a good record for himself in the management of the various charitable institutions of Cook Country that I feel confident his ability and his power of organization will be of lasting benefit to the city."[47] Chicago Democratic women were less at odds with their party leaders and had mayoral candidates whom they could support with less ambivalence. But, as chapter 8 more fully demonstrates, Democratic women did not get more of what they wanted for the city. Bemis was elected to the Cook County Board in 1922; Fairbank and Smith were delegates to the national convention in 1924; Dever did appoint Mary McDowell to head the department of Public Welfare and Grace Temple and Helen Hefferan to seats on the Board of Education.[48] Beyond these "token" appointments, Democratic women acquired little influence within the party system. Both Republican and Democratic party leaders preferred to use women as the foot soldiers in the campaigns for male candidates and male agendas for the city. It was clear by the end of the decade that the male party leadership had no intention of listening to women's ideas for the city's development. Despite their exclusion from the seats of power, activist women persevered throughout the 1920s, trying to influence municipal development by using their voluntary organizations and the methods they had perfected over the past decades.

Municipal Activism of Women's Organizations

Activist Chicago women were on the ground floor as women's political focus shifted from obtaining suffrage to how to proceed with suffrage. In February 1920 the final meeting of the National American Woman Suffrage Association was held in Chicago, where women formally dissolved that organization and reorganized into the LWV. The most immediate question for the new national organization was whether to function primarily as an informational and educational organization or to engage directly in politics.[49] Most activist Chicago women refused to settle for the former method. One of the most vocal proponents of direct political engagement was Elizabeth Bass, former president of the CWC and a fervent Democrat.[50] But after decades of working together, Chicago activists were also unwilling to abandon their past organizations and strategies to work only inside the parties, and Bass herself was no exception. For many activist Chicago women, the LWV was a perfect compromise because they could make of it what they wanted on the local level.[51] Throughout the 1920s Chicago women used the LWV as the vehicle for continuing to draw women into working together to promote a women's agenda for the city even as they simultaneously engaged in electoral politics.

During the 1920s, in fact, Chicago women ran the LWV's state and local organizations; the league's headquarters were in the city. The Illinois LWV's first president was Flora Cheney, a member of the WCC who later would enter politics. Former Hull House resident and head of the Children's Bureau Julia Lathrop (1922–1924) and activist Mary Foulke Morrison (1924–1928) followed Cheney into that office. Serving on the Board of Directors and as chairs of standing committees were such familiar women as Bowen, McDowell, Hefferan, Purvin, Abbott, Nestor, and Yarros, suffrage leader Harriet Taylor Treadwell, Rose Murfey, Katherine Goode, and prominent WCC member Sarah Tunnicliff. African American women were represented by Ada S. McKinley, head resident of the Community House (later renamed South Side) Settlement and CWTUL leader Irene Goins. Madeleine Wallin Sikes and Annie Bemis were LWV speakers to city and county women's organizations.[52]

Unlike the Boston League of Women Voters, the Cook County league focused its activities on grassroots women's organizations, targeting neighborhood, ward, settlement house, religious, ethnic, and African American women's clubs. Chicago women's organizations hosting LWV speakers in 1922 and 1923 included: the Catholic Chicago Woman's Club, Edgewater and South Side Catholic women's clubs; women's clubs of Neighborhood House, and of the West Pullman, Woodlawn, Englewood, and Ravenswood neighborhoods; and clubs of the Independent German-American, Swedish, and Norwegian women. LWV speakers addressed women of the Woodlawn Baptist Church, the Central Catholic Meeting, the Conference of Jewish Presidents, Council of Jewish Women, Chicago Woman's Aid, the 26th, 47th, and 50th ward civic leagues, the 5th and 6th ward LWV, the Central Eleanor Club, and the Colored Women of the 1st and 3rd senatorial districts. With a few exceptions, the leaders of neighborhood and ward LWV groups are unfamiliar figures. Yet the fact that there were so many groups during the 1920s, and that their leaders are not readily recognizable, attests to widespread political activity and municipal engagement among Chicago women that penetrated far below the leadership levels of the most visible organizations.[53]

Although the women of the LWV in Chicago, as elsewhere, remained non-partisan in the sense of not working inside the parties and not endorsing specific political candidates, their activities were quite political in the sense suggested by Kristi Andersen in her examination of women and politics after suffrage. Andersen's caution against confusing nonpartisan with non-political is particularly valuable for understanding the political agenda of the ILWV.[54] In its forty-year retrospective, the ILWV explained the underlying basis of its work in a dual belief in the efficacy of democratic participation and in government responsibility to resolve social problems. The ILWV, these women declared, had been founded on the

> unshakable conviction that self-government should include all the people; that citizens need training for their responsibilities; that certain social problems moving into the area of government had long been of particular concern to women and still should have their special attention.

The ILWV thus was open to women of all parties and did not recommend candidates but rather took stands "on specific issues" and worked for "measures which it believed were in the public interest."[55]

The ILWV's work on the federal Sheppard-Towner Maternity and Infancy Act exemplifies both the means and desired ends of its work. By constituting a joint committee of women's organizations—including the WCC, the Catholic Women's League, the Chicago Conference of Jewish Women, Women's Department of the Chicago Church Federation, Chicago Woman's Aid, the Chicago chapter of the American Association of University Women, the Illinois WCTU, the YWCA, Illinois Republican Women's Organization and the Illinois Women's Democratic Club, the CWTUL, the Illinois Business and Professional Women, the Illinois Federation of Colored Women's Clubs, the Chicago Infant Welfare Society, the League of Cook County Women's Clubs, and Illinois Federation of Women's Clubs—the ILWV orchestrated the women's campaign for the state that would enable the state to participate in the Sheppard-Towner program.[56]

For activist Chicago women, Sheppard-Towner was important not only because it would implement new public policy safeguarding the health of women and children, but also because it would increase the power of government and reshape the relationship of citizens to that government. Activist women welcomed the fact that Sheppard-Towner would transfer women's voluntary health and welfare efforts into the hands of government. For more than two decades, activist Chicago women had founded,

Figure 20. Summer Fresh Air Baby Camp, 1903. (Chicago *Daily News*, Chicago Historical Society, DN-0001270)

funded, and run such voluntary health and welfare efforts in the city. The WCC had helped maintain children's neighborhood health centers; black women's organizations had supported an infant feeding program and a well-baby clinic at Provident Hospital; and the Elizabeth McCormick fund, established by wealthy Chicago woman Harriet McCormick in 1908 in memory of her deceased daughter, had been used to support summer baby tents.[57] Federal funding and matching state funds from Sheppard-Towner would turn these voluntary efforts into systematic provision for health care, which women believed would ensure healthier people and a healthier city. But it would do so by institutionalizing health care as a government activity, and many activist Chicago men opposed this shift. Representatives from the mainstream reform organization, the Chicago Civic Federation, testified before Congress in 1921 against the Sheppard-Towner legislation, calling it "unsound fiscal policy" that would result in "extravagance in local government . . . and greater tax burdens."[58] The Federation cautioned that this federal funding would take more money from Illinois taxpayers' pockets than it would return. Newspapers railed against such "government paternalism." Male doctors fought Sheppard-Towner as encroaching upon their professionalism, and a business-medical alliance in Illinois argued that "both state and federal government largesse had grown out of control in the years since World War I." The WCC countered by pointing out that men who opposed accepting federal funds for infant and maternal health care as "government paternalism" and as extending "improper functions upon the federal government," were simultaneously willing to accept $7.7 million in federal funds for other purposes. Chicago and Illinois women were not alone in believing that men gladly spent state or federal funds to profit male enterprises. After Governor Nathan Miller vetoed the enabling legislation for Sheppard-Towner in New York, an incensed Florence Kelley pointed out that after he had spent $125,000 of state funds for building a hog barn on the state fairgrounds, women voters might not be amused to "know that swine shelters appeal to him more strongly than dying mothers and babies."[59]

The arguments over Sheppard-Towner in the early 1920s again reflect fundamental differences in outlook between activist women and men in Chicago. Business and professional men, such as those belonging to the Civic Federation, did not want more taxes; they resisted having government raise and spend tax revenues on social programs, and continued to seek "good government" by professional experts such as themselves.[60] Regarding Sheppard-Towner, activist Chicago women separated the funding and development of social programs from good government issues, as they had done previously with lakefront development and housing. They also refused to put "good" government before people's health and welfare.[61] But as with too many municipal issues, activist women lost the struggle to make public health the responsibility of government. Illinois in 1923 became one of only three states not to pass the legislation that would have authorized the state to participate in the Sheppard-Towner program. Birth control was one women's health issue that remained definitely a private responsibility. Under the leadership of activist Rachelle Yarros and the Illinois Birth Control League, during the 1920s women succeeded despite legal obstacles posed by the Chicago Health Department in opening six birth control clinics in the city.[62]

Group experience and commonality of interest undergirded Chicago women's activism and regularly drew women into common cause rather than splintering them into groups pursuing particularistic interests. But because the city had never witnessed a monolithic women's movement, the determination of the ILWV to craft and facilitate such contacts gave these women a vehicle through which to work together across the 1920s. Moreover, the close connections between the League and Chicago women's activism is evident in the fact that most of the Chicago women who were appointed or elected to local offices and those who ran for state offices in the early 1920s belonged to the League. Annie Bemis (Cook County Commissioner), Mary Bartelme (assistant to the Judge, and then Judge, of the Juvenile Court), Mary McDowell (Commissioner of Public Welfare),

Helen Hefferan and Grace Temple (Board of Education), and Bridget Sullivan (Cook County Public Guardian), as well as Katherine Goode and Flora Cheney, were all League members.[63] Ward and neighborhood branches of the organization—including African American women's league branches—proliferated in the city throughout the decade. In 1920s Chicago disentangling women's municipal activism from the actions of the League is impossible.[64]

But Chicago women also kept working within their traditional women's organizations to secure political changes that would give the city's residents more power to govern Chicago. In 1920–21, as a constitutional convention met to draft a new state constitution, the CWC vigorously lobbied it to include home rule provisions for Chicago, a change that the women had been promoting for several years in the hopes that a city freer to control its own development would then present women with a greater possibility of achieving their ends. The CWC wanted Chicago to have the power to frame, adopt, and amend its own municipal charter, the right to own and operate public utilities and regulate any utilities that remained privately owned, the power to subject all franchise grants to a municipal referendum, and the right to bar the state from granting public franchises that would require permanent fixtures on city streets without the city's consent. Former suffrage leader and 1907 anti-charter leader Catharine Waugh McCulloch chaired the CWC's Committee on the Constitutional Convention of 1920. Madeleine Wallin Sikes chaired its subcommittee on municipal home rule. The WCC had earlier urged its members to vote "yes" on a November 1919 advisory ballot that demanded the initiative and referendum powers in a new constitution and supported municipal ownership, saying that "the people should have the power to acquire public utilities."[65] Women of the CWC and the WCC seemingly did not fear popular democracy.[66]

In the 1920s the CWC continued to work on municipal affairs, but the WCC had always been the most municipally oriented woman's organization and it led much of women's activism through the decade. The WCC had five thousand members at the beginning of 1920; by 1923 its membership included an additional 26 ward branches with another fifteen hundred members and a young women's auxiliary of six hundred members. There were at least three African American ward branches: the 2nd, 3rd, and 4th ward branches were designated as "colored." On the one hand, this is a sad commentary on continuing racial discrimination, but on the other, it shows African American women were still working with white women and actively participating in citywide politics directed by the WCC. Mrs. Eva Wells headed the 2nd ward branch, and Mrs. Bessie G. Smith led the 3rd and 4th ward branches.[67] The WCC expanded its citizenship training classes, intended to train women in how to teach other

Figure 21. Woman's City Club of Chicago Citizenship Class. (Woman's City Club Collection, Chicago Historical Society, ICHi-34341)

women about politics, voting, and elections so that they might become more involved in municipal politics. Among the women certified in its first post-1920 class was African American activist Elizabeth Lindsay Davis, who was also active in the ILWV. The WCC's monthly *Bulletin* remained filled with notices of political and citizenship meetings, instructions on registering to vote, explanations of the rules of the partisan primary, and details of the records of candidates for municipal offices.[68]

The WCC continued throughout the 1920s to monitor the municipal agencies that oversaw activities essential to the Club's conception of general welfare. The WCC demanded the appointment of women to the park boards, contending that "women will understand the principles of recreation for children and adults. . . . We know how it should be administered, when and where it is most needed, and who should be recreation leaders." In 1922, with Thompson appointees to the school board under grand jury investigation for graft and inappropriate use of school funds, the WCC renewed its fight for a smaller, elected board that would be subject to

Figure 22. Candidates' Day at the Woman's City Club, September 1922. Candidates for Cook County commissioner: Annie Bemis and Emily Washburn Dean and club leaders Mary Langworthy and Louise de Koven Bowen are pictured (Photo by Raymar Studios, Chicago; Woman's City Club Collection, Chicago Historical Society, ICHi-34340)

popular recall. In 1924 the WCC demanded that the municipal government restore funding to the Bureau of Social Surveys, the office charged with investigating municipal living conditions, vagrancy, crime, poverty, and unemployment—work that the women believed should be an integral part of the Department of Public Welfare, created by municipal ordinance in 1914. The WCC continued to work for better safety conditions in public theaters, with WCC president Bowen and Mayor Dever exchanging correspondence on this issue in 1924. In 1925 the WCC was still pursuing a campaign to reduce the "smoke nuisance" and calling on members to function as chimney observers throughout the city. In 1927 the WCC held a housing conference long after Chicago men had ceased to be interested in this problem, and again demanded that the board of education be removed from political control.[69]

As Chicago men and political leaders continued to resist most of women's demands and as the state legislature consistently failed to pass women's proposed legislation, activist women regularly turned toward the federal government as a means of implementing the municipal changes that they were unable to secure through local and state initiatives. The WCC reported in 1923 that virtually every piece of legislation that women had introduced and worked for in Springfield had failed, including Sheppard-Towner, the eight-hour work day for women, raising the number of compulsory years of education from six to eight, jury service for women, a bill to protect the rights of illegitimate children, and more and better distribution of school funds to ensure equal education opportunities. The women were clearly discouraged by this lack of results on the local level. One of the area's few female legislators told the WCC that "as voting citizens women were certainly not prepared in their blindness to find themselves practically without influence" and to find "their deepest interests of small concern to the men who were supposed to be representing them." Adding insult to injury, she reported to the WCC of having been told by male legislators that women's bills failed because "the women asked too much." "Was it unreasonable," she asked rhetorically, "if women agreed upon some twelve or fourteen bills . . . when there were some 1,300 bills introduced by men?"[70] She also could not help but notice that all of the women's bills had to do with the general welfare.

As early as February 1920, in conjunction with the formation of the LWV, the WCC must have had some of doubts about being able to convince the state legislature to listen. That year, the WCC proposed a women's national political platform, which demanded increased federal government support for the Children's Bureau and the Bureau of Women in Industry, passage of Sheppard-Towner legislation, and a constitutional amendment against child labor, but it also called for federal funds for education and the creation of a federal bureau of housing and living conditions. In defending a federal bureau of housing, the WCC articulated the gulf between activist women's and men's visions of a good society by contrasting government actions on economic activities favored by men with the social concerns of women. The United States, the Club wrote, "has spent large sums of money on the promotion of scientific farming, the care of cattle, sheep and bees, on the development of commerce and manufacturing . . . [but it] has taken no cognizance of the problem of housing its citizens." The WCC platform also demanded that "as the homemakers of the nation" women be given equal participation with architects and town planners in the "work of such a bureau."[71]

Just as Chicago men had earlier resisted demands for a municipal housing policy, so too in the 1920s they rejected such a federal housing bureau, and the self-designated male "experts" continued to ignore women's expertise.[72] The City Club's last venture into the problem of municipal housing had been to host a housing conference in late 1920. There, the men ignored Harriet Vittum's eloquent pleas, rejected government engagement in housing development, and instead urged the city council to provide financial incentives for private enterprise.[73] By 1921, Mary McDowell had witnessed so many failures of private enterprise to provide adequate, decent housing that she flatly declared that only "the police power of the state" would solve the housing problem.[74] As activist women in Chicago grew more determined to seek government intervention in housing, activist men increasingly lost interest in projects that promised them no immediate economic rewards or political gains. The City Club disbanded its committee on housing in 1922, while the WCC doggedly pursued the issue throughout the 1920s, holding a housing conference in 1927 and reiterating its belief that resolution of the municipal housing crisis was a key element to creating a good city. These activist women held fast to the vision expressed by the CWC in 1914 that it was "wasteful and inefficient" to spend money on social welfare without first providing adequate housing for all the city's residents.[75]

Activist white women also took a much stronger stand against racial discrimination than did white men. White activist Celia Parker Woolley and black activist Ida B. Wells-Barnett had earlier co-founded the Frederick Douglass Settlement, on South Wabash Avenue, to "promote just and amicable" race relations. Wells-Barnett's association with the Douglass Center and with Woolley was never easy. She was attacked by those in Chicago's African American community who followed the "temporizing" approach advocated by Booker T. Washington, but also clashed with Woolley who was content to have a white woman, rather than Wells-Barnett, as president of the Douglass Center Woman's Club.[76] Then, racial rioting in the summer of 1919 forced white Chicagoans to confront the consequences of racist practices. As historian William Tuttle observed, the riots terrified many white Chicagoans because unlike in earlier episodes, African Americans in Chicago left their segregated neighborhoods and took the offensive to their white tormentors.[77] Many white Chicago men took the riots as a sign that the city should be more strictly segregated. Even progressive-minded philanthropist Julius Rosenwald abandoned plans to build housing in the so-called Black Belt.[78] Although private institutions run for women, such as the Women's Model Lodging House, the YWCA, and the Chicago Women's Shelter, apparently refused shelter for African American women,[79] activist Chicago women responded to the racial rioting by speaking out against racism as a threat to the common good. McDowell told the WCC that "civic patriotism demands that for the welfare of the city as a whole, race prejudice must be lost in a constructive program to provide proper housing . . . [and] that it is not possible to have a well governed city with a segregated group of any kind." The WCC's newly formed committee on race relations wrote letters protesting the city's failure to arrest white rioters. The committee was explicitly charged to explore the links between race and housing and other social problems. Addams, McDowell, and Vittum appeared in public with Ada S. McKinley to make a show of cross-race community in the midst of the upheaval.[80]

Reconstructing a complete picture of the dynamics of black and white women's relationships during the early decades of the century is impossible. Too little has been left to us by Chicago black women's organizations in the 1920s for one thing. Yet numerous instances of women's interaction across race may well suggest a greater division between activist white men and women than among white and black women when it came to confronting municipal racism. In 1905 the Visiting Nurses Association (VNA), established in 1889 by a group of wealthy white women, hired Tallahassee Smith as one of the first African American public health nurses in the United States. In 1920 the VNA employed four black nurses. Most of black VNA nurses, of course, saw only a black clientele, but that the organization had hired at least a few black nurses rather than only giving money to support them outside the organization signaled a willingness of black and white women to work together, a willingness that had never existed within male circles. In 1912 activist Celia Parker Woolley wrote a strong letter to the superintendent of the contagious diseases department at the Cook County Hospital to protest the decision not to admit black nurses to practice sessions. "Yours is a county institution," protested Woolley. "[It is] supported by public funds, gathered in the form of taxes from every class of citizens, no one of which can be properly deprived of any of its benefits either in the wards or in any department of practice, study and instruction." Joanna Snowden belonged to the Juvenile Protective Association and was a juvenile court probation officer assigned to a white neighborhood. The CPEL heeded Wells-Barnett's plea in 1914 that it reject a prominent African American man's request that the group endorse the white Republican candidate for alderman in the 2nd ward rather than the black challenger; the CPEL endorsed the black candidate. Fannie Barrier Williams and Ida B. Wells-Barnett joined Grace Abbott, Addams, Breckinridge, Anna Wilmarth Ickes, and Nestor on the campaign committee to elect Vittum and McDowell to the Cook County Board in 1914. As president of the WCC, Louise Bowen refused to speak out against hiring a black doctor, Dr. Roscoe Giles, at the Municipal Tuberculosis Sanitarium, saying, "I cannot comply with your request as personally I believe that a colored physician has every right to be in the . . . Sanitarium." Mayor Thompson, on the other hand, quickly approved his removal. As an individual, Bowen wrote a letter of protest to Chicago activist and businessman B. E. Sunny, president of the Chicago Telephone Company, against his company's exclusion of black women from jobs as telephone operators. McDowell and Irene Goins together worked to organize African American stockyard workers. In 1921 the WCC organized ward-based employment services, including a 2nd ward service led by Irene McCoy Gaines.[81]

In a number of instances, black women were invited to address white women's organizations, rather than vice versa, or to serve on committees together with white women. The ILWV invited Sadie Adams to represent the IFCWC at a conference in early 1923 to discuss Sheppard-Towner. The IFCWC was a member of the Joint Committee for Sheppard-Towner. Representatives from the organization also attended a 1931 ILWV meeting, which discussed tax relief bills pending in the state legislature. Ruth Hanna McCormick invited African American activists Blanche Gilmer, Helen Sayre, and Irene McCoy Gaines to join the board of a women's republican campaign committee that she organized in 1922. The WCC still had its committee on race relations in 1932, which in March of that year sponsored a talk by A. Philip Randolph.[82] Group experiences and a sense of common interest again seem to have pushed Chicago's activist women to forge at least tenuous alliances across race in pursuit of common causes. They recognized in each other a commonality of interests that at times transcended, although never eradicated, racial divisions.[83]

Activist women, of course, had never been a cohesive block on any municipal issue, and continuing differences of opinion among them helped men ignore women on such matters as school reform. Reconciling a general vision of a good city with the labor concerns of teachers had always been a thorny issue for activist women. By late in the decade, activist middle-class women in the WCC and public school teachers again found themselves at odds over the school superintendent, William McAndrew, who had been appointed by former Mayor Dever. Activist women remained incensed at how politicians, businessmen, and labor leaders worked the school board for political favors. In late 1922 a grand jury investigating the school board's spending practices brought graft indictments against several Thompson appointees. Five years later former board member Grace Temple accused the new Thompson board appointees of carrying out Thompson's political agenda for the schools, saying that the previous board members, many of whom had been appointed by Dever, had never been subjected to political pressures by the former mayor. The WCC charged that the current board had awarded a million dollar contract for school building to the board president's construction company. Labor leaders John Fitzpatrick and Victor Olander, who had opposed Thompson's election, now sought jobs and favors from the board. Leaders of another men's organization, the Cook County Wage Earners' League, had supported Thompson; in return their president was appointed director of labor for the board of education.[84] In late 1927 the WCC supported McAndrew because they believed he was trying to stop such practices, but the teachers opposed him because they believed he was trying to reduce their authority. The WCC declined to judge the teachers' claim because the Club was pursuing its longstanding goal of a school system free of all politics—whether on the part of businessmen, labor, teachers, or politicians—as best for all children and thereby for the city as a whole.[85] Sorting out the McAndrew affair is complicated. The teachers were furious with him, yet it was alleged that he was suspended by the board because of his "defense of the teachers," and the WCC remained a strong supporter of teachers' "rights and job protection."[86]

Despite their differences on the matter of the superintendent, teachers and clubwomen were still motivated by a common goal—the best education for the children of the city. That they disagreed on how best to pursue that goal does not undermine the commonality. And it was abundantly clear that by the end of the 1920s that the school system was still suffering from political corruption and a lack of priority given to funding instructional activities, without which, activist women believed, a good system of public education was impossible. In early 1930 the National Education Association issued a report claiming that Chicago "underpays for instruction and overpays for cleaning and operation of schoolhouses . . . that Chicago cheats the teachers out of money to give to employees who operate the plant." The latter employees, of course, were men; the teachers were women. Independent accountants assessing the state of the Chicago schools concurred with the NEA's conclusions. Activist women had been decrying this situation for years: in the early 1890s the IWA had fought against the lumping of operating costs into the instructional budget; in 1915 teachers had urged Superintendent Ella Flagg Young to find a way to pay engineers and janitors and light and heat expenses from the building fund rather than the education fund.[87] It was equally clear that white middle-class activist men were no longer terribly interested in the school situation. They opposed the Thompson graft, of course, but the state Otis Law of 1917 had satisfied many of their reform goals by centralizing the schools under a more powerful superintendent and guaranteeing civil service regulations. Thereafter, even if the board engaged in blatant political maneuvering or exploited the schools for personal gain, activist men could point to the achievement of basic progressive goals. The City Club's legislative agenda for 1923 shows the organization growing less interested in specific municipal reforms, concentrating instead on electoral reforms and investigating the possibilities of the City Manager Plan of government.[88] The Cook County LWV, by contrast, retained a Committee on Chicago Schools, which included Madeleine Sikes among its members from 1928–31.[89]

Beyond this shift in emphasis within the City Club, the attitudes of male activists George Sikes (husband of Madeleine) and Charles Merriam reveal that they saw the city differently from activist middle-class women. Sikes contended that the legislative program of the City Club was "entirely political," thus the Club "would not embrace the more social issues of the

ILWV."[90] The ILWV, of course, was interested in such "political" issues as electoral reforms, but a deeper difference of vision was at work here beyond whether they were interested in the mechanisms of politics. Sikes could distance himself from female activism because male reformers did not see schools, housing, and infant and maternal care as pressing urban political problems. They justified their attitude by stating that these issues were not the "real" stuff of politics as were taxation and the economic growth of the city.[91] Charles Merriam's memoir on Chicago politics expressed similar sentiments.

> In my experience women have shown the keenest interest in the problems of schools, recreation, health, city waste, housing, the protection of women and children, the case of the immigrant, and in general all measures for the protection of the weak and the helpless. Questions of finance, engineering, most public works, industrial controversies, and public utility problems, have been of less interest, although not without capable students.[92]

It suited male reformers to consign women's municipal concerns to a category separate from their own in order to pursue their agenda unhampered by alternatives. If activist women's concerns could be categorized as non-political—as merely interested in aiding the "weak and the helpless"—or ignored, then male activists did not have to address them as the real stuff of urban decision-making.

Political scientist Kristi Andersen sees this attitude as a strategic part of men's resistance to women's post-suffrage attempts to change the boundaries of political concerns. "When women held office, the myth of disinterestedness was preserved by the idea that women were in politics for the sake of their families or communities." According to Andersen, the extent to which this was in fact a "myth" was attested to by steadfast male resistance to women's actual political ambitions and demands.[93] For Chicago, historians generally either view women within this "myth" or focus attention on select women and issues to portray their municipal involvement as elitist.[94] In this way, they do not have to take seriously the idea that women were actually proposing to challenge male ideas and goals for the city, any more than did the men of Chicago.

But activist Chicago women had addressed precisely those issues that Merriam claimed did not interest them. In 1919 the WCC had wanted a new state constitution to provide municipal ownership of public utilities and a reorganization of municipal taxing powers and debt limitation. In 1928 the WCC held an institute on municipal government attended by representatives from the Cook County and Chicago LWV, the Cook County Federation of Women's Clubs, the CWA, and the PTA. In early 1930 it held a day-long institute on Chicago political issues and topics. The 1928 LWV legislative agenda demanded a larger state school distribu-

tive fund and expanded compulsory school legislation. In late 1931 the
ILWV, the WCC (plus several of its ward branches), the CWC, the Catholic Women's Club, the Federation of Colored Women's Clubs, the Council
of Jewish Women, the women's department of the Chicago Church Federation, the Chicago Conference of Jewish Women's Organizations, the
Women's Bar Association, several women's political party organizations,
and a number of neighborhood women's clubs all supported bills to reorganize the assessment machinery of Cook County and to broaden the tax
base "so as to provide a more equitable distribution of the tax burden
among all sources of revenue."[95]

The WCC's restatement in 1926 of its political principle "that it is the
first duty of Chicago to protect [the] health of its citizens" showed that
the different vision's of a good city expressed by Chicago activist women
and men in their 1919 debate about the qualities for a good mayor, were
still there later in the decade. Harriet Vittum told clubmembers in 1926
to "urge upon the city administration all sanitary measures to protect the
milk and water supply; to guarantee against contagious diseases; to insist
upon Birth registration; to suppress the smoke evil; . . . to make hospital
provision for liquor and drug addicts; to keep streets, alleys and parks
scrupulously clean." The 1926 and 1929 platforms of the WCC still promoted as municipal priorities the construction of numerous and well-
staffed recreation facilities, adequate and safe school buildings, increased
education revenue, suppression of the "smoke evil," municipal responsibility for providing better housing, laws to protect children from exploitation, and "scrupulously" clean streets, alleys, and parks.[96] Almost every
facet of these platforms reiterated that of the Woman's Municipal Platform
of 1916. On the other hand, the municipal platform espoused by the *Tribune* in 1928, sandwiched between the 1926 and 1929 WCC platforms,
envisioned a completely different set of municipal priorities. The *Tribune*'s
priorities were economic development and making Chicago "the first city
in the world." The newspaper called for municipal government to give
priority to building a subway, electrifying all railroads, erecting the best
convention hall in the country, and constructing more and safer streets
and highways.[97] As Chicago women vainly struggled to extract more
money from the state legislature for maternal and infant health care, Chicago men twice successfully persuaded the legislature to raise the city's
debt limit to fund street improvements. Between 1915 and 1930, 112
miles of streets were widened or opened at an average cost of one million
dollars per mile.[98] Chicago in the 1920s measured its progress in bricks
and mortar: bridges built, roads widened, buildings erected, and the transformation of "a city of brick into a city of marble." Big Bill Thompson's
administrations improved 75.5 miles of major streets, built 78 percent of
the city's bridges (including the Michigan Avenue bridge linking the

north and south sides of the Chicago River in the Central Business District), and straightened a branch of the Chicago River. Progress, according to Charles Merriam, was a Chicago Plan that

> includes some 200 miles of street widenings, extensions and improvements, looks to the reorganization of the passenger and freight terminal facilities, considers the city's harbors, and envisages as one of its central features a striking development of the Chicago Lake Front. . . . [I]t may be said that the total cost of city plan projects thus far completed is in the neighborhood of two hundred fifty million dollars, and additional projects already approved by the official authorities contemplate the expenditure of fifty millions more. . . . [I]mportant units have reached their conclusion. The widening of Michigan Avenue and of Roosevelt Road, the construction of Wacker Drive, the opening of Western and Ashland avenues.[99]

Activist women measured progress in more human terms. Chicago's infant mortality rate did not compare well with other major U.S. cities. In 1916 the death rate for children under two years in Chicago was 141.4 per every 1,000 births; in Detroit it was 129.3; in Philadelphia 88.3; in New York 58.1; and in Boston 49.4. The average death rate for children under one year in 1920–21 in Chicago was 89.3 for every 1,000 births; in 1927, the number was 66.5. In Chicago in 1914, 8 percent (392) of deaths of women of childbearing age were caused by infection immediately following childbirth. Maternal death rates remained unchanged from 1915 to 1935 both in Chicago and nationally. The lower rates of infant mortality, as welcome as they were, were not nearly enough for Chicago women activists, especially because much of that improvement had resulted from women's voluntary and medical efforts not from government money spent on infant and maternal welfare. And even as government was not dramatically increasing its responsibility for such health care services, women activists found their efforts increasingly assailed by the male medical establishment, which, in 1927 complained that the women of the Infant Welfare Society of Chicago were "trying to overcome [maternal] ignorance by educating mothers to keep away from their neighborhood physicians and giving the impression that the physicians employed by the Infant Welfare Society are highly competent."[100]

Funds for education and other matters of child welfare were also not forthcoming from government. Women's goal of securing a larger state school distributive fund that would make educational opportunity equal throughout the state was not passing through the legislature. Chicago juvenile court workers complained to other women that fiscal efficiency and spending reductions were first priority of the County Board, that there were inadequate facilities for African American dependent children, and that men preferred building institutions to house children rather than placing them into homes. Judge Mary Bartelme told the LWV how one of the city's leading businessmen was delighted by institutions "because everyone seemed to respond quickly and in unison and he considered this a most 'efficient system.' But [said Bartelme] children do not like to be herded together in institutions and can we blame them?"[101]

As commissioner of public welfare in the middle of the decade, Mary McDowell tried to make solving the city's dreadful housing situation a municipal priority. Here, too, activist women found their path blocked by apathy or hostility to the problem, or by the power of men to shape solutions to their own economic and political advantage. McDowell's experiences are instructive. According to historian Thomas Philpott, she was "sure that a public solution was required but aware that government would not act." As a result, she had to keep begging "business interests to 'do something.' " Mayor Dever's response was to create an advisory Housing Commission, but it lacked both power and money. It was "an official body, but it was a private group in spirit, controlled by commerce, industry, and real estate, not by government." Not surprisingly, these men sent a bill to the legislature that suited their economic interests, which did nothing beyond requesting that the legislature lift existing limitations on how much land, and for how long, could be held vacant and unimproved.[102]

Thus the 1920s proved to be a frustrating decade for activist Chicago women's hopes for the city. They met continual defeat in the political arena and were unable to secure either municipal support or state legislation for many of their cherished welfare measures. The older generation of women activists was also running out of time, as its numbers dwindled because of death, retirement from public work, and removal to Washington, D.C. In 1928, however, these women undertook one last big push to make a difference in how and for whom the city worked.

Eight

"I Am the Only Woman on Their Entire Ticket": The End of an Era

BY THE end of the 1920s, three factors would make it impossible for activist Chicago women to pursue the municipal activism in which they had engaged for decades. First, women's activism was much more diffuse than in the past. Suffrage had given women more actual political opportunities; partisan political organizing now competed with traditional women's organizations for their attention. Generational change meant that younger women had neither experienced the group solidarity that had been forced upon the older generation by social and political customs nor grown up squarely in a women's political culture. They could choose from among a broader range of professional and work opportunities that would not leave them room for the type of voluntary, grassroots activities in which women's organizations had specialized.

Second, important elements of urban institutions and structures had remained essentially static and continued to work against women. Women now realized how difficult it was to secure a primary nomination for office, without which they could not win political office. District-based electoral seats precluded rallying female solidarity for women candidates across the city. Women could not secure appointed municipal offices unless the men controlling the political system had a reason for appointing them. So many of these appointed offices controlled the municipal services identified by activist women as most important to achieving their vision of the city— health and welfare, parks and recreation, housing, and schools, for instance—that failing to change the composition of these offices or to relocate their responsibilities into government meant that men could continue to ignore women.

Third, the Progressive Era was over. Men holding the balance of political power had either resolved to their satisfaction the problems created by massive urbanization, or the problems had proven virtually intractable because they were tied too closely to a political system with other priorities. No matter what women had done, they had been unable to break the hold of real estate, banking, business, and even labor interests on, for example, schools and housing. Decisions made on these issues had sufficiently satisfied enough men to allow them to turn their attention elsewhere. The intraparty struggles for dominance that had characterized

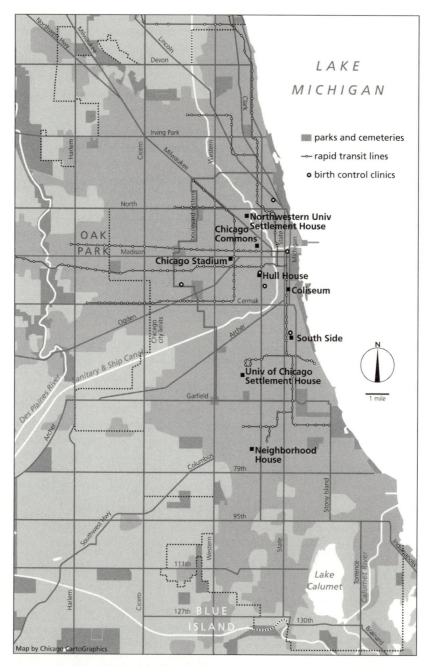

Figure 23. Map of Chicago, 1930. Showing rapid transit lines, and sites of women's activities from 1920 to 1933, including six birth control clinics (Drawn by Dennis McClendon, Chicago CartoGraphics)

both the Democratic and Republican parties for decades had proven often more important than formulating municipal reform programs.[1] Thompson won his three mayoral terms by adroit exploitation of these divisions inside the Republican Party but also by playing upon the lack of unity in the Democratic Party. Twelve years of Thompsonian rule brought bricks-and-mortar development but little government resolution to social problems, and no faction within either party wanted to shift the focus of municipal government responsibility, public policy, and spending decisions away from economic development. In the face of this intransigence, during the 1920s activist women turned their attention to forces outside the city. But once again, they were generally thwarted, as with the failure of enabling legislation for Sheppard-Towner funds.

These various developments were at work in 1928 when four longtime activist Chicago women ran for state and federal political office, and again two years later when other women sought seats on the Cook County Board of Commissioners. We can also see in these races that women supported these candidates, believing that they would better represent many of women's concerns, and that the male political leadership's continued opposition to activist women's concerns added fuel to their determination to deny women nomination and election.

Labor leader Agnes Nestor sought the Democratic nomination in the 6th district of the Illinois House. Of all of the situations of women running for office in 1928, hers was the most dramatic representation of activist women's declining possibilities to wield influence within the city and the political parties.[2] The Democrats supposedly were the party of labor in Chicago, and Nestor was both a working woman and a union organizer. But, as she pointed out, the party's incumbent in her district, Charles Weber, had not only opposed the bill for an eight-hour work day for women that women's organizations had been trying to push through the legislature, he had also boasted that he would win renomination *because* he opposed this bill. Nestor believed that the party's response to her candidacy would be a test case of its acceptance of women. She told Margaret Dreier Robins that because she was "the only women on their entire ticket through the county and the only labor person," if the "Democratic chiefs . . . endorse Weber we can take it as turning down women and labor."[3] But Nestor's situation was worsened by Illinois's district-based, partisan representation system. Each congressional district sent three representatives to the state house: the candidate receiving the most votes in each party, and then the candidate receiving the next highest total of votes. This meant that a Democratic district sent two Democrats and one Republican, while a Republican district did the opposite. The 6th district, which covered the city's north side and stretched into the suburb of Evanston, traditionally sent only one Democrat. Nestor's political agenda, which focused on the needs of working women and education, was not what Democratic men in her district wanted from their one representative in Springfield.

Longtime activists Anna Wilmarth Ickes and Flora Cheney sought Republican nominations for House seats from the 7th and 5th districts, respectively. Their situation was somewhat different, although neither woman ran on a platform that was particularly palatable to most men. Wilmarth Ickes belonged to both the WCC and the CWC, among other women's organizations, and in 1924 had been elected to the board of trustees of the University of Illinois. Cheney was a former public school teacher who was a leader in several Chicago women's clubs and had been the first president of the Illinois LWV. Anna's mother, Mary Wilmarth, had been a leading activist for decades until her death in 1919 and had raised Anna in the culture of women's progressive activism; Jane Addams and Ellen Gates Starr had first discussed founding Hull House in Mary's living room in 1889.[4] Wilmarth Ickes and Cheney, however, were seeking Republican nominations in districts that always sent two Republicans to the state house. Despite the activist credentials that had brought them into conflict with many activist Chicago men, they posed less of a threat than did Nestor to men's control of their districts.

The fourth woman was the staunchly Republican, politically connected Ruth Hanna McCormick, who sought the nomination for representative-at-large to the U.S. Congress—a post created because the state legislature had refused to redistrict the state since the 1900 census. Her situation was different still from the other three, yet it too was constrained by the political system and Republican party politics. First, McCormick declared her candidacy, as did most women, without party support. "Nobody asked me to run," she declared candidly.[5] Republican Party leaders were unenthusiastic about her candidacy, but once they realized how popular she was with women, whose registration totals in Chicago had increased 46 percent from 1924 to 1928, and that she stood a good chance of winning the nomination, many of them jumped on her bandwagon as part of their maneuvering to control the party in the state. McCormick acknowledged that "no doubt it was the women who gave me my chance in the primary," which she won by over ninety thousand votes, with more than half of her votes cast in Cook County.[6] But in light of the vicious opposition of male party leaders to her subsequent candidacy for U.S. Senate in 1930, it is debatable whether she would have won the nomination in 1928 without certain Republican politicians supporting her for their own purposes. Furthermore, that two at-large seats were up for election, so the top two vote-getters in the primary would be on the ballot in the general election, meant that it would remain theoretically possible until then to elect the runner-up, who in this case was Congressman Henry Rathbone.

Chicago women both as individuals and in their organizations rallied behind these four candidates as offering positions that many women were seeking in politics. When the Democrats refused to slate her, Nestor mounted a primary challenge without party support or financing. Her campaign's organizational meetings focused on the traditional women's alliances for support, votes, and campaigners: it targeted neighborhood and citywide women's clubs, the Uptown branch of the LWV, and long-time activists. The WCC enthusiastically endorsed Nestor, who also asked the president of the CWC to write letters to members living in the district asking them to support her. Nestor spoke to Chicago teachers and working women's groups and at settlement houses and neighborhood women's clubs. Letters of support and money came to the Nestor campaign from women throughout the city. Mrs. Elsie Lofgren, a former member of the Postal Clerks' Union and a WTUL convention delegate, wrote that she supported Nestor's campaign "because of the fact that you are a woman and whenever there is a chance to help advance the sphere of womanhood, I shall do all in my power to help." Marie O. Andresen, a lawyer and former assistant state's attorney, wrote that she supported Nestor even though she herself was a Republican. Andresen also indicated that she had indeed been contacted by the president of the CWC. Beulah Berolzheimer, president of the Federation of Women High School Teachers, sent a letter of support and a check. Margaret Haley sent an open letter to all teachers urging them to support Nestor. Mary Langworthy, a Republican and current president of the WCC, contributed money to Nestor's campaign, as did Katherine Fisher, whose contribution came with the notation "to show my enthusiastic interest." Julia Lathrop, whose father had organized the Illinois Republican Party, contributed a small sum; Mrs. Charles R. Crane, the wife of one of the city's leading industrialists, contributed two hundred dollars; ten dollars came from Mrs. Dora Nordloe, who identified herself as the wife of a teamster; teachers' leader Lillian Herstein made a contribution, as did committed activists Frances Crane Lillie, Ella Stewart, and Edith Wyatt.[7]

McCormick's campaign, like Nestor's, was largely a women's crusade. She depended heavily on the support of Republican women's organizations and Chicago women volunteers organized by section of the city, especially by wards, and managed by a general campaign headquarters directed by women. McCormick's biographer recounts the frustration felt by one of the few men working in her Chicago headquarters at operating in such unfamiliar surroundings. He was working, he wrote to a friend, "in this campaign with 16 women in this office and no one to swear at."[8] Democrat Elizabeth Bass was a campaign speaker for McCormick, as were Vittum, McDowell, and Mabel Sippy. Judith Loewenthal, Emily Napieralski, Harriet Treadwell, and Myrtle Blacklidge worked in her campaign.

Republican women allied with both the Thompson and Deneen factions of the party worked for her even though neither man supported her. Other women campaigners belonged to the WCC and ward-based WCC and LWV groups.[9]

Wilmarth Ickes and Cheney also depended on the established network of women's clubs and women's political party organizations to support their campaigns and to vote for them. The WCC endorsed both women. Unfortunately, we have little more information on how these women conducted their campaigns, an all-too-common problem for tracing women in urban history. Neither women left any papers as did Nestor and McCormick. Wilmarth Ickes was the first wife of Harold Ickes, and although by 1928 he had turned Democratic, he ran her campaign. He only mentions the campaign in terms of his role in it, along with a comment that Raymond and Margaret Dreier Robins convinced the anti-saloon league not to oppose her even though Harold was a "wet" and Anna was barely "dry."[10]

We do have evidence that McCormick and Nestor in particular experienced considerable male resistance to their candidacies. McCormick received a letter from one man informing her that he "would not think of voting for a woman for Congressman-at-Large any more than to vote for one of my cows for such a responsible office." Representative Weber's boast that he would defeat Nestor because he opposed the eight-hour day for working women was not much different from Chicago democratic leader George Brennan's declaration that "Men won't vote for a women." As Nestor told Margaret Dreier Robins, Weber "is depending upon the organization putting him over, and I am trying to break down that support."[11]

The WCC endorsed Nestor, Cheney, and Wilmarth Ickes because of these candidates' ongoing concern with making government function to further human welfare. Cheney, the WCC noted, believed that the "first purpose of government is to promote the welfare of the largest number of citizens." Wilmarth Ickes, if elected, would direct her efforts to forwarding "the welfare and social legislation which women have at heart." Nestor was backed for her particular interests in the eight-hour day for women and educational equality.[12] After Wilmarth Ickes secured her nomination, she expounded on her agenda. She declared first that she had as her aim "the accomplishment of the greatest good for the greatest number." She emphasized that technological progress "has brought in its wake a new sequence of duties, pure food, sanitation, education, health and dozens of allied questions" upon which women had to have a voice.[13] She optimistically believed that men wanted to hear women's voices, an optimism that her first term experiences in the legislature would temper.

Running for a national office that required her to campaign throughout the state, McCormick's specific aims somewhat differed from those of the three Illinois house candidates. Yet she too was working to try to insert more women into the political system so that they could begin to change it. She hoped that a woman elected to such an office would encourage other women to become political candidates. She also believed that if she were elected on the strength of women's votes, men would "be impressed" and could then "be influenced to reform."[14]

Any cross-party, cross-class, and citywide support women candidates experienced could not overcome the district-based election system in which only those living in the district can vote. Furthermore, the rules of the partisan primary system worked against Nestor's chances of winning. If Republican women voted for her in the Democratic primary, they could not vote Republican in the general election. Nestor lost the primary by a vote of 14,774 to 6,224 in a district that was heavily Republican in its northern, suburban part. Catharine Waugh McCulloch conceded that Republicans were "so interested in cleaning up the Republican party and 'saving' [progressive candidate] Ralph Church" that they could not vote in the Democratic primary.[15]

Wilmarth Ickes and Cheney were nominated and subsequently elected. What guaranteed their victories was neither their ideas nor men's agreement with them, but rather the fact that they were Republicans running in districts that always sent two Republicans to the state house. In such cases, party leadership and male voters could calculate that they could afford to support one woman for office. McCormick was resoundingly nominated and elected in 1928. Two years later she fell victim to male political machinations when she attempted to run for a U.S. Senate seat as her primary challenger, Charles Deneen, and Mayor Thompson both worked against her despite her nomination by the party.[16]

In other areas of municipal politics, three longtime activist women won seats on the Cook County Board of Commissioners in 1930. Their fates also were largely determined by party politics and the structure of the system. Labor activist Mary McEnerny, longtime welfare advocate and Assistant General Superintendent of the United Charities Amelia Sears, and Mrs. Glenn Plumb, whose first name I have never found, but who was described as the widow of a friend of labor, entered the Democratic primary. Democrats were usually guaranteed to win the city's ten seats on the board, so their chances were at least good. Considering the board's responsibility for providing much social welfare in the city at the time, McEnerny and Sears were especially suited for these positions. All three women secured a nomination, but just barely, finishing finished eighth, ninth, and tenth. Judith Loewenthal, president of the CWA and member of the WCC, again a qualified candidate, ran for the board as a Republican from the city. She was not even nominated by that party's voters.[17] That seven men finished ahead of Sears, McEnerny, and Plumb in the primary indicates that neither the party nor its male voters was convinced that they wanted women in a public office where they would decide on the distribution of tax revenues. That so public a figure as Judith Loewenthal could not even win nomination in the Republican primary gives further evidence of male voters' refusal to consider women candidates. The *Tribune*, a Republican newspaper, refused to endorse any of the few women candidates who actually made it to the general election.[18]

Several African American women also ran in the primaries in 1930 but could not overcome the double obstacles of racism and sexism. Attorney Georgia Jones-Ellis stood for state house from the 5th district, a majority white district where a black candidate stood little chance. Moreover, Jones-Ellis believed that she had the endorsement of regular Republican men, only to discover on election day that the men of the party did not deliver on their promise. Wells-Barnett's situation was somewhat different. She ran for state senate from the 3rd district, where the winner was certain to be African American, but she finished a distant fourth to the winner, a career party man. According to Wells-Barnett's most recent biographer, she faced two problems. First, Republican men felt that "female independence potentially upset the balance of political debts in relationships already tilted again the African American community," and thus they wanted to nominate only a strict party regular. Second, men figured that women candidates could not muster enough political clout to ensure that regular party voters would support them. As Wells-Barnett herself noted, African American Republican leaders remained "stubborn about helping women."[19] Her situation was not much different from that of Louise Bowen when she explored the possibility of running for mayor in 1923.

So by the end of the decade, Chicago women had little to show in the way of political victories. No women sat on the city council. The only high-ranking appointed municipal office occupied by a woman was that of commissioner of public welfare, where Mary McDowell, Anna L. Smith, and then Elizabeth Conkey served from 1924. But even here women were not equal: only women held this post, the salary of which in 1931 was five thousand dollars, when all other commissioners in the city were paid eight to ten thousand dollars.[20] In terms of achieving a broader municipal influence, activist women felt similarly stymied. They had been unable to stop the Thompson renomination and election in 1927. Then they had to endure the removal from office of health commissioner Herman Bundeson, who had been an ally in the women's public health campaign. Bundeson was forced to resign because he had refused to insert Thompson campaign materials into a Chicago Board of Health pamphlet on baby care in 1927. Those activist women who had worked against Thompson were obviously appalled by the cynical exercise of political power by someone they detested. But even those women who had supported Thompson were dismayed by the loss of a municipal official who had supported one of their cherished aims and who had challenged Thompson on this issue. In 1928 the CTF turned against Thompson when it gave Bundeson its unanimous endorsement as Democratic candidate for the office of coroner.[21]

In influencing the political parties, activist women fared no better. In 1928, after fifteen years of suffrage, no women served on the Cook County central committees of either party—the bodies that controlled the decision-making and nominating procedures for all levels of politics. The central committees were composed primarily of ward committeemen who refused to slate women for these positions. In 1928 no women were elected as national convention delegates for either party. Ida B. Wells-Barnett overwhelmingly lost in her challenge to Thompson's handpicked candidate from her district, Oscar DePriest.[22] In the 1920s women still had to fight the men in control of the institutions of the parties and government to achieve complete equal political rights and treatment. The Illinois attorney general had tried to mute women's voices within the parties by ruling that women were ineligible to vote for delegates to the national party conventions. Not until 1928 did the Illinois legislature pass a law "authorizing women to act as election judges and clerks."[23] Newspapers still published misleading stories whose only purpose could have been to denigrate women's political participation. A story on the 1928 presidential campaign, for example, was headlined, "Women, North Siders Batter Down Al's [Smith's] lead," implying that women were voting against Smith although, in fact, the straw poll on which the article was based revealed women supporting Smith over Hoover, 1,043 to 990, while men supported Hoover, 2,961 to 2,484.[24]

As this newspaper story shows, women's positions on political issues were constantly subject to manipulation. Nestor's opponent, Charles Weber, had singled out two positions with which to attack her and to boast of his certain victory. One was his opposition to the eight-hour workday for women; the other was proclaiming himself the candidate of beer and wine.[25] He could not directly accuse Nestor of being a proponent of Prohibition because there is no evidence that she was or that she even addressed this issue in her campaign. But his implication that electing a woman would guarantee the extension of Prohibition directs our attention back to unresolved urban problems and how bound up they had become with urban politics. Prohibition was never popular in Chicago, and a wet-dry tension underlay all the city's politics. Weber's stress on "wetness" was a familiar political ploy. As mayor, William Dever had chosen to enforce the Prohibition laws. In the 1927 campaign, Thompson had made this a centerpiece of his attack on Dever. Many activist women, as we have seen, had supported Dever. Thus, connecting women to Prohibition and playing upon male, as well as ethnic, fears of women in public office was easy. Beyond a lack of evidence that Nestor favored Prohibition, the city's leading women's organizations from the CWC to the WCC to the CWTUL to the CTF rarely made Prohibition part of any of their campaign discussion, literature, or endorsements, beyond supporting the upholding of the law. In its 1926 "Statement of Principles," the WCC agreed that the Volstead Act ought to be enforced as part of a concerted campaign to reduce crime, a campaign that included enforcing laws regulating sale of firearms, laws to protect children's welfare, and laws against child labor.[26] Crime concerned these women, again because it harmed the welfare of children and women. Its statement on the Volstead Act appeared under the heading "Crime"; there was no heading for "Prohibition." When Ruth McCormick ran for U.S. Senate in 1930, the issue was used against her again in misleading ways. McCormick declared that being "dry" was her personal preference, but that she intended to abide by popular opinion, which was turning decisively against Prohibition, if the issue of repeal came up. McCormick's 1930 primary opponent was Charles Deneen, whom the Woman's Christian Temperance Union endorsed as a faithful supporter of Prohibition. After McCormick won the nomination, Illinois Prohibition supporters were so fearful of her views on this issue that they ran a "dry" opposition Independent candidate. But as with Nestor, Prohibition was one weapon that men used against political rivals even though other issues were clearly more important and perhaps more decisive for any particular electoral race. Women candidates were a favorite target for this tactic because male politicians and voters rarely listened to what they said or did. Women were assumed to favor Prohibition, and activist women were assumed to be even more in favor of it.[27]

The evidence that activist women were still pursuing a different vision of the purpose of government reappears in Wilmarth Ickes's reelection campaign in 1930. In speeches directed to women's clubs she pointed out,

> Matters of education, health and quarantine, child welfare, sanitation, garbage disposal, pure food laws, working hours for women, employment of children, all with which in the past government had little or nothing to do but which now have been made the subject of legislation . . . certainly brings the work of the legislature near to women's hearts. Would we keep our rightful influence in these matters we must go to the polls.

Men and women, Wilmarth Ickes also stressed, still possessed different ideas about the purpose of politics. "What is legislation anyway," she asked women, "except the passing of laws designed for the welfare of the State and to abate pollution of our streams or to regulate the drivers of autos affects the lives and welfare of our children as do good school laws and more direct health measures"[28] But the men of the legislature, according to her, saw things differently. The bill that she had introduced to form a sanitary water board to abate and prevent water pollution had passed because the Illinois Manufacturers' Association had not blocked it. Wilmarth Ickes quickly appreciated how business interest still determined any new policy development. "The woman who goes to Springfield," she pointed out, "enters a man's world. . . . So to speak of woman's influence at Springfield has a touch of humor." And she recounted how one of the five bills that she had introduced during her first term quickly died in committee, "the argument advanced against it being that it contained an 'entirely new idea.' A man's reason surely. . . . I cannot imagine a group of women scrapping a bill because its contents were new."[29]

Anna Wilmarth Ickes was an extremely wealthy woman. She was neither insensible to issues of taxation nor did she think that only women were interested in social issues. She disagreed with the LWV's proposed revenue amendments to the state constitution, writing that she would not support their propositions because

> this amendment would make possible the imposition of an income tax in ADDITION to our present personal property tax, and that the members from down state control the legislature and could (under the amendment) vote taxes upon Cook County to be spent down state.[30]

So Wilmarth Ickes combined a women's concern for a common welfare with an eye to tax issues in ways that made her acceptable, as one of two representatives, to her highly middle-class Republican district. But this did not mean that she succeeded in pushing through many of the bills that she introduced in Springfield, especially if the bill threatened male economic interests.

As a longtime advocate of social welfare, Amelia Sears confronted the limits on women's activism as the economic depression settled on Chicago. Private charity could not begin to meet the crisis, and the county board struggled to meet its welfare obligations to growing numbers of desperate people. As Sears stressed government responsibility to help, the business perspective prevailed over the human one. Sears called for "immediate development of public work [as] the only hope of preventing needless suffering this winter." Harriet Vittum agreed, saying, "Chicago must find some way to put to work the men and women who are willing to work, whose children must be fed." Here were the echoes of the IWA's call for immediate municipal public work to solve the unemployment caused by the depression of 1893. But men countered with such proposals as meeting unemployment with a nationwide employment system "administered by industry."[31] They never considered municipal employment through public works. Then in 1932 Sears called for civic, business, and labor organizations to come together and help the board regain the confidence of the public. Sears called for citizen involvement, which had always been a hallmark of women's activism, as the welfare situation in Chicago was growing desperate. Unemployment reached 40 percent in Chicago during 1932, and one hundred thousand families were on the relief rolls, an increase of eighty-four thousand since late 1930.[32] The support Sears and Vittum may have had from other women on the issue of relief was counteracted by men's control of the institutions of government. The men on the county board did not want citizen involvement, and they ridiculed Sears's suggestion. The board's decision to raise two million dollars for relief through a bond issue failed, and Mayor Cermak decided not to contribute any municipal monies to public relief.[33] No female activism could have asserted primacy over male control of the institutions of government.

While Cermak's decision can be seen as logical in the face of depression and declining municipal revenues—between May 1928 and July 1930, the city had levied no general property taxes and in fact had cut the assessments of Central Business District (the Loop) property[34]—it was also a reflection of how men decided to spend existing funds. Cermak and the other men in power now made choices about where to put municipal revenues, choices that were rooted in decisions made in the past about the main interests of government. Since the school system was separate from the municipal government and its revenues were restricted by a legally imposed cap on the percentage of tax revenues that could be levied for the schools, as tax assessments and levies fell so, automatically, did school funds, and no monies could be moved into the school fund from other municipal sources. Given these institutionalized restrictions, the crucial question was what to cut from the school budget. The board of education did what it had always done in times of financial crises: it cut teachers and educational programs. The board fired fourteen hundred public school teachers, slashed teacher pay by 23.5 percent, and cut educational programs by closing special schools and special departments that activist women had fostered since the turn of the century. On the other hand, the board chose to maintain budgets for buildings and equipment. At least one historian of municipal finances claims the close relationship of the city's politicians with the janitors and building contractors with keeping school revenues flowing to these two groups rather than to the teachers or the instructional budget. Moreover, the city's bankers demanded that the school board pay all outstanding debts, including the interest on the bonds that had paid for school buildings, before it paid the teachers. By early 1933, the school board owed the teachers more than twenty million dollars in back pay.[35] The CTF and the Women High School Teachers called a mass meeting in January 1932, held at the old Chicago Stadium on west Madison Street, to try to protect teachers and programs. The female teachers supported Mayor Cermak's tax reorganization plan that would shift tax assessment power from elected to appointed bodies. This support for the Cermak plan split the teachers from the CFL and IFL, whose objections that such a change would undermine the voters' right to choose its tax assessors echoed Georg Leidenberger's findings about why male unionists favored municipal ownership of utilities.[36] In the 1930s, as at the turn of the century, male unionists fought to maintain control over their tax monies through elected tax assessment offices to protect their political and economic power in the city. But Chicago's female teachers neither had gained control over their economic situation nor had they been able to establish any political power in the city. Cermak's plan, they hoped, would at least restore some of their jobs.[37]

As the economic crisis of the early 1930s severed teachers from organized labor, it also illuminated the ongoing differences between women activists, who still made a common welfare in the city their primary concern, and the male politicians and businessmen running the city, who continued to focus on economic development and male professional expertise to cope with the Great Depression. In early 1930 the LWV held a forum, "The Tax Muddle and the Way Out." In December 1931 the LWV organized a meeting attended by representatives from the WCC, the CWC, the Catholic Women's Club, the Chicago Conference of Jewish Women's Organizations, the IFCWC, the IWRC, the Women's Department of the Chicago Church Federation, and numerous neighborhood women's organizations. These women also strongly supported the reorganization of the Cook County assessment machinery.[38] Edith Abbott, Jane Addams, Mary McDowell—professed Republicans—and the leaders of the WCC were so concerned about the city's neglect of social welfare services that in 1932 they formed the Social Services Non-partisan Committee of Cook County to campaign for Thomas Courtney, the Democratic nominee and Cermak man, for state's attorney. They hoped his election would result in more attention to protecting the needs of a ravaged citizenry. Courtney won in Chicago by a margin of nearly three hundred thousand votes.[39]

But male politicians, businessmen, and labor leaders did not consult women's organizations, did not include women in their various citywide meetings to consider the city's economic crisis, and ignored women's suggestions about the schools, unemployment, public health, and a whole range of urban welfare problems. The city remained firmly in control of men whose first priority as always was economic protection. When businessmen and bankers remained impervious to the dire situation of teachers, thousands of the teachers participated in a violent demonstration, marching through the streets of downtown. When a compromise was finally reached, it was negotiated between businessmen and representatives of the Men's Federation of Teachers. No women teachers were allowed to participate in the discussions. Margaret Haley summed up the gendered nature of the situation: "They were all men." In the depths of the school crisis in 1933, Madeleine Wallin Sikes castigated in language reminiscent of Elizabeth Morgan and the IWA four decades earlier the businessmen on the board of education for their decisions. "No amount spent on buildings and equipment, or operation," she contended, "compares with the importance of the instructional service. The teacher and the pupils make the school."[40]

Considering their only limited success over the decades at working on the local level to implement key elements of their urban vision, it was logical that activist women turned away from municipal institutions to seek power in the Cook County board of commissioners or state offices or Federal government agencies such as the Children's Bureau. This circumstance may well explain why activist women, including Republicans Addams, Bowen, Breckinridge, McDowell, and Vittum, were working to elect democrat Henry Horner as governor. Horner was supported by Mayor Anton Cermak, and when elected he became the state's first Jewish governor.[41] McEnerny, Nestor, and Bass also campaigned for Horner. Many of these women also supported Franklin Roosevelt for president that year, as both the state and federal governments were seeming more receptive to women's agendas for increasing state-sponsored social welfare. The impact of Chicago's activism on the national level can be seen in the fact that the Children's Bureau was headed by Julia Lathrop from 1912 to 1921 and then Grace Abbott from 1921 to 1934. CWTUL activist Mary Anderson headed the Women's Bureau from 1920 to 1944. Florence Kelley, of course, had gone on to head the National Consumers' League. Lathrop had been one of the principal architects of the Sheppard-Towner legislation while at the Children's Bureau. The links could work backwards also. After resigning from the Children's Bureau, Lathrop returned to Chicago to assume a leadership position in the LWV.[42] But as historian Robyn Muncy has pointed out, legislation passed by and programs designed and administered almost exclusively by men, had the almost contradictory effect of muting women's voices even as they gained more positions within the New Deal administrative structure.[43]

The shift toward promoting federal programs to address social welfare also further weakened the women's coalition through which activists had attempted to exercise power on the local level for several decades. The national WTUL, for example, now focused on federal government protections for working women. Building the Children's Bureau as a power base from which to secure federal legislation on public health and child welfare had had its negative effects, much of which Chicago activists could have neither foreseen nor prevented. Having staked their public health campaign on Sheppard-Towner legislation, the backlash generated by this initiative from professional men had seriously damaged women's health care efforts in the city. The city's only African American run hospital, Provident, was forced to bear almost the entire burden of health care for Chicago's rapidly expanding African American population because the medical establishment's hostility forced the closing of neighborhood health centers previously supported by women, and that women had hoped to keep alive through Sheppard-Towner funds.[44] By the early 1930s, the kinds of public health services previously supported by women had been sorely undermined by pressure from the medical establishment and failure to secure any federal or state funds through the Sheppard-Towner legislation.[45] Even securing positions on the Cook County board did little to further women's ideas on the providing of social welfare. In late 1932 Irene Kowin, deputy chief probation officer of the juvenile court, lamented to a meeting of the LWV how other fiscal exigencies limited funding for the court's operations. "The Juvenile Court goes to the County Board for its budget. Bankers insist that the city reduce expenditures. . . [An] efficiency expert attempts to even further reduce expenditures." The result, she said, was inadequate funding that led to inadequate facilities for dependent children.[46] Because no municipal body had made provision of social welfare its top priority, when economic recession forced budget cuts, social welfare institutions were the first to feel the pinch, just as teachers and educational programs were the first targets of the school board. As historian Joanne Goodwin has shown, such fiscal constraints and municipal prioritizing had gradually forced activist women working to secure mothers' pensions as "right" and "just" to change their rhetoric to emphasize the need of the state to care for children.[47]

On the other hand, by 1933 circumstances in Chicago had made activist women fully aware that they and their organizations had been effectively marginalized in municipal politics. The Republican Party, which had not listened to activist women for years anyway, was so moribund that it could provide these women with no political power base. The Democratic Party gained uncontested control of all municipal elections after 1931 by solidifying the allegiance of the white male working class. The 1916 Loeb rule had effectively blocked the CTF from becoming a municipal power, and the parties' appointments to the school board remained almost exclusively businessmen and male labor figures who continued to make decisions on the schools based on male economic priorities. Labor's flirtation with the Republican Party under Thompson ended as it became disillusioned with him during his final term. His successor, Democrat Anton Cermak, set out to build the Democratic "machine." After his death in early 1933 the party ensured that organized labor would never return to the Republicans by systematically wooing the men in new industrial unions into the party organization.[48] It had already gained the allegiance of the CFL through, among other measures, its policies of maintaining prevailing wages for city workers and consulting with the CFL on appointments to the judiciary and the school board.[49] Although it has always been a cardinal principal of the American party system to lure groups of voters away from the other party, neither party in Chicago ever vied for the women's vote, nor were activist women consulted about judicial or school board appointments.

The WCC and the CWC did keep working to influence municipal affairs. Not until into the 1930s did the LWV lose significance for activist women. The Chicago *Daily News, Almanac* from 1927 to 1932 lists numerous ward- and neighborhood-based branches of both the LWV and the WCC across the city. These include several branches listed as "Colored," such as the 2nd ward branch (colored) WCC, as well as branches that were probably African American because they were listed as being headed by an African American woman, for instance, the Douglas Branch of the LWV headed by Irene Goins and Helen Sayre.[50] But the tight control of the party system over municipal development effectively blocked any progress by these organizations. If historian Robert Slayton is correct in his final analysis of Chicago politics, that "any group that wanted to work with the political structure—be it labor union, community organization, or ethnic club—had to structure itself along [machine hierarchical] lines if it wanted to become part of the system of rewards," then activist Chicago women could never have made any substantial inroads into the system in the 1930s even if their coalition had remained intact and their focus steadfastly on the city. Activist women did not believe that "power flowed from the top," as Slayton described it.[51] Rather, they believed in and practiced the idea that power flowed from democratic cooperation across society. Over the decades activist women had honed the practices of cooperation, personal investigation, and broad public education on municipal issues, and they were unwilling to become a cog in the party machinery. They also refused to play by exactly the same political party rules. Their partisan adherence weakened and sometimes shattered when their party pursued policies to which they objected.

Placed in this overall urban context, it made sense that by the 1932 elections, a new generation of Chicago women would turn toward working within the party system. All prevailing circumstances seemed to tell them that only through the political party system, not women's organizations, could they hope to exercise any political power. Even Agnes Nestor remained faithful to the Democratic Party, declining the request of rising Illinois politician Paul Dougles and the League for Independent Political Action that she support the Farmer-Labor Party of Cook County. When Lillian Herstein did run in the primary for the U.S. House on that party's ticket in 1932, she came in last.[52] In an ironic twist for activist women, as more women participated in party politics and increased their voter registration numbers—women's registration totals in the city in 1932 had reached 43 percent of men's—and as the influence of women's organizations such as the WCC over municipal politics diminished, women would find that they had not replaced this lost power with increased standing and power within the parties. They still were not slated for municipal offices, still not given positions of importance, and still not invited to be equal members with men. As the older generation of activist women faded away, younger women with political visions and aspirations had to content themselves with being the parties' foot soldiers. They worked for their party, but they had little say over Chicago's development.

Conclusion

Chicago Remains the City of Big Shoulders

FROM THE fire of 1871, growing numbers of activist Chicago women began to construct a vision of Chicago as a livable city in which municipal government would be used above all to foster and protect a common welfare for all residents. The history of women's activism in Chicago clearly exposes that many women developed, on the basis of their experiences as women in the city, a vision of the city as a socially just "home" for all its residents, a home created by municipal public policy. Across several decades, these women worked to put their vision into practice. The leaders built coalitions of women's organizations. Both leaders and members engaged in grassroots, personalized work to bring all citizens into the decision-making process by going into public spaces and then door-to-door with petitions, defying men who were trying to confine them to the private world of the home so that men might control the public world. They organized mass rallies and parades in which thousands of women participated. They investigated schools, housing, workplaces, and public venues all across the city. They agitated for free parks and beaches and environmental protections for neighborhoods and the entire city. Striking women workers, allied with middle-class women, confronted the city's businessmen, police force, and unsympathetic politicians, demanding safer working conditions and better pay as well as the right to demonstrate and strike. Activist black and white women tried to forge alliances to address the range of urban problems caused by racist attitudes and urban policies. They had worked together in the Juvenile Protective Agency and the CWTUL and the ILWV, and directly confronted the issue of how restricted opportunity based on racial thinking would prevent Chicago from becoming a good city. Activist women, in short, confronted the men of the city on every issue that they deemed important for securing a general welfare and creating a good city. Once women attained suffrage, they worked to secure votes and win political offices so that they could have a more direct political voice in determining their city's growth and development.

Whether activist women's vision for a good city was a better one than most men's, or whether implementing women's solutions for urban problems of education, the environment, social welfare, recreation, racism, public health, and housing earlier in the century would have prevented the crises that beset the city in the post–World War II years, are not the issues of this book. Clearly, many of the urban problems that activist women had tried to remedy before the 1930s, but over which they had lost their battles to find a socially just solution, had in many ways worsened by that decade. Chicago's public school system has been a chronic problem ever since. Failure to more directly address the problem of racism earlier in the century continued to plague the city's school, housing, employment, and recreation situations as the African American population grew, and as new immigrants from Mexico, Puerto Rico, and Latin America have come to the city seeking jobs and a better future. Failure of the city to accept direct responsibility for health and welfare provisions has left it with only one public hospital, and even that and the entire welfare system are still dependent on funding from the Cook County Board of Commissioners.

As other scholars have astutely observed, this latter situation has kept the city out of fiscal trouble. But the price has been paid by the city's poor, and still more so by its children, who also continue to pay the price for the city's recurring school crises and insufficient health care or social services.[1] Since the end of the 1920s, the city has continued to concentrate municipal spending on what political scientists call "common functions"—government building, highways, sewerage and sanitation infrastructure, and the safety functions of police and fire. Not only has it little developed its spending on "non-common functions"—a major segment of which is public services such as health, hospitals, and welfare—the city has devolved many of these expenses onto the county or state. Non-common functions, again according to political scientists, are those considered "poor people's services."[2]

Moreover, the inability or unwillingness of Chicago—indeed, of cities around the world—to address these problems in ways desired by activist women early in the twentieth century was addressed again at the end of the century by the Organization for Economic Cooperation and Development at its international conference on women and the city, using much the same language as activist Chicago had used a century earlier. According to the conference's participants, women had to participate more forcefully in urban development because "women are more often sensitive to the quality of life which they confront on a day to day basis"; because "women's use of cities differs from that of men"; because most solutions to urban problems are "typically put forward in terms of calculation [of costs and benefits] and technology [that] crowd out moral and aesthetic views of environmental care." Conference participants echoed the sentiments and ideas of activist Chicago women when they contended that "the experience of nurturing and household management is one in which moral principle, emotional sensitivity and material interest are constantly in play together. It is this experience many women can and do bring forward in their approach to environmental problems." In 1914 nurse Anna

Allen had made exactly those points when urging the members of the University of Chicago Settlement Woman's Club to register and vote. There were enormous problems in the city, she said, "because we have not been making the proper connection between our homes and the big machine down there at the City Hall and County Building." Women, she believed, had to link women's experiences and expertise in the home to city problems and municipal government.[3]

Rather than entering into a discussion about which was the better vision, or whether women's vision was fiscally possible, this book has sought to examine the ideas and actions of activist women so that we can see urban development and contestations for power differently than we have before and recognize that there were alternatives suggested and roads not taken. This book also has sought to show why the alternatives were rejected. Activist Chicago women developed a gendered vision of the city, a vision with an underlying premise of the correct nature and purpose of municipal government that often contradicted and sometimes profoundly threatened the male vision of the profitable city in which the purpose of government was to foster and protect male economic desires. Although they might compete among themselves about whose economic desires they wanted protected, Chicago men across class, ethnicity, and race remained committed to preserving their vision of the good city, never surrendering to the women's vision.[4] And since the 1930s Chicago mayors worked hard to reconcile the economic desires of businessmen with those of laborers. Informal agreements between the city government and the CFL to pay the prevailing wage without collective bargaining agreements meant that the city guaranteed the economic security of a significant portion of the city's male laborers. Businessmen also won. One of Mayor Richard J. Daley's first actions upon becoming mayor in 1955 was to win the "approbation of Chicago's business community by launching an ambitious building program concentrated in the Loop." Daley also created a municipal department of city planning, whose budget grew from $149,500 to $914,500 in its first seven years. In the words of historian Roger Biles, "In every phase of the building boom, from conceptualization to construction, Daley and city hall planners worked closely with the business community."[5] Examining activist women earlier in the century enables us to see progressive-era Chicago as the site of multiple contestations to control the city's future that were not limited to male struggles to control the political parties and votes but that in the end were contests won largely by men.

By looking at activist women in the context of urban development, we can also see that it was not the primary goal of activist Chicago women to create more public spaces for themselves; occupying public space was a means to an end, not the end itself. For activist women, the end was a better city with different priorities. Machine politics, ethnic politics, and class politics were clearly present in Chicago in these decades, but so too was gender politics. Urban historians ought to be able by now to see that they can no longer ignore this dimension of any city's history.

The majority of activist Chicago women also never adhered to a simplistic version of political non-partisanship. With suffrage, they were quick to acknowledge the enduring power and place of the party system in American politics. By 1924 the WCC, which had previously shunned direct involvement in political campaigns, started inviting all major political candidates to address the club. In 1927 the WCC officially encouraged women to participate in all facets of party politics, declaring that "political parties are the most powerful instruments in our governmental life," through which "women have the opportunity to do their best work if they will study party organization and take an intelligent part in its operations." The following year the WCC told women that "nothing is more important for the voters who wish to secure good government than to become associated with their party organization." The Women's Worlds Fair of 1927 included a Democratic Day and a Republican Day, along with a Club Women's Day. In 1930 the CWC announced that it would hold an "all-partisan candidate meeting."[6] Individual activist women openly declared their allegiance to one party or the other.

This is not an inconsequential matter in a democratic society run by party politics. To acknowledge that women accepted partisanship means that we must thereafter acknowledge that the politicians and parties treated women differently from men. Such scholars as Dianne Pinderhughes have shown us how the democratic process has not accorded equal opportunity to African Americans. This acknowledgment must also be extended to women. Yet at the same time, many of these women did want to redefine partisan politics away from the nineteenth-century male model toward a more flexible and less hierarchical system that would incorporate new members and new ideas and allow for more direct citizen participation in policy development. As Kristi Andersen has shown, women made some headway during the 1920s with these aims.[7] Yet those gains came gradually and at different rates at different levels of politics. Chicago activist women discovered how intractable the system could be on the local level, where daily decisions were likely immediately to affect the economic and political fortunes of men who were used to controlling the city to their desired ends. Chicago men dismissed women as lacking knowledge and interest in the "hard" political issues of taxation and finance. Yet a wealth of evidence exists to show that neither was true. The true problem was that activist women had offered a different vision of the means and ends of municipal taxation and financing, as early as the IWA's proposals in the early 1890s.

Figure 24. Women's Worlds Fair Organizers. Louise de Koven Bowen (Progressive Republican), Elizabeth Bass (Democrat), and Helen Bennett (Regular Republican). (Chicago *Daily News*, Chicago Historical Society, DN-85605)

The attitude of many Chicago men toward activist women in Chicago resembled that which historian Sandra Haarsager sees confronting Bertha Knight Landes, a Seattle activist who served in that city's council and then for one two-year term as mayor. When Landes ran for city council in 1922 she focused on the idea that municipal government should make the city a home rather than on the business model of the city. For Landes, this meant a municipal government that paid attention to the so-called "hard" issues of municipal government—assessment procedures, tax revenues and budgets, regulation of public utilities, grading and paving of streets, and building and maintaining water mains and sewers—but at the same time making municipal sanitation, garbage collection, food and building inspection, and moral conditions part of the central concerns of government. In her mayoral campaign of 1926 she summed up her philosophy in language that greatly resembled that of Anna Nicholes thirteen years earlier. "City governments," Landes asserted, "exist largely because of the family and the home, and their first duty is to serve these two institutions. . . . No city is greater than its homes." In her short time in office, Landes worked to balance the focus on the city as primarily concerned with business and economic development with a focus on the city as concerned with meeting social needs. She fought for a good public hospital, municipal recreation committee, and environmental protections, and proposed more government attention to child welfare, tuberculosis, and other health problems. In November 1926 she laid out her ideas in a speech to the ILWV.

Landes had won office in Seattle through a combination of political fortunes: a disgraced opponent and a nonpartisan system that had weakened party politics. Once elected to public office, business and labor interests opposed her administration. Landes did not ignore "our industrial future," as she termed it. But her proposals for economic development ran counter to what most private industries wanted. For example, her appointee to head the municipal lighting department promoted publicly owned power as the way to attract new industry by offering cheap rates while simultaneously providing better service and better lives to Seattle's residents. It was not accidental that the city's private power companies opposed her re-election. Landes was defeated for re-election in 1928 by old-style male politics. Big business interests funneled campaign funds to her opponent, who in turn derided her as bringing "petticoat rule" to Seattle, and the ranks of male municipal employees actively worked against her.[8]

Activist Chicago women's livable city was not the *Tribune*'s economic paragon or the world-class city extolled by Charles Merriam when he declared the city as transforming itself from "a city of brick into a city of marble; shaping lakes and parks, streets, ways and playgrounds into a beautiful and useful whole, which soon will be one of the physical marvels of the world, adding to the urban beauty spots of historic fame." This does not mean that activist women were not proud of the city and did not want it to be a beautiful one also. At the end of her memoir, Louise de Koven Bowen gazed out over the city and marveled at its beauty.[9] But the memoirs of Merriam and Bowen, written at virtually the same time by two activist Chicagoans, differ in important ways that reflect the different gender perspectives on the city. Merriam's city is one of political structures, politicians, and political campaigns. In his memoir, he seems to float above the city as a disinterested observer. The only true exception to this perspective comes when he describes his own political campaigns. Bowen, on the other hand, situates herself directly into the city. The first chapter of each book sets the tone and perspective. Merriam's is an analytical account of "How Chicago Came to Be," in which political and economic growth tell the story. In Bowen's first chapter, "A Grandchild in Early Chicago," the growth of the city is seen through the experiences of a young girl. The city's rough and tumble character is exposed in her account of another little girl being crushed against a lamppost by a runaway horse. But this was not just a story of an accident in a "frontier" city. Bowen went on to describe how the little girl's family had no money to pay for a doctor. Witnessing this incident and its aftermath gave Bowen her first direct experience with poverty and social injustice. Then, when she attempted to collect money to pay for a doctor for the little girl, she discovered the limits to private charity and dependence on "the kindness of strangers."

Merriam, of course, had not been born in Chicago but arrived there as a young man, so he could not speak of such early experiences. Yet aside from his own political campaigns, his experiences of the city and its people are never revealed. He forthrightly declares on his first page that his is a backward view that "only for the purposes of a more intimate view of urban politics, there are sketched [in this account] the broad features of this great drama of urban life, losing to be sure much of the color and motion of the picture." Among those "broad features" that he says he only "sketches" are "racial elements . . . measures for communication, health, safety, comfort and culture." One finishes his book knowing much about important people, political campaigns, organizations, and statistics on race, religion, and sex, but little about life in the city. When Louise Bowen situates herself in the city, on the other hand, she is able to convey to us how she grew and learned to see the city through other people's eyes and to understand their experiences from their perspective.

In an analysis of the differences between men's and women's novels about Chicago, Sidney Bremer found this same distinction in tone and perspective. Bremer contends that "men's novels use objectifying observations to comprehend the city, while the women's novels advance personal experience to understand urban reality." This distinction is clearly at work in the memoirs of Merriam and Bowen. Merriam begins his introduction saying, "The observations contained in the following chapters are based upon some twenty-eight years of residence in Chicago." Bowen, in her preface begins, "In writing the following record I feel as though I had dug up my whole life." Their last pages reflect the same differences. Merriam closes with abstract observations that might well fit any number of cities.

> The strength of Chicago lies in its broad economic basis, in its new blend of racial types, in its dynamic energy and drive, in its free spirit and its free position, in its open way to leadership of urban progress. These are not destiny itself, but the materials out of which the garment may be woven on the loom of time.

Bowen ends her memoir again personalizing the city.

> Chicago—peopled by indomitable early settlers with energy, courage and perseverance, and, above all, with vision. They saw the great advantages of a situation at the foot of the Great Lakes, surrounded by the fertile corn and wheat fields of the West, and they laid the foundation of what is soon to be, not only one of the largest, but one of the most beautiful cities in the world.

This same distinction between objectifying and personalizing character-izes the differences between architect Jens Jensen and activist Anna Nicholes when they spoke about a city of homes.

Several other elements of Bremer's analysis apply to the analysis of the gender differences between women and men activists. "Women's novels," Bremer argues, "present Chicago through its inhabitants, not as phenom-enon over and apart from them." Women's novels also "present urban interdependence" rather than emphasize "masculine individualism." Women novelists were "more participants than observers in local affairs." The Chicagoans of Edith Wyatt's novel *True Love*, according to Bremer, "are all part of a family network. . . . [I]ts Chicago is not a socially frag-mented, profiteering machine."[10] The novelist Edith Wyatt was also a di-rector of the WCC and a member of the Consumers' League and other women's organizations.

Activist Chicago women did have some victories at fashioning a more livable city that emphasized homes as well as business. It seems plausible to conclude that their efforts helped save the city's lakefront for free, public recreation rather that turning it into a working harbor. They secured pub-lic bathhouses at a time when many of the city's residents had no other alternatives for bathing. They were responsible for forcing the city to ac-cept responsibility for citywide garbage collection, a move that promised to improve health and sanitation in all areas of the city, not just in those that could, or would, pay for it. They opened the city's spaces to women. By the early 1930s, Chicago women refused to be excluded from any pub-lic places—social, economic, or political. If they had not officially made it onto the city council, they did appear there as citizens. Courts and jails, the Cook County Board of Commissioners, mayoral administrations, picket lines, mass outdoor meetings, hospitals and clinics, and at least a few appointed positions, were open to women. Their presence in these places and the voices they raised once there, did change the relationship of Chicago residents to their city in important ways. Women workers gained more protection on picket lines. Working-class children were not automatically tracked into vocational education. Orphaned children were not simply warehoused into institutions. Women and children did receive better health care. Better and more readily available recreational facilities dotted the city as well as the lakefront. The special milk commission set up by women's organizations resulted in 1908 in Chicago's becoming the first municipality to require that its milk supply be pasteurized.[11]

The Women's Worlds Fairs, which activist women held for four years beginning in 1925, must have braced women's optimism, convincing them that by working together as women they would continue to effect change. The purpose of the fairs was to exhibit women's ideas, work, and products, and to serve as a vocational clearinghouse for women and girls

seeking employment, trades, and professions, while at the same time raising money for women's political party and voluntary organizations. The
1925 Fair, held in the American Exhibition Palace, drew over one hundred
sixty thousand visitors to a week-long exhibit "demonstrating the progress
made by women in the Arts, in Literature, in Science, and in Industry."
There were almost three hundred booths representing one hundred occu-
pations. The 1927 Fair, held in May at the Coliseum, showed activist
women's continuing concern with supporting women's causes and organizations. Proceeds from that year's fair, with its 238 booths, were ear-
marked for the Immigrants' Protective League and the Chicago Public
School Art Society. The exhibitors at the fairs reflected a continuing wom-
en's alliance in the city: Hull House, the Illinois Federation of Women's
Clubs, the Illinois Club for Catholic Women, the IFCWC, Business and
Professional Women, the CWTUL, the YWCA, the Auxiliary House of
the Good Shepherd (run by Roman Catholic nuns), the Visiting Nurses
Association, and the Women's Bar Association. African American clubwomen presented a pageant at the 1927 fair. The connections that activist
women still made between politics and female voluntary organizations
was reflected in their holding a Democratic Day, a Republican Day, and a
Club Women's Day. Neither party politics nor women's groups was to take
precedence, but they were to work together for a better city. That the chair
of the 1927 Fair was staunch Democrat Elizabeth Bass and the honorary
chair was progressive Republican Louise de Koven Bowen also showed
how activist Chicago women believed during the 1920s that they had to
come together across party lines on issues of concern to women.[12]

Yet beyond all the expansion of women's role and place in the city,
beyond all their hard work and successes, activist women could not
achieve their big goal. They could not turn Chicago from the City of Big
Shoulders into a City of Homes. In the end, men tightly held to the reins
of political power in the city. A city organized on a model of social interdependence did not replace a city organized on a model of masculine individualism and striving. The City Profitable largely triumphed over the
City Livable.

NEITHER appendix A nor B is meant to be a conclusive listing of all these women's club memberships or public and political activities. Tracking the lives, memberships, and activities of all but the most prominent of women in this time period is difficult. Even the entries of the most prominent of them, such as Ellen Henrotin, are undoubtedly incomplete. Rather, I include these appendixes to provide as much information as I can that shows the connections women made through their voluntary organizations, their common concerns, and their common crusades. But even more important, they help illustrate what I mean by activist women as defined in the introduction. Whenever possible, I listed a woman's family name or her husband's first name because women often listed themselves by their married name. In a few cases I have never discovered a woman's first name.

Selection Criteria

Appendix A includes women who were active in multiple organizations, worked over decades, participated in more than one public or political action. Appendix B includes women who were active in fewer organizations and worked over less time, but who contributed to women's activism. I also used this category to include some ethnic, African American, and working-class women about whom it is difficult to construct a fuller picture of their possible activities and for whom it seemed important to show that they were active.

For both appendixes, I usually excluded the following: membership or work not exclusively tied to Chicago, for example the Women's Board of the Columbian Exposition; investigations undertaken principally as occupational duties or privately within clubs, for example the Breckinridge and Abbott housing surveys; women whose only activities seemed confined to suffrage, for example Antoinette Funk.

Names of women are sometimes spelled differently in various sources, and organizations can be referred to as a league or a club. I have tried to choose the most common version.

Appendix A

Abbott, Edith, 1876–1957. Occupation: faculty member Chicago School of Civics and Philanthropy. Clubs and organizations: WCC, CPEL, LWV, IPL. Public and political activities: investigator in 1914 waitresses' strike; Social Service

Non-partisan Committee of Cook County Supporting Thomas Courtney, 1932 Democratic candidate for state's attorney

Abbott, Grace, 1878–1939. Occupation: social reformer, second head of U.S. Children's Bureau. Clubs and organizations: WCC, CPEL, IPL, JPA. Public and political activities: citizens' committee to investigate 1910 garment workers' strike; directed campaign committee for Vittum and McDowell for county commissioner in 1914; WCC 19th ward leader; addressed 1916 Woman's Municipal Platform meeting; 1916 suffrage parade

Addams, Jane, 1860–1935. Occupation: settlement house director. Clubs and organizations: Bureau of Justice, CWC, WCC, CPEL, CWTUL. Public and political activities: speaker at 1900 mass meeting to support teachers' tax crusade; member board of education; leader in women's 1907 anti-charter campaign; lobbied for woman suffrage in Springfield in 1909; citizens' committee to investigate 1910 garment workers' strike; attended 1912 Progressive Party national convention in Chicago; led delegation of women protesting Ella Flagg Young's dismissal as superintendent of schools in 1913; speaker at first anniversary celebration of founding of ASC; speaker at February 1914 women's registration rally; financial contribution to Harriet Vittum's 1914 aldermanic campaign and served on campaign committee; investigator in 1914 waitresses' strike; Committee of 100 women for Charles Merriam in 1919; marched with McKinley, McDowell, and Vittum in 1919 against recent racial rioting; attended 1920 LWV organizational meeting; participant in 1927 women's mass march to re-elect Mayor Dever; 1932 women's Independent Horner for Governor committee

Bass, Elizabeth (Mrs. George), -1950. Clubs and organizations: CWC, CPEL, WDC. Public and political activities: speaker at 1913 CWC symposium on "The Colored People of Chicago"; led delegation of women protesting Ella Flagg Young's dismissal as superintendent of schools in late 1913; speaker at February 1914 women's registration rally; co-chair, CWC Public Affairs committee that monitored the city council, Cook County Board of Commissioners and board of education; 1915 meeting to protest county board plan to eliminate Public Welfare Bureau; campaign speaker for Democratic mayoral candidates, 1915, 1919, 1927; addressed 1916 Women's Municipal Platform meeting; speaker at 1920 LWV organizational meeting; chaired 1927 Women's Worlds Fair; 1927 women's mass march to re-elect Mayor Dever; speaker's committee for Ruth Hanna McCormick congressional campaign, 1928; 1932 campaign rallies for Horner for Governor and Roosevelt for President

Bowen, Louise (deKoven), 1859–1953. Clubs and organizations: Bureau of Justice, Hull House Woman's Club, WCC, CPEL, CESA, LWV, Juvenile Court Committee [became Juvenile Protective Agency in 1909], JPA, WRRC. Public and political activities: citizens' committee to investigate 1910 garment workers' strike; speaker at February 1914 women's registration rally; financial contribution to Harriet Vittum's 1914 aldermanic campaign; investigator in 1914 waitresses' strike; 1915 meeting to protest county board plan to eliminate Public Welfare Bureau; chaired 1916 Woman's Municipal Platform meeting; attended 1920 LWV organizational meeting; chaired 1922 women's republican rally against municipal candidates linked to William Hale Thompson; considered running for mayor in 1923; chaired Women's Worlds Fairs; member 1927 Independent Republican [Mayor] Dever committee; active supporter of Ruth Hanna McCormick's 1928 congressional campaign; 1932 women's Independent Horner for Governor committee

Breckinridge, Sophonisba, 1866–1948. Occupation: faculty member Chicago School of Civics and Philanthropy, Professor of Social Economy University of Chicago. Clubs and organizations: WCC, CPEL, IPL, CWTUL, LWV, Legal Aid Society. Public and political activities: citizens' committee to investigate 1910 garment workers' strike; speaker at 1913 CWC symposium on "The Colored People of Chicago"; campaign committee for Vittum and McDowell for county commissioner in 1914; 1915 meeting to protest county board plan to eliminate Public Welfare Bureau; addressed 1916 Woman's Municipal Platform meeting; women's campaign committee for Charles Merriam for mayor 1919; Committee of 100 women to elect Representative Morton Hull in 1923; 1932 women's Independent Horner for Governor committee

Brown, Corinne (Stubbs), 1849–1914. Occupation: teacher. Clubs and organizations: LFLU, IWA, PAWC, CWTUL, Woodlawn Reading Club, Woodlawn Woman's Club, Economics Club, Socialist Women's League of Chicago, West Side Equal Suffrage Association. Public and political activities: 1893 Socialist Party candidate for University of Illinois trustee; patron for CTF "Tax Fund" Benefit and rally; speaker for 1907 anti-charter campaign

Cheney, Flora (Sylvester), 1872–1929. Occupation: teacher. Clubs and organizations: WCC, CPEL, IESA, LWV, League of Women Voters' Forum (successor to CESA). Public and political activities: Committee of 100 women to elect Representative Morton Hull in 1923; People's Dever for Mayor committee and participant in women's mass march to re-elect Dever in 1927; elected to Illinois house from 5th District in 1928

Davis, Elizabeth (Lindsay), 1855–1944. Occupation: teacher and writer. Clubs and organizations: Ida B. Wells, IFCWC, City Federation of Colored Women's Clubs [later renamed Chicago and Northern District], Phyllis Wheatley Women's Club, WCC, Hyde Park Woman's Club, 2nd ward branch of WCC, CPEL [this was possibly a CESA membership], League of Women Voters' Forum. Public and political activities: established the Phyllis Wheatley Home for African American girls; member first WCC citizenship training class

Flower, Lucy (Coues), 1837–1921. Clubs and organizations: CWC, Woman's League, PAWC, JPA. Public and political activities: led movement to establish Illinois Training School for Nurses (subsequently Cook County School of Nursing); member of board of education; led movement to enact compulsory school attendance laws; trustee of the University of Illinois; helped establish the Juvenile Court; patron for CTF "Tax Fund" Benefit and rally

Gaines, Irene (McCoy), 1892–1964. Occupation: stenographer in Juvenile Court, case worker for Cook County welfare department. Clubs and organizations: CWTUL, IFRCWC, Chicago Northern District Federation of Colored Women's Clubs, WCC, LWV. Public and political activities: marched in 1914 Chicago suffrage parade; 2nd ward leader for WCC employment services; industrial secretary of YWCA; leader in Ruth Hanna McCormick's 1930 senatorial campaign

Haley, Margaret, 1861–1939. Occupation: teacher and labor organizer. Clubs and organizations: CTF, CFL, CPEL, IESA, Hull House Woman's Club. Public and political activities: led teachers' corporate tax reassessment crusade; organized CTF citizen vigilance committees in 1902; speaker at February 1914 women's registration rally; attended 1920 LWV organization meeting; speaker for municipal Democratic candidates 1923, 1924; supported Agnes Nestor's Illinois house campaign, 1928

Hefferan, Helen (Maley), 1865–1953. Occupation: teacher trainer. Clubs and organizations: Englewood Woman's Club, Illinois Catholic Women's Association, Illinois Congress of Parents and Teachers, LWV, WCC, CWC, Women's Legislative Congress. Public and political activities: speaker for 1907 anti-charter campaign; member Voluntary Advisory Board to Department of Welfare; public endorsement of Sweitzer for mayor in 1915; addressed 1916 Woman's Municipal Platform meeting; Committee of 100 women for Charles Merriam for mayor in 1919; member board of education; public speaker for LWV; participant in 1927 women's mass march to re-elect Mayor Dever; 1932 campaign rallies for Horner for Governor and Roosevelt for President; Citizens' School Committee in 1933

Henrotin, Ellen (Martin), 1847–1922. Clubs and organizations: CWC, WCC, CPEL, Fortnightly, CWTUL, PAWC, juvenile court committee, Amanda Smith Industrial School for Girls, Children's Hospital Society. Public and political activities: led CWC petition drive for women on board of education; addressed eight-hour work day rally in 1894; worked for female taxpayer suffrage in 1902; honorary chair, Committee for Extension of Equal Municipal Suffrage; presided at municipal suffrage forum at 1907 NAWSA convention in Chicago; lobbied for the juvenile court bill and for woman suffrage in Springfield; chaired citizens' committee to investigate 1910 garment workers' strike; trustee of University of Illinois; public endorsement of Sweitzer for mayor in 1915

Ickes, Anna (Wilmarth), 1873–1935. Clubs and organizations: CWC, Fortnightly, WCC, CWTUL, LWV. Public and political activities: furnished bond for arrested women pickets and gave court testimony against police in waitresses' strike of 1914; campaign committee for Vittum and McDowell for county commissioner in 1914; member of Chicago Government Planning Commission in mid-1920s; served on board of trustees of University of Illinois and three terms in Illinois House

Lathrop, Julia, 1858–1932. Occupation: social worker, settlement house resident, faculty of Chicago School of Civics and Philanthropy. Clubs and organizations: CWC, Juvenile Court Committee, Hull House Woman's Club, WCC, LWV. Public and political activities: lobbied for the juvenile court bill in Springfield; speaker to neighborhood women's clubs; first head of the U.S. Children's Bureau; financial contributor to Agnes Nestor's 1928 congressional campaign

McCormick, Ruth (Hanna), 1880–1944. Clubs and organizations: CWC, WCC, CWTUL, IESA. Public and political activities: investigator in 1914 waitresses' strike; marched with Irene McCoy Gaines in 1914 suffrage parade; picketed in support of arrested striking garment workers in 1915; organized Women's Worlds Fairs; served one term in the U.S. Congress, 1928; ran for U.S. Senate seat in 1930

McCulloch, Catharine (Waugh), 1862–1945 Occupation: lawyer. Clubs and organizations: CWC, CPEL, CESA, IESA, WCC, IWDC, LWV. Public and political activities: proposed a township suffrage bill in 1901; leader in women's 1907 anti-charter campaign; lobbied for woman suffrage in Springfield in 1909; speaker at February 1914 women's registration rally; chaired CWC Constitutional Convention Committee; publicly supported Dever for mayor in 1923; attended 1920 LWV organizational meeting; supported Agnes Nestor's 1928 congressional campaign

McDowell, Mary, 1854–1936. Occupation: settlement house director. Clubs and organizations: CWC, CWTUL, WCC, IESA, LWV. Public and political activities: speaker for 1907 anti-charter campaign; lobbied for woman suffrage in Springfield in 1909; led women's campaign for municipal ownership of garbage collection and reduction; speaker at 1913 CWC symposium on "The Colored People of Chicago"; ran for Cook County commissioner in 1914; organized 29th ward Woman's Civic League; spoke to Women's Socialist League during 1914 municipal elections; 1915 meeting to protest county board plan to eliminate Public Welfare Bureau; attended 1915 mass meeting to support the CTF against the Loeb Rule; led women's delegation to Mayor Thompson to protest his appointments to Department of Welfare; member of Independent Dever Club; marched with McKinley, Addams, and Vittum in 1919 against recent racial rioting and helped form an Interracial Cooperative Committee of women's clubs; appointed commissioner of public welfare by Mayor Dever; Dever appointee to city housing commission; participant in 1927 women's mass march to re-elect Mayor Dever; speaker's committee for Ruth Hanna McCormick 1928 congressional campaign; 1932 women's Independent Horner for Governor committee; led WCC civic welfare committee meeting endorsing Horner for governor in 1932

Morrison, Mary (Foulke). Clubs and organizations: LWV, CESA, WCC. Public and political activities: picketed with striking garment workers in 1915; 1915 meeting to protest county board plan to eliminate Public Welfare Bureau; addressed 1916 Woman's Municipal Platform meeting; president of ILWV

Nestor, Agnes, 1880–1948. Occupation: gloveworker and union organizer. Clubs and organizations: CWTUL, LWV, WCC, CFL. Public and political activities: lobbied in Springfield for municipal suffrage; investigator in 1914 waitresses' strike; campaign committee for Vittum and McDowell for county commissioner in 1914; addressed 1916 Woman's Municipal Platform meeting; attended 1920 LWV organization meeting; public speaker for LWV; participant in 1927 women's mass march to re-elect Mayor Dever; member of Chicago Government Planning Commission in mid-1920s; ran as Democratic challenger for nomination to Illinois House of Representatives in 1928; member of 1932 Woman's Independent Horner for Governor Committee

Nicholes, Anna, 1865–1917. Occupation: social worker, settlement house resident. Clubs and organizations: Englewood Woman's Club, Neighborhood House Woman's Club, CWTUL, WCC. Public and political activities: spoke at municipal suffrage forum at 1907 NAWSA convention in Chicago on need for ballot for working women; speaker for 1907 anti-charter campaign; lobbied in Springfield for municipal suffrage; member of Cook County Civil Service Commission; 1915 meeting to protest county board plan to eliminate Public Welfare Bureau

Purvin, Jennie (Franklin), 1873–1958. Clubs and organizations: CWC, CWA, WCC, LWV. Public and political activities: organized WCC 3rd ward branch; considered running for 3rd ward alderman in 1914; leader of WCC Bathing Beach Committee's movement to build small recreational beaches along the lake especially for children; member Voluntary Advisory Board to Department of Welfare; 1915 meeting to protest county board plan to eliminate Public Welfare Bureau; Committee of 100 women for Charles Merriam in 1919; member of 1923 Women's Independent Dever committee

Robins, Margaret (Dreier), 1868–1945. Occupation: union organizer. Clubs and organizations: CWTUL, WCC, CFL. Public and political activities: spoke at municipal suffrage forum at 1907 NAWSA convention in Chicago on civic duty of women; led 1907 WTUL parade to protest murder charges against members of Industrial Workers of the World; speaker for 1907 anti-charter campaign; lobbied in Springfield for municipal suffrage; treasurer of WTUL strike committee during 1910 garment workers' strike; speaker at February 1914 women's registration rally; executive committee for Harriet Vittum's aldermanic campaign; investigator in 1914 waitresses' strike; 1915 meeting to protest county board plan to eliminate Public Welfare Bureau; Committee of 100 women for Charles Merriam for mayor in 1919; member of 1923 Women's Independent Dever club; member of 1927 People's Dever for Mayor campaign

Sears, Amelia. Clubs and organizations: WCC, CWTUL. Public and political activities: Director Cook County bureau of public welfare; assistant general superintendent of United Charities; women's campaign committee for Charles Merriam for mayor in 1919; participant in 1927 women's mass march to re-elect Mayor Dever; elected Cook County commissioner in 1930

Sikes, Madeleine (Wallin), 1868–1955. Clubs and organizations: Association of Collegiate Alumnae, Woman's Club of Austin, CWC, WCC, Consumers' League, League of Cook County Clubs, 33rd ward civic league, LWV. Public and political activities: speaker to neighborhood women's clubs for ACA and LWV; campaign to stop dismissal of Ella Flag Young as superintendent of schools; women's campaign committee for Charles Merriam for Mayor in 1919

Smith, Julia (Holmes Abbot), 1838–1930. Occupation: doctor. Clubs and organizations: PAWC, Bureau of Justice, Cook County Suffrage Association, Fortnightly, CWC, WCC, CPEL, Illinois Women's Democratic League, 1923 Women's Democratic Club for Dever. Public and political activities: trustee of University of Illinois; public support for Maclay Hoyne for mayor in 1919 and Dever for mayor in 1923; attended 1920 LWV organization meeting

Solomon, Hannah (Greenebaum), 1858–1942. Clubs and organizations: CWC, WCC, Council of Jewish Women, Women's Democratic Council for Good Government. Public and political activities: helped found Bureau of Associated Charities in 7th ward [later Bureau of Personal Service]; public endorsement of Sweitzer for mayor in 1915; 1915 meeting to protest county board plan to eliminate Public Welfare Bureau; marched in 1916 suffrage parade; women's campaign committee for Charles Merriam for mayor in 1919; led WCC Civic Welfare Committee meeting endorsing Horner for governor in 1932

Starr, Ellen Gates, 1859–1940: Occupation: settlement house director. Clubs and
organizations: Chicago Public School Art Society, CWTUL, Bureau of Justice.
Public and political activities: member 1910 garment workers' strike committee;
arrested for supporting striking waitresses in 1914; ran for University of Illinois
trustee; arrested while picketing with striking garment workers in 1915; ran for
alderman of 19th ward as a Socialist

Vittum, Harriet, 1872–1953. Occupation: nurse, settlement house director. Clubs
and organizations: WCC, CWC, JPA, CWTUL, Chicago League of Mothers'
Clubs, Children's Home and Aid Society. Public and political activities: citizens'
committee to investigate 1910 garment workers' strike; investigator in 1914
waitresses' strike; ran for Cook County commissioner and alderman of 17th
ward in 1914; co-chair, CWC Public Affairs Committee that monitored the
city council, Cook County Board of Commissioners, and board of education;
meeting to protest county board plan to eliminate Public Welfare Bureau; member Voluntary Advisory Board to Department of Welfare; addressed 1916 Woman's Municipal Platform meeting; spoke at City Club; women's campaign committee for Charles Merriam for mayor in 1919, then backed Hoyne for mayor;
marched with Addams, McKinley, and McDowell in 1919 against recent racial
rioting; committee to elect Arthur Lueder mayor in 1923; participant in 1927
women's mass march to re-elect Mayor Dever; speaker's committee for Ruth
Hanna McCormick's 1928 congressional campaign; women's independent
committee for Horner for governor

Wells-Barnett, Ida, 1862–1931. Occupation: journalist, civil rights activist. Clubs
and organizations: Ida B. Wells Club, Alpha Suffrage Club, Negro Fellowship
League, Frederick Douglass Center Woman's Club, CPEL, IESA, Conference
of Women's Republican Clubs. Public and political activities: co-founder of
Frederick Douglass Center; speaker to settlement house women's clubs; first
African American adult probation officer in municipal court; led delegation of
African American women to Springfield to lobby against racist legislation in
1913; campaign committee for Vittum and McDowell for county commissioner
in 1914; organized campaign to elect African American alderman in 2nd ward
1914 and 1915; founded women's 2nd ward Republican club and 3rd ward
women's political club; public support for Maclay Hoyne for mayor in 1919;
attended 1920 LWV organization meeting; ran for delegate to Republican national convention in 1928; ran for state senate in 1930

Williams, Fannie (Barrier), 1855–1944. Clubs and organizations: Prudence Crandall Study Club, Phyllis Wheatley Club, IWA, CWC, CPEL [this was possibly
a CESA membership]. Public and political activities: co-founder of Frederick
Douglass Center; spoke at municipal suffrage forum at 1907 NAWSA convention in Chicago; speaker at 1913 CWC symposium on "The Colored People of
Chicago"; campaign committee for Vittum and McDowell for county commissioner in 1914; member Chicago library board

Wilmarth, Mary (Hawes), 1837–1919. Clubs and organizations: Fortnightly,
CWC, WCC, CPEL, Consumers' League, Bureau of Justice. Public and political
activities: trustee of Frederick Douglass Center; 1st ward leader of WCC; citizens' committee to investigate 1910 garment workers' strike; picketed during
1910 garment workers' strike and bailed out arrested strikers; attended 1912

Progressive Party national convention in Chicago; speaker at 1913 CWC symposium on "The Colored People of Chicago"; financially supported Harriet Vittum's aldermanic campaign; investigator in 1914 Waitresses' Strike; 1915 meeting to protest county board plan to eliminate Public Welfare Bureau; furnished bond for Ellen Gates Starr in 1915

Woolley, Celia (Parker), 1848–1918. Occupation: minister. Clubs and organizations: Fortnightly, CWC, PAWC, CPEL, WCC. Public and political activities: patron for CTF "Tax Fund" Benefit and rally; held interracial meetings in her home; co-founder of Frederick Douglass Center

Yarros, Rachelle (Slobodinsky), 1869–1946. Occupation: doctor. Clubs and organizations: CWTUL, WCC, LWV, Illinois Birth Control League, Chicago Citizens' Committee on Birth Control. Public and political activities: led WCC Social Hygiene Committee and movement to disseminate birth control information; opened nation's second birth control clinic; speaker for LWV

Appendix B

Adams, Sadie. Clubs and organizations: Ida B. Wells-Barnett Club, Alpha Suffrage Club, CFCWC. Public and political activities: marched under ASC banner in Washington, D.C., suffrage parade; attended IESA meetings

Allen, Anna. Occupation: nurse, settlement house resident. Clubs and organizations: WCC, University of Chicago Settlement Woman's Club. Public and political activities: spoke to University of Chicago Settlement Woman's Club urging the women to register and vote.

American, Sadie, 1862–1944. Clubs and organizations: Young Ladies' Aid Society [renamed Chicago Woman's Aid Society in 1896]; CWC. Public and political activities: secured money from the city council to build small parks; member of citizens' education committee to amend the Harper education proposal

Anderson, Mary. Occupation: boot and shoe maker, union organizer. Clubs and organizations: CWTUL, WCC. Public and political activities: headed Women's Bureau in Washington, D.C.

Barnum, Gertrude. Clubs and organizations: CWC, Hull House Woman's Club, CWTUL. Public and political activities: member 1910 garment workers' strike committee and strike speakers' committee

Bartelme, Mary, 1866–1954. Occupation: lawyer, judge. Clubs and organizations: CWC, CPEL, WCC, LWV. Public and political activities: Cook County public guardian; juvenile court judge; financial contribution to Harriet Vittum's 1914 aldermanic campaign

Bedell, Leila. Occupation: doctor. Clubs and organizations: Woman's League, CWC, PAWC, Industrial Art Association. Public and political activities: organized the Woman's League

Bemis, Annie (Sargent). Clubs and organizations: WCC, LWV. Public and political activities: member Voluntary Advisory Board to Department of Welfare; attended trustee meetings of the Sanitary District and addressed women's clubs on municipal sanitation issues; speaker to Chicago women's organizations for LWV; elected Cook County commissioner

Berolzheimer, Beulah. Occupation: teacher. Clubs and organizations: WCC, Federation of Women High School Teachers. Public and political activities: publicly supported Agnes Nestor's 1928 congressional campaign

Blackwelder, Gertrude (Mrs. I.S.). Clubs and organizations: CWC, WCC, CPEL. Public and political activities: member of citizens' education committee to amend the Harper education proposal. Public and political activities: leader of the CWC Public Affairs Committee that monitored the city council, Cook County Board of Commissioners and board of education

Blacklidge, Myrtle. Clubs and organizations: Illinois Women's Republican League. Public and political activities: directed 1919 Olson for mayor women's organization; ran for Cook County commissioner in 1922; worked in Ruth Hanna McCormick's 1928 congressional campaign

Britton, Gertrude (Howe). Clubs and organizations: Hull House Woman's Club, WCC. Public and political activities: member board of education; investigated and published in 1906 study on truancy problem at public schools; supported Ida Fursman's legal challenge to the Loeb Rule; public support for Maclay Hoyne for mayor in 1919

Brown, Caroline M (Mrs. Frank B). Clubs and organizations: CWC, Bureau of Justice, PAWC

Byron (Bryon), Mary C. Occupation: employed by Juvenile Court. Clubs and organizations: WCC. Public and political activities: NAWSA suffrage organizer for African American women

Deach, Inez (Rodgers). Clubs and organizations: WCC 18th ward leader. Public and political activities: 1915 meeting to protest county board plan to eliminate Public Welfare Bureau; member Voluntary Advisory Board to Department of Welfare

Dean, Emily (Washburn), 1870–1956. Clubs and organizations: WCC, WRRC, IWRC. Public and political activities: delegate-at-large candidate to 1924 Republican convention; 1922 candidate for Cook County commissioner; Women's Worlds Fair of 1925; publicly supported Anton Cermak for mayor in 1931

DeBey, Cornelia, 1865–1948. Occupation: doctor. Clubs and organizations: CWC, WCC, CPEL. Public and political activities: patron for CTF "Tax Fund" Benefit and rally; lobbied state legislature for a child labor bill; mediator in 1904 stockyards' and 1905 teamsters' strikes; member board of education

Dickinson, Frances, 1856–1945. Occupation: doctor. Clubs and organizations: IWA, PAWC, CWC, LFLU, CPEL, Socialist Women's League. Public and political activities: organized and led the IWA Ward and Precinct Committee; presided at 1914 Socialist Women's League meeting to consider suffrage and the garbage question [addressed by Mary McDowell]

Dobyne, Margaret. Clubs and organizations: CPEL, IESA, WCC. Public and political activities: a leader of the CWC Public Affairs Committee that monitored the city council, Cook County Board of Commissioners and board of education; member Voluntary Advisory Board to Department of Welfare; 1915 meeting to protest county board plan to eliminate Public Welfare Bureau; worked in 1915 William Hale Thompson campaign

Drake, Marion. Occupation: lawyer. Clubs and organizations: CWC, CPEL, WCC, WCC 1st ward leader. Public and political activities: 1914 candidate for

1st ward alderman; spoke to Wage Earners' Suffrage League urging working women to register to vote; leader of the CWC Public Affairs Committee that monitored the city council, Cook County Board of Commissioners and board of education

Emanuel, Fannie (Hagen), 1871–1934. Occupation: doctor. Clubs and organizations: Ida B. Wells Club, IFCWC, Phyllis Wheatley Home, president of Alpha Suffrage Club, Frederick Douglass Center Woman's Club, president of YWCA. Public and political activities: established Emanuel Settlement (1908–12) especially for African American children

Fairbank, Janet (Ayer), 1879–1951. Occupation: novelist. Clubs and organizations: Fortnightly, WCC, IWDC. Public and political activities: delegate-at-large to 1924 Democratic convention; publicly supported Dever for mayor in 1923; led 1927 women's mass march to re-elect Mayor Dever

Fisher, Katherine (Dummer). Clubs and organizations: WCC. Public and political activities: attended CWTUL meetings and made financial contribution to support 1910 striking garment workers; financial contribution to Agnes Nestor's 1928 congressional campaign

Fulmer, Harriet, 1877–1952. Occupation: nurse and superintendent VNA. Public and political activities: instituted summer tent colonies for poor tuberculosis patients, summer baby tents for sick babies, and placement of nurses in industrial plants; speaker to women's neighborhood clubs

Fursman, Ida (Mrs. Frederick). Occupation: teacher. Clubs and organizations: CPEL, CTF. Public and political activities: addressed 1916 Woman's Municipal Platform meeting; 1919 Labor Party candidate for 27th ward alderman

Gallagher, Helen. Clubs and organizations: Catholic Women's League. Public and political activities: member of board of education; speaker at Ella Flagg Young's golden anniversary gala; supported Ida Fursman's legal challenge to the Loeb Rule

Goggin, Catharine, 1855–1916. Occupation: teacher, union organizer. Clubs and organizations: CTF, CPEL. Public and political activities: organized the CTF; sued City of Chicago and board of education in 1899 for not paying teachers according to set pay schedules; presided at 1900 mass meeting to protest non-enforcement of corporate tax laws

Goins, Irene. Occupation: owned millinery shop. Clubs and organizations: LWV, Douglas Branch LWV, CFCWC, IFCWC, CWTUL, YWCA. Public and political activities: worked with Mary McDowell to organize African American stockyards workers; worked with other women in LWV for passage of child labor amendment; organized IFRCWC

Goode, Katherine (Hancock), –1928. Clubs and organizations: WCC Schools Committee, LWV. Public and political activities: speaker to women's clubs for LWV; elected to Illinois House in 1924 and 1926

Gudeman, (Mrs. Edward). Clubs and organizations: CWA, WCC. Public and political activities: made public endorsement of female candidates for Cook County commissioner in 1922

Haines, (Mrs. John C.). Clubs and organizations: Woman's Industrial Aid, Good Samaritan Society. Public and political activities: women's fire relief activities after 1871 fire

Hart, Sara (Mrs. Harry). Clubs and organizations: WCC, CPEL, WRRC. Public and political activities: 1915 meeting to protest county board plan to eliminate Public Welfare Bureau

Hedger, Caroline, 1868–1951. Occupation: doctor. Clubs and organizations: CWC, WCC, CPEL. Public and political activities: helped organize 1913 Chicago child welfare exhibit; medical consultant for Elizabeth McCormick Memorial Fund; campaigned for the Sheppard-Towner legislation

Henry, Alice, 1857–1943. Occupation: journalist and labor organizer. Clubs and organizations: CWTUL, Political Equality League of Self-Supporting Women, West Side Equal Suffrage Association, and IESA. Public and political activities: worked in 1907 anti-charter campaign

Herstein, Lillian, 1886–1983. Occupation: teacher. Clubs and organizations: CTF, CWTUL, CFL. Public and political activities: campaigned for child labor legislation; 1922 candidate for metropolitan sanitary district trustee and 1932 candidate for U.S. House of Representatives both on Farm-Labor Party ticket; financial contribution to Agnes Nestor's 1928 campaign

Hitchcock, Annie (McClure). Clubs and organizations: Fortnightly, CWC, Society of Decorative Art. Public and political activities: organized women's relief activities after the 1871 fire

Huling, Caroline, 1856–1941. Occupation: journalist. Clubs and Organizations: CCSA, IWA. Public and political activities: led campaign to monitor women's treatment in Justice of the Peace courts; spoke to Trades and Labor Assembly about supporting compulsory education laws

Kaneko, Josephine (Conger). Occupation: journalist and socialist party organizer. Clubs and organizations: Socialist Party. Public and political activities: 1914 Socialist candidate for 6th ward alderman; speaker to neighborhood women's clubs

Kavanaugh, Fanny. Clubs and organizations: LFLU, IWA, Chicago Trades & Labor Assembly. Public and political activities: personally visited courts and police stations to observe treatment of arrested women; worked to resolve Pullman Strike

Kelley, Florence, 1859–1932. Occupation: social welfare reformer. Clubs and organizations: Consumers' League. Public and political activities: coauthored 1892 report with Corrine Brown on condition of public schools especially in poorer wards; led anti-sweatshop movement in Chicago; appointed chief state factory inspector in 1893

King, Florence. Occupation: lawyer. Clubs and organizations: WCC, CPEL, IESA, LWV. Public and political activities: 1915 meeting to protest county board plan to eliminate Public Welfare Bureau; public supporter of Hoyne for mayor in 1919

Kretzinger, Clara (Wilson). Clubs and organizations: CWC, CPEL. Public and political activities: helped lead CWC efforts to reform the board of education and place more women on it at turn of the century; member of citizens' education committee to amend the Harper education proposal

Langworthy, Mary (Mrs. B. F.). Clubs and organizations: WCC, CPEL, WRRC. Public and political activities: urged women to vote for women as Cook Country commissioners in 1922; leader in women's mass march to re-elect Dever in

1927; member Chicago Government Planning Commission; financial contribution of Agnes Nestor's 1928 congressional campaign

Lillie, Frances (Crane), 1869–1954. Occupation: physician. Clubs and organizations: PAWC. Public and political activities: funded the children's day nursery at Hull House; 1915 meeting to protest county board plan to eliminate Public Welfare Bureau; arrested while picketing with striking garment workers in 1915; publicly supported 1919 workers' strike against the Crane company (her family's company); financially supported Agnes Nestor's 1928 congressional campaign

Loewenthal, Judith (Mrs. Edward). Clubs and organizations: CWA , CPEL, WCC. Public and political activities: member Chicago Government Planning Commission; active supporter of Ruth Hanna McCormick's 1928 congressional campaign

Loughridge, Jenny. Clubs and organizations: Trades Union Label League, CWTUL, Hull House Woman's Club.

Low, Minnie, 1867–1922. Occupation: social worker. Clubs and organizations: JPA. Public and political activities: headed Bureau of Personal Service; helped found the juvenile court; probation officer for juvenile court; 1915 meeting to protest county board plan to eliminate Public Welfare Bureau; member Voluntary Advisory Board to Department of Welfare

Maloney, Elizabeth, 1880–1921. Occupation: waitress, union leader. Clubs and organizations: CWTUL, Political Equality League of Self-Supporting Women, Wage Earners' Suffrage League. Public and political activities: worked in 1907 anti-charter campaign; lobbied in Springfield for municipal suffrage and labor laws; investigator in 1914 waitresses' strike

Martin, Ellen. Clubs and organizations: CWC, CPEL, CCSA

McDermut, Lida (Mrs. W. E.). Clubs and organizations: WCC, CPEL. Public and political activities: Socialist candidate for 7th ward alderman in 1914

McEnerny, Mary. Occupation: bindery worker and labor organizer. Clubs and organizations: CWTUL, Wage Earners' Suffrage League. Public and political activities: elected Cook County commissioner in 1930; worked in 1932 Horner for governor campaign

McKinley, Ada S. (Dennison), 1868–1952. Occupation: social welfare advocate. Clubs and organizations: LWV, Douglas branch LWV, IFRCWC. Public and political activities: marched with Addams, McDowell and Vittum in 1919 against recent racial rioting; founded South Side Settlement House at 32nd and Wabash; organized African American Douglas branch of LWV

Meder, Leonora (Mrs. John). Occupation: lawyer. Clubs and organizations: Federation of Catholic Women's Charities. Public and political activities: 1915 meeting to protest county board plan to eliminate Public Welfare Bureau; headed Social Services Bureau of Cook County; first appointed city commissioner of public welfare; first woman to serve on a jury in Illinois in 1933

Medill, Katherine (Mrs. Joseph). Woman's Industrial Aid, Chicago Hospital for Women and Children. Public and political activities: organized women's relief activities after the 1871 fire

Mitchell, Ellen. Public and political activities: first woman appointed to the board of education

Morgan, Elizabeth (Chambers), 1850–1944. Clubs and organization: LFLU, IWA. Public and political activities: led IWA committee on public baths; secured appointment by the health commissioner of the first women factory inspectors; secured passage of 1893 state Sweatshop Act; played an important role is convincing city council to fund public baths

Murfey, Rose (Mrs. Edward). Clubs and organizations: Anti-Smoke League, WCC, LWV, CWC. Public and political activities: candidate for delegate-at-large to 1924 Republican convention

Napieralski, Emily. Clubs and organizations: WCC, Polish Women's Alliance. Public and political activities: women's campaign committee for Charles Merriam for mayor 1919, then backed Hoyne for mayor; publicly supported Arthur Lueder for mayor in 1923; active supporter of Ruth Hanna McCormick's 1928 congressional campaign

Nicholes, Grace, 1875– Occupation: social worker, settlement house resident. Clubs and organizations: Englewood Woman's Club, Neighborhood House Woman's Club, WCC, CPEL, IESA. Public and political activities: speaker for 1907 anti-charter campaign

O'Connor, Nellie (Johnson). Clubs and organizations: CWC, WCC, CPEL. Public and political activities: participant in 1913 housing conference organized by City Club; active supporter of Hoyne for mayor in 1919

Pine, Bessie. Public and political activities: organized Northwest Side Jewish Woman's Democracy

Piucinski, Clara. Clubs and organizations: Non-partisan Club of Polish Women of the 29th ward. Public and political activities: petitioned for women's right to serve as poll judges; organized Women's Democratic clubs of Irving Park, Mayfair, Avondale and Jefferson Park neighborhoods

Randall, (Mrs. J. H.). Clubs and organizations: LFLU, IWA, Women's Refuge. Public and political activities: led IWA committee on public baths

Rodgers, Elizabeth (Flynn), 1847–1939. Occupation: labor organizer. Clubs and organizations: Woman's League, Working Women's Union No. 1. Public and political activities: organized first union of household workers

Rutherford, Kathryn. Clubs and organizations: CPEL. Public and political activities: William Hale Thompson supporter in 1915; supported Hoyne for mayor in 1919; candidate for Illinois house in 1924

Sergel, Annie (Mrs. Charles). Clubs and organizations: Anti-Smoke League, CWC, WCC. Public and political activities: organized the women's 1908 anti-smoke crusade; leader of 6th ward WCC

Severin, (Mrs. William). Clubs and organizations: Englewood Woman's Club, WCC, WRC. Public and political activities: 1915 meeting to protest county board plan to eliminate Public Welfare Bureau; publicly supported Olson for mayor in 1915

Sippy, Mabel (Mrs. Bertram). Clubs and organizations: CPEL, WCC. Public and political activities: led Chicago National Woman's Party 1916 campaign to defeat Woodrow Wilson; Committee of 100 women for Charles Merriam in 1919; speaker's committee for Ruth Hanna McCormick 1928 congressional campaign;

Smith, Bessie. Clubs and organizations: Forrestville branch 3rd and 4th ward (colored) WCC

Smith, Maud E. Clubs and organizations: IFCWC, Chicago and Northern District Federation of Colored Women's Clubs

Snowden, Joanna. Occupation: social worker in the juvenile court. Clubs and organizations: JPA, Northwestern Federation of Colored Women's Clubs. Public and political activities: worked in Ruth Hanna McCormick's 1930 senatorial campaign

Steghagen, Emma. Occupation: bootmaker, labor organizer. Clubs and organizations: CWTUL, Wage Earners' Suffrage League. Public and political activities: actively recruited members into the WESL

Stevens, Alzina (Parsons), 1849–1900. Occupation: printer. Clubs and organizations: Working Women's Union No. 1, Dorcas Federal Labor Union, Hull House Woman's Club. Public and political activities: CWC-supported police station juvenile probation officer before founding of juvenile court; juvenile court probation officer

Stevenson, Sarah Hackett, 1841–1909. Occupation: doctor. Clubs and organizations: Fortnightly, PAWC, Children's Aid Society, MOL, CWC. Public and political activities: led movement to establish Illinois Training School for Nurses (subsequently Cook County School of Nursing); led movement to establish free public baths

Stewart, Ella (Seass), 1871–1945. Clubs and organizations: IESA, CWC, WCC, CPEL. Public and political activities: worked for female taxpayer suffrage in 1902; speaker for women's 1907 anti-charter campaign; addressed Bohemian Women's Citizens Club urging members to register to vote in 1914; 1915 meeting to protest county board plan to eliminate Public Welfare Bureau; financial contribution to Agnes Nestor's 1928 congressional campaign

Sweet, Ada, 1852–1928. Occupation: U.S. pension agent and journalist. Clubs and organizations: CWC, MOL, PAWC. Public and political activities: presided over an 1892 mass public meeting to protest against private contracting of street cleaning; speaker for 1907 anti-charter campaign

Temple, Frances (Mrs. Richard). Clubs and organizations: CWC, CPEL, WCC. Public and political activities: member of citizens' education committee to amend the Harper education proposal

Temple, Grace. Clubs and organizations: CWC, CPEL, WCC, LWV. Public and political activities: picketed with striking garment workers in 1915; member of board of education; vice-chair CWC Public Affairs Committee that monitored the city council, Cook County Board of Commissioners and board of education; urged women to vote for women as Cook Country commissioners in 1922

Trainor, Rose. Clubs and organizations: Catholic Women's League, WCC

Treadwell, Harriette Taylor (Mrs. C. H.). Clubs and organizations: LWV, WCC, CPEL. Public and political activities: speaker at February 1914 women's registration rally; 1915 meeting to protest county board plan to eliminate Public Welfare Bureau

Tuley, Katherine (Mrs. Murray). Clubs and organizations: CWC. Public and political activities: leader in movement to place women on board of education; patron for CTF "Tax Fund" Benefit and rally; speaker for 1907 anti-charter campaign

Tunnicliff, Sarah. Clubs and organizations: WCC, LWV, Women's Section Department of Fuel Conservation. Public and political activities: as head of WCC clean air and transportation committee, spoke at public hearings, investigated theaters, and coordinated work of women's organizations on these issues; worked with LWV for passage of Sheppard-Towner legislation

Van Der Vaart, Harriet. Occupation: teacher, settlement founder and resident. Clubs and organizations: WCC, CTF, CWTUL. Public and political activities: speaker for 1907 anti-charter campaign; citizens' committee to investigate 1910 garment workers' strike, investigated working conditions of women and children for Illinois bureau of labor

Vosbrink, Florence (Mrs. George). Public and political activities: member of board of education

Waful, Ella. Public and political activities: 1923 candidate for alderman; worked in Ruth Hanna McCormick's 1928 congressional campaign

Waring, Mary (Fitzbutler), 1869–1958. Occupation: teacher and doctor. Clubs and organizations: IFCWC, Women's Second Ward Suffrage League, JPA. Public and political activities: ran for delegate-at-large to 1924 Republican convention

Wells, Eva. Clubs and organizations: 2nd ward (colored) WCC

Witkowsky (Mrs. James). Clubs and organizations: CWA, WCC, CWC. Public and political activities: lobbied in Springfield for municipal suffrage

Wyatt, Edith, 1873–1958. Occupation: writer and novelist. Clubs and organizations: JPA, WCC, Consumers' League, Children's Home & Aid Society. Public and political activities: wrote and published in *Harper's Weekly* an account of the 1915 garment workers' strike

Young, Ella (Flagg), 1845–1918. Occupation: teacher, administrator. Clubs and organizations: CPEL, WCC. Public and political activities: speaker at February 1914 women's registration rally; publicly supported Carter Harrison for major in 1915

Young, Goldie. Public and political activities: organized Northwest Side Jewish Woman's Democracy

Young, Laura (Mrs. William). Clubs and organizations: WCC, Austin Woman's Club. Public and political activities: candidate for 33rd ward alderman in 1919

Notes

Introduction
City of Big Shoulders or City of Homes?

1. Carl Sandburg, "Chicago," in *Chicago Poems* (New York, 1916). Banker quoted in Anna Nicholes, "How Women Can Help in the Administration of a City," *The Woman's Citizen Library* v. 9 (New York, 1913), 2150.

2. Donald L. Miller, *City of the Century: The Epic of Chicago and the Making of America* (New York, 1996), 16–17, and Robert G. Spinney, *City of Big Shoulders: A History of Chicago* (DeKalb, IL, 2000).

3. Sandburg, "Chicago." Joanne Meyerowitz, *Women Adrift: Independent Wage Earners in Chicago, 1880–1930* (Chicago, 1988), used the term "women adrift" to signify both working women's independence and the fear that this new group raised among other urban residents. The images Sandburg used in his much longer poem about Chicago, "Windy City," are little different. In ten sections of hundreds of lines, one stanza speaks of "monotonous houses" (section 5), and the closest he comes to seeing the city as a home is one line: "I am the woman, the home, the family" (section 6). More common are such images as, "Out of the pay day songs of steam shovels, . . . the wages of structural iron rivets, the living lighted skyscrapers. . . . I am Chicago" (section 1), and "The city is a tool chest . . . a time clock . . . a shop door" (section 7). Sandburg, "Windy City," in *Slabs of the Sunburnt West* (New York, 1922). In "Streets Too Old," the old and tired are women: "How old, how old we are:—the walls went on saying, street walls leaning toward each other like old women of the people, like old midwives tired and only doing what must be done." Sandburg, "Streets Too Old," in *Smoke and Steel* (New York, 1920).

4. Nicholes, "How Women Can Help in the Administration of a City," 2150–51.

5. Chicago *Record-Herald*, October 1908.

6. Frederic C. Howe, *The City: The Hope of Democracy* (New York, 1905), *Confessions of a Reformer* (New York, 1925), and *Wisconsin: An Experiment in Democracy* (New York, 1912); Charles E. Merriam, *Chicago: A More Intimate View of Urban Politics* (New York, 1929); Lincoln Steffens, *The Shame of the Cities* (New York, 1904); Brand Whitlock, *Forty Years of It* (New York, 1914); and Clinton R. Woodruff, ed., *City Government by Commission* (New York, 1911) and *A New Municipal Program* (New York, 1919) are representative examples of this literature.

7. See Robert Crunden, *Ministers of Reform: The Progressives' Achievement in American Civilization, 1889–1920* (Urbana, 1984); Ray Ginger, *Altgeld's America: The Lincoln Ideal Versus Changing Realities* (New York, 1958); Samuel P. Hays, *The Response to Industrialism, 1885–1914* (Chicago, 1957) and *Conservation and the Gospel of Efficiency: The Progressive Conservation Movement, 1890–1920* (Cambridge, MA, 1959); Richard Hofstadter, *The Age of Reform: From Bryan to*

F.D.R. (New York, 1955); Michael P. McCarthy, "Businessmen and Professionals in Municipal Reform: The Chicago Experience, 1887–1920" (Ph.D. Dissertation, Northwestern University, 1970); George Mowry, *The California Progressives* (Berkeley, 1951); Martin Schiesl, *The Politics of Efficiency: Municipal Administration and Reform in America, 1880–1920* (Berkeley, 1977); Robert H. Wiebe, *Businessmen and Reform: A Study of the Progressive Movement* (Cambridge, MA, 1962) and *The Search for Order, 1877–1920* (New York, 1967). The overwhelming emphasis on the Progressive Era as a struggle between bosses and reformers can be grasped in review essays by Jon Teaford, "*Finis* for Tweed and Steffens: Rewriting the History of Urban Rule," *Reviews in American History* 10 (December 1982): 133–49, and David Thelen, "Urban Politics Beyond Bosses and Reformers," *Reviews in American History* 7 (September 1979): 406–12. See also Terrence J. McDonald, "The Burdens of Urban History: The Theory of the State in Recent American Social History," *Studies in American Political Development* 3 (1989): 3–29. See Samuel P. Hays, "The Politics of Reform in Municipal Government in the Progressive Era," *Northwest Pacific Quarterly* 55 (October 1964): 157–69 for beginning the upper-class middle-class debate.

   8. John Buenker, *Urban Liberalism and Progressive Reform* (New York, 1973), and J. Joseph Huthmacher, "Urban Liberalism and the Age of Reform," *Mississippi Valley Historical Review* 44 (September 1962): 231–41.

   For examples see James J. Connolly, *The Triumph of Ethnic Progressivism: Urban Political Culture in Boston, 1900–1925* (Cambridge, MA, 1998); Alan Dawley, *Struggles for Justice: Social Responsibility and the Liberal State* (Cambridge, MA, 1991); William Issel, "Class and Ethnic Conflict in San Francisco Political History," *Labor History* 18 (1977): 341–59; Georg Leidenberger, "Working-Class Progressivism and the Politics of Transportation in Chicago, 1895–1907" (Ph.D. Dissertation, University of North Carolina, 1995); Richard Oestreicher, "Urban Working-Class Political Behavior and Theories of American Electoral Politics, 1870–1949," *Journal of American History* 74 (March 1988): 1257–86; Richard Schneirov, *Labor and Urban Politics: Class Conflict and the Origins of Modern Liberalism in Chicago, 1864–1897* (Urbana, 1998); and Shelton Stromquist, "The Crucible of Class: Cleveland Politics and the Origins of Municipal Reform in the Progressive Era," *Journal of Urban History* 23 (January 1997): 192–220.

   9. In this regard, see Amy Bridges, *Morning Glories: Municipal Reform in the Southwest* (Princeton, 1997); Paul Barrett, *The Automobile and Urban Transit: The Formation of Public Policy in Chicago, 1900–1930* (Philadelphia, 1983); Robert B. Fairbanks, *Housing Reform and the Community Development Strategy in Cincinnati, 1890–1960* (Urbana, 1988); Kenneth Finegold, *Experts and Politicians: Reform Challenges to Machine Politics in New York, Cleveland, and Chicago* (Princeton, 1995); David Hammack, *Power and Society: Greater New York at the Turn of the Century* (New York, 1987); Harold L. Platt, *City Building in the New South: The Growth of Public Services in Houston, 1830–1915* (Philadelphia, 1983). For urban political reform as a broader, more general movement, see Philip J. Ethington, *The Public City: The Political Construction of Urban Life in San Francisco, 1850–1900* (Cambridge, UK, 1994); Maureen A. Flanagan, *Charter Reform in Chicago* (Carbondale, IL, 1987); and Terrence J. McDonald, *The Parameters of*

Urban Fiscal Policy: Socioeconomic Change and Political Culture in San Francisco, 1860–1906 (Berkeley, 1986).

10. John Buenker, "Sovereign Individuals and Organic Networks: Political Cultures in Conflict in the Progressive Era," *American Quarterly* 40 (June 1988): 199, and Robert B. Fairbanks, "Rethinking Urban Problems: Planning, Zoning, and City Government in Dallas, 1900–1930," *Journal of Urban History* 25 (September 1999): 810.

11. For examples, see Dawley, *Struggles for Justice*; James Kloppenberg, *Uncertain Victory: Social Democracy and Progressivism in European and American Thought, 1870–1920* (New York, 1986); Daniel T. Rodgers, *Atlantic Crossings: Social Politics in a Progressive Age* (Cambridge, MA, 1998); and Schneirov, *Labor and Urban Politics*. In urban history specifically, see Fairbanks, *Housing Reform*, and Karen Sawislak, *Smoldering City: Chicagoans and the Great Fire, 1871–1874* (Chicago, 1995). For urban environmentalism, see David Stradling, *Smokestacks and Progressives: Environmentalists, Engineers, and Air Quality in America, 1881–1951* (Baltimore, 1999). For examples of works that argue for the importance of gender experiences for shaping ideas, actions, and policy decisions, see Maureen A. Flanagan, "The City Profitable, the City Livable: Environmental Policy, Gender, and Power in Chicago in the 1910s," *The Journal of Urban History* 22 (January 1996):163–90; Angela Gugliotta, "Class, Gender, and Coal Smoke: Gender Ideology and Environmental Injustice in Pittsburgh, 1868–1914," *Environmental History* 5 (April 2000): 165–93; and Landon R. Y. Storrs, *Civilizing Capitalism: The National Consumers' League, Women's Activism, and Labor Standards in the New Deal Era* (Chapel Hill, 2000).

12. Sarah Deutsch, "Learning to Talk More Like a Man: Boston Women's Class-Bridging Organizations, 1870–1940," *American Historical Review* 97 (April 1992): 379–404, and *Women and the City: Gender, Space, and Power in Boston, 1870–1940* (New York, 2000); Gayle Gullett, *Becoming Citizens: The Emergence and Development of the California Women's Movement, 1880–1911* (Urbana, 2000); Sandra Haarsager, *Organized Womanhood: Cultural Politics in the Pacific Northwest, 1840–1920* (Norman, OK, 1997); Judith N. McArthur, *Creating the New Woman: The Rise of Southern Women's Progressive Culture in Texas, 1893–1918* (Urbana, 1998); Anne Meis Knupfer, *Toward a Tenderer Humanity and a Nobler Womanhood: African-American Women's Clubs in Turn-of-the-Century Chicago* (New York, 1996); and Priscilla Murolo, *The Common Ground of Womanhood: Class, Gender, and Working Girls' Clubs, 1884–1928* (Urbana, 1997). In addition see, Mary Murphy, *Men, Women, and Leisure in Butte, 1914–41* (Urbana, 1997); Mary Ryan, *Civic Wars: Democracy and Public Life in the American City during the Nineteenth Century* (Berkeley, 1997); Anne Firor Scott, *Natural Allies: Women's Associations in American History* (Urbana, 1991); and Kathryn Kish Sklar, *Florence Kelley and the Nation's Work: The Rise of Women's Political Culture, 1830–1900* (New Haven, 1995). See also several essays in Noralee Frankel and Nancy S. Dye, eds., *Gender, Class, Race and Reform in the Progressive Era* (Lexington, 1991).

13. For a discussion of the difference, see Maureen A. Flanagan, "Women in the City, Women of the City: Where Do Women Fit in Urban History?" *Journal of Urban History* 23 (March 1997): 251–59. See also Platt, *City Building in the*

New South, for his argument of how urbanization involves the creation of an urban environment, the structuring and restructuring of which constantly pressures urban residents to decide how to maintain and improve it.

14. Paula Baker, "The Domestication of Politics: Women and American Political Society, 1780–1920, *American Historical Review* 89 (June 1984): 641; William Chafe, "Women's History and Political History," in Nancy Hewitt and Suzanne Lebsock, eds., *Visible Women: New Essays on American Activism* (Urbana, 1993), 105 [emphasis mine]; and Sara Evans, "Women's History and Political Theory: Toward a Feminist Approach to Public Life," in Hewitt and Lebsock, eds., *Visible Women*, 119–39. See also Ethington, *The Public City*, 346, for his conclusion that progressivism was a discourse "distinguished by the way people became mobilized and integrated into relations with the state"; and Connolly, *The Triumph of Ethnic Progressivism*, for his discussion of "style" and women's social reform in that city.

15. The first quotation is from Nicholes, "How Women Can Help in the Administration of a City," 2184; the second quotation is from Woman's City Club of Chicago, "Some Reasons" (October 1926), Woman's City Club Manuscript Collection, Box 1, folder 1, Chicago Historical Society. See also this argument applied to environmental issues in Flanagan, "The City Profitable, the City Livable."

16. See Laura Lee Downs, "If 'Woman' Is Just an Empty Category, Then Why Am I Afraid to Walk Alone at Night? Identity Politics Meets the Postmodern Subject," *Comparative Study of Society and History* (1993): 414–51. This essay is an extensive critique of discourse analysis as promoted by Joan Scott. The original essay includes a response from Scott and a counter response from Downs.

17. Louise Tilly, "Gender, Women's History, and Social History," *Social Science History* 13 (Winter 1989): 439–62. And the OECD Conference on Women in the City, *Women in the City: Housing, Services and the Urban Environment, 4–6 October 1994* (Paris, 1995); the quotation is from 13. See also Maureen A. Flanagan, "Women and the Urban Environment: Crossing Borders and Boundaries to Investigate a Gender Perspective," paper presented at "The City in North America: Historical and Comparative Perspectives on Public Works and Urban Services, the Environment, and Political Culture," Mexico City, Mexico, October 2001.

18. The city of Chicago annexed a number of surrounding towns in 1889 and 1893. For the earlier decades covered by this study, thus, some of the women may have lived outside the actual city limits. In the later decades, some activist women lived in surrounding suburbs, although a number of them, such as Catharine Waugh McCulloch, worked in the city. The vast majority of the women and organizations examined in this book, however, lived in and were located in the city itself.

19. Nancy Love, "Ideal Speech and Feminist Discourse: Habermas Re-Visioned," *Women and Politics* 11 (1991): 101–22. Love points out that there can never be a complete community of interest among women because social groups by definition have to decide on inclusion and exclusion and have to emphasize some issues at the expense of others. But human existence is not neat and tidy, and to speak of community or solidarity does not mean to speak of unambiguous homogeneity. Deborah Gray White, *Too Heavy a Load: Black Women in Defense of Themselves, 1894–1994* (New York, 1999), 17–18, makes exactly this point when she describes how African American women have always been divided by social identifications, but how at crucial points in their history they could focus on their

common needs and agendas as black women. Connolly, *The Triumph of Ethnic Progressivism*, makes this same general point for Boston women, although his emphasis on ethnicity precludes a sustained examination of these women; instead he concludes that no female solidarity could succeed when confronted by the ethnic, religious, and neighborhood politics of Boston men (183–84).

20. For some of the general overviews on Chicago's growth, see William Cronon, *Nature's Metropolis: Chicago and the Great West* (New York, 1991); Flanagan, *Charter Reform in Chicago*; Harold M. Mayer and Richard C. Wade, *Chicago: Growth of a Metropolis* (Chicago, 1969); Miller, *The City of the Century*; Bessie Louise Pierce, *A History of Chicago*, vols. 2 and 3 (New York, 1940 and 1957); Harold L. Platt, *The Electric City: Energy and the Growth of the Chicago Area, 1880–1930* (Chicago, 1991); and Donald F. Tingley, *The Structuring of a State: The History of Illinois, 1899–1928* (Urbana, 1980). For Chicago's foreign-born population, see Howard Chudacoff, *The Evolution of American Urban Society* (Englewood Cliffs, NJ, 1981).

21. For industrial accidents, see James R. Barrett, *Work and Community in the Jungle: Chicago's Packinghouse Workers, 1894–1922* (Urbana, 1987), 69 and 109n.10, and Rick Halpern, *Down on the Killing Floor: Black and White Workers in Chicago's Packinghouses, 1904–54* (Urbana, 1997), 42. For streetcar accidents, see Paul Barrett, *The Automobile and Urban Transit*, 18.

22. Jane Addams, *Twenty Years at Hull House* (New York, 1910); Lynne Curry, *Modern Mothers in the Heartland: Gender, Health, and Progress in Illinois, 1900–1930* (Columbus, OH, 1999); and Harold Platt, "Jane Addams and the Ward Boss Revisited: Class, Politics, and Public Health in Chicago, 1890–1930, *Environmental History* 5 (April 2000): 194–222.

23. For a general description of how the attitude that government was more a threat to liberty than a means to implement collective values had limited local government power during the nineteenth century, see Ballard Campbell, *The Growth of American Government: Governance from the Cleveland Era to the Present* (Bloomington, IN, 1995). On the limits of Chicago's early governing system, see Robin L. Einhorn, *Property Rules: Political Economy in Chicago, 1833–1872* (Chicago, 1991). Jon Teaford, *The Unheralded Triumph: City Government in America, 1870–1900* (Baltimore, 1984), and Eric Monkkonen, *America Becomes Urban: The Development of U.S. Cities and Towns, 1780–1980* (Berkeley, 1988), both emphasize the positive activities of municipal government at this time.

24. Sandburg, "Chicago." See Addams, *Twenty Years at Hull House* and *Democracy and Social Ethics* (New York, 1902), 222–23.

25. See Flanagan, *Charter Reform in Chicago*, for conflicting arguments about increasing the power of the municipal government through writing a new municipal charter.

26. Deutsch, *Women and the City*. See her introduction, especially 4–5 and 16, and Daphne Spain, *How Women Saved the City* (Minneapolis, 2001), 14.

27. Protective Agency for Women and Children, "Report from the President 1887," in *Annual Reports, 1887–1905*, Chicago Historical Society.

28. See Flanagan, "Gender and Urban Political Reform: The City Club and the Woman's City Club of Chicago in the Progessive Era," *American Historical Review* 95 (October 1990): 1032–50.

29. As Kristi Andersen put it in her study of women's politics after suffrage, party organizations were not willing to give real power to women activists but "were quite willing to have women share the burden of canvassing, staffing party headquarters, and serving as poll watchers and election judges." Andersen, *After Suffrage: Women in Partisan and Electoral Politics before the New Deal* (Chicago, 1996), 144.

30. See Flanagan, "Gender and Urban Political Reform" and "The City Profitable, the City Livable"; Gugliotta, "Class, Gender, and Coal Smoke"; Robyn Muncy, "Gender and Professionalization in the Origins of the U.S. Welfare State: The Careers of Sophonisba Breckinridge and Edith Abbott, 1890–1935," *Journal of Policy History* 2 (1990): 290–315; and Kathryn Kish Sklar, "Two Political Cultures in the Progressive Era: The National Consumers' League and the American Association for Labor Legislation," in Linda Kerber, Alice Kessler-Harris, and Kathryn Kish Sklar, eds., *U.S. History As Women's History: New Feminist Essays* (Chapel Hill, 1995), 36–62.

31. In analyzing the experience of activist Chicago women, this book draws upon the insights of feminist political theorists Carole Pateman, *The Disorder of Women: Democracy, Feminism and Political Theory* (Stanford, 1989) and Anne Phillips, *Engendering Democracy* (University Park, PA, 1991) on the gendered nature of western democratic thinking and political institutions.

32. Louise de Koven Bowen, *Speeches, Addresses and Letters*, v. 1 (Ann Arbor, 1937), 61.

Chapter 1
"The Whole Work Has Been Committed to the Hands of Women"

1. By comparison, Boston's fire of 1872 destroyed 750 buildings and sixty-five acres of the commercial area, and the 1904 fire in Baltimore ravaged one hundred acres. See Christine Meisner Rosen, *The Limits of Power: Great Fires and the Process of City Growth* (Berkeley, 1986), especially 186, where she notes that Boston people "were not burnt out of 'home as well as office.' "

2. The historiography of urban history discusses the weak nature of U.S. municipal government in the nineteenth century. For representative examples, see David Hammack, *Power and Society: Greater New York at the Turn of the Century* (New York, 1982); Eric H. Monkkonen, *America Becomes Urban: The Development of U.S. Cities and Towns, 1780–1980* (Berkeley, 1988); and Martin Schiesl, *The Politics of Efficiency: Municipal Administration and Reform in America, 1880–1920* (Berkeley, 1977). For Chicago government before the fire, see Robin L. Einhorn, *Property Rules: Political Economy in Chicago, 1833–1872* (Chicago, 1991).

3. The members of the Board of Directors and Executive Committee of the Relief and Aid Society from 1871 to 1873 were the dry goods merchants Marshall Field, Henry W. King, John V. Farwell, and Abijah Keith; manufacturers George Pullman and Nathaniel K. Fairbank; lumber merchants Turlington W. Harvey and Thomas M. Avery; lawyers Wirt Dexter, Edwin C. Larned, Julius Rosenthal, E. B. McCagg, B. G. Caulfield, and C.H.S. Mixer; manufacturers N. S. Bouton, A. B. Meeker, and J. T. Ryerson; commission merchants Murry Nelson and J. Mason Loomis; Dr. H. A. Johnson, physician; railroad executives C. G. Hammond and

H. E. Sargent; railway supply dealer J. MacGregor Adams; and R. Laird Collier, a minister. Kathleen McCarthy, *Noblesse Oblige: Charity and Cultural Philanthropy in Chicago, 1849–1929* (Chicago, 1982), provides the most comprehensive discussion of the work of the Relief and Aid Society before the fire.

4. Chicago Relief and Aid Society, *First Special Report to the Common Council* (November, 1871); Rev. E. J. Goodspeed, *History of the Great Fires in Chicago and the West* (Chicago, 1871), 420, prints the text of Mayor Roswell Mason's decree to this effect. The Society did make annual reports to the Common Council from 1871 to 1874, but the Council had no authority over the Society; the Society could, and did, defy the wishes of the Council.

5. See Karen Sawislak, *Smoldering City: Chicagoans and the Great Fire, 1871–1874* (Chicago, 1995), and John A. Mayer, "Private Charities in Chicago from 1871–1915" (Ph.D. Dissertation, University of Minnesota, 1978) for extensive discussions of the aims and methods of the Society over fire relief.

6. Chicago Relief and Aid Society, "Minutes of the Executive Committee," October 14, 1871, *Minute Books*, United Charities of Chicago MS Collection, Box 1, folders 3 and 5, Chicago Historical Society; Chicago *Tribune*, October 16 and October 18, 1871; and Relief and Aid Society, *Report of the Chicago Relief and Aid Society of the Disbursement of Contributions for the Sufferers by The Chicago Fire* (Chicago, 1874), 181, 196–201.

7. Relief and Aid Society, *Report of the Disbursement of Contributions*, 158–59. The city's newspapers published the notice of the requirement for written applications with references. See *Tribune*, February 10, 1872. Samples of both blank and completed applications are in United Charities MS Collection, Box 1, folders 3 and 5.

8. Shelter committee applications are in United Charities MS Collection, Box 1, folder 5.

9. Margaret Hubbard Ayer and Isabella Taves, *The Three Lives of Harriet Hubbard Ayer* (Philadelphia, 1957), 62.

10. Hallie Q. Brown, comp., *Homespun Heroines and Other Women of Distinction* (New York, 1988; facsimile of 1926 publication).

11. James W. Sheahan and George P. Upton, *The Great Conflagration: Chicago: Its Past, Present and Future* (Chicago, 1872), 300–301; Relief and Aid Society, *First Special Report*, 15 and 18, briefly mentions the work of women in general and Medill in particular.

12. Letter of Aurelia King to "My Dear Friends All," October 21, 1871, reprinted in Paul M. Angle, ed., *The Great Chicago Fire: Described in Seven Letters by Men and Women Who Experienced It* (Chicago, 1946). Original letter in Chicago Fire—Personal Narratives MS Collection, Chicago Historical Society.

13. All the quoted material is from a letter of Annie McClure Hitchcock to Mrs. Jewell, December 8, 1871, in Annie McClure Hitchcock MS Collection, Chicago Historical Society.

14. The *Tribune*, October 18, 1871, printed the notice of this regulation.

15. Ibid., October 19, 1871. Annie Hitchcock was married to a Charles Hitchcock, and it would be fascinating to know whether the signatory of this letter was her husband. None of my attempts to track this down, however, has produced any definitive answer. No reference to Hitchcock that I have found gives his middle

initial, while none of the city directories for this period records a "C. Hitchcock" with the middle initial "T."

16. See, for example, the Society's description of women in its *First Special Report*, 15.

17. For an example of a contemporary account, see Sheahan and Upton, *The Great Conflagration*, which contains several hundred pages on the fire, of which it devotes two pages to the work of women.

18. Relief and Aid Society Directors Field, Fairbanks, Ryerson, and Farwell, for instance, sat on the advisory board of the Ladies' Christian Union, one of the women's organizations participating in relief work.

19. Lori D. Ginzberg, *Women and the Work of Benevolence: Morality, Politics, and Class in the 19th-Century United States* (New Haven, 1990) chapter six, especially 149–51, 155, and 159–60, suggests that the public crisis of the U.S. Civil War (1861–65) and the task of organizing sanitary and other relief to meet it, changed women's attitudes toward the purpose of their work and how to accomplish it in ways that opened a gulf between how women viewed themselves and their work and how men viewed women and their work. See also Judith A. Giesberg, *Civil War Sisterhood: The U.S. Sanitary Commission and Women's Politics in Transition* (Boston, 2000). For the different ways in which Catholic nuns pursued fire relief in Chicago, see Suellen Hoy, "Caring for Chicago's Women and Girls: The Sisters of the Good Shepherd, 1859–1911," *Journal of Urban History* 23 (March 1997): 260–94.

20. Circular, letters, and two accounts of items received by women of the First Congregational Church from Cincinnati and St. Louis, in United Charities MS Collection, Box 1, folder 1.

21. *Tribune*, March 23, 1872.

22. Ibid., October 18, 1871.

23. Barbara Berg, *The Remembered Gate: Origins of American Feminism, the Woman and the City 1800–1860* (New York, 1978), 265–68,

24. The *Tribune*, November 4, 1871, printed notice of the formation of both societies.

25. Chicago Relief and Aid Society, *Report to the Common Council*, October 1871–January 1872 (Chicago, 1872), and *Fifteenth Annual Report, 1872* (Chicago, 1873), list all the cash disbursements made for this time period.

26. Charles C. P. Holden, President of the Common Council, "To the Mayor and Aldermen of the City of Chicago in the Common Council Assembled," *Journal of the Proceedings of the Common Council of the City of Chicago* (November 13, 1871), 347, describes the operation of the kitchen.

27. Dexter made his statements in a letter sent to and published in the Chicago *Republican*, January 26, 1872.

28. *Tribune*, February 7, 1872, and A. T. Andreas, *The History of Chicago*, vol. 2 (Chicago 1884–86), 769–70, give further accounts of these events.

29. *Tribune*, February 7 and March 4, 1872; and *Republican*, February 8, 1872.

30. Letter to the Cincinnati newspapers from J. L. Keck, chair of the relief committee sent from Cincinnati to Chicago, reprinted in Andreas, 2: 769.

31. *Tribune*, March 23, 1872.

32. Letter printed in *Republican*, March 6, 1872.

33. Chicago Relief and Aid Society, *Report to the Common Council, October 1871-January 1872* and *Fifteenth Annual Report*.

34. Relief and Aid Society, *First Special Report*, 15.

35. Nancy Hewitt, *Women's Activism and Social Change: Rochester, New York, 1822–1872* (Ithaca, 1984), 219–20 and 147–48, and McCarthy, *Noblesse Oblige*, 6–13. But see also, Berg, *The Remembered Gate*, especially the summary chapter, for conclusions about women's early to mid-nineteenth-century voluntary associations' giving women the opportunity to expand their view of themselves, their work, and their connections to other women.

36. See for example, Karen Sawislak, *Smoldering City*, 87 and 104–105.

37. Chicago Relief and Aid Society, *First Special Report*, 18–19. United Charities MS Collection, Box 1, folder 1 contains a copy of the sewing machine application. See also *Republican*, March 9, 1872.

38. United Charities, MS Collection, Box 1, folder 1.

39. Sawislak, *Smoldering City*, and Mayer, "Private Charities in Chicago from 1871–1915," give detailed accounts of the Society's concern with property and work relationships.

40. Mayer, "Private Charities in Chicago from 1871–1915," 19, 23–24.

41. Letter from Hitchcock to Mrs. Jewell, December 8, 1871, Hitchcock Collection. Many female teachers who were now unemployed because the schools had been destroyed were facing even bleaker prospects because the school board was proposing to save money after the fire by eliminating music, drawing, and language teachers. *Republican*, November 13, 1871.

42. Hitchcock to Jewell, December 8, 1871.

43. Goodspeed, *History of the Great Fires in Chicago and the West*.

44. Sara M. Evans, "Women's History and Political Theory: Toward a Feminist Approach to Public Life," in Nancy Hewitt and Suzanne Lebsock, eds., *Visible Women: New Essays on American Activism* (Urbana, 1993), 128–30, discusses women using their organizations to critique the shortcomings of male stewardship in public affairs. Maureen A. Flanagan, "Gender and Urban Political Reform: The City Club and the Woman's City Club of Chicago in the Progressive Era," *American Historical Review* 95 (October 1990): 1032–50, explores this issue for the early twentieth century.

45. *Tribune*, November 4, 1871, and October 18 and 20, 1871.

46. See the account of these fears in Timothy Naylor, "Responding to the Fire: The Work of the Chicago Relief and Aid Society," *Science and Society* 39 (1975–76): 252–54.

47. Relief and Aid Society, *First Special Report*, 30.

48. Ibid.

49. Open letter from the Good Samaritan Society published in *Tribune*, March 11, 1872.

50. *Republican*, November 24, 1871; see *Tribune*, March 11, 1872, for Good Samaritan Society in this regard.

51. See James Leiby, *A History of Social Welfare and Social Work in the United States* (New York, 1978); Josephine Shaw Lowell, *Public Relief and Private Charity* (1884); McCarthy, *Noblesse Oblige*; and Walter Trattner, *From Poor Laws to Welfare State*, 2nd ed. (New York, 1979).

52. I have chosen to describe these women and men as "prominent middle class" because it seems the best way to designate the status of a group of people, not all of whom could be classified as upper class in terms of wealth and property, but whose position in Chicago's social structure was surely prominent. In Chicago in 1871 the men and women described here would seem to fit both Frederic Jaher and Stuart Blumin's respective definitions of an upper strata—in terms of influence and power—and an emerging middle class—in terms of sentiment and lifestyle. See Frederic Cople Jaher, *The Urban Establishment: Upper Strata in Boston, New York, Charleston, Chicago, and Los Angeles* (Urbana, 1982), and Stuart Blumin, *The Emergence of the Middle-Class: Social Experience in the American City, 1760–1900* (New York, 1989).

The people discussed in this chapter are white. A valid gender comparison necessitates comparing white women's organizations to the Relief and Aid Society. Chicago's African American community totaled 1 percent of the total population in the 1870s. I have found only one description of an African American woman's fire relief activities, as mentioned earlier in this chapter.

For representative examples of work on fire relief, see McCarthy, *Noblesse Oblige*; Timothy Naylor, "Responding to the Fire"; Otto Nelson, "The Chicago Relief and Aid Society, 1850–1874," *Journal of the Illinois State Historical Society* 59 (1966): 48–66; and Karen Sawislak, "Smoldering City," *Chicago History* (Fall and Winter, 1988–89): 70–101, and *Smoldering City.* Sawislak's essay, "Relief, Aid, and Order: Class, Gender and the Definition of Community in the Aftermath of Chicago's Great Fire," *Journal of Urban History* 19 (November 1993): 3–18, discusses the role of women, but her class interpretation of fire relief analyzes gender differences as a conflict between male "abstract measures of community" and women's "direct markers of belonging."

53. Hewitt, *Women's Activism and Social Change*, and McCarthy, *Noblesse Oblige*, provide excellent descriptions of how this worked in mid-nineteenth century cities. The quotation is from Sawislak, "Relief, Aid, and Order," 14.

54. Sawislak, "Relief, Aid, and Order," 15–16.

55. See Ginzberg, *Women and the Work of Benevolence*, 190.

56. Bradwell and Livermore became active women suffragists, and Hoge continued her charity work. Organizing sanitary fairs during the war undoubtedly contributed to Chicago women's learning how to organize, and the founding of the Hospital for Women and Children was a direct result. See McCarthy, *Noblesse Oblige*, 10, 21–22, and 39, and Adade Mitchell Wheeler and Marlene Stein Wortman, *The Roads They Made: Women in Illinois History* (Chicago, 1977), 41–44, 52–54, and 61.

57. Letter from Pullman to Mayor Roswell Mason, October 23, 1871, in Pullman Family MS Collection, Box 1, folder 2, Chicago Historical Society.

58. See Chicago *Tribune*, February 7, March 6 and 31, 1872, for the new regulations, and Relief and Aid Society, *First Special Report*, 17. We can assume the Good Samaritan Society's standard for discrimination was much lower than the Relief Society's because Katharine Medill had worked with the Special Bureau before she quit in disgust over her inability to sufficiently help those she saw in need.

59. *Tribune*, March 11, 1872, printed the women's letter [emphasis in the original].

60. Relief and Aid Society, *First Special Report*, 17.

61. *Tribune*, March 11, 1872 [emphasis mine].

62. Chicago Relief and Aid Society, *Report(s) of the Chicago Relief and Aid Society to the Common Council of the City of Chicago* (1872, 1873, and 1874), list the names of all individuals and businesses in Chicago and throughout the country and world who donated to the relief fund. None of the directors of the Society made any monetary contributions. Because these men never modestly hid their own largesse, as a glance through the annual reports of any charitable organization that they directed will show, it is not plausible that they might just not have listed any donations they made to the relief fund.

63. Editorial from a Cincinnati newspaper, reprinted in *Tribune*, February 7, 1872.

64. Prominent white men were accustomed to order and control because they viewed the city as their own—even as other groups within the city were beginning to threaten this power. Thus, the Cincinnati men who were of comparable status in their own city would have accorded the Chicago men this privilege. See Amy Bridges, *Morning Glories: Municipal Reform in the Southwest* (Princeton, 1997); Einhorn, *Property Rules*; Harold L. Platt, *City Building in the New South: The Growth of Public Services in Houston, Texas, 1830–1915* (Philadelphia, 1983); and Jon Teaford, *The Unheralded Triumph: City Government in America, 1870–1900* (Baltimore, 1984).

65. The dry goods companies of Marshall Field, Henry W. King, and J. V. Farwell, for example, were paid $88,248, $24,375, and $37,526, respectively, to furnish relief supplies. These figures are compiled from the lists of cash disbursements contained in the Chicago Relief and Aid Society, *Reports . . . to the Common Council* (1872, 1873, 1874) and the final accounting of the Society, *Report of the . . . Disbursements* (1874). For the lumber tariff, see Bessie Pierce, *History of Chicago*, vol. 3 (Chicago, 1957), 16–17; *Tribune*, February 17 and 20, 1872; and *Republican*, February 12 and 15, 1872.

66. Letter printed in Andreas, 2:770; see note 30 of this chapter.

67. William Bross, *History of Chicago, Historical and Commercial Statistics, Sketches, Facts and Figures* (Chicago, 1876), 97–100, prints text of speech he gave to New York businessmen directly after the fire, appealing to them to lend capital to Chicago businesses.

68. United Societies Collection, Box 1, folder 1, contains accounting dated 1 November 1871 of items received by the Ladies of the First Congregational Church from outside of the city as well as a letter from Mrs. Dickinson of St. Louis, see p. 325. Missouri, regarding supplies she was bringing to the city.

69. See Ginzberg, *Women and the Work of Benevolence*, for a discussion of how the women's philanthropic activities in the mid-nineteenth century began to pose a threat to male prerogatives to power and politics.

70. See Einhorn, *Property Rules*; Bross, *History of Chicago*; "The Anniversary Fire Number," *The Lakeside Monthly* (October 1872); and *Tribune* May 4, 1872.

71. Much current work on women in cities emphasizes their political culture and style and thereby misses the overt challenge to male power that an episode such as women's fire relief illustrates. S. Sara Monoson, "The Lady and the Tiger: Women's Electoral Activism in New York City Before Suffrage," *Journal of Women's History* 2 (Fall 1990), 100–35, examines urban women's pre-suffrage activism

and ideas that challenged male power. For additional discussion of the conjunction of women's public exercise of power and women's culture, see also Kathryn Kish Sklar, *Florence Kelley and the Nation's Work: The Rise of Women's Political Culture, 1830–1900* (New Haven, 1995).

72. Eric Foner, *Politics and Ideology in the Age of the Civil War* (New York, 1980), 7–10.

73. See *Tribune*, March 12 and 21, 1872, and *Proceedings of the Common Council of the City of Chicago*, Regular Meetings of March 11, 1872, 122, and December 22, 1873, 29; and *Tribune*, December 23, 1873.

Chapter Two
"Thoughtful Women Are Needed"

1. Kathleen D. McCarthy, *Noblesse Oblige: Charity and Cultural Philanthropy in Chicago, 1849–1929* (Chicago, 1982), chapter 1, describes the charitable work of Chicago women before 1871. The Hoge quotation is from page 21.

2. Good Samaritan Society, *Annual Reports* (1877–79 and 1881), Chicago Historical Society, list the officers.

3. See Lana Ruegamer, "The Paradise of Exceptional Women: Chicago Women Reformers, 1863–1893," (Ph.D. Dissertation, Indiana University, 1982); Bessie Louise Pierce, *A History of Chicago*, v. 2 (New York, 1940), 456; and *Tribune*, June 19, 1868. Immediately upon its founding, Sorosis was embroiled in the question then vexing the larger suffrage movement: whether to concentrate on women's rights or to promote universal suffrage that included black suffrage and rejected any property or educational requirements for voting. This dilemma split Sorosis into two opposing factions, as it did the national suffrage movement. In February 1869, the two factions within the Chicago Sorosis held woman suffrage conventions to debate the issues, and each group formed its own suffrage association. Sorosis's preoccupation with suffrage and its avowedly social agenda meant that these women did not actively engage in municipal affairs. *Tribune*, January 10, 14, 21, 28, and 31, 1869, reported on this disagreement, often in the most disparaging terms. Steven M. Buechler, *The Transformation of the Woman Suffrage Movement: The Case of Illinois, 1850–1920* (New Brunswick, NJ, 1986), 67–76, describes this controversy.

4. Ruegamer, "The Paradise of Exceptional Women," 148.

5. Brown is quoted in Henriette Greenebaum Frank and Amalie Hofer Jerome, *Annals of the Chicago Woman's Club for the First Forty Years of Its Organization, 1876–1916* (Chicago, 1916), 15–16. Until 1895, the club was called the Chicago Women's Club.

6. For 1880, see Frank and Jerome, *Annals*, 35; for 1893 see "Annual Meeting," May 27, 1893, *Club and Board Minutes*, Chicago Woman's Club MS Collection, Box 20, 2nd book, Chicago Historical Society; for 1913 see Frank and Jerome, *Annals*, 324–25. By January 1914, 2,362 different women had been members of the Club.

7. Ruegamer, "The Paradise of Exceptional Women," 150.

8. "Meeting Minutes," December 19, 1877, January 2, 1878, April 17, 1878, and March 16, 1887, *Board Minutes*, CWC Collection, Box 1. See Kathryn Kish

Sklar, "The Historical Foundations of Women's Power in the Creation of the American Welfare State, 1830–1930," in Seth Koven and Sonya Michel, eds., *Mothers of a New World: Maternalist Politics and the Origins of Welfare States* (New York, 1993), 43–93.

9. "Meeting Minutes," February 4, 1880, *Board Minutes*, CWC Collection, Box 1, and Frank and Jerome, *Annals*, 48.

10. Frank and Jerome, *Annals*, 40–41.

11. Ruegamer, "The Paradise of Exceptional Women," 161.

12. Frank and Jerome, *Annals*, 28–29.

13. Ibid., 66–67; and letter of Katherine E. Tuley to Ernst Prussing, (dated received October 1, 1888 at top), Katherine E. Tuley MS Collection, Chicago Historical Society.

14. Frank and Jerome, *Annals*, 69–71.

15. "Meeting Minutes," June [day obliterated], 1892, November 9, 1892, and "Regular Meeting of Board of Directors," December 14, 1892, *Club and Board Minutes*, CWC Collection, Box 20, book 2.

16. "Regular Meeting," April 25, 1894, *Club Minutes*, Box 20.

17. "Regular Meeting," April 28, 1897, *Club Minutes*, Box 20.

18. See "Minutes," Chicago Woman's Aid MS Collection (formerly Young Ladies' Aid), folder 112, Special Collections, University of Illinois Chicago, Chicago; for Union of Bohemian Women, see Adade M. Wheeler and Marlene S. Wortman, *The Roads They Made: Women in Illinois History* (Chicago, 1977), 63; and for the Wells Club, see Anne Meis Knupfer, *Toward a Tenderer Humanity and a Nobler Womanhood: African American Women's Clubs in Turn-of-the-Century Chicago* (New York, 1996).

19. See Ruth Bordin, *Woman and Temperance: The Quest for Power and Liberty, 1873–1900* (New Brunswick, NJ, 1990), for her assessment of the organization's difficulties in maintaining membership and pursuing a public agenda from the 1890s.

20. Frank and Jerome, *Annals*, 51–52.

21. Protective Agency for Women and Children, "Report from the President 1887," contained in *Annual Reports, 1887–1905*, Chicago Historical Society.

22. Frank and Jerome, *Annals*, 51, reports that a Mrs. Wallace gave five hundred dollars to start the Protective Agency.

23. Protective Agency, *Annual Reports*, 1886–1890, Chicago Historical Society.

24. *Justitia: A Court for the Unrepresented*, May 1, 1888, records this aim from the Cook County Suffrage Association meeting of April 17, 1888, in Caroline A. Huling MS Collection, folder 7, Special Collections, University of Illinois Chicago Library.

25. See Philip Ethington, *The Public City: the Political Construction of Public Life in San Francisco, 1850–1900* (Cambridge, UK, 1994), for his reflections on the importance of newspapers for disseminating political agendas.

26. Ralph Scharnau, "Elizabeth Morgan, Crusader for Labor Reform," *Labor History* 14 (1973): 341–42.

27. See Jane Addams, *Twenty Years at Hull House* (New York, 1910); Paul Avrich, *The Haymarket Tragedy* (Princeton, 1984); and Thomas Philpott, *The*

Slum and the Ghetto: Neighborhood Deterioration and Middle-Class Reform, Chicago 1880–1930 (New York, 1978).

28. *Tribune*, October 5, 1888.

29. Her name is spelled as both Rogers and Rodgers. Local 1789 was almost moribund by late 1888, and Rodgers had apparently left the Trades and Labor Assembly before joining the Woman's League following a dispute with the Assembly leadership. See Meredith Tax, *The Rising of the Women: Feminist Solidarity and Class Conflict, 1880–1917* (New York, 1980), 41, 47, and 51–52; and "Meeting Minutes," June 19, 1887, *Minute Book*, Chicago Trades and Labor Assembly MS Collection, Chicago Historical Society.

30. *Tribune*, October 12, 1888.

31. Ibid., October 7, 1888.

32. Bureau of Justice, *Annual Report* (1889), Chicago Historical Society.

33. *Tribune*, October 7, 1888.

34. Ethington, *The Public City*, 363–401, frames his discussion of women and public life in San Francisco in ways that consider urban reform proposals from the male perspective. Ethington does not include an examination of what women might have been doing or saying, for instance, to provoke the anti-women remarks of Mayor James Phelan that are recorded in his book.

35. The most complete account of the Alliance's history is found in Tax, *The Rising of the Women*, chapter 4. See also Scharnau, "Elizabeth Morgan, Crusader for Labor Reform," and Mari Jo Buhle, *Women and American Socialism, 1870–1920* (Urbana, 1983), 72–73 and 91–92.

36. "Meeting Minutes," October 25 and November 8, 1888, *Minute Book*, Trades and Labor Assembly Collection; Tax, *The Rising of the Women*, 68; and *Tribune*, October 13, 1888.

37. Illinois Women's Alliance, "Organizations and Delegates," *First Annual Report* (year ending November 1, 1889), in Huling Collection, folder 39; and Women's Baptist Home Mission Society, *Historical Sketches of the Women's Baptist Home Mission Union and Women's Baptist Foreign Mission Union* (Chicago, 1903), and miscellaneous pamphlets of Women's Baptist Home Mission Society, Chicago Historical Society. See Glenna Matthews, *The Rise of Public Woman: Woman's Power and Woman's Place in the United States, 1630–1970* (New York, 1992), chapter 7, on the tendency to overemphasize religious motivations.

38. See, for example, Richard Schneirov, *Labor and Urban Politics: Class Conflict and the Origins of Modern Liberalism in Chicago 1864–97* (Urbana, 1998), 272, who labels IWA leaders such as Elizabeth Morgan, Corinne Brown, and Fanny Kavanaugh as "prolabor socialists."

39. For an excellent examination of this thinking and its application to municipal government for pre-fire Chicago, see Robin L. Einhorn, *Property Rules: Political Economy in Chicago, 1833–1872* (Chicago, 1991). Eric H. Monkkonen makes the distinction between "passive regulation" and "active service" in *America Becomes Urban: The Development of U.S. Cities and Towns, 1780–1980* (Berkeley, 1988), 93, but also see chapters 4 and 5 for a general urban synthesis in this regard.

40. John Jentz, "Class and Politics in an Emerging Industrial City: Chicago in the 1860s and 1870s," *Journal of Urban History* 17 (May 1991): 227–63; and Rich-

ard Schneirov, "Political Cultures and the Role of the State in Labor's Republic: The View from Chicago, 1848–1877," *Labor History* 32 (Summer 1991): 376–400.

41. Schneirov, "Political Cultures," 397.

42. Monkkonen, *America Becomes Urban*, 115–16. For working-class men, see Alexander Keyssar, *Out of Work: The First Century of Unemployment in Massachusetts* (New York, 1986), 262.

43. Unidentified newspaper clipping, January 16, 1894, in Thomas and Elizabeth Morgan Collection, Book 2, in Illinois Historical Survey, University of Illinois Library, Urbana, Illinois.

44. See Monkkonen, *America Becomes Urban*, 206–209, for his discussion of the gradual shift that took place in U.S. city government toward practicing some types of "active, systematic intervention." See the discussion below of the IWA and its concept of government's duty toward its people.

45. *Tribune*, January 2, 1874.

46. Citizens' Association, "Report of the Committee on Tenement Houses" (1884), Citizens' Association MS Collection, Chicago Historical Society.

47. *Tribune*, January 22, 1894.

48. *Tribune*, May 4, 1889, quotes President Huling to this effect; the declaration was also printed in "Meeting Minutes," May 5, 1889, *Minute Book*, Trades and Labor Assembly Collection.

49. IWA, "Report of Committee on Visiting Institutions," *First Annual Report*, Huling Collection, folder 39, and "Meeting Minutes," June 16, 1889, *Minute Book*, Trades and Labor Assembly Collection.

50. Unidentified newspaper clipping, January 3, 1891, in Morgan Collection, Book 2.

51. See Allan H. Spear, *Black Chicago: The Making of a Negro Ghetto, 1890–1920* (Chicago, 1967), 58, 66–67, and 108–109; and *Tribune*, October 28, 1888, interview with founding member Fannie Barrier Williams. The United Labor Party included African American male laborers, but this was a class and gender specific organization. See Schneirov, *Labor and Urban Politics*, 220.

52. IWA, "Organizations and Delegates," *First Annual Report*, Huling Collection, folder 39.

53. Clipping from the *Tribune*, November 2, 1889, in Morgan Collection, Book 2. Williams' name was also mentioned earlier in a newspaper article on the IWA. See unidentified newspaper clipping, dated June 7, 1889, in Morgan Collection.

54. Invitation circular from meeting of October 6, 1888, in Morgan Collection, Book 2, and "Meeting Minutes," October 25, 1888, *Minute Book*, Trades and Labor Assembly Collection.

55. Unidentified newspaper clippings, December 16 and 18, 1888, and January 20, 1889, in Morgan Collection, Book 2; and Tax, *The Rising of the Women*, 72–74 and 78–79, and letters of Trades and Labor Assembly to Illinois Women's Alliance, January 28, 1889, and Illinois Women's Alliance to Trades and Labor Assembly, March 17, 1889, in Morgan Collection, Book 2.

56. *Tribune*, May 14, 1890.

57. Unidentified newspaper clipping, 1889 (on page with other clippings marked January 1889), in Morgan Collection, Book 2.

58. Unidentified newspaper clipping, January 13, 1889, in Morgan Collection, Book 2.

59. *Tribune*, May 4, 1889.

60. Illinois Women's Alliance, "Report of the Committee on Compulsory Education," *First Annual Report*, Huling Collection, folder 39.

61. Unidentified newspaper clipping, August 3, 1889, in Morgan Collection, Book 2.

62. Chicago *Inter-Ocean*, April 4, 1891, carried an account of the IWA's charges regarding this legal policy and its demands for arresting men equally with women.

63. Tax, *The Rising of the Women*, 69–71; unidentified newspaper clippings from 1890 (probably May) and July 1890, and Chicago *Evening Post*, September 18, 1890, in Morgan Collection, Book 2; and *Tribune*, September 19, 1890.

64. Kavanaugh, quoted in Tax, *The Rising of the Women*, 70.

65. Unidentified newspaper clippings, (May), June, and December 1890, Morgan Collection, Book 2.

66. "Meeting Minutes," July 3, 1887, *Minute Book*, Trades and Labor Assembly Collection.

67. "Report of the Committee on Free Baths," *First Annual Report*, Huling Collection, folder 39. See undated note from Elizabeth Morgan to Trades and Labor Assembly, *Record Book*, 1889–1890, Trades and Labor Assembly Collection, and unidentified newspaper clippings, June 7, September 7 and October (no day), 1889, in Morgan Collection, Book 2.

68. Lucy Cleveland, "The Public Baths of Chicago," *Modern Sanitation* 5 (October 1908), 6–7; "Regular Meeting," December 28, 1892, *Club and Board Minutes*, CWC Collection, Box 20, 2nd book. For the public bath movement in the U.S., see Marilyn Thornton Williams, *Washing "The Great Unwashed": Public Baths in Urban America, 1840–1920* (Columbus, OH, 1991).

69. Cleveland, "The Public Baths," 8, which also provides a quick overview of the public bath movement in Chicago. Alderman's quotation appears in Daphne Spain, *How Women Saved the City* (Minneapolis, 2001), 234.

70. The accounts written by women stress their own responsibility, while those of men avoid the issue. See Cleveland, "The Public Baths"; Jane Addams, "Woman's Work for Chicago," *Municipal Affairs* (September 1898): 506–507; and The Free Bath and Sanitary League, "Souvenir of Dedication of the South Side Bath" (1897), Newberry Library, Chicago. I am indebted to Suellen Hoy for alerting me to these sources.

71. *Tribune*, May 4, 1889 and Tax, *The Rising of the Women*, 69.

72. IWA, "Report of Ward and Precinct Committee," *First Annual Report*, Huling Collection, folder 39. The term "vigilante" here means citizens exercising vigilance in seeing that government worked.

73. Tax, *The Rising of the Women*, 81–84. Tax (302, fn 40) justifiably took Jane Addams to task for attributing to Hull House a greater share of the credit for securing factory legislation in Illinois, a sentiment echoed by Kathryn Kish Sklar, "Hull House in the 1890s: A Community of Women Reformers," *Signs: Journal of Women in Culture and Society* 10 (Summer 1985): 665–66. On the other hand,

David John Hogan, *Class and Reform: School and Society in Chicago, 1880–1930* (Philadelphia, 1985), 25–27, and Glenna Matthews, *The Rise of Public Woman*, 158–59, assume the primacy of social settlements in developing social legislation. Hull House officially opened in September 1889.

74. IWA, "Report of the Committee on Compulsory Education," *First Annual Report*, Huling Collection, folder 39.

75. IWA, "Report of Committee on Compulsory Education," Huling Collection, folder 39, and letter from Elizabeth Morgan to Trades and Labor Assembly, December 6, 1889, *Record Book, 1889–1890*, Trades and Labor Assembly Collection.

76. Letter from Elizabeth Morgan to the Chicago Trades and Labor Assembly explaining the most recent meeting of the IWA, December 6, 1889, *Record Book, 1889–1890*, in Trades and Labor Assembly Collection; and Tax, *The Rising of the Women*, 71.

77. The Stewart quotation appears in IWA, "Report of Committee on Compulsory Education," *First Annual Report*, Huling Collection, folder 39. The second quotation comes from an unidentified newspaper clipping that has been put together with other clippings from November 1891, in Morgan Collection, Book 2.

78. IWA, "Report of Committee on Compulsory Education," *First Annual Report*, Huling Collection, folder 39.

79. Unidentified newspaper clipping, November 1, 1890, in Morgan Collection, Book 2.

80. See "Report of the Committee of the Citizens' Association on Education," (1881), *Reports of Committees*, Citizens' Association Collection. For a summary of men's ideas on education, see Hogan, *Class and Reform*, 57–60.

81. Frank and Jerome, *Annals*, 71.

82. IWA, "Report of the Committee on Compulsory Education," Huling Collection, folder 39.

83. Political theorist Anne Phillips, *Engendering Democracy* (University Park, PA, 1991), 4 and 6, has described how, by "grounding the abstractions of economic or foreign policy in a more compassionate understanding of daily need" as they entered formal politics, women challenged the historically dominant definition of democratic politics that "in identifying politics with (a very particular definition of) the public sphere [had] made democracy coterminous with the activities that have been historically associated with men." See also Carole Patemen, *The Disorder of Women: Democracy, Feminism and Political Theory* (Stanford, 1989). I follow this conception of women's ideas about government rather than the idea that divides men's and women's public activities into the "politics of needs" and the "politics of rights." For this latter analysis, see Nancy Fraser, "Struggle Over Needs: Outline of a Socialist-Feminist Critical Theory of Late Capitalist Political Culture," in *Unruly Practices: Power, Discourse, and Gender in Contemporary Social Theory* (Minneapolis, 1989).

84. Tax, *The Rising of the Women*, gives the most complete description of the Alliance's demise. See also Buhle, *Women and American Socialism*, especially 92 for "misalliance."

85. Copy of speech in Huling Collection, folder 42.

86. Unidentified clipping, March 28, 1894, Morgan Collection, Book 2; clipping simply dated "1894" records the IWA as passing a resolution favoring the eight-hour day "almost without opposition."

87. For Chicago, see Knupfer, *Toward a Tenderer Humanity and a Nobler Womanhood*, and Wanda Hendricks, "The Politics of Race: Black Women in Illinois, 1890–1920" (Ph.D. Dissertation, Purdue University, 1990) and *Gender, Race, and Politics in the Midwest: Black Club Women in Illinois* (Bloomington, IN, 1998). For recent work on the African American clubwomen's movement as well as the general history of African American women, see Eileen Boris, "The Power of Motherhood: Black and White Activist Women Redefine the 'Political,' " in Koven and Michel, eds., *Mothers of a New World*, 213–45; Nancy A. Hewitt, "Politicizing Domesticity: Anglo, Black, and Latin Women in Tampa's Progressive Movements," in Noralee Frankel and Nancy S. Dye, eds., *Gender, Class, Race and Reform in the Progressive Era* (Lexington, KY, 1991), 24–41; Evelyn Brooks Higginbotham, *Righteous Discontent: The Women's Movement in the Black Baptist Church, 1880–1920* (Cambridge, MA, 1993); Darlene Clark Hine, "The Housewives' League of Detroit: Black Women and Economic Nationalism," in Nancy Hewitt and Suzanne Lebsock, eds., *Visible Women: New Essays on American Activism* (Urbana, 1993), 223–41; Stephanie J. Shaw, "Black Club Women and the Creation of the National Association of Colored Women," *Journal of Women's History* 3 (Fall 1991): 10–25; and Deborah Gray White, "The Cost of Club Work: the Price of Black Feminism," in Hewitt and Lebsock, eds., *Visible Women*, 249–69.

88. Elisabeth Lasch-Quinn, *Black Neighbors: Race and the Limits of Reform in the American Settlement House Movement, 1890–1945* (Chapel Hill, 1993), explores the failure of the settlement house movement to promote true racial equality.

89. *Tribune*, October 26, 1888, contains an interview with Fannie Barrier Williams about the Crandall Club. The first description of the Ida B. Wells Club is from Spear, *Black Chicago*, 101, and the second is from Knupfer, *Toward a Tenderer Humanity*, 36. See Patricia A. Schechter, *Ida B. Wells-Barnett and American Reform, 1880–1930* (Chapel Hill, 2001) for the most recent details of the Club's social activities.

90. Elizabeth L. Davis, *The Story of the Illinois Federation of Colored Women's Clubs* (Des Moines, IA, 1925), 25; and Wheeler and Wortman, *The Roads They Made*, 68.

91. See unidentified newspaper clippings, June 7, 1889, and *Tribune*, November 2, 1889, in Morgan Collection, Book 2.

92. "Report of the Illinois Women's Alliance to the Meeting of May 5, 1889 of the Trades and Labor Association," *The Record*, Trades and Labor Association Collection.

93. The quotations is from *Women's Era* (June 5, 1894), cited in Maude Jenkins, "The History of the Black Women's Club Movement in America" (Ed.D. Dissertation, Columbia University, 1984), 52–53.

94. Fannie Barrier Williams, "The Club Movement among Colored Women of America," in J. E. MacBrady, ed., *A New Negro for a New Century* (Chicago, n.d.): 417–18.

95. Sklar, "Hull House in the 1890s," 665; Hendricks, "The Politics of Race," 80–81; and Davis, *Story of the Illinois Federation of Colored Women's Clubs*.

96. Hendricks, "The Politics of Race," 80–81.

97. Woolley was an ordained minister in addition to being actively engaged in club work and the suffrage movement; a few years later she would be instrumental in founding Chicago's first interracial social settlement, the Frederick Douglass Center.

98. Typescripts of the meetings of the whole to discuss the issue are in CWC Collection, Box 48, folder 7. Vote totals are from "Regular Meetings," December 26, 1894 and January 23, 1895, *Club and Board Minutes*, CWC Collection, Box 20, 3rd book.

99. "Annual Meeting," May 18, 1895, *Club and Board Minutes*, CWC Collection, Box 20, 4th book.

100. I compared available membership lists for these organizations with names of African American men taken from Spear, *Black Chicago* and Charles Branham, "Black Chicago: Accommodationist Politics before the Great Migration," in Melvin G. Holli and Peter d'A. Jones, eds., *The Ethnic Frontier: Group Survival in Chicago and the Midwest* (Grand Rapids, MI, 1977), 211–62.

101. Presidential address of Ada Sweet is quoted in Frank and Jerome, *Annals*, 145–46.

102. "Regular Meeting," January 23, 1901, *Club and Board Minutes*, CWC Collection, Box 21.

103. See Alfreda Duster, ed., *Crusade for Justice: The Autobiography of Ida B. Wells* (Chicago, 1970), 275–78. Wells-Barnett belonged to the predominantly white Chicago Political Equality League from at least 1897 to 1907. See Chicago Political Equality League, "List of Members," *Annual Reports* (1897 and 1907), Chicago Historical Society. For the CPEL, see chapter 3.

104. "Report of Education Department," April 23, 1902, *Annual Report*, CWC Collection, Box 21, 4th book. Alton was making the case for segregation based on the 1896 Supreme Court ruling *Plessy v. Ferguson*, which allowed separate but equal public facilities.

105. Davis, *The Story of the Illinois Federation of Colored Women's Clubs*, 45–46 and 48.

106. White, "The Cost of Club Work, the Price of Black Feminism," 255–57. See also the conclusions of Shaw, "Black Club Women."

107. Boris, "The Power of Motherhood," 216.

108. Charles Branham, "Black Chicago," 211–62.

109. Boris, "The Power of Motherhood," 215. See also Schechter, Ida B. Wells-Barnett.

Chapter Three
"The First Thing Is to Create Public Sentiment and Then Express It at Every Opportunity"

1. Helen Lefkowitz Horowitz, *Culture and the City: Cultural Philanthropy in Chicago from the 1880s to 1917* (Chicago, 1976), 27–28.

2. These and other responses are recorded in Paul M. Angle, ed., *Prairie State: Impressions of Illinois, 1673–1967* (Chicago, 1968), and Bessie L. Pierce, *As Others See Chicago: Impressions of Visitors, 1673–1933* (Chicago, 1933).

3. Pierce, *As Others See Chicago*, 251.

4. See William Stead, *If Christ Came to Chicago* (Chicago, 1894). For short accounts of Stead's impact on middle-class Chicagoans, see Jane Addams, *Twenty Years at Hull House* (New York, 1910), 122–23; Allen F. Davis, *Spearheads for Reform: The Social Settlements and the Progressive Movement, 1890–1914* (New York, 1967), 187–88; and Ray Ginger, *Altgeld's America: The Lincoln Ideal Versus Changing Realities* (New York, 1958), 248–50.

5. Adade Wheeler and Marlene Wortman, *The Roads They Made: Women in Illinois History* (Chicago, 1977), 67–71.

6. "Regular Meeting," November 30, 1892, *Club and Board Minutes*, Chicago Woman's Club MS Collection, Box 20, 1st book; and Henriette Greenebaum Frank and Amalie Hofer Jerome, *Annals of the Chicago Woman's Club* (Chicago, 1916), 106–107. Opposition to mandatory Sunday closings in this instance would be repeated often enough in subsequent years to clearly indicate that temperance was not, as has been suggested, a driving force of women's municipal activism either in the 1890s or later in the Progressive Era. For instance, in 1908 local women's clubs began to declare themselves dissatisfied with the "Puritan Sunday"; or a few years later, not one women's organization signed a call for organizing a permanent campaign to close Chicago's saloons. See *Tribune*, April 7, 1908, and April 6, 1914.

7. Ann Massa, "Black Women in the 'White City,' " *Journal of American Studies* 8 (December 1974): 319–37, provides the best overview of this issue.

8. Wheeler and Wortman, *The Roads They Made*, 80, and Meredith Tax, *The Rising of the Women: Feminist Solidarity and Class Conflict, 1880–1917* (New York, 1980), 49–51.

9. Lana Ruegamer, "The Paradise of Exceptional Women: Chicago Women Reformers, 1863–1893" (Ph.D. Dissertation, Indiana University, 1982), 164; the Meeting Minutes of the Chicago Woman's Club contain no discussion of Haymarket. In spring 1887, however, the CWC discussed various aspects of the "Labor Question." See "Regular Meeting," March 16, 1887, *Board and Meeting Minutes*, Chicago Woman's Club MS Collection, Box 1.

10. Stanley Buder, *Pullman: An Experiment in Industrial Order and Community Planning, 1880–1930* (Chicago, 1967), 171–72, and Addams, *Twenty Years*, 158–61.

11. Janice Reiff, "A Modern Lear and His Daughters: Gender in the Model Town of Pullman," *Journal of Urban History* 23 (March 1997): 316–41, esp. 318–19. Kathryn Kish Sklar rightly contends that middle-class women would not go so far in their support for the strikers as Florence Kelley wished them to. Yet this does not vitiate the facts that activist Chicago women were publicly engaged in the Pullman strike and that middle-class Chicago men disagreed with women about how much support to give the strikers. See Sklar, *Florence Kelley and the Nation's Work: The Rise of Women's Political Culture, 1830–1900* (New Haven, 1995), 273–74.

12. Buder, *Pullman*, 272.

13. Philip J. Ethington, *The Public City: The Political Construction of Public Life in San Francisco, 1850–1900* (Cambridge, UK, 1994), 332–36; Marsha Wedell, *Elite Women and the Reform Impulse in Memphis, 1875–1915* (Knoxville,

1991), 128–32; and Philip J. Ethington, "Recasting Urban Political History: Gender, the Public, the Household and Political Participation in Boston and San Francisco during the Progressive Era," *Social Science History* 16 (Summer 1992): 321–24. Ethington's quantitative analysis produces an interpretation of this event that differs from that of Sarah Deutsch, *Women and the City: Gender, Space, and Power in Boston, 1870–1940* (New York, 2000), 221.

14. Marjorie Murphy, *Blackboard Unions: The AFT and the NEA, 1900–1980* (Ithaca, 1990), 12–13.

15. Marjorie Murphy, "From Artisan to Semi-Professional: White Collar Unionism Among Chicago Public School Teachers, 1870–1930" (Ph.D. Dissertation, University of California, Davis, 1981), and *Blackboard Unions*, give the best overview of the teachers' situation at the turn of the century.

16. Murphy, "From Artisan to Semi-Professional," 42, and *Blackboard Unions*, 28 and 29, including fn.18. David John Hogan, *Class and Reform: School and Society in Chicago, 1880–1930* (Philadelphia, 1985), does not mention this particular aspect of the Harper Report.

17. *Tribune*, March 2, 1899.

18. Ibid., July 3, 8, and 10, 1902.

19. Newspaper clipping (undated), "Scrapbook," Lucy Flower MS Collection, Chicago Historical Society. The Chicago *American*, December 29, 1900, reprinted a speech given by Professor Charles DeGarmo.

20. *Tribune*, June 8, 1899.

21. "Regular Meeting," March 27, 1895, and February 26 and March 26, 1902, *Club and Board Minutes*, CWC Collection, Box 20, 3rd and 4th books. The Lake View Woman's Club had initiated this resolution.

22. "Minutes of Meetings," January 18, 1896, American Association of University Women—Chicago Branch (formerly called Chicago Association of Collegiate Alumnae) MS Collection, Box 1, folder 1, Chicago Historical Society, and Frank and Jerome, *Annals of the Chicago Woman's Club*, 163.

23. *Tribune*, June 8, 1899.

24. Ibid., February 26, 1899. See Murphy, "From Artisan to Semi-Professional," especially 42, 185, and 206 n.55, for her conclusions in this regard. Murphy's analysis is confusing also because some newspaper articles that she cites do not appear to support her conclusions. The *Tribune*, February 24, 1899, for example, contains only a short article on teacher opposition to the Harper Report that does not mention the CWC, and the *Tribune*, April 7, 1901 contains no story supporting a claim that "[t]he Chicago Woman's Club had already helped defeat the Chicago Teachers' Federation in its bid to maintain the mandatory pension fund." The only article regarding teachers and pensions that day is about the split developing on that issue between the elementary and high school teachers.

25. "Annual Meeting," April, 1902, *Board Minutes*, CWC Collection, Box 3, 4th book.

26. "Regular Meeting," October 23, 1901, *Club Minutes*, CWC Collection, Box 21, 4th book, and *Tribune*, October 19, 1901.

27. "Regular Meeting," March 27, 1895, *Club and Board Minutes*, CWC Collection, Box 20, 3rd book.

28. Speech of Ellen M. Henrotin to unnamed teacher's organization (marked 1897 or 1898) in Ellen M. Henrotin MS Collection, Box 2, folder 26, Schlesinger Library, Cambridge, MA.

29. For examples, see "Meeting Minutes," January 15 and February 19, 1898, Chicago Association of Collegiate Alumnae MS Collection, Box 1, folder 1; "Regular Meeting," February 27, 1901, *Club Minutes*, CWC MS Collection, Box 21, 3rd book; and *Tribune*, July 15, 1902.

30. The quotation is from Hogan, *Class and Reform*, 203. He is correct to acknowledge the strength of the alliance but fails to appreciate how the quest for public power, not just social reform, drove women's municipal work and alliances.

31. Marjorie Murphy, "Taxation and Social Conflict: Teacher Unionism and Public School Finance, 1898–1914," *Illinois State Historical Journal* (Winter 1981): 242–60, and *Blackboard Unions*, 66–68, convey a sense of teacher awareness of the political context of school reform.

32. Robin Einhorn, *Property Rules: Political Economy in Chicago, 1833–1872* (Chicago, 1991), 44–46.

33. From 1895 to 1905, the paper was contracted to pay $30,000 annually, then $31,000 until 1985. Murphy, "From Artisan to Semi-Professional," 40.

34. See "Open Letter to the Mayor," from George A. Schilling, June 6, 1895, in Chicago Teachers' Federation MS Collection, Box 35, folder 3, Chicago Historical Society.

35. See Murphy, "Taxation and Social Conflict," 243, for new state laws allowing this.

36. Murphy, "From Artisan to Semi-Professional," 33–34. See also open letter to "Newspapers of the State of Illinois," from Catharine Goggin and Margaret Haley, representing the Tax Investigating Committee of The Chicago Teachers' Federation and typescript of suit filed by CTF against City of Chicago, et al., in CTF Collection, Box 35, folder 3. Letter from Mayor Carter Harrison to Helen B. Eastman, Corresponding Secretary of the Chicago Teachers' Federation, March 8, 1900; letter from Helen Eastman to Harrison, March 17, 1900; and letter from Catharine Goggin to Graham H. Harris (n.d), in CTF Collection, Box 35, folder 4.

37. See letter of Catharine Goggin to G. H. Harris, n.d., in CTF Collection, Box 35, folder 4, wherein Goggin tells Harris that the teachers know that taxpayers would never support the teachers in such a challenge.

38. Robert L. Reid, ed., *Battleground: The Autobiography of Margaret Haley* (Urbana, 1982), esp. 43–44, 55, and 58–59. Haley's autobiography must be used judiciously, but this version has been carefully edited with explanatory footnotes, and her account of the tax battle as related here is supported by other documentation. See typescript of "Mass Meeting of the Teachers' Federation at the Central Music Hall, Monday, October 29th, 1900," in CTF Collection, Box 35, folder 4; Murphy, "Taxation and Social Conflict," 244–46; and Chicago Teachers' Federation, *Bulletin* (November 22, 1901).

39. Reid, *Autobiography of Margaret Haley*, 63.

40. Hogan, *Class and Reform*, 202.

41. "Meeting Minutes," October 19, 1900, *Club Minutes*, CWC Collection, Box 21, 3rd book.

42. For the janitors, see Hogan, *Class and Reform*, 202.

43. *Tribune*, July 1, 2, 3, 9 and 10, 1902; and Murphy, "Taxation and Social Conflict," 248–49.

44. *Tribune*, July 1, 1902.

45. See Ibid., July 8, 1902, for authorization of these pay raises, and "Regular Meeting," April 28, 1900, *Club Minutes*, CWC Collection, Box 21, 2nd book.

46. Copy of the League resolution is found in "Regular Meeting," April 28, 1900, *Club Minutes*, CWC Collection, Box 21, 4th book; the CWC's actions are from "Report of the Education Department," April 23, 1902, in Ibid.

47. *Tribune*, February 19 and 24, 1899.

48. Murphy, "Taxation and Social Conflict," 248–49, and "From Artisan to Semi-Professional," 42–48 and 206n.55.

49. *Tribune*, March 5 and 9, 1899.

50. Ibid., February 26, 1899.

51. "Meeting Minutes," March 22, 1899, April 26, 1899, and April 28, 1900, *Club Minutes*, CWC Collection, Box 21, 1st and 2nd books.

52. *Tribune*, March 5 and 12, 1899.

53. See *Tribune*, February 19 and 26, March 5 and 12, 1899, for original plans to replace Harper committee, and January 6 and 13, 1901, for additional information on teacher participation in Committee of 100. See also Murphy, "From Artisan to Semi-Professional," 47–49. At some point, CTF leader Catharine Goggin was added to the committee. See *Tribune*, January 6, 1901. For CWC members, see "Minutes of Meetings," February 27, 1901, *Club Minutes*, CWC Collection, Box 21, 3rd Book.

54. *Tribune*, October 19, 1901.

55. Ibid., June 8, 1899.

56. For examples, see CTF Collection, Box 35, folder 4, account of a mass meeting and letter to Catharine Goggin from Mary McDowell, expressing support and thanks from University of Chicago Settlement Woman's Club for the teachers' fight; and Box 35, folder 5 and Box 36, folder 1 for lists of leaders of the CWC, various local women's clubs, other prominent Chicago women, and the two Chicago women on the University of Illinois Board of Trustees as supporting a fund raising drive. For account of a tax fund benefit, giving total of eight thousand attendees, see *Tribune*, January 19, 1901.

57. "Meeting Minutes," February 27, 1901, *Club Minutes*, CWC Collection, Box 21, 3rd book.

58. Both quotes from typescript of "Mass Meeting of the Teachers' Federation," in CTF Collection, Box 35, folder 4.

59. Ibid. For the Central Labor Union, see chapter 2.

60. Jane Addams, *Democracy and Social Ethics* (New York, 1902), 222–23.

61. "Meeting Minutes," November 23, 1898, *Club Minutes*, CWC Collection, Box 21, 1st book.

62. See Murphy, "From Artisan to Semi-Professional," 49 for the quote, and 75 for her assessment of the teachers' conception of democratic education.

63. *Tribune*, January 8, 1902. Lathrop left Chicago in 1912 to head the Children's Bureau. She returned to the city in 1921, and in 1922 became president of the Illinois League of Women Voters.

64. See, for example, Michael McGerr, *The Decline of Popular Politics: The American North, 1865–1928* (New York, 1986), and Richard L. McCormick, *From Realignment to Reform: Political Change in New York State, 1893–1910* (Ithaca, 1981).

65. Marjorie Murphy, "The Pioneer Work of Women in Building the Teacher Union Movement in Chicago," *American Teacher*, in CTF Collection, Box 1, folder 2.

66. Reid, *Battleground*, 61.

67. Chicago Teachers' Federation, *Bulletin*, January 31, 1902, and *Tribune*, January 12, 1902.

68. Reid, *Battleground*, 72. For Shanahan's opposition to the teachers, also see Murphy, "Taxation and Social Conflict," 246.

Chapter Four
"The Welfare of the Community Requires the Admission of Women to Full Citizenship"

1. See Steven M. Buechler, *The Transformation of the Woman Suffrage Movement: The Case of Illinois, 1850–1920* (New Brunswick, NJ, 1986) for an overview of the Illinois movement including Chicago women's activities, esp. 106–108 for the IWSA. For Funk, see Elizabeth Clemens, "Organizational Repertoires and Institutional Change: Women's Groups and the Transformation of U.S. Politics, 1890–1920," *American Journal of Sociology* 98 (January 1993): 755–98. African American Chicagoan Mary C. Bryon (whose surname in sources is also spelled "Byron") was employed by NAWSA to campaign for suffrage among African American women in Illinois and seven other states. See *The Crisis* (November 1914), 10. For examples of how other urban women's suffrage movements were clearly tied to the national effort and thus less connected to the urban context, see Ellen Carol DuBois, "Working Women, Class Relations, and Suffrage Militance: Harriot Stanton Blatch and the New York Woman Suffrage Movement, 1894–1909," *Journal of American History* 84 (June 1987): 34–58, and *Harriot Stanton Blatch and the Winning of Woman Suffrage* (New Haven, 1997); Sara Hunter Graham, *Woman Suffrage and the New Democracy* (New Haven, 1996), esp. chapter 4; Gayle Gullett, *Becoming Citizens: The Emergence and Development of the California Women's Movement, 1880–1911* (Urbana, 2000); and Judith N. McArthur, *Creating the New Woman: The Rise of Southern Women's Progressive Culture in Texas, 1893–1918* (Urbana, 1998).

2. Caroline Huling MS Collection, especially folders 7 and 35, Special Collections, University of Illinois Chicago Library, Chicago, IL. The quotation is from the Association's meeting of April 17, 1888, printed in *Justitia: A Court for the Unrepresented*, May 1, 1888, folder 7.

3. S. Sara Monoson, "The Lady and the Tiger: Women's Electoral Activism in New York City Before Suffrage," *Journal of Women's History* 2 (Fall 1990): 100–35, examines the Woman's Municipal League, a fairly exclusive group, formed in 1894 and how its early work broadened by the 1910s. According to Elisabeth Perry, "Women's Political Choices After Suffrage: The Women's City Club of New York, 1915–1990," *New York History* (October 1990): 421, the New York Wom-

en's City Club was founded by "a group of about one hundred New York suffrage leaders," who once suffrage was gained "would want an environment of their own in which to study, debate, and take stands on political issues relevant to their life in the city." Chicago women's suffrage activities also differed from those in Los Angeles and San Francisco. See Gullett, *Becoming Citizens*, esp. 162–63 and 182–84, and Philip J. Ethington, *The Public City: The Political Construction of Urban Life in San Francisco, 1850–1900* (Cambridge, UK, 1994), 398–401.

4. See Gullett, *Becoming Citizens*, for her discussion of Los Angeles and San Francisco elite women's clubs in this regard. See also Sarah Deutsch, *Women and the City: Gender, Space, and Power in Boston: 1870–1940* (New York, 2000). In Boston the leading suffrage organization was named the Boston Equal Suffrage Association for Good Government. Note especially Deutsch's assessment of how the women of this organization could not picture themselves as like, or as acting like, working-class women (224).

5. "Regular Meetings," May 24, October 3, 17 and 24, 1894, *Club Minutes*, Chicago Woman's Club MS Collection, Box 20, 3rd book, Chicago Historical Society.

6. The League excluded women who remained in the CWC but moved from the Chicago area. "By-Laws" and "Membership List," *First Annual Report* (1895–96); "Membership List," *Sixth Annual Report* (1900–01); and "Membership List," *Yearbook* (1913–14), Chicago Political Equality League, Chicago Historical Society. The 1913–14 membership list also gives the ward and precinct for all Chicago residents.

7. CPEL, "Program Public Meetings," *Annual Reports* (1896–1897 and 1897–1898).

8. CPEL, *By-Laws and Annual Reports* (1895–1900). Addams's topics were "Present Day Attitudes toward Social Problems," "City Politics," "Charitable Relations," "Trades Unions," "Contemporary Efforts at Social Control of Industrial Communities," and "Contemporary Efforts at Social Control through the Agency of Government."

9. Flyer titled "Illinois Women Tax-payers should have the Ballot," June 1[8], 1902, signed by Catharine Waugh McCulloch and Ella S. Stewart, in Catharine Waugh McCulloch MS Collection, Reel #1 (folder 22), Schlesinger Library, Cambridge, MA. See also, Chicago *Tribune*, July 2, 1902, and clipping from *Woman's Journal* (Boston, 1894) in Lucy Flower Scrapbooks, Lucy Flower MS Collection, Chicago Historical Society.

10. For a full examination of the charter reform movement in Chicago, see Maureen A. Flanagan, *Charter Reform in Chicago* (Carbondale, IL, 1987).

11. In addition to the municipal government, these included the Cook County government, which had among its powers the authority to distribute public welfare in the city; the school board; the public library board; the three park boards; and the Municipal Sanitary District.

12. See Flanagan, *Charter Reform in Chicago*, 24–26.

13. Ibid., 58–64, for discussion of the overwhelmingly middle-class, professional, and business-oriented membership of the Charter Convention.

14. Whether, and to what extent, women participated in the charter reform campaigns of the Progressive Era depended on the context of the individual city, a

circumstance that has hardly been investigated by urban historians. Older studies, such as David Hammack, *Power and Society: Greater New York at the Turn of the Century* (New York, 1987), Harold L. Platt, *City Building in the New South: The Growth of Public Services in Houston, Texas, 1830–1910* (Philadelphia, 1983), and Martin Schiesl, *The Politics of Efficiency: Municipal Administration and Reform in America: 1880–1920* (Berkeley, 1977), were written before urban historians even thought about women's involvement in political reform. James J. Connolly, *The Triumph of Ethnic Progressivism: Urban Political Culture in Boston, 1900–1925* (Cambridge, MA, 1998), integrates women into his study, but he emphasizes ethnicity and progressivism. As a result, activist Boston women remain in the background of his study of political reform. He says that "the one group that might have jumped into the [charter] fray, the Boston Equal Suffrage Association for Good Government, had by 1909 shifted its emphasis almost entirely to suffrage work" (97). It would be interesting to know the reasons for this shift, and to know if other women's groups might have been interested in this issue, and if not, why not.

Women's historians rarely connect women to such political events as charter reform. Gullett, *Becoming Citizens*, discusses only the 1880s charter reform efforts in Los Angeles, not later efforts. According to Gullett, elite women in the 1880s supported "the city charter movement, a reform that promised to make city government more efficient and rational by replacing elected officials with appointed experts." She emphasizes elite women interested in "good government progressivism" and not the context of the city itself. Deutsch, *Women and the City*, does not investigate Boston charter reform. Yet the precise urban context may well help dictate differences for women from city to city. According to Gullett, in California cities, organized women and city fathers began building alliances with one another and created "progressivism" there. She rejects the existence of a connection between the strengthening of the suffrage movement in California and women's participation in the good government movement as a "moot point." See 46, 150, and 170.

15. "Preliminary Report on the Need for a New City Charter," Chicago Civic Federation MS Collection, Box 3, Chicago Historical Society; and "Regular Meeting," April 9, 1902, *Club Minutes*, CWC Collection, Box 21, 4th Book.

16. Letter from Ellen Henrotin to Catharine Waugh McCulloch, January 15, 1906, McCulloch Collection, Microfilm Reel #1.

17. "Minutes of Meetings," April 1, 1906, Chicago Federation of Labor. Microfilm at Chicago Historical Society.

18. Letter from the Illinois Equal Suffrage Association, May 14, 1906, in McCulloch Collection, Microfilm Reel #1.

19. McCulloch to A. G. Ingraham, June 12, 1906, McCulloch Collection, Microfilm Reel #1.

20. Letters of R. T. Crane, June 20, 1906, and A. C. Bartlett, June 18, 1906, to Catharine Waugh McCulloch, McCulloch Collection, Microfilm Reel #1.

21. Gullett, *Becoming Citizens*, reports that elite Los Angeles men and women cooperated on suffrage because they had the same vision of "good government" urban reform. McArthur, *Creating the New Woman*, 104, says that Texas women "could argue the need for married women's property law, and a vote, to defend their interests and those of their children. Reconceptualized and de-radicalized by

an infusion of Progressive-Era maternalism, both demands gained popularity." Neither situation pertained to the activism of Chicago women.

22. "Regular Meeting," September 26, 1906, *Board Minutes*, CWC Collection, Box 4. A letter to this effect was sent to all members.

23. McCulloch to Raymond Robins, November 30, 1906, Raymond Robins MS Collection, State Historical Society of Wisconsin, Madison, Wisconsin.

24. Chicago Charter Convention, 1906–1907, *Proceedings*, December 4, 1906, 130–31.

25. Ibid., December 27, 1906, 767–78, contains the delegates' arguments on municipal suffrage.

26. Robins to McCulloch, December 17, 1906, in McCulloch Collection, Microfilm Reel #1.

27. McCulloch Collection, Microfilm Reel #2.

28. Note from Addams to Sophonisba Breckinridge, n.d., inviting her to a meeting to consider plans for defeating the charter, in Breckinridge Family MS Collection, Microfilm Reel #2 (corresponds to folders 740 and 741), Library of Congress, Washington, D.C.; see also Ellen M. Henrotin MS Collection, Box 1, folder 2, Schlesinger Library, Radcliffe College, Cambridge, MA.

29. Jane Addams, *Twenty Years at Hull House* (New York, 1910), 203–206 and 237–38. Henrotin said there were 110 women's groups. Henrotin MS Collection, Box 1, folder 2. See Chicago *Record-Herald*, March 7, 1906, for Addams's talk.

30. See *Charter Reform in Chicago*, 77–83, for a discussion of this issue and the charter.

31. "Minutes of Meetings," November-December 1906, CTF MS Collection, Box 39, folder 2.

32. Letter of Maloney and Henry to the CTF, printed in Chicago Teachers' Federation, *Bulletin*, June 29, 1907. Maloney was an Irish immigrant and leader of the Chicago Local 484 Waitresses' Union from 1902–1921, and served on the General Executive Board of the National Women's Trade Union League. See Dorothy Sue Cobble, *Dishing It Out: Waitresses and their Unions in the Twentieth Century* (Urbana, 1991), 66, 75, and 81.

33. "Minutes of Meetings," CFL June 16, 1907, and Chicago *American*, June 16, 1907.

34. Addams, *Twenty Years*, 237.

35. Chicago *American*, August 4, 1907. This was a Hearst-owned newspaper that opposed the charter.

36. Chicago *Inter-Ocean*, September 9, 1907.

37. CPEL, *Twelfth Annual Report* (1906–07).

38. One obvious lesson here is that if scholars just pay attention to the newspapers and to men's sources, urban women's political efforts will go unnoticed.

39. See Flanagan, *Charter Reform*, chapters 4 and 5.

40. "Report of the Legislative Department," (1906–07), McCulloch Collection, Microfilm Reel #1.

41. Sikes quoted in Karen M. Mason, "Testing the Boundaries: Women, Politics, and Gender Roles in Chicago, 1890–1930" (Ph.D. Dissertation, University of Michigan, 1991), 127.

42. See Mason's overall assessment of Sikes, in "Testing the Boundaries," esp. 118–19 and 141–47.

43. Letter from Madeleine Wallin Sikes to Alfred Wallin, February 16, 1909, in George and Madeleine Wallin Sikes MS Collection, Box 3, Chicago Historical Society.

44. Hilda Satt Polacheck MS Collection, Box 2, folder 11, Special Collections, University of Illinois Chicago Library, Chicago. Polacheck's writings have been edited into a biography by Dena J. Polacheck Epstein, *I Came A Stranger: The Story of a Hull-House Girl* (Urbana, 1989).

45. Letter of Charles Merriam to Catharine Waugh McCulloch, November 4, 1908, Charles Merriam MS Collection, Box 12, folder 25, Special Collections, Regenstein Library, University of Chicago. Merriam and Fisher are also both quoted in *Record-Herald*, November 11, 1909.

46. See *Record-Herald*, February 8 and 23, 1909.

47. See accounts of this lobbying effort in Agnes Nestor MS Collection, Box 1, folder 4, Chicago Historical Society. See letters from Grace Nicholes to Nestor, December 8, 1908, and February 3, 1909, Box 1, folders 3 and 4, asking Nestor to speak to the CWC. See also the suffrage resolution adopted by second interstate conference of National Women's Trade Union League meeting in September 1908. Delegates specifically representing Chicago women's unions, and not the WTUL as an organization, were the dominant force at this conference. See the *Union Labor Advocate* (December 1908), for the resolution (32) and for the list of delegates (40).

48. See Flanagan, *Charter Reform in Chicago*, 144–45, for failure of the 1909 charter legislation.

49. See Buechler, *The Transformation of the Woman Suffrage Movement*; Adade Mitchell Wheeler, "Conflict in the Illinois Woman Suffrage Movement of 1913," *Illinois State Historical Journal* (Summer 1983): 95–114; and Adade Wheeler and Marlene Stein Wortman, *The Roads They Made: Women in Illinois History* (Chicago, 1977).

50. "Minutes of Meetings," March 28, 1912, University of Chicago Settlement Woman's Club, in Nestor MS Collection, Box 1, folder 6.

51. Daily *Socialist*, March 18, 1912, clipping in Chicago Women's Trade Union League Scrapbooks, Box 1, folder 3, Special Collections, University of Illinois Chicago Library, Chicago. See also *Tribune*, March [21?], 1912 (with photos).

52. Unidentified newspaper clipping, March [30?] 1912, CWTUL Scrapbooks, Box 1, folder 3.

53. In 1911 the Chicago Woman Suffrage party was chaired by CWTUL leader Margaret Dreier Robins. Margaret Haley also belonged to the party. Elizabeth A. Payne, *Reform, Labor, and Feminism: Margaret Dreier Robins and the Women's Trade Union League* (Urbana, 1988), 144, and Marjorie Murphy, "The Pioneer Work of Women in Building the Teacher-Union Movement in Chicago," *The American Teacher* (n.d.), in CTF Collection, Box 1, folder 2.

Chapter Five
"To Bring Together Women Interested in Promoting the Welfare of the City"

1. See membership lists in Woman's City Club of Chicago, *Yearbook* (1910), *Its Book* (1915), and *Bulletin* (May 1919 and 1920).

2. In 1915–16, 16 percent of women belonging to the WCC were married to men in the City Club; 55 percent of married women officers and directors of the WCC in that same year were married to men in the City Club, while 75 percent of married women chairing the WCC's standing and civic committees had husbands in the City Club. WCC, *Its Book*. The WCC was primarily a middle-class organization. Many upper-class women did belong, and the WCC was not free of class and ethnic prejudices, but its members came from every city ward, and included settlement house residents, public school teachers, professional women, University of Chicago professors, a few labor leaders, Catholic and Jewish women, and African American clubwomen. Most of the members were nowhere else mentioned as "prominent" or identified with "prominent" Chicago men. So the WCC is not an "upper-class women's club," as described by Steven M. Buechler, *The Transformation of the Woman Suffrage Movement: The Case of Illinois, 1850–1920* (New Brunswick, NJ, 1986), 166, nor was it a club of "elite" women such as those in Los Angeles and San Francisco or the Women's Municipal League of Boston. See Gayle Gullett, *Becoming Citizens: The Emergence and Development of the California Women's Movement, 1880–1911* (Urbana, 2000), and James J. Connolly, *The Triumph of Ethnic Progressivism: Urban Political Culture in Boston, 1900–1925* (Cambridge, MA, 1998), 48–50.

3. In general, the City Club membership was smaller—172 at its founding to around 2,400 by 1916; it took only one vote to blackball nominees, who had to be "those who are sincerely interested in practical methods of improving public conditions." Letter of Walter L. Fisher to Messrs. Marx and Door, November 16, 1903, Walter L. Fisher MS Collection, Library of Congress, Washington, D.C. Acceptance into the WCC required only the testimony of one member that a prospective new member sympathized with the WCC's objectives. For an extended analysis of the membership of the two clubs, see Maureen A. Flanagan, "Gender and Urban Political Reform: The City Club and the Woman's City Club of Chicago in the Progressive Era," *American Historical Review* 95 (October, 1990): 1032–50. For membership information on the City Club, see "List of Members," December 1903 and February 2, 1905, in City Club of Chicago MS Collection, Box 20, folder 1, Chicago Historical Society, and City Club, *Yearbook* (1905–06). In 1906, the City Club had considered actually fixing the total membership at no more than one thousand. See "Circular," March 26, 1906, CC Collection, Box 20, folder 2.

4. WCC, *Its Book* (1915), and monthly issues of the *Bulletin* contain accounts of the ward committee activities. Gwendolyn Wright, *Moralism and the Model Home: Domestic Architecture and Cultural Conflict in Chicago, 1873–1913* (Chicago, 1980), 281, observed the different methods practiced by the men and women in the two clubs.

5. "Membership Circular," March 23, 1904, CC Collection, Box 20, folder 1. Until 1913, women could not participate in City Club discussions.

6. Julius Rosenwald MS Collection, Box 20, folder 2, Special Collections, Regenstein Library, University of Chicago.

7. Jane Addams, "Mary Hawes Wilmarth," in *The Excellent Becomes the Permanent* (New York, 1932), 103.

8. Anna E. Nicholes, "How Women Can Help in the Administration of a City," *The Woman's Citizen Library*, v. 9 (New York, 1913), 2143–2208.

9. See Maureen A. Flanagan, "Gender and Urban Political Reform" and "The City Profitable, the City Livable: Environmental Policy, Gender, and Power in Chicago in the 1910s," *Journal of Urban History* 22 (January 1996): 163–90; and Suellen Hoy, "Municipal Housekeeping: The Role of Women in Improving Urban Sanitation Practices, 1870–1917," in Martin V. Melosi, ed., *Pollution and Reform in American Cities, 1870–1930* (Austin, 1980): 173–98 . Judith N. McArthur, *Creating the New Woman: The Rise of Southern Women's Progressive Culture in Texas 1893–1918* (Urbana, 1998) sees municipal housekeeping as emanating from the home economics movement. Philip J. Ethington, "Recasting Urban Political History: Gender, the Public, the Household, and Political Participation in Boston and San Francisco during the Progressive Era," *Social Science History* 16 (Summer 1992): 301–33, and Connolly, *The Triumph of Ethnic Progressivism*, 49, 72–73, detail the political nature of municipal housekeeping.

10. Both quotations are from Nicholes, "How Women Can Help in the Administration of a City," 2150–51. Dallas men and activist women differed over the issue of a municipal water system. Men "proposed building a new reservoir and allowing the new water from purer sources to mix with supply in the old reservoirs, and treating the whole with chemicals when circumstances required it," while the Dallas Federation of Women "undertook a three-year campaign to persuade the male electorate to approve a bond issue for a filtration plant." See McArthur, *Creating the New Woman*, 34.

11. Anne Phillips, *Engendering Democracy* (University Park, PA, 1991).

12. Nicholes, "How Women Can Help," 2143, 2163, and 2184.

13. See again McArthur's example of the different approach of activist Dallas men and women on water filtration. Women wanted government to prevent problems; men wanted to reserve government action to respond *if* something happened. See chapter 7, below, for a similar difference regarding Sheppard-Towner legislation.

14. Nicholes, "How Women Can Help," 2205–2206. For Fulmer, see *Tribune*, October 28, 1905.

15. Wright, *Moralism and the Model Home*, 281, for quotations, and 271 for her statement of the WCC's turn away from housing reform.

16. Thomas Philpott, *The Slum and the Ghetto: Neighborhood Deterioration and Middle-Class Reform, Chicago 1880–1930* (New York, 1978).

17. Ibid., 108–109.

18. "Report of the Committee on Tenement Houses," Citizens' Association of Chicago (1884), pamphlet at Chicago Historical Society.

19. Unidentified newspaper clipping, January 3, 1891, in Thomas and Elizabeth Morgan Collection, Book 2, in Illinois Historical Survey, University of Illinois Library, Urbana, IL.

20. Robert Hunter, *Tenement Conditions in Chicago: A Report by the Investigating Committee of the City Homes Association* (Chicago, 1901). Jane Addams had secured financial support for this endeavor from Anita Blaine McCormick. See Philpott, *The Slum and Ghetto*, 100–101, for the 1902 ordinance.

21. Philpott, *The Slum and the Ghetto*, 102–106, and Harold Platt, "Jane Addams and the Ward Boss Revisited: Class, Politics, and Public Health in Chicago, 1890–1930," *Environmental History* 5 (April 2000): 194–222, esp. 209.

22. When the issue was discussed at the 1907 charter convention, the majority resolutely opposed giving the city council police powers to compel property owners to comply with tenement ordinances. Property rights, not a corrupt city council, was the foremost concern. Chicago Charter Convention, meeting of February 23, 1907, *Proceedings* (October 1906 to March 1907), 1017–19.

23. Philpott, *The Slum and Ghetto*, 107 [emphasis in original] and "Minutes of Meetings," June 17, 1912, City Club Collection, Box 15, folder 1.

24. Sadie T. Wald, "1900—Housing Conditions—1905," *Charities and the Commons* (December 30, 1905), 455.

25. Philpott, 101–102.

26. Wald, "Housing Conditions," 461.

27. Ibid., 455.

28. Men and women did not abandon the effort to force sanitary inspections of the city's housing stock, but this idea was gradually subordinated to the objective of constructing new housing. See, for examples, "The Housing Problem in Chicago," pamphlet of Housing Committee, the Chicago Association of Commerce (1912), Chicago Historical Society; and Chicago *Record-Herald*, November 11 and 12 and December 27, 1911, and December 15, 1912.

29. City Club of Chicago, "The Philadelphia Housing Conference," *Bulletin* 5 (December 20, 1912): 409–17. With one exception, the papers reflected these preoccupations. The one woman speaker at the Philadelphia conference, Johanna von Wagner, spoke on "Instructive Sanitary Inspection." See "Second Housing Conference," *The Survey* (November 23, 1912), 219. "Minutes of Meetings," June 17, 1912, *Committee on Housing Conditions*, CC MS Collection, Box 14, folder 2.

30. City Club, "The Philadelphia Housing Conference."

31. The City Club, for example, had been following this course for some time as it studied housing problems. See also Wright, *Moralism and the Model Home*, 261–62.

32. City Club, "The Third National Conference on Housing," *Bulletin* 7 (January 12, 1914), 2–10.

33. Breckinridge earned a Ph.D. in political science with a dissertation on the development of legal tender in the United States and Britain. Abbott's was in political economy, with a dissertation titled "A Statistical Study of the Wages of Unskilled Labor, 1830–1900"; Ellen Fitzpatrick, *Endless Crusade: Women Social Scientists and Progressive Reform* (New York, 1990), 50–52, 66–67, and 176–83, discusses the professional training of both women.

34. City Club, *Bulletin* 7, 11–12. According to Ellen Fitzpatrick (52), Breckinridge "saw government power as malleable. . . . When government served a public good, she deemed sweeping actions justifiable . . . [and] viewed as legitimate the exercise of federal authority in regulating economic affairs. This idea was an intellectual precondition for the modern welfare state Breckinridge would later endorse."

35. City Club, *Bulletin* 7, 11–12. Abbott, too, emphasized the crucial role of government, saying, "[U]ntil we have an efficient city government in this city and in every other city in this country, we will never get housing reform." If that quotation is taken out of its context and not correlated with many other of Ab-

bott's statements, it could be mistaken as a plea for good government before all else. Yet in its context, it is clear that for her efficient government was necessary because only then could urban residents get from it the housing and other welfare measures that they needed. See below in this chapter, subsection on fire prevention, for elaboration on this idea.

36. For the committee's almost total preoccupation with these issues, see "Minutes of Meetings," February 16 and March 2, 1913, November 18, 1915, and January 27, 1916 (which contains quote on paternalism), *Committee on Housing Conditions*, City Club MS Collection, Box 15, folder 1, and Box 17, folder 3.

37. "Minutes of Meetings," April 27, May 11, 18 and 25, 1914, *Committee on Housing*, City Club Collection, Box 16, folder 3.

38. "Final Year's Report," *Committee on Housing* (1916), City Club Collection, Box 17, folder 3. "Minutes of Meetings," March 2, 9, and 16, 1916, *Committee on Housing*, City Club Collection, Box 17, folder 3, and May 25, 1916, Box 18, folder 7.

39. Ibid., March 2, 9 and 16, *Committee on Housing*, City Club Collection, Box 17, folder 3, and May 25, 1916, Box 18, folder 7. See also Alfred B. Yeomans, *City Residential Land Development: Studies in Planning, Competitive Plans for Subdividing a Typical Quarter Section of Land in the Outskirts of Chicago* (Chicago, 1916), and Wright, *Moralism and the Model Home*, 281, for accounts of this work. City Club, *Bulletin* 12 (December 22, 1919). See also, Robert B. Fairbanks, "Planning, Zoning, and City Government in Dallas, 1900–1930," *Journal of Urban History* 25 (September 1999): 809–37.

40. *Tribune*, April 1, 1914.

41. "Annual Report of the Civics Committee," April 1914, *Club Minutes*, and "Annual Report," *Club Minutes*, April 1915, Chicago Woman's Club MS Collection, Box 23 and 24, Chicago Historical Society. WCC, *Its Book*, 73–74.

42. "Minutes of Meetings," March 8, 1915, *Committee on Housing Conditions*, City Club Collection, Box 16, folder 3, Chicago Historical Society, and Yeomans, *City Residential Land Development*.

43. Philpott, *The Slum and the Ghetto*, A. Scott Henderson, *Housing and the Democratic Ideal: The Life and Thought of Charles Abrams* (New York, 2000), and Lawrence Vale, *From the Puritans to the Projects: Public Housing and Public Neighbors* (Cambridge, MA, 2000), 72 and 130.

44. Allan H. Spear, *Black Chicago: The Making of a Negro Ghetto, 1890–1920* (Chicago, 1967), 216–18, summarizes white male response to the racial rioting of 1919. Philpott, *The Slum and the Ghetto*, 207–208 and 259–69, discusses the housing ideas of Chicago philanthropist Julius Rosenwald in this regard.

45. Fitzpatrick, 180–82; and Breckinridge to Julia Lathrop, December 23, 1909, in Breckinridge Family MS Collection, Microfilm Reel #2 (Container 740–41), Library of Congress, Washington, D.C.

46. Sophonisba Breckinridge, "The Color Line in the Housing Problem," *The Survey* 29 (February 1, 1913): 575–76.

47. Letter of Celia Parker Woolley to Breckinridge, November 26, 1913, Microfilm Reel #2, Breckinridge Collection; "Regular Meeting of December 10, 1913," *Club Minutes*, CWC Collection, Box 23.

48. See the WCC, *Bulletin* (February 1920) for call for a national bureau, and City Club, *Bulletin* (January 17, 1921) for Vittum. After March 1918 no additional committee minutes for the City Club Housing Committee are extant; after 1922, the *Bulletin* contains no further mentions of a housing committee.

49. For additional details on this entire issue, see Flanagan, "Gender and Urban Political Reform," 1038–39.

50. Reduction produced soap, grease, and fertilizer as profitable by-products but necessitated that people first separate their pure garbage from unreducible refuse and admittedly produced noxious odors; incineration, instead, burned everything at a high heat, generated electricity that could be captured by the city, and was virtually odorless. City Club, "Chicago's Garbage Problem," *Bulletin* 6 (December 20, 1913): 336. See Martin Melosi, *The Sanitary City: Urban Infrastructure in America from Colonial Times to the Present* (Baltimore, 2000), 199–200.

51. Jane Addams, *Twenty Years at Hull House*, 203–205; Nicholes, "How Women Can Help," 2192–93.

52. *Tribune*, April 10, 1908; Nicholes, "How Women Can Help," 2173–75; and WCC, *Its Book*, 52–56.

53. *Tribune*, February 22, 1914. See Philpott, *The Slum and the Ghetto*, 101–103, for his description of how the city council cynically passed regulations that they could then be bribed not to enforce. Maureen A. Flanagan, *Charter Reform in Chicago* (Carbondale, IL, 1987), describes the practices of the aldermanic ring, the Grey Wolves, that in the 1890s awarded a franchise to a non-existent company so that other bidders would be forced to raise their bids.

54. For the CWTUL, see clipping from Chicago *Examiner*, May 15, 1911, in Chicago Women's Trade Union League MS Collection, Box 1, folder 1, Special Collections, University of Illinois Chicago Library. WCC, *Its Book*, 55, and *Bulletin* 4 (September 1915): 2, describe and summarize the WCC efforts.

55. Nicholes, "How Women Can Help," 2194

56. "Yearly Report," April 7, 1914, *Committee on Garbage and Refuse Disposal*, CC MS Collection, Box 14, folder 6.

57. See "Minutes of Meeting," January 29, 1917, WCC MS Collection, Box 1, folder 1, Chicago Historical Society, for Agnes Nestor's summary of women's concerns on this issue, and Chicago Daily *News*, May 5, 1911, and Evening *Post* June 9, 1911, clippings in CWTUL Collection, Box 1, folder 1.

58. This may seem anomalous in a city that was often in the grip of venal machine politicians of both parties. But, at least since Jane Addams' victory in attacking the corrupt bargain between politicians and businessmen that had helped produce a typhoid epidemic in 1902, many Chicago activists were optimistic about conquering political corruption. For activist women, then, it seemed possible that they could achieve both clean government through citizen action and make government responsible for the common welfare. See mentions, above, of Breckinridge and housing, and below in chapter 7 for Sheppard-Towner legislation. In this regard, the activist Chicago women considered in this book differed markedly from the California clubwomen described by Gullett, *Becoming Citizens*, as aligning themselves with male reformers. Much more systematic study of women's direct relationship to the urban context needs to be done before we can have an

accurate picture of urban women and reform in the Progressive Era. For Addams and the typhoid epidemic, see Platt, "Jane Addams and the Ward Boss Revisited," 208–14.

59. See Flanagan, *Charter Reform in Chicago.*

60. Daily *World*, July 23, 1912, clipping in CWTUL Collection, Box 1, folder 4.

61. For these demands and justifications, see *Record-Herald*, October 14, 1912, clipping in CWTUL Collection, Box 1, folder 4; WCC, *Bulletin* 2 (July 1913); and "Minutes of Meeting," January 29, 1917, WCC MS Collection, Box 1, folder 1.

62. "Minutes of Meetings," January 29, 1917, WCC MS Collection, Box 1 folder 1. For New York City, see Sara E. Wermiel, *The Fireproof Building: Technology and Public Safety in the Nineteenth-Century American City* (Baltimore, 2000), 206–10.

63. And, as Eric Monkkonen has pointed out, businessmen could approve of municipal expenditures to create a modern fire department because such capital expenses "provided an important investment opportunity for the private money market." Monkkonen, *America Becomes Urban: The Development of U.S. Cities and Towns, 1780–1980* (Berkeley, 1988), 109.

64. WCC, "Report of Clean Air and Transportation Committee for 1913/14 and 1914/15." *Its Book*, 62–63.

65. Stradling, *Smokestacks and Progressives: Environmentalists, Engineers, and Air Quality in America, 1881–1951* (Baltimore, 1999), 101–102.

66. *Record-Herald*, October 1908 covered this campaign. See also, WCC, *Yearbook* (1910–1911) and Henriette Greenebaum Frank and Amalie Hofer Jerome, *Annals of the Chicago Woman's Club for the First Forty Years of Its Organization, 1876–1916* (Chicago, 1916), 270. I want to thank Harold Platt for sharing his research on the Anti-Smoke League.

67. WCC, *Bulletin* (April 1915): 7; and for the quotation see, WCC, *Its Book*, 64. R. Dale Grinder, "The Battle for Clean Air: The Smoke Problem in Post-Civil War America," in Martin V. Melosi, ed., *Pollution and Reform in American Cities, 1870–1930* (Austin, 1980), 83–103, discusses differences in types of coal. Viewing the Anti-Smoke League primarily as a minor aspect of anti-smoke environmentalism risks trivializing these women as housewives who were a mere sideshow to male environmentalism. When placed in the broader context of urban development, it is not persuasive to argue that these women were assuming "their high moral ground and with a sense of the dramatic [were denouncing] the greedy soilers of civilization," as Stradling, *Smokestacks and Progressives*, 119–20, contends. The Anti-Smoke League was a small element of a larger women's movement concerned about public health and safety in the city.

68. "Minutes of Meetings," September 5, 1913, *Committee on Smoke Abatement*, City Club MS Collection, Box 15, folder 5. For the gender differences exhibited by Pittsburgh women and men on smoke pollution, see Angela Gugliotta, "Class, Gender, and Coal Smoke: Gender Ideology and Environmental Injustice in Pittsburgh, 1868–1914," *Environmental History* 5 (April 2000): 165–93.

69. For the CAC's work and its reports, see Harold L. Platt, "Invisible Gases: Smoke, Science, and the Redefinition of Environmental Policy in Chicago, 1900–1920," *Planning Perspectives* 10 (1995): 67–97. The committee categorized five

coal-burning services: central power plants, locomotives, low pressure heating plants, domestic heating plants, and marine stacks.

70. Melosi, *The Sanitary City*, 107, states explicitly that "the Progressives' advocacy of environmental reform was often constrained by less enthusiasm for social welfare programs that weakened their ability to direct political and social change."

71. See Chicago *Defender*, September 19, 1914, for African American women. Nicholes, "How Women Can Help," 2196–98; Wright, *Moralism and the Model Home*, 265; WCC, *Its Book*, 65–66; and WCC, *Bulletin* (April 1915): 4–5. See Flanagan, "The City Profitable, the City Livable," for a more extensive discussion of this issue.

72. Stanley Schultz, *Constructing Urban Culture: American Cities and City Planning, 1800–1920* (Philadelphia, 1989), 148–49, emphasizes how male sanitarians dismissed this type of clean-up as aesthetic urban housekeeping. Stradling, *Smokestacks and Progressives*, tends in this direction.

73. Chicago *Defender*, September 19, 1914.

74. WCC, *Bulletin* (July 1915): 4–8.

75. *Defender*, September 19, 1914.

76. "Minutes of Meetings," April 8, 1914, *Committee on Streets, Alleys, and Bridges*, City Club MS Collection, Box 16, folder 5. This attitude undoubtedly contributed to the relative ineffectualness of clean-up campaigns. See Melosi, *The Sanitary City*, 186.

77. See Wanda Hendricks, "The Politics of Race: Black Women in Illinois, 1890–1920" (Ph.D. Dissertation, Purdue University, 1990), for the development among Chicago African American women of a sense about the possibilities of using government to secure a broader social welfare.

78. Mary McDowell, "Civic Experiences," (1914), typescript in Mary McDowell MS Collection, folder 19, Chicago Historical Society.

79. See Kriste Lindenmeyer, *"A Right to Childhood": The U.S. Children's Bureau and Child Welfare, 1912–46* (Urbana, 1997), 146–47. Such an analysis is not wrong, but it is also not sufficient for urban historians. Monkkonen, *America Becomes Urban*, chapter 9, discusses the shift beginning around 1870 toward constructing a more active, service-providing city in the United States. Within this overall shift of perspective, however, there still existed distinctly male and female visions of how activist the municipal government should be, and for what purposes this activism would be taken.

80. See Michael McCarthy, "Chicago Businessmen and the Burnham Plan," *Illinois State Historical Journal* (Autumn 1970): 228–56.

81. City Council of Chicago, "Proceedings of the Subcommittee on Harbor Development of the Committee on Harbors, Wharves and Bridges of the City Council of Chicago," *Journal of the Proceedings of the City Council* (Chicago, 1911): 17–18.

82. City Club, "Harbor Development and the Proposed Bond Issue," *Bulletin* 5 (March 29, 1912): 84, 87–89. Letters of support for lakefront harbor plans came from prominent merchants Marshall Field and John V. Farwell, and a representative of the Association of Commerce also spoke strongly in favor. Sentiment remained the same a few years later. See "Annual Report for 1915," *Committee on Harbors, Wharves, Waterways*, 317B–317G, CC Collection, Box 17, folder 5.

83. See WCC, *Bulletin* (November 1916): 7–8, for a description of this proposal. Burnham's *Plan* had envisioned such grand-scale recreational possibilities for the lakefront; both it and the Special Parks Commission's plan would have taken years and huge sums of money to complete.

84. See description of this group above in chapter 2. "Souvenir of Dedication of South Side Bath at 39th Street and Wentworth Avenue" (March 30, 1897), 35, The Newberry Library. I want to thank Suellen Hoy for sharing her research on cleanliness with me. The League's phrasing is pertinent to the historical debate that characterizes women of this period as pursuing a "politics of *needs*" distinct from the "politics of *rights*" typical of men, a distinction posed most notably by Nancy Fraser, "Struggle over Needs: Outline of a Socialist-Feminist Critical Theory of Late Capitalist Political Culture," in *Unruly Practices: Power, Discourse, and Gender in Contemporary Social Theory* (Minneapolis, 1989). Kathryn Kish Sklar, *Florence Kelley and the Nation's Work: The Rise of Women's Political Culture, 1830–1900* (New Haven, 1995), 258–59, analyzes Florence Kelley's shifting the argument from one of rights of property to one of "a new civil and economic right for women to be protected from abuse and ill health."

85. Frank and Jerome, *Annals of the Chicago Woman's Club*, 248.

86. Thomas S. Hines, *Burnham of Chicago: Architect and Planner* (Chicago, 1979), 324 and 332, quotation on 327.

87. WCC, *Bulletin* (September 1916): 4, and *Bulletin* (November 1916): 8. Capitalization in the original.

88. Paul Barrett, *The Automobile and Urban Transit: The Formation of Public Policy in Chicago, 1900–1930* (Philadelphia, 1983), 109.

89. See "Minutes of Meetings," July 7, 1889, *Minute Book*, Trades and Labor Assembly MS Collection, Chicago Historical Society. Not *all* businessmen at *all* times thought only of the lakefront's economic potential. Aaron Montgomery Ward had filed suit in 1890 to remove unsightly structures from what is now the Grant Park area and keep it an open public space. See Lois Wille, *Forever Open, Clear, and Free: The Struggle for Chicago's Lakefront*, 2nd ed. (Chicago, 1991), chapter 7.

90. City Club, *Bulletin* (March 29, 1912): 82.

91. The first quotation is from the WCC, *Bulletin* (October 1916): 13; and the second, *Bulletin* (November 1916): 7–8. See also *Bulletin* (July 1916): 9.

92. See letters from Greater Chicago Federation to Chicago City Council and from 10th Ward Taxpayers, *Journal of the Proceedings of the Chicago City Council* (April 26, 1915), 19 and (July 6, 1915), 979. See also *Journal of the Proceedings* (April 4, 1917), 4198.

93. *Record-Herald*, July 11, 1911.

94. Accounts of this project are in WCC, "Ten Years of Civic Work," *Bulletin* (May 1920): 3–4; and *Its Book*, 38–41.

95. WCC, *Bulletin* (September 1916): 4.

96. For the City Club proposals, see "Minutes of Meetings," October 9, 1916, *Committee on Parks and Playgrounds*, City Club Collection, Box 19, folder 1; for an earlier example of the statistical approach to beach building, see "Minutes of Meetings," May 27, 1913, *Committee on Water Front*, Box 15, folder 7. Consolidation of the park districts did not come until the 1930s. See Ellen Fitzpatrick,

Endless Crusade, and Robyn Muncy, *Creating a Female Dominion in American Reform, 1890–1935* (New York, 1991), for evidence of women, professionalism, and statistical analyses.

97. WCC, *Bulletin* (October 16, 1916): 13, and *Its Book*, 74. Parts of recreational schemes proposed by various women's and men's organizations sometimes overlapped. Many activist women had supported aspects of Burnham's plan and park consolidation. But by focusing on male groups and proposals and neglecting the women's records, historians have missed important points of disagreement on lakefront plans. In 1916, for instance, the CWC declared in favor of consolidation but opposed the scheme being proposed by male organizations. "Annual Report of the Playground Committee," April 1914, *Club Minutes*, CWC Collection, Box 23, and "Annual Report of the Playground Committee," *Club Minutes*, April 1916, Box 25.

98. "Minutes of Regular Meeting," December 3, 1913 undated resolution in section marked March 1914; and "Annual Report of the Playground Committee," April 1914, *Club Minutes*, CWC Collection, Box 23. WCC, *Its Book*, 74.

99. WCC, *Its Book*, 74, states this explicitly for parks and playgrounds in the city.

100. Elizabeth A. Payne, *Reform, Labor, and Feminism: Margaret Dreier Robins and the Women's Trade Union League* (Urbana, 1988), 88–91, cites forty thousand; twenty-five thousand is the figure given in "Concerning the Garment Workers' Strike: Report of the Sub-Committee to the Citizens' Committee, Nov. 5th, 1910," in Ellen Henrotin MS Collection, folder 48, Schlesinger Library, Radcliffe College, Cambridge, MA.

101. Payne, *Reform, Labor, and Feminism*, 90–91.

102. Women's ability to cooperate across class on labor issues in the city is often ignored by labor historians, who stress class divisions or working women's actions. By doing so, they have buried an important argument in the process of urban development in Chicago. Historians of American socialism rarely address the cross-class alliances women made in this and other strikes. See, for example, Mari Jo Buhle, *Women and American Socialism, 1870–1920* (Urbana, 1981), 194–96. For a different perspective, see Janice L. Reiff, "A Modern Lear and His Daughters: Gender in the Model Town of Pullman," *Journal of Urban History* 23 (March 1997): 316–41, which links gender and labor in the context of competing visions about a good urban society. A similarly titled but different flyer was co-authored by Starr and socialist sympathizer Gertrude Barnum and lists the CFL, CWTUL, and Bowen as raising funds to help striking workers and their families. "Garment Workers' Strike," Ellen Gates Starr MS Collection, Box 1, folder 18, Smith College Library, Northampton MA. For Smith, the CPEL, and Woodlawn Woman's Club, see *Tribune*, November 7 and 15, 1910. See also, Deutsch, *Women and the City*, 224

103. "Concerning the Garment Workers' Strike."

104. *Tribune*, December 20, 1910. "Garment Workers' Strike," quotes the Association of Commerce on minimizing worker grievances: the "grievance causing the original walkout was apparently confined to one shop of one concern and spread through the trade as a sympathetic action rather than from the general prevalence of this grievance in the trade as a whole."

105. Chicago *Examiner*, November 1, 1910, clipping in Louise de Koven Bowen Scrapbooks, Chicago Historical Society.

106. *Tribune*, November 23, 1910.

107. Flyer in Ellen Gates Starr MS Collection, Box 1, folder 18.

108. Women's Trade Union League of Chicago, "Official Report of Strike Committee, Chicago Garment Workers' Strike, October 29, 1910–February 18, 1911," Chicago Historical Society. Katherine Fisher's mother was Ethel Sturges Dummer, who was for decades active in Chicago civic affairs, including investigating issues of municipal administration. The work of Dummer can be followed through her voluminous Collection at the Schlesinger Library, Radcliffe College. For Fisher's attendance at the meeting, and the clergy, see *Tribune* November 14 and 22, 1910.

109. Emma Steghagen, "Report on the Chicago Strike," *Life and Labor* (July 13, 1913), quoted in Marjorie Murphy, *Blackboard Unions: The AFT and the NEA, 1900–1980* (Ithaca, 1990), 74.

110. "Garment Workers' Strike" and *Tribune*, November 7, 1910, for the CPEL's actions.

111. See *Tribune*, December 17 and 20, 1910, for the Association of Commerce. See *Tribune*, December 21, 1910 for the CWTUL.

112. This was Section 1921 of the Chicago Code of 1911. See also the explanation of this code in "Report of City Council Committee on Schools, Fire, Police and Civil Service to the Council," *Journal of the Proceedings of the Chicago City Council* (October 25, 1915): 1789–92.

113. *Tribune*, February 21, 23, 24, and 26, and March 6 and 10, 1914, and Chicago Daily *News*, March 2, 1914.

114. List of "Sympathetic Pickets," compiled by *Committee on Labor Conditions*, October 1915, City Club MS Collection, Box 17, folder 7. See also, *Tribune*, November 15 and 17, and December 7, 1915, and Daily *News*, December 18, 1915, and March 2, 1914 for Starr in 1914.

115. Clippings from *Tribune*, December 7, 1915, in Crane-Lillie Family MS Collection, Box 9, folder 4 (Scrapbook), Chicago Historical Society, and from *Day Book*, December 9, 1915, Starr MS. Collection, Box 1, folder 18. Amalgamated Clothing Workers' leader Sidney Hillman sent Lillie a letter of appreciation, saying, "You may never understand how much it meant to me to have a woman like yourself defy the edicts of society and boldly espouse the cause of the weak and oppressed." Crane-Lillie Collection, Box 7, folder 7.

116. Edith Wyatt, "The Chicago Clothing Strike," *Harper's Bazaar*, December 11, 1915.

117. Police testimony from *National News*, October 1915, Starr Collection, Box 1, folder 18.

118. Among other charges that the committee claimed to have substantiated was that undercover police officers had been sent to infiltrate meetings of strikers and then report back to the department. "Report of City Council Committee," *Journal of the Proceedings of the Chicago City Council* (October 25, 1915). The City Club heard a report on this recommendation in January 1916, and a copy of report is contained in City Club, *Bulletin* 9 (January 10, 1916): 9–11.

119. "Minutes of Meetings," January 7, 1916, *Committee on Labor Conditions*, City Club Collection, Box 17, folder 7. See also City Club "The Henrici Strike," *Bulletin* 7 (June 13, 1914), for the City Club's refusal to condemn the police activities during the waitresses' strike.

120. City Club, "The Garment Workers' Strike," *Bulletin* 9 (January 10, 1916): 3–5.

121. "Report of the Proceedings: Mass Meeting of Women to Protest Against the Spoils System and Adopt a Woman's Municipal Platform," March 18, 1916, WCC MS Collection, Box 1, folder 1.

122. *Post*, December 8, 1915, clipping in Starr Collection, Box 1, folder 18. Douglas Bukowski, *Big Bill Thompson, Chicago, and the Politics of Image* (Urbana, 1998), 48, concluded that the middle class was happy with Thompson's actions in the 1915 strike. Activist Chicago women obviously disagreed.

123. "Report of the Proceedings: Mass Meeting of Women," 35–37. The AFL perspective, which often brought the organization into conflict with women workers, has been well-documented. For a recent assessment of this gender conflict in regard to standardized wage laws during the 1930s, see Landon R. Y. Storrs, *Civilizing Capitalism: The National Consumers' League, Women's Activism and Labor Standards in the New Deal Era* (Chapel Hill, 2000).

124. See Flanagan, "Gender and Urban Political Reform," 1032–50, for more on vocational education. For primary source material on men's ideas about vocational education, see "Reports," *Committee on Public Education and Subcommittee on Vocational Education* (1907 to 1916), City Club Collection, and City Club, *Bulletin* 5 (December 4, 1912). City Club Collection, Box 14, folder 1, and Box 18, folder 5, contain letters sent to board of education, association of commerce, Commercial Club, and Hamilton Club. David J. Hogan, *Class and Reform: School and Society in Chicago, 1880–1930* (Philadelphia, 1985), makes a class analysis that does not distinguish gender differences.

125. Karen M. Mason, "Testing the Boundaries: Women, Politics, and Gender Roles in Chicago, 1890–1930" (Ph.D. Dissertation, University of Michigan, 1991), 141–42, and 147.

126. Maureen A. Flanagan, "Mayor Fred A. Busse: A Silent Mayor in Turbulent Times," in Paul Green and Melvin Holli, eds., *The Mayors: A Chicago Political Tradition* (Carbondale, IL, 1987), 57–58. See Hogan, *Class and Reform*, 206–207 for Busse's "Business board."

127. "Report of the President," April 25, 1914, *Club Minutes*, CWC Collection, Box 23, Book labeled 1913–1914. Joan K. Smith, "Progressive School Administration: Ella Flagg Young and the Chicago Schools, 1905–1915," *Illinois State Historical Journal* 73 (Spring 1980): 36–42.

128. See the discussion of this issue in chapters 2 and 3.

129. Marjorie Murphy, "Taxation and Social Conflict: Teacher Unionism and Public School Finance, 1898–1914," *Illinois State Historical Journal* (Winter 1981): 251.

130. *Tribune*, March, 14, 1915.

131. Don T. Davis, "The Chicago Teachers' Federation and the School Board," typescript (February 1917), Chicago Teachers' Federation Collection, Box 1, folder 2, Chicago Historical Society. Urion wanted four board members and four

teachers instead of the current configuration of two board members and six teachers. See Smith, "Progressive School Administration," 34 and Hogan, *Class and Reform*, 208 fn. 49.

132. Smith, "Progressive School Administration," 40–42, and Davis, "The Chicago Teachers' Federation and the School Board." The board member who engineered the reappointment of Young was Mrs. Tena MacMahon, who three years later would oppose the Loeb Rule, breaking the CTF. See below, and Smith, 40–46, for MacMahon.

133. Robert Reid, *Battleground: Autobiography of Margaret A. Haley* (Urbana, 1982), 171, contains text of the Loeb Rule.

134. Gallagher's speech opposing the rule was printed in the court brief filed by the CTF. "Statements, briefs, etc., 'The People of the State of Illinois . . . upon the relation of Ida L. Fursman . . . vs. The City of Chicago, the Board of Education of the City of Chicago, et.al.; Further Abstracts of Record, by Appellees," at Chicago Historical Society. The women voted 4 to 1 against the Loeb rule; the men voted 10 to 5 in favor.

135. Nestor to Buck, September 29, 1915, in Nestor Collection, Box 1, folder 7

136. "Report of the Proceedings," WCC Collection, Box 1. CTF representative Ida Fursman also spoke to the meeting, which is discussed in more detail in chapter 6. See also, WCC, *Bulletin* (July 1916).

137. *Tribune*, July 3, 1916. See Hogan, *Class and Reform* 209 and 311 n.11, for examples of Loeb's anti-union sentiments directed against the teachers.

138. "Statements, briefs, etc." Hogan, *Class and Reform*, 209, cites the Loeb rule as one of the first examples "of the application of the open shop philosophy to public employees." See Smith, "Progressive School Administration," 40–42, for Sotheby.

139. Daily *News*, December 1, 1915. Otis was excoriated for his willingness to talk to Margaret Haley, Ella Flagg Young, and former president of the CWC, Elizabeth Bass. The quotations are from Smith, "Progressive School Administration," 43.

140. When Margaret Haley achieved a measure of influence in the administration of Mayor Edward Dunne (1907–1911), newspapers and businessmen constantly referred to her as a "short-haired woman" (and labeled her male supporters "long-haired men") to indicate that she had left her proper place in respectable womanhood. See Flanagan, "Mayor Fred A. Busse." Loeb quoted in Hogan, *Class and Reform*, 209.

141. WCC, *Bulletin* (July 1916): 6–7.

142. See Leidenberger, "Working-Class Progressivism and the Politics of Transportation in Chicago, 1895–1907" (Ph.D. Dissertation, University of North Carolina, 1995). There are other examples. Union members on the Chicago school board promoted male interests rather than the interests of female teachers. See previous examples of the action of John Sonsteby. Board member John C. Harding was more interested in having the schools adopt union-made textbooks than in increasing or protecting teacher pay. See Murphy, "Taxation and Social Conflict," 252. That some middle-class liberal men may have developed a "new ethical sensibility . . . together with new kinds of cross-class alignments" in the

late 1880s, as Richard Schneirov argues, may well be the case. But this is still a male-oriented perspective, for as he points out, this new sensibility created "strength and legitimacy" for "labor and labor issues." That is, its focus was re-forming the economic system not providing social welfare. Richard Schneirov, *Labor and Urban Politics: Class Conflict and the Origins of Modern Liberalism in Chicago, 1864–97* (Urbana, 1998), 275. Philip J. Ethington, *The Public City: The Political Construction of Urban Life in San Francisco, 1850–1900* (Cambridge, UK, 1994), 403–405, discusses the struggle between classes of San Francisco men to control municipal government to advance a specific male agenda.

143. Leidenberger, "Working-Class Progressivism," 121, describes one female activist as "[s]omewhat like a wife chiding her husband, one teacher criticized 'This body of unreliable and obscure men [in City Hall] for having been a protection to the greed of capital and a detriment to the state and the city.' " But likening a teacher to a nagging wife can effectively distract attention from her as possessing a serious political agenda and toward seeing her as a stereotype; even if that was not the author's intent, it can and often will be read that way. David Stradling achieves the same effect in *Smokestacks and Progressives* when he assesses women's approach to smoke pollution as the moral, civilizing voice of the city.

144. Eileen Boris, *Home to Work: Motherhood and the Politics of Industrial Homework in the United States* (Cambridge, UK, 1994); Joanne L. Goodwin, "An American Experiment in Paid Motherhood: The Implementation of Mothers' Pensions in Early Twentieth Century Chicago," *Gender and History* 4 (1992): 323–42, and *Gender and the Politics of Welfare Reform: Mothers' Pensions in Chicago, 1911–1929* (Chicago, 1997); Linda Gordon, *Pitied but Not Entitled: Single Mothers and the History of Welfare, 1890–1935* (New York, 1994); and Elisabeth Lasch-Quinn, *Black Neighbors: Race and the Limits of Reform in the American Settlement House Movement, 1890–1945* (Chapel Hill, 1993).

145. Dorothy Sue Cobble, *Dishing It Out: Waitresses and Their Unions in the Twentieth Century* (Urbana, 1991), 77, and Adade M.Wheeler and Marlene S. Wortman, *The Roads They Made: Women in Illinois History* (Chicago, 1977), 79.

146. Kathryn Kish Sklar, "The Historical Foundations of Women's Power in the Creation of the American Welfare State, 1830–1930," in Seth Koven and Sonya Michel, eds., *Mothers of a New World: Maternalist Politics and the Origins of Welfare States* (New York, 1993), 75, and Sklar, *Florence Kelley and the Nation's Work*. See also Flanagan, "The City Profitable, the City Livable."

147. Cobble, *Dishing It Out*, 77, and Leidenberger, "Working-Class Progressivism," 108–10. Leidenberger, 121 n.18, chides Marjorie Murphy, *Blackboard Unions*, for underestimating "the productive relations" between teachers and middle-class clubwomen in order "to underline the working-class nature of the CTF." Payne, *Reform, Labor, and Feminism*, 125–27.

148. For Chicago, see, in addition to Leidenberger, John Jentz, "Class and Politics in an Emerging Industrial City: Chicago in the 1860s and 1870s," *Journal of Urban History* 17 (May 1991): 227–63; Richard Schneirov, "Political Cultures and the Role of the State in Labor's Republic: The View from Chicago, 1848–1877," *Labor History* 32 (Summer 1991): 376–400, and *Labor and Urban Politics*. For general examples, see Leon Fink *Workingmen's Democracy: The Knights of Labor in American Politics* (Urbana, 1983); Richard Oestreicher, "Urban Work-

ing-Class Political Behavior and Theories of American Electoral Politics, 1870–1940," *Journal of American History* 74 (March 1988): 1257–86; and Martin Shefter, "Trade Unions and Political Machines: The Organization and Disorganization of American Working Class Life in the Late Nineteenth Century," in Ira Katznelson and Aristide R. Zolberg, eds., *Working-Class Formation: Nineteenth-Century Patterns in Western Europe and the United States* (Princeton, 1986): 199–276. By 1917, the Chicago WTUL's vision of political and social democracy so clearly clashed with national goals that Samuel Gompers engineered Robins' removal from her position on the Chicago Federation of Labor executive council despite the support of the CFL's visionary leader John Fitzpatrick for women workers. Payne, *Reform, Labor, and Feminism*, 107.

149. Payne, *Reform, Labor, and Feminism*, 134; Wheeler and Wortman, *The Roads They Made*, 73 and 98; and WCC, *Bulletin* (May 1920). Recognizing the multiplicity of identifications of female activists, such as Yarros, would help urban historians broaden their understanding of women's municipal work. For Robins's rejection, see *Tribune*, April 26, 1908. Even within the CWC, the tides constantly shifted, and in 1908 the "conservative" candidate won the presidency by one vote, only to be succeeded at the next election by a "radical" candidate, who in turn was succeeded by an even more "radical" candidate.

150. "[The] boundaries of symbolic orders are more ambiguous, more tenuous than they seem. An 'ethic of solidarity' presents gender, class, race, and ethnicity as unstable categories. They are isolated aspects of complex and fluid individual and social identities. New social movements . . . unite individuals around aspects of their identities." Nancy Love, "Ideal Speech and Feminist Discourse: Habermas Revisioned," *Women and Politics* 11 (1991): 101–22. The longer quotation is from Ibid., 116–17. Deborah Gray White, "The Cost of Club Work, the Price of Black Feminism," in Nancy Hewitt and Suzanne Lebsock, eds., *Visible Women: New Essays on American Activism* (Urbana, 1993): 249–69, and *Too Heavy a Load: Black Women in Defense of Themselves, 1894–1994* (New York, 1999), make this case for African American women. For Wells-Barnett, see Patricia Schechter, *Ida B. Wells-Barnett and American Reform, 1880–1930* (Chapel Hill, 2001), 172–73.

151. Wright, *Moralism and the Model Home*, 263. The first quotation is Jensen's own words; the second is Wright's synthesis of Jensen's ideas.

152. Nicholes, "How Women Can Help in the Administration of the City," 2151 and 2153.

153. "Report of the Proceedings: Mass Meeting of Women," 33.

Chapter Six
"I Do Not Think the Husband Will Influence the Wife's Vote in Municipal Affairs"

1. Bowen, *Growing Up with a City* (New York, 1926; reissue Urbana, 2002), 106–107.

2. Kristi Andersen, *After Suffrage: Women in Partisan and Electoral Politics before the New Deal* (Chicago, 1996), and Nancy Cott, "Across the Great Divide: Women in Politics before and after 1920," in Patricia Gurin and Louise Tilly, eds., *Women, Politics, and Change* (New York, 1990), 153–76.

3. See Adade Mitchell Wheeler, "Conflict in the Illinois Woman Suffrage Movement of 1913," *Illinois State Historical Journal* (Summer 1983): 95–114, for an overview of the final lobbying for suffrage and the text of the Illinois law. Restricting women's local suffrage was a blow to activist women's municipal hopes because the fifteen at-large commissioners (five from the county and ten from the city) oversaw the county's welfare system. Under the existing decentralized municipal governing structure, much public welfare was dispensed by the county with the city having only minimal control over welfare issues within its boundaries. The WCC had actively participated in appealing to the court to rule in women's favor on this issue. See *Tribune*, November 4, 1914, and WCC, *Bulletin* (November 1914). In early 1915 women showed their frustration with the county board, and specifically with not being able to vote for it, by calling a woman's conference to protest the board's plans to eliminate both the public welfare bureau and the children's summer outage program. Chicago *Tribune*, February 17 and 18, 1915. See below in this chapter for women being barred from serving as election judges in 1915 and additional restrictions applied against women.

4. WCC, *Bulletin* (March 1915): 3. The first national Progressive Party convention in Chicago in 1912—which many women attended, at which Jane Addams was a keynote speaker, and where from presidential nominee Theodore Roosevelt down through the ranks men congratulated themselves on being the party that eagerly sought women's participation—had raised women's consciousness about their uphill battle to effect change. Chicago activist Mary Wilmarth watched in dismay as the convention's male delegates rousingly passed a strong military measure despite women's vigorous protests, and remarked to Addams, "How frail a barrier woman's influence seemed to be in spite of its vaunted power." Wilmarth quoted in Jane Addams, "Mary Hawes Wilmarth," in *The Excellent Becomes the Permanent* (New York, 1932), 106–107. Nor did the prospects seems much brighter to Wilmarth for her first presidential election. "I am oppressed with the call for decision as to my first vote for President," she wrote to her close friend and ally Ellen Gates Starr. "I have no great hopes of an important improvement by change of administration." Letter from Mary H. Wilmarth to Ellen Gates Starr, October 21, 1916, Ellen Gates Starr Collection, Box 12, folder 143, The Sophie Smith Collection, Smith College Library, Northampton, MA.

5. See Charles Branham, "Black Chicago: Accommodationist Politics Before the Great Migration," in Melvin G. Holli and Peter d'A. Jones, eds., *The Ethnic Frontier: Group Survival in Chicago and the Midwest* (Grand Rapids, MI, 1977), 212–62, for an account of African American men and political possibilities after 1870. The Republicans immediately nominated John Jones for county commissioner in 1871, then John W. E. Thomas for state senator in 1876. Both men won office, which, according to Branham, they could not have done without white votes (see 222–23). For some of the city's European immigrant groups and their incorporation into the political process, albeit never without prejudice, see Humbert Nelli, *Italians in Chicago: 1880–1930: A Study in Ethnic Mobility* (New York, 1970), chapter 4, and Edward Kantowicz, *Polish-American Politics in Chicago 1888–1940* (Chicago, 1975), chapters 5–8. But also see Dianne M. Pinderhughes, *Race and Ethnicity in Chicago Politics: A Reexamination of Pluralist Theory* (Urbana, 1987), for the differences in the political fortunes between African Ameri-

cans and European ethnics. For laboring men, see Richard Schneirov, *Labor and Urban Politics: Class Conflict and the Origins of Modern Liberalism in Chicago, 1864–97* (Urbana, 1998), chapters 1 and 2, and Robert A. Slayton, "Labor and Urban Politics: District 31, Steel Workers Organizing Committee, and the Chicago Machine," *Journal of Urban History* 23 (November 1996): 29–66. The difference between the parties' response to male and female voters, groups, and organizations will be discussed in this and following chapters.

6. The Chicago Daily *News*, February 3, 1914 has a photo of seventy-seven-year-old Mary Wilmarth registering to vote. For the most part the CWC let its offspring, the Political Equality League, lead the citywide registration drive while the CWC itself concentrated on getting all of its members to register and vote and raised funds to help fight the inevitable legal challenges that the anti-suffrage forces were making against the state suffrage law. "Annual Report of the Equal Suffrage Committee," April 1913 to April 1914, *Club Minutes*, CWC MS Collection, Box 23, Chicago Historical Society.

7. For Kaneko and Barnum see Ellen C. DuBois, "Working Women, Class Relations, and Suffrage Militance: Harriot Stanton Blatch and the New York Woman Suffrage Movement, 1894–1907," *Journal of American History* 73 (June 1987): 47 and 57; for McEnerny, see *Tribune*, April 3, 1913; and for WTUL meeting, see *Union Labor Advocate* (December 1908): 32 and 40, in Ellen M. Henrotin Collection, Box 2, folder 47, Schlesinger Library, Radcliffe College, Cambridge, MA. For Socialist women and suffrage, see also Sally Miller, ed., *Race, Ethnicity, and Gender in Early Twentieth-Century American Socialism* (New York, 1996). Here again, the Chicago experience differs from that of Boston women as described by Sarah Deutsch, *Women and the City: Gender, Space, and Power in Boston, 1870–1940* (New York, 2000), chapter 7 and especially 222.

8. *Tribune*, July 1, clipping in the Chicago Women's Trade Union League Collection, Box 2, folder 6, Special Collections, University of Illinois at Chicago Library, Chicago.

9. For Steghagen's goal, see unnamed newspaper clipping in CWTUL Collection, Box 2, folder 7.

10. *Tribune*, October 11, 1913, clippings in the CWTUL Collection, Box 2, folder 6.

11. For McEnerny specifically, see *Tribune*, January 22 and 23, 1914; for Drake, see clipping from Chicago *Record-Herald*, January 22, 1914, in CWTUL, Box 2, folder 7. Drake was also a member of the CWC and the WCC, and in charge of organizing the women of the city's first ward for the latter organization. See also WCC, *Bulletin* (June 1914).

12. For Wells-Barnett's name, see Chicago Political Equality League, *Annual Reports*. Dorothy Sterling, *Black Foremothers* (New York, 1979), 109, says that Wells-Barnett was a member of a "white-led" Women's Suffrage Association; see also Mildred I. Thompson, *Ida B. Wells-Barnett: An Exploratory Study of an American Black Woman, 1893–1930*, v. 15 in Darlene Clark Hine, ed., *Black Women in U.S. History* (Brooklyn, 1990), 129, and Patricia Schechter, *Ida B. Wells-Barnett and American Reform, 1880–1930* (Chapel Hill, 2001), 198–200. Williams is listed as a speaker in *Program of the Annual Convention* (February 13–17, 1907), at Chicago Historical Society. Chicago *Broad-Ax*, March 12, 1910 and September

20, 1913. For McCormick, Gaines and McCormick's strong ties to African American women through the 1920s, see Kristie Miller, *Ruth Hanna McCormick: A Life in Politics, 1880–1944* (Albuquerque, 1992), 93 and 131. The *Crisis*, November 1914, cites Byron as an African American women working with NAWSA on the midwest suffrage campaign. In 1916 the president of the Illinois Equal Suffrage Association spoke before the Alpha Suffrage Club, and the Chicago *Defender* noted that in April that year Wells-Barnett had attended a reception given by that same association. Wells-Barnett, in fact, had been a member of the IESA for several years. See, *Broad-Ax*, March 25, 1916; Chicago *Defender*, April 15, 1916; and Jo Freeman, *A Room at a Time: How Women Entered Party Politics* (Lanham, MD, 2000), 56n.36.

13. Wanda Hendricks, "The Politics of Race: Black Women in Illinois, 1890–1920" (Ph.D. Dissertation, Purdue University, 1990), 87–88, 150, and 167. The *Crisis* (September 1912): 242–43 for Logan, and (August 1915): 191, for Davis; and *Defender*, February 21, 1914

14. An account of the rally from *L'Italia*, February 1, 1914.

15. Statements for Norwegian women from WCC, *Bulletin* (October 1917).

16. *Tribune*, January 21 and 29, 1914. Again, one must note the difference between Chicago women's suffrage activities and those of the Boston Equal Suffrage Association for Good Government, which Deutsch, *Women and the City*, 223–24, describes as scheduling meetings at times when working women could not attend, hiring neighborhood canvassers rather than do the work themselves, and generally holding themselves aloof from non-elite Boston women.

17. See Virginia Sapiro, "Women, Citizenship, and Nationality: Immigration and Naturalization Policies in the United States, *Politics and Society* 13 (1984): 1–26. Under this law, even native-born women lost their citizenship if they married a non-citizen.

18. Instructions on this were printed, for example, in *L'Italia*, February 1, 1914.

19. Typescript in Hilda Satt Polacheck Collection, Box 1, folder 4, Special Collections, University of Illinois at Chicago Library.

20. "Meeting Minutes," Monday Evening, January 29, 1917, WCC MS Collection, Box 1, folder 1, Chicago Historical Society.

21. *Tribune*, January 17 and 22, February 1, 2, 4, and 8, 1914, and Chicago *Record-Herald*, gave publicity and accounts of the meeting and its aftermath.

22. Mary McDowell, "Civic Experiences, 1914," 17, typescript, Mary McDowell Collection, folder 19, Chicago Historical Society, and Joel Goldstein, *The Effects of the Adoption of Woman Suffrage: Sex Differences and Voting Behavior— Illinois, 1914–21* (New York, 1984), 87–93. Illinois law required eligible voters to register to vote before every local and national general election (Goldstein, 81).

23. WCC, *Bulletin* (November 1914); *Tribune*, February 4, 1914; Alfreda Duster, ed., *Crusade for Justice: The Autobiography of Ida B. Wells* (Chicago, 1970), 346, and Schechter, *Ida B. Wells-Barnett*, 199–200.

24. For the quotation, see *Tribune*, February 1, 1914. See Gullett, *Becoming Citizens: The Emergence and Development of the California Women's Movement, 1880–1911* (Urbana, 2000), 186, for more ambivalence on the part of California suffragists. Activist Chicago women also differed from the California suffragists,

who Gullett says supported woman suffrage because "people like themselves—white, native-born, and middle-class—represented American's best hope for civic improvement" (192.) In Chicago, these women believed that *women* represented the best hope for civic improvement.

25. Text of talk given by Anna Allen in Madeleine Wallin Sikes Collection, Box 7, Chicago Historical Society. The text has no original date and was subsequently marked February 1912; the content clearly indicates that this is a mistake and that the year should be 1914.

26. "Meeting Minutes," Monday Evening, January 29, 1917, WCC Collection, folder 1.

27. Oral interview between the author and Mrs. Anne Hagerty Kennedy, August 21, 1993, North Riverside, Illinois.

28. See suggestions of this in Andersen, *After Suffrage*, and Sara Evans, "Women's History and Political Theory: Toward a Feminist Approach to Public Life," in Suzanne Lebsock and Nancy Hewitt, eds., *Visible Women: New Essays on American Activism* (Urbana, 1993), 119–39.

29. *Tribune*, March 7, 1915.

30. Ibid., January 31, 1896.

31. Ibid., February 5, 1914. Trout had also attempted to keep Ida B. Wells-Barnett from marching with the Chicago contingent to the Washington, D.C., suffrage parade in 1913. Wells-Barnett herself refused to accede to Trout, and other white Chicago women, including Catharine Waugh McCulloch, had supported her determination to march with them. See Schechter, *Ida B. Wells-Barnett*, 200.

32. *Tribune*, February 23 and 24, 1914. A measure of the breadth of Chicago women's activism can be seen in the list of these women. They were Mrs. W. F. Mulvihill, Mrs. Nellie Wallingford, Mrs. J. M. Schollenberg, Miss Edna B. Potter, Mrs Anna C. Blockside, Mrs. Sarah Mellinger, Mrs. Mary A. White, Miss Cora Fuke, Mrs. J. B. Kern, Mrs. A. S. Irvine, Mrs. Dora M. Donohoe, Mrs. Carrie E. Fry, and Mrs. Lillie McCarthy. None is recognizable as a "leading" or "elite" activist; just middle-class women wishing to exercise their political right to vote.

33. Ibid., March 1, 1914.

34. Gullett, *Becoming Citizens*, emphasizes the "clean government" concerns of elite women working for suffrage. See below for differences in male and female voting patterns.

35. *Tribune*, January 18, 19, and 20, 1914.

36. For discussions of women's post-suffrage politics, see Anne Martin, "Women's Inferiority Complex," *New Republic* (July 20, 1921): 210; Sara Alpern and Dale Baum, "Female Ballots: The Impact of the Nineteenth Amendment," *Journal of Interdisciplinary History* 15 (Summer 1985): 43–67; Robyn Muncy, *Creating a Female Dominion in American Reform, 1895–1935* (New York, 1991), 125–28, especially 127n.11; Susan Ware, *Beyond Suffrage: Women in the New Deal* (Cambridge, MA, 1981), 6; Kristi Andersen, "Women and Citizenship in the 1920s," in Tilly and Gurin, eds., *Women, Politics, and Change*, 177–98; Paul Kleppner, "Were Women to Blame? Female Suffrage and Voter Turnout," *Journal of Interdisciplinary History* 12 (Spring 1982): especially 623n.3; Paul Allen Beck, "A Socialization Theory of Partisan Realignment," in Richard Niemi and Herbert Weisberg, eds., *Controversies in American Voting Behavior* (San Francisco, 1976); Paula

Baker, *The Moral Frameworks of Public Life: Gender, Politics, and the State in Rural New York, 1870–1920* (New York, 1991); and Michael McGerr, "Political Style and Women's Power, 1830–1930," *Journal of American History* 76 (December 1990): 864–85. See also Andersen, *After Suffrage*, for evidence that enough available national electoral and registration data exist to show that women did *not* vote exactly as did men.

37. See accounts of women's activities in *Record-Herald*, August 4 and 25, 1913; and *Tribune*, November 25, 1913, January 19, 20, 21, 22, 25, 26, and 29, 1914, and March 7 and 10, 1915. Clara Piucinski [possibly Plucinski] had been a member of the Non-Partisan Club of Polish Women of the 29th ward when she had signed a petition the previous year demanding that women be declared eligible to serve as poll judges. See *Tribune*, November 25, 1913.

38. The legal challenge was based on wording in the existing regulations that stated that poll judges had to be "head of the family." *Tribune* November 25 and 28, 1913. See also "Minutes of Regular Business Meeting," December 10, 1913, *Club Minutes*, CWC Collection, Box 23. *Tribune*, January 24, 1914, lists some of the women appointed as poll judges, and the list displays a range of ethnic names. Women were subsequently barred from acting as polling judges by a new ruling the following year.

39. *Tribune*, January 21 and 23, 1914.

40. *Record-Herald*, March 2, 1914, clipping in CWTUL Collection, Box 2, folder 7.

41. P. Orman Ray, *An Introduction to Political Parties and Practical Politics*, 3rd ed. (New York, 1917), 185–86. I would like to thank Jo Freeman for this citation.

42. *Tribune*, February 25, 1914, and Goldstein, *The Effects of the Adoption of Woman Suffrage*, 101, for turnout in the February 1914 primary. Tenth ward totals were 56.4 percent for women and 51.2 percent for men; 17th ward totals were 51.1 percent to 52.6 percent; 5th ward totals were 48.9 percent and 50.8 percent. I have also used Goldstein's calculations on the class and ethnic composition of the city's thirty-five wards. As was the pattern with new voters, women registered for their first elections in smaller percentages of the eligible population than did men, with societal norms and legal impediments contributing as much as reluctance to enter partisan politics to slow rising registration.

43. Mary McDowell to Voters of 29th Ward, McDowell Collection, folder 19. In the April election, women in the largely Jewish 15th ward were credited with helping re-elect regular Republican Alderman Beilfuss because he had supported their efforts to secure more small parks and playgrounds in the city. *Tribune*, April 9, 1914.

44. Unless otherwise noted, vote totals for the 1914 elections are from the *Tribune*, February 25 and 26, 1914, and April 8 and 9, 1914.

45. Although I have not been otherwise able to confirm it, the *Tribune*, February 24, contended that Hopkins' campaign manager was a black woman doctor.

46. Napieralski was a member of the ward's Polish Women's Progressive Club who had run as a write-in candidate for the Progressive Party nomination. In the primary she had received 47 votes, 42 of which came from women. See Goldstein, 133.

47. *Tribune*, February 27, 1914.

48. Campaign flyer entitled "Headquarters, 17th Ward Mothers' Independent Club with the salutation 'Cara Amica.' " The Italian reads: "Per il bene del vostro quartiere e della città, voi avete un dovere verso voi stessa ed i vostri bambini di osservare che le vostre condizioni vitali siano tali da dare ai vostri ragazzi i medesimi vantaggi che sono concessi ai ragazzi in altre parti della città, come decenti scuole con relative palestre ginnastiche, strade pulite convenientemente illuminate, spaccio di latte salubre per i piccini, e tutte le altre misure che voi come madre, meglio conoscete essere necessarie per la salute dei vostri bambini." "Vittum, Harriet E.—election Bid Materials, 1914," Northwestern University Settlement MS Collection, Box 66, folder 19, at Northwestern University, Evanston, Illinois. I am particularly grateful to Michigan State University graduate student Amy Hay for finding these materials for me. English translation is mine. Any infelicities in the Italian text are in the original.

49. List of campaign contributors in Harriet Vittum Collection, folder 1, at Special Collections, University of Illinois Chicago Library.

50. For lumping women into male voting behavior patterns, see John Buenker, "Sovereign Individuals and Organic Networks: Political Cultures in Conflict During the Progressive Era," *American Quarterly* (June 1988): 187–204. Vote totals are from *Tribune*, April 8, 1914.

51. Napieralski had received 7.5 percent of women's votes and 5.1 percent of men's. Two of the four women who tried for city council in 1916 received significantly higher percentages of women's vote; one received .02 percent more of women's vote; while the fourth received more votes from men. *Tribune*, March 1, 1916 and *Daily News, Almanac*, 1917.

52. The complete text of Kaneko's speech, and McDermut's campaign statement, were printed in the socialist women's paper, *The Coming Nation*, March 1914. I am extremely indebted to Cliff Hawkins for informing me of this speech and providing me a xerox copy. For how other Socialist women candidates tried to combine a socialist appeal with an appeal to all women, see Sherry J. Katz, "Redefining 'The Political': Socialist Women and Party Politics in California, 1900–1920," in Melanie Gustafson, Kristie Miller, and Elisabeth Israels Perry, eds., *We Have Come to Stay: American Women and Political Parties, 1880–1960* (Albuquerque, NM, 1999), 23–32.

53. *Memorial: Corinne Stubbs Brown* (1914), at Chicago Historical Society.

54. See Mari Jo Buhle, *Women and American Socialism: 1870–1920* (Urbana, 1983), 149–52 and 156–58, and the documents in Miller, ed., *Race, Ethnicity and Gender in Early Twentieth Century American Socialism*, for consideration of how socialist men and women clashed over the issue of women suffrage and whether a feminist agenda could be reconciled with a socialist one.

55. Schechter, *Ida B. Wells-Barnett*, 172.

56. So few women ran for municipal office in the years when male and female vote totals were kept separately that data is limited of course. In Vittum's race, women cast 1.7 percent of their vote for the Socialist candidate; men cast 4.5 percent for him. In Drake's race, 1.4 percent of women voted for the Socialist, while 3.1 percent of men did so. In the heavily foreign-born 12th ward, 9.5 percent of women voted for the Socialist, and 7.5 percent for the Progressive, Napieralski; but men voted 9.9 percent for the Socialist and 5.1 percent for Napieralski.

From total ballots cast in the aldermanic races that spring, women voted 14 percent for Independents, 11.6 percent for Progressives, and 7.26 percent for Socialists; the comparable statistics for men were 6.63 percent, 9.7 percent, and 8.7 percent. In the 7th ward, independent Republican Kimball won with 43.9 percent of women's votes as opposed to 29.8 percent of men's. *Tribune*, April 8 and 9, 1914. In the November 1914 ballot for University of Illinois trustees (women had been able to vote for this office since the 1890s), women cast 21 percent of their votes for Progressive Party candidates, including giving 6.94 percent to Ellen Gates Starr, against 16 percent for Progressive candidates from men, who gave 5 percent of their votes to Starr. Goldstein, *The Effects of the Adoption of Woman Suffrage*, 138.

57. See *Tribune*, November 2 and 4, 1914. Assessing women's politics a few years later, Ray, *An Introduction to Political Parties and Practical Politics*, 185, described both leagues as having "appointed precinct captains . . . assisted in enrolling voters and in conducting house-to-house canvasses, and looked after the appointment of women watchers and workers at the polls."

58. WCC, *Bulletin* (September and November 1914).

59. Goldstein, *The Effects of the Adoption of Woman Suffrage*, 102–105. For the April 1914 election, women's turnout was especially higher in the 1st ward (ethnic, foreign-born), 82.2 percent of registered women and 64.4 percent of registered men; in the 2nd ward (African American), 69 percent of women and 58.4 percent of men; in the affluent 6th ward, 72.2 percent of women and 63 percent of men.

60. Ibid., 102. Taking a representative sample of twelve wards covering class and race, the average turnout rate for women was 87.8 percent; for men, 88.9 percent.

61. Ibid., 87, 89–93, 101. *Tribune*, March 21, 1916 and *Daily News*, *Almanac* (1919). Registered men numbered 470,029 and 493,578 for those years, respectively.

62. *Tribune*, February 17 and 22, 1915 and WCC, "February 1915 Calendar," in WCC MS Collection, folder 1, Special Collections, University of Illinois Chicago Library.

63. *Tribune*, February 15, 1915.

64. Ibid., February 26, 1915. See WCC, *Bulletin* (March 1915), for the Club's frustration with their choices. During the 1915 primary campaign, activist women had been especially concerned about the plan of the Cook County board to eliminate its public welfare and children's summer outages bureaus, and they were particularly frustrated with having the right to vote for county commissioners taken from them.

65. *Tribune*, February 17, 22, and 25, and March 10, 1915.

66. Figures are from Edith Abbott, "Are Women a Force for Good Government? An Analysis of the Returns in the Recent Municipal Elections in Chicago," *National Municipal Review* 4 (1915): 437–38.

67. Activists Henrotin, Helen Hefferan, and Hannah Soloman endorsed Sweitzer, and Bass spoke at Sweitzer rallies. *Tribune*, February 24 and April 2 and 4, 1915.

68. Ibid., February 28 and April 3, 1915.

69. Ibid., April 2 and 3, 1915. In other categories, garment workers were recorded as favoring Thompson 52 to 41; tobacco and cigar workers, 65 to 38; and bookbinders, 54 to 46. The tally for housewives was 334 to 354.

70. Women cast 59.8 percent of their votes for Thompson and 36.2 percent for Sweitzer; men's respective figures were 58.2 percent and 37.5 percent. Abbott, "Are Women a Force for Good Government," 429–30.

71. Ibid., 444.

72. WCC, *Bulletin* (April 1915).

73. *Tribune*, March 1 and April 5, 1916.

74. Addams in a presentation to the City Club on the topic, "Should the Chicago Aldermanic Elections Next Spring Be Non-Partisan?" City Club, *Bulletin* (November 29, 1913): 304.

75. See below this chapter for a discussion of Thompson and the office of commisioner of public welfare, and chapter 7.

76. "Report of the Proceedings: Mass Meeting of Women to Protest against the Spoils System and Adopt a Woman's Municipal Platform," 1–2, WCC MS Collection, Box 1, folder 1, Chicago Historical Society.

77. *Tribune*, February 26 and March 4, 18, and 19, 1916.

78. WCC, "Report of the Proceedings."

79. Ibid., 19. Activist women organized a women's Joint Committee on Education to form the proposed citizens' school committee.

80. Douglas Bukowski, *Big Bill Thompson, Chicago, and the Politics of Image* (Urbana, 1998), especially 44–46, and see Deutsch, *Women and the City*, for Boston.

81. WCC, "Report of the Proceedings," 38.

82. Ibid., 7.

83. In this sense, the Woman's Municipal Platform and its various points must be distinguished from the ideas and rhetoric of the Boston Good Government Association. According to James J. Connolly, *The Triumph of Ethnic Progressivism: Urban Political Culture in Boston, 1900–1925* (Cambridge, MA, 1998), 184, the male BGGA had a "vision of a single public interest . . . [and] endorsed candidates . . . based on the issues of fiscal responsibility and public honesty." As he also notes, the BGGA did not have women members until passage of the Nineteenth Amendment. In Chicago, women were initiating a vision of the public interest, which emphasized human betterment not the type of fiscal responsibility promoted by the BGGA.

84. *Tribune*, February 17 and September 11, 1915, and February 17, 1916. An existing Lake Town ordinance, left over from before annexation, specified that no saloon could be established in the town unless a majority of qualified voters within a one-eighth mile radius of the proposed establishment agreed to it.

85. See Charles Branham, "Black Chicago," 243–56. But see also Pinderhughes, *Race and Ethnicity in Chicago Politics*, and Allan Spear, *Black Chicago: The Making of a Negro Ghetto, 1890–1920* (Chicago, 1967). Rosalyn Terborg-Penn, "African American Women and the Vote: An Overview," in Ann D. Gordon, ed., *African American Women and the Vote, 1837–1965* (Amherst, MA,1997), 13–15, discusses how racism and sexism created a perpetual tension between race and gender in black women's politics. It is noteworthy to consider that African American men's belief that they were part of the system meant that African American women

under Wells-Barnett's leadership first challenged the practice of nominating only white men as aldermen in the 2nd ward.

86. Daily *News, Almanac*, 1916, 1917, and 1924; and *Tribune*, March 1, 1916 and April 2, 1919.

87. For Rowe, see *Tribune*, April 6, 1915, and Adade Wheeler and Marlene Wortman, *The Roads They Made: Women in Illinois* (Chicago, 1977), 119. For McDowell, see *Tribune*, February 25, 1916.

88. City of Chicago, *Chicago City Manual* (1915), lists the members of the voluntary advisory board. In 1923, Mayor Dever appointed Mary McDowell as commissioner of public welfare.

89. *Tribune*, February 26, 1916.

90. Chicago *Broad-Ax*, March 7, 1914, and February 6 and March 13, 1915; *Defender*, February 27, 1915; and Abbott, "Are Women a Force for Good Government?" 444.

91. Deborah Gray White, "The Cost of Club Work, the Price of Black Feminism," in Lebsock and Hewitt, *Visible Women*, 251–53, discusses how black women's activism challenged black men who believed it their right to control black politics and who repulsed the demands of black women for equal political standing. Trying to understand the differences between white and black women's activities in this time period, some scholars have unfortunately failed to distinguish between political possibilities for African Americans in the North and in the South. Eileen Boris, "The Power of Motherhood: Black and White Activist Women Redefine the 'Political,' " in Seth Koven and Sonya Michel, eds., *Mothers of a New World: Maternalist Politics and the Origins of Welfare States* (New York, 1993), 216, declares that "we must reconceptualize [the Progressive Era] as an era of disenfranchisement of all women and black men," but black women and men did vote in various northern and western states. Grace Wilbur Trout tried to keep Wells-Barnett from marching with white suffragists in the 1913 Washington, D.C., suffrage parade, but other Chicago white women refused to exclude Wells-Barnett. In the May 1914 Chicago suffrage parade Ruth Hanna McCormick marched with Irene McCoy Gaines and "two companies of black women." See Hendricks, "The Politics of Race," 142–43, and Miller, *Ruth Hanna McCormick*, 92–93.

92. In the 1914 primary, Wells-Barnett and the Alpha Suffrage Club supported African American challenger W. R. Cowan. Women gave Cowan 53.4 percent of their votes against 40.9 percent from men. Forty percent of the registered women of the 2nd ward voted compared to 33.9 percent of registered men. In the April general election, 69 percent of registered women voted compared to 58.4 percent of registered men. Women's voting record emboldened African American men to force the Republican party to nominate Oscar DePriest for alderman the next year. See Hendricks, "The Politics of Race," 167–70 and 180–84. See also *Tribune*, February 25, 1914; *Broad-Ax*, February 28, 1914; *Defender*, February 21 and 28, 1914; and Goldstein, *The Effects of the Adoption of Woman Suffrage*, 101–102.

93. Native Americans were excluded from the political system and until the World War I era most were not citizens; Southern states individually disfranchised black voters; and restrictions prevailed on citizenship for Asian immigrants. Women, on the other hand, were citizens but were ineligible to vote. See Linda

Kerber, "A Constitutional Right to Be Treated Like American Ladies: Women and the Obligations of Citizenship," in Linda Kerber, Alice Kessler-Harris, and Kathryn Kish Sklar, eds., *U.S. History as Women's History: New Feminist Essays* (Chapel Hill, 1995), 17–35, and *No Constitutional Right to Be Ladies: Women and the Obligation of Citizenship* (New York, 1998).

94. Evans, "Women's History and Political Theory," 119–39.

95. On the national level, and certainly in many localities, both parties had by the early twentieth century formulated political agendas that reflected the wishes and needs of their male membership. Theda Skocpol, *Protecting Soldiers and Mothers: the Political Origins of Social Policy in the United States* (Cambridge, MA, 1992), 76–81, provides a comprehensive overview of the recent literature on the process of solidifying the two-party system. Karen Beckwith, "Comparative Research and Electoral Systems: Lessons from France and Italy," *Women and Politics*, 12 (1992): 1–33, discusses the potential impact of "party types" on women's access to politics. Whether parties "view women as an important societal group—as mothers, as workers"—or whether there are leftwing parties "which are purported more inclusive," seems to make a difference for women's political possibilities. Neither circumstances existed in the United States in the early twentieth century. See also the theoretical discussions of Carole Patemen, *The Disorder of Women: Democracy, Feminism and Political Theory* (Stanford, 1989), and Anne Phillips, *Engendering Democracy* (University Park, PA, 1991).

96. See J. Morgan Kousser, "Are Political Acts Unnatural?" *Journal of Interdisciplinary History* 15 (Winter 1985): 467–80, and "Restoring Politics to Political History," in *Journal of Interdisciplinary History* 12 (Spring 1982): 569–95. Skocpol, *Protecting Soldiers and Mothers*, 54, calls this "the fit" between institutions and individuals or groups in the polity, while Anne N. Costain, *Inviting Women's Rebellion: A Political Process Interpretation of the Women's Movement* (Baltimore, 1992), describes it as a manifestation of the political process in which "the receptivity of the political process" to a group's desires largely determines its policy success. See also Cynthia Harrison, *On Account of Sex: The Politics of Women's Issues, 1945–1968* (Berkeley, 1988).

97. *Tribune*, April 2, 1919.

98. Nancy F. Cott, *The Grounding of Modern Feminism* (New Haven, 1987), 109–11; Ellen Fitzpatrick, *Endless Crusade: Women Social Scientists and Progressive Reform* (New York, 1990), 146–57; and Elisabeth I. Perry, "Women's Political Choices After Suffrage: The Women's City Club of New York, 1915–1990," *New York History* (October 1990): 417–34, have speculated on male intransigence to women and politics.

Chapter Seven
"Looking Out for the Interests of the People"

1. WCC, *Bulletin* (February 1919). See Maureen A. Flanagan, "The City Profitable, the City Livable: Environmental Policy, Gender, and Power in Chicago in the 1910s," *Journal of Urban History* 22 (January 1996): 163–90, for an analysis of a similar divergence over specific environmental issues.

2. Stephen Buechler, *The Transformation of the Woman Suffrage Movement: The Case of Illinois, 1850–1920* (New Brunswick, NJ, 1986); Lynne Curry, *Modern Mothers in the Heartland: Gender, Health and Progress in Illinois, 1900–1930* (Columbus, OH, 1999); Ellen Fitzpatrick, *Endless Crusade: Women Social Scientists and Progressive Reform* (New York, 1990); Joanne Goodwin, *Gender and the Politics of Welfare Reform: Mothers' Pensions in Chicago, 1911–1929* (Chicago, 1997); Gayle Gullett, *Becoming Citizens: The Emergence and Development of the California Women's Movement, 1880–1911* (Urbana, 2000); Molly Ladd-Taylor, *Mother-Work: Women, Child Welfare, and the State, 1890–1930* (Urbana, 1994); Judith McArthur, *Creating the New Woman: The Rise of Southern Women's Progressive Culture in Texas, 1893–1918* (Urbana, 1998); Robyn Muncy, *Creating a Female Dominion in American Reform, 1890–1935* (New York, 1991); Anne Firor Scott, *Natural Allies: Women's Associations in American History* (Urbana, 1991); and Theda Skocpol, *Protecting Soldiers and Mothers: the Political Origins of Social Policy in the United States* (Cambridge, MA, 1992). Kristi Andersen, *After Suffrage: Women in Partisan and Electoral Politics before the New Deal* (Chicago, 1996); Felice D. Gordon, *After Winning: The Legacy of the New Jersey Suffragists, 1920–1947* (New Brunswick, NJ, 1986); and Sandra Schackel, *Social Housekeepers: Women Shaping Public Policy in New Mexico, 1920–1940* (Albuquerque, NM, 1992) tackle the 1920s, but without an urban dimension.

3. Sandra Haarsager, *Bertha Knight Landes of Seattle: Big-City Mayor* (Norman, OK, 1994).

4. Amy Bridges, *Morning Glories: Municipal Reform in the Southwest* (Princeton, 1997); Douglas Bukowski, *Big Bill Thompson, Chicago and the Politics of Image* (Urbana, 1998); Howard Gillette, *Between Justice and Beauty: Race, Planning, and the Failure of Urban Policy in Washington, D.C.* (Baltimore, 1995); John Hancock, " 'Smokestacks and Geraniums': Planning and Politics in San Diego," in Mary Corbin Sies and Christopher Silver, eds., *Planning the Twentieth-Century American City* (Baltimore, 1996), 161–86; and John R. Schmidt, *"The Mayor Who Cleaned Up Chicago": A Political Biography of William E. Dever* (DeKalb, IL, 1989). Environmental historians Martin Melosi, *The Sanitary City: Urban Infrastructure in America from Colonial Times to the Present* (Baltimore, 2000), and David Stradling, *Smokestacks and Progressives: Environmentalists, Engineers, and Air Quality in America, 1881–1951* (Baltimore, 1999), both include women in their discussion of the Progressive Era but rarely mention them afterward.

5. Sarah Deutsch, *Women and the City: Gender, Space, and Power in Boston, 1870–1940* (New York, 2000), and James J. Connolly, *The Triumph of Ethnic Progressivism: Urban Political Culture in Boston, 1900–1925* (Cambridge, MA, 1998).

6. Mary P. Ryan, *Women in Public: Between Banners and Ballots, 1825–1880* (Baltimore, 1990), and *Civic Wars: Democracy and Public Life in the American City during the Nineteenth Century* (Berkeley, 1997).

7. Deutsch, *Woman and the City*, introduction and chapter 7. It is not inconsequential that she titles her work *Women and the City*, rather than Women *in* the City, or Women *of* the City, a distinction made by myself and the contributors in a special issue of the *Journal of Urban History* 23 (March 1997).

8. See Deutsch, *Women and the City*, 262, and Mildred Adams, "What Are Women Mayors Doing?" *The American City* 26 (June 1922): 543–44, for information on women mayors. Again, it is important to realize the differences between big cities and smaller towns. Andersen, *After Suffrage*, 117–21, contends that it was easier for women to hold office on the local level than on the state and federal, but she is talking about smaller localities, especially county offices. Even then, it is necessary to distinguish among the kinds of county offices and their powers, and Andersen admits that those dealing with education were most open to women.

9. Connolly, *The Triumph of Ethnic Progressivism*, 179–82.

10. Ibid., 182–83. See also 65–66 and 72–74, for more information on the Jewish and Catholic Leagues.

11. Nancy Love, "Ideal Speech and Feminist Discourse: Habermas Re-Visioned," *Women and Politics* 11 (1991): 116–17.

12. Connolly, *The Triumph of Ethnic Progressivism*, 183.

13. Ibid., 183. See also Suellen Hoy, "Caring for Chicago's Women and Girls: The Sisters of the Good Shepherd, 1859–1911," *Journal of Urban History* 23 (March 1997): 260–94, for suggestions about how Chicago Catholic nuns, although not allied with other women's organizations, can be integrated into Chicago women's municipal activism.

14. Sarah Deutsch, "Learning to Talk More Like a Man: Boston Women's Class-Bridging Organizations, 1870–1940," *American Historical Review* 97 (April 1992): 379–404. Gullett, *Becoming Citizens*; McArthur, *Creating the New Woman*; and Pamela Tyler, *Silk Stockings and Ballot Boxes: Women and Politics in New Orleans, 1920–1963* (Athens, GA, 1996). Mary Murphy, *Mining Cultures: Men, Women and Leisure in Butte, 1914–1941* (Urbana, 1997), never strays from its specific focus to consider the possibilities of women's roles in the city's overall development. See Deutsch, *Women and the City*, 190 and 199, for the Boston WTUL and elite women.

15. For Blacklidge see *Daily News, Almanac* (1917). *Tribune*, February 17, 22, 23 and 24, 1919, gives the most complete account of women's primary election activities. See also a letter dated February 28, 1919, from Merriam to Wallin Sikes thanking her for supporting his mayoral campaign, George and Madeleine Wallin-Sikes MS Collection, Box 8, Chicago Historical Society. Wallin-Sikes's activities underscore the connections between women's organizations and subsequent political action. She developed her political interests while chairing the education legislation committee of the Association of Collegiate Alumnae, steering the committee toward a "political" agenda of monitoring state legislatures and campaigning for federal education legislation. See Karen M. Mason, "Testing the Boundaries: Women, Politics, and Gender Roles in Chicago, 1890–1930" (Ph.D. Dissertation, University of Michigan, 1991), 141–42, and Wallin-Sikes Collection, Box 7, folder "Educational Reform." In the 1920s, Napieralski was president of the Polish Women's Alliance of America. *Daily News, Almanac* (1929).

16. In fact, the bureau of public welfare, which had been created by municipal ordinance, was virtually defunct by 1919, and the office of commissioner of public welfare was vacant. This bureau had given activist women a particular entree into municipal government because the commissioner was to consult with a volunteer

advisory board, which, as originally constituted, included a number of the city's most politically active women. See chapter 6, above.

17. *Tribune*, February 22, 1919. Before she moved to Boston, labor organizer Mary Kenney O'Sullivan had founded, with Hull House support, the Jane Club, the prototype for the Eleanor Clubs. See Adade M. Wheeler and Marlene S. Wortman, *The Roads They Made: Women in Illinois History* (Chicago, 1977), 38.

18. The 1919 mayoral election was further complicated by the appearance of a short-lived Labor Party, which slated Chicago Federation of Labor leader John Fitzpatrick for mayor. One of the only two women who stood for alderman in this election was CTF leader Ida Fursman, labor party candidate in the 17th ward, who had legally challenged the Loeb Rule, belonged to the Political Equality League, and addressed the women's mass meeting of March 1916. See *Tribune* March 25 and April 2, 1919.

19. Ibid., March 26, 29, and 31, 1919. The West Side Women's Club was also mentioned as supporting Hoyne. Other references to a club with this name indicate that it might have been an African American women's club. Anne Meis Knupfer, *Toward a Tenderer Humanity and a Nobler Womanhood: African American Women's Club in Turn-of-the-Century Chicago* (New York, 1996), identified a West Side Women's Club as active in suffrage matters; more than one club existed in Chicago with a variation on this name and I have located no source that gives definitive information on which one supported Hoyne.

20. See Alfreda Duster, ed., *Crusade for Justice: The Autobiography of Ida B. Wells* (Chicago, 1970), 348 for De Priest, and 350–53 for Thompson campaign.

21. When she ran for delegate to the Republican national convention in 1928, the *Tribune*, April 5, 1928, quoted her: "I am out on half a dozen meetings a night telling our people that Thompson has betrayed them, that he has appointed men who have sold them into political slavery." Patricia A. Schechter, *Ida B. Wells-Barnett and American Reform, 1880–1930* (Chapel Hill, 2001), 205–207, describes Wells-Barnett and the ASC in the 1915 campaign, and her fury with Hoyne later in 1919, but says nothing about the 1919 mayoral campaign.

22. WCC, *Bulletin* (December 1920).

23. Young belonged to the CWC and the Austin Woman's Club, but I have not found her name listed with other women's organizations. Final count in mayoral vote was Thompson 259,828; Sweitzer, 238,206; Hoyne, 110,901; and Fitzpatrick, 55,990. Vote totals are from *Tribune*, April 2, 1919, and *Daily News, Almanac* (1920); Young's challenge in *Tribune*, March 25, 1919.

24. WCC, *Bulletin* (May 1920).

25. All quotes from *Tribune*, November 5 and 8, 1922. Cook County Bureau of Public Welfare was distinct from the city department of public welfare.

26. Text of speech, Emily Washburn Dean to Woman's Roosevelt Republican Club (March 10, 1922), in Emily Washburn Dean MS Collection, folder 12, Chicago Historical Society.

27. *Tribune*, October 20 and 23, 1922. On October 26, on the other hand, the *Tribune* reported that a meeting of six hundred women "enthusiastically" endorsed the entire party ticket and supported Righeimer for appointing women election judges and clerks. The newspaper does not identify these women.

28. WCC, *Bulletin* (January 1923).

29. For a detailed discussion of Bowen's mayoral gambit, see Sharon Alter, "A Woman for Mayor?" *Chicago History* (Autumn 1986): 53–68. *Tribune*, December 11 and 19, 1922. The *Daily News*, December 9, 1922 mentioned that the Brundage / Crowe faction of the party might support Bowen, but this was probably an anti-Thompson feint, as subsequent support for a Thompson challenger in the primary demonstrates. See Haarsager, *Bertha Knight Landes of Seattle*, 226–27, for male characterization of her one term in office as "petticoat rule." Seattle provides both an instructive comparison with Chicago, and an example of the pervasive male hostility toward women in politics. Landes was a leading clubwoman. Her first-place finish in the nonpartisan mayoral primary in 1926 had virtually assured her election because the second-place finisher was the scandal-ridden incumbent. But she lost re-election two years later, despite a list of impressive administrative accomplishments in what was clearly a backlash against a woman in power. Among those who worked hard to defeat her were male city employees who clearly, as Bowen had contended, resented being governed by a woman. See Haarsager, *Bertha Knight Landes of Seattle*, 123–42 and 219–25.

30. *Tribune*, March 19, 22, and 25, 1923. See Schmidt, *"The Mayor Who Cleaned Up Chicago"* for a general account of this election. For Bowen's position, see Alter, "A Woman for Mayor?" 68.

31. *Tribune*, March 23 and April 2, 1923. See also Schmidt, *"The Mayor Who Cleaned Up Chicago"*, 69.

32. Chicago *Daily News, Almanac* (1924).

33. *Tribune*, April 3, 6, and 8, 1924. For description of Waring, see Knupfer, *Toward a Tenderer Humanity and a Nobler Womanhood*, 155–56.

34. *Tribune*, April 9 and 10, 1924. Women's political possibilities were always greater in at-large, rather than district-based, races.

35. *Tribune*, February 18, 19 and 20, 1927, provides nearly the only information on women and the primary election, including a report of five thousand female Republican precinct workers reported attending a Litsinger rally.

36. Agnes Nestor MS Collection, Box 3, folder 3, Chicago Historical Society; *Tribune*, April 1 and 2, 1927; and Schmidt, *"The Mayor Who Cleaned Up Chicago"*, 157. See photos of this march in *Tribune*, April 1, 1927.

37. Schmidt, *"The Mayor Who Cleaned Up Chicago"*, 103–109, 157–58, 162, and 165–67. One interesting note is that McAndrew was then suspended from his post in late 1927 by action of Thompson's board members because he supported the teachers. *Tribune*, March 1, 1928.

38. Louise de Koven Bowen, *Speeches, Addresses and Letters*, v. 2 (Ann Arbor, MI, 1937), 684–90.

39. In a speech of February 1, 1926, to the WRRC, Bowen recounted that the organization had backed the entire slate in 1924 in return for the nomination of one woman, Mary Bartelme, to the circuit court. But two years later, the party again ignored Republican women at candidate selection time. Bowen, *Speeches*, v. 2, 768–74.

40. While the white and black women's Republican groups often worked together, the progressive leanings of the WRRC, the inherent racism of white women's organizations, and the need for African American women activists to pursue a race as well as a gender agenda, often impeded cooperation among Republican

women. Ruth Hanna McCormick generally had the enthusiastic support of the African American women's Republican organization, but even she drew Wells-Barnett's wrath for inviting Mary Church Terrell—a rival of Wells-Barnett—to campaign for McCormick's election to Senate at the end of the decade. Unidentified newspaper clipping, October 19, 1929, in Irene McCoy Gaines MS Collection, Box 1, folder 1927–1929, Chicago Historical Society, with a resolution signed by Wells-Barnett and other politically active African American women declaring "we hereby serve notice on Mrs. Ruth Hanna McCormick that we resent the slight thus put upon the Negro women of Illinois, whose vote she solicits, by the employment of an outsider to influence that vote."

41. Hays quoted in Andersen, *After Suffrage*, 103.

42. Chicago's was not an isolated incident of this attitude, for in New York the progressive Republican leader, Nicholas Butler Murray, had puzzled over women's demands for equality, wondering what more they could want now that they had the vote. See Elisabeth I. Perry, "Negotiating Political Space after Suffrage: Republican Women in New York, 1917–1926," paper presented to the Organization of American Historians, April 1994. Copy in my possession.

43. Bowen, *Speeches*, v. 2, 639–42.

44. Application in Dean MS Collection, folder 11.

45. See Schmidt, *"The Mayor Who Cleaned Up Chicago,"* 151–54, for this split and for Thompson's machinations in playing one reform wing against the other. See also Bukowski, *Big Bill Thompson*, for an extensive discussion of the factions and personalities in the Chicago Republican Party.

46. Schechter, *Ida B. Wells-Barnett*, 216–17 and 238–39.

47. Dean supported Cermak "believing his election will insure the defeat of Thompsonism and a better administration of our City's affairs." She said that Bowen and Addams were asked to serve on the Women's Independent Committee for Cermak. Correspondence of March 6, 10, and 16, 1931, between Dean and Anne Forsyth, another leader of the WRRC, Dean Collection, folder 13. I have been unable to verity whether Addams did so, but Bukowski, *Big Bill Thompson*, 248, says that Addams endorsed Cermak. The Bowen quotation is from *Tribune*, April 5, 1931, clipping in Louise Hadduck de Koven Bowen Scrapbooks, vol 3, Chicago Historical Society.

48. He also appointed clubwoman Fannie Barrier Williams to the library board.

49. National American Woman Suffrage Association and First National Congress of the League of Women Voters, February 12–18, 1920, *Program*, at the Chicago Historical Society.

50. She made her point in a speech titled "Why Should Women Enroll in Political Parties," in *Program*, NAWSA and the First National Congress of the League of Women Voters.

51. The League of Women Voters organized along national, state, and local lines, similar to the organizational structure of the General Federation of Women's Clubs. The ILWV Manuscript Collection at the Chicago Historical Society focuses on the activities of the Chicago / Cook County branch, as well as providing information on ward based leagues. In this chapter I generally refer to the organization as the ILWV since that is the name of the manuscript collection, but I focus on the activities of the local league women and groups.

52. Various lists are contained in ILWV MS Collection, Box 3, folder 17, Box 2, folder 11, and Illinois League of Women Voters, "Forty Years of Faith and Works," pamphlet, Chicago Historical Society. McKinley was listed as a committee chair on ILWV stationery in 1924; Goins was listed as a director in 1921 and headed the Douglas branch LWV in the city.

53. ILWV MS Collection, "List of Speakers and Women's Groups," October 27, 1922, Box 5, folder 35. For lists of ward and neighborhood LWV branches later in the decade, see *Daily News, Almanac* (1927–32).

54. Andersen, *After Suffrage*, chapter 6.

55. LWV, "Forty Years of Faith and Works."

56. ILWV Collection, Box 6, folders 53 and 54. See also, WCC, *Bulletin* (June 1923). The fourth annual convention of the ILWV in 1924 featured an open session on Sheppard-Towner that was jointly conducted with the child welfare committee of the WCC. See ILWV, "Miscellaneous Pamphlets," Chicago Historical Society. On other "political" matters, the ILWV urged women to consider the potential benefits for women of changing the electoral system to one of proportional representation, promoted legislation for the eight-hour day, supported the proposed national child labor amendment and the Cable Bill on woman's citizenship, helped to develop a women's legislative program, spoke to women's groups about the national elections and standards for political candidates, discussed the work of the Federal Trade Commission and the World Court, and promoted women's participation in a movement for international peace. See ILWV Collection, Box 5, folder 35.

57. See Curry, *Modern Mothers in the Heartland*, 21, 36, and 47–48, for Chicago women's voluntary efforts. The Elizabeth McCormick fund gave the money to establish the first children's day hospital at the Northwestern University settlement where Harriet Vittum was a trained nurse and Head Resident. "Testimonial" (1947), Northwestern University Settlement MS Collection, Northwestern University.

58. See Curry, *Modern Mothers in the Heartland*, 120–23 and 128–31, for Chicago women and Sheppard-Towner, and 131 for the Civic Federation.

59. WCC, *Bulletin* (July-August 1923). See Curry, 131, for *Daily News* editorial using these arguments, and 139 for other male responses. Kelley quoted in Kriste Lindenmeyer, *"A Right to Childhood": The U.S. Children's Bureau and Child Welfare, 1912–46* (Urbana, 1997), 94. Miller, in fact, lost re-election in fall 1923.

60. See Charles Merriam, *Chicago: A More Intimate View of Urban Politics* (New York, 1929). From its founding in 1894 through the 1920s, bankers were among the prominent leaders of the Civic Federation. See David L. Beito, *Taxpayers in Revolt: Tax Resistance during the Great Depression* (Chapel Hill, 1989), for bankers and the Civic Federation during the late 1920s.

61. When viewed in the urban context, male opposition to Sheppard-Towner was more than a backlash against "politicized motherhood," and Chicago women's support for the legislation went far deeper than "personal concerns about their children's health," both of which were suggested by Molly Ladd-Taylor, *Mother-Work*, 168–69. Neither Connolly, *The Triumph of Ethnic Progressivism*, nor Deutsch, *Women and the City*, examines Boston women's activities on Sheppard-Towner. According to Ladd-Taylor, 173, the Boston Women's Municipal

League—which Connolly says lost all influence early in the decade—had supported a pre-natal care program under the leadership of Elizabeth Lowell Putnam, who then opposed Sheppard-Towner. The actions of Boston women would be especially interesting because Massachusetts, Illinois, and Connecticut were the only states ultimately to reject these federal funds.

62. I would like to thank Rose Holz for the information on the location of the six birth control clinics. For more information, see her forthcoming Ph.D. dissertation from the University of Illinois, "The Birth Control Clinic in American: Live Within; Life Without, 1923–1972."

63. "Partial List of Women . . . Recently . . . Appointed or Elected to Public Office in Chicago, Cook County, and the State of Illinois," July 31, 1923, ILWV Collection, Box 3, folder 21. I have never found an extensive membership list for the ILWV, but the names mentioned here appear in various places in the manuscript collection and in the ILWV pamphlet, "Forty Years of Faith and Works."

64. See ILWV, "Forty Years of Faith and Works," and Daily *News, Almanac* (1927 and 1929) for list of ward and neighborhood branches, including information that Irene Goins headed one of the African American branches; Goins was an original member of the ILWV Board of Directors and her name also appears as one of the women working in the ILWV on behalf of the child labor amendment. See Box 2, folder 11 (1925); List of Speakers and Organizations (1927–28), Box 5, folder 35; Meeting of December 14, 1931, Box 4, folder 31; and Meeting of September 30, 1932, Box 3, Ledger Book ILWV Collection.

65. Wallin-Sikes MS Collection, Box 8. Also see the letter from Catharine Waugh McCulloch to the WCC, January 20, 1920, in WCC MS Collection, Box 1, folder 1, Chicago Historical Society. The WCC also supported including in any new constitution municipal home rule powers to acquire public utilities. WCC, *Bulletin* (November 1919).

66. The proposed constitution did not pass; among its other problems for Chicagoans was its proposal to permanently restrict Chicago's representation in the state legislature. The problems of Chicago's municipal ownership movement can be tracked through Paul Barrett, *The Automobile and Urban Transit: The Formation of Public Policy in Chicago, 1900–1930* (Philadelphia, 1983), Harold Platt, *The Electric City: Energy and the Growth of the Chicago Area, 1880–1930* (Chicago, 1991), Schmidt, *"The Mayor Who Cleaned Up Chicago"*. Women do not figure in any of these accounts.

67. For lists of club branches and leaders see the *Daily News, Almanac* . For African American women, the WCC, *Bulletin* (October 1923), listed both Wells and Smith as members and ward leaders; WCC, *Directory* (December 1920), listed Irene McCoy Gaines as a member.

68. For citizenship classes, see WCC, *Bulletin* (May 1919 and October 1923). For other information, see also *Bulletin* (February and September 1923 and March 1924). A photo taken of the first meeting of a citizenship training school includes an African American woman, presumably Davis. See also Elizabeth L. Davis, *The Story of the Illinois Federation of Colored Women's Clubs* (Des Moines, IA, 1925).

69. WCC, *Bulletin* (October 1920, January 1917, July-August, 1922, January 1923, February and April 1924, November 1925, October 1927, January 1928).

70. WCC, *Bulletin* (July-August 1923).

71. WCC, *Bulletin* (February 1920). When ex-Chicago activist Florence Kelley (who had relocated to New York City) testified before Congress in December 1920 in support of Sheppard-Towner, she made a similar argument. She told Congress that "women deeply resented the fact that Congressmen legislated salary and pension increases for postal employees and veterans, but claimed that the government could not afford to provide health care for women and children." Quoted in Ladd-Taylor, *Mother-Work*, 170.

72. Flanagan, "The City Profitable, the City Livable," and "Women, Men, and the Housing Problem: Chicago Activists, 1900–1920," paper presented at annual meeting of the Social Science History Association, Baltimore, 1993, elaborate on this point.

73. City Club, *Bulletin* (January 17, 1921). See also Gail Radford, *Modern Housing for America: Policy Struggles in the New Deal* (Chicago, 1996), for a complete discussion of the role played by businessmen in enacting housing policy that favored private enterprise.

74. University of Chicago Settlement, "Annual Report," May 1921, Mary McDowell MS Collection, Chicago Historical Society.

75. WCC, *Bulletin* (January 1928), and *Yearbook* (1929–1930). See also *Tribune*, April 9, 1914, for CWC.

76. Phrase quoted in Knupfer, *Toward a Tenderer Humanity and a Nobler Womanhood*, 44. See also Schechter, *Ida B. Wells-Barnett*, 184–87, and Duster, *Crusade for Justice*, 281–88.

77. William Tuttle, *Race Riot: Chicago in the Red Summer of 1919* (New York, 1970).

78. Allan H. Spear, *Black Chicago: The Making of a Negro Ghetto, 1890–1920* (Chicago, 1967), 216–18, summarizes the white male response to the riots. Philanthropist Julius Rosenwald justified the abandonment of the housing project by observing that to ensure a 5 percent return on investment, rents would exceed the capabilities of even higher-paid African Americans. "I made up my mind that unless the building could be built and rented on a business basis, there was no virtue in putting it up." See also Thomas Philpott, *The Slum and the Ghetto: Neighborhood Deterioration and Middle-Class Reform, Chicago 1880–1930* (New York, 1978), 207–208, 259–69.

79. Philpott, *The Slum and the Ghetto*, 302–304.

80. WCC, *Bulletin* (January and December 1920). Davis, *The Story of the Illinois Federation of Colored Women's Clubs*, 36–40. For the four women, see the entry for "Ada S. McKinley," in Rima Lunin Schultz and Adele Hast, eds., *Women Building Chicago, 1790–1990: A Biographical Dictionary* (Bloomington, IN, 2001), 572.

81. For the VNA, see Curry, *Modern Mothers in the Heartland*, 21 and 59; for Woolley, see letter from Celia Parker Woolley to Charlotte Johnson, November 27, 1912, in Julius Rosenwald MS Collection, Box XIV, folder 3, Special Collections, Regenstein Library, the University of Chicago; for the CPEL, see Wanda Hendricks, *Gender, Race, and Politics in the Midwest: Black Club Women in Illinois* (Bloomington, IN, 1998), 108; for Williams and Wells-Barnett and Snowden, see Joanne Goodwin, *Gender and the Politics of Welfare Reform: Mothers' Pensions in Chicago, 1911–1929* (Chicago, 1997), 122 and 135; for Bowen, see letter printed

in Chicago *Examiner*, January 30, 1917, and *Speeches*, v. 1, 503; for Thompson and Giles' removal, see Bukowski, *Big Bill Thompson*, 49; for McDowell and Goins, see Elizabeth Anne Payne, *Reform , Labor, and Feminism: Margaret Dreier Robins and the Women's Trade Union League* (Urbana, 1988), 53–54; for employment services see, Chicago *Herald and Examiner*, December 23, 1921, clipping in Louise de Koven Bowen *Scrapbooks*, v. 2, Chicago Historical Society. The 2nd ward branch of the WCC was designated "colored" as were the 3rd and 4th ward WCC (Forrestville Branch), and the Douglas LWV. See Goodwin, *Gender and Politics of Welfare Reform*, 247 n. 113, for confusion on this point. In 1913–14, the CWC reported working with the Phyllis Wheatley Home for Colored Girls and of making financial contributions both to it and to the Douglass Center. "Annual Report," April 1914, *Philanthropy Department*, CWC Collection, Box 23.

82. Fannie Barrier Williams had been on the program of the annual suffrage convention meeting in Chicago in 1907 and presented a paper at a regular meeting of the CWC in 1913 on "The Colored People of Chicago." Ida B. Wells-Barnett addressed the University of Chicago Settlement Woman's Club in 1912 and was invited to attend the Illinois Equal Suffrage Association reception in 1916. See "Program of the Annual Convention," February 13–19, 1907, and "Minutes of Regular Meeting," December 10, 1913, *Club Minutes 1911–14*, CWC Collection, Box 23; "Minutes of University of Chicago Settlement Woman's Club, January 25, 1912," in Agnes Nestor MS Collection, Box 1, folder 6, Chicago Historical Society; and ILWV Collection, Box 6, folders 52 and 53 and Box 4, folder 31; and Kristie Miller, *Ruth Hanna McCormick: A Life in Politics* (Albuquerque, 1992), 131–32. See *Tribune*, March 27, 1932 for Randolph. Knupfer, *Toward a Tenderer Humanity and a Nobler Womanhood*, reiterates how black and white women's organizations, civic and suffrage, forged alliances. Despite such instances of black women addressing white women or working side-by-side, white women did generally set the agenda and spoke more often to black women than vice versa.

83. In this regard, see Susan Lynn, *Progressive Women in Conservative Times: Racial Justice, Peace and Feminism, 1945 to the 1960s* (New Brunswick, NJ, 1992), for her discussion of the earlier cross-race cooperation in women's organizations such as the YWCA, where in 1923 the executive committee of the Student YWCA "approved the demands of black student members who called for social equality at Y conferences and meetings" (42). An unfortunate tendency of scholars to convict all white women of racism leaves no room for appreciating how men and women held different ideas about municipal conditions. To acknowledge this does not excuse white racism but brings a fuller perspective to Chicago's development. Elisabeth Lasch-Quinn, *Black Neighbors: Race and the Limits of Reform in the American Settlement House Movement, 1890–1945* (Chapel Hill, 1993), focuses on the failure of white settlement workers to insist upon "social equality" to lump together all white men and women; Fitzpatrick, *Endless Crusade*, 139, contends that "few white Progressive reformers shared [Frances] Kellor's consistent concern for the plight of black Americans."

84. *Tribune*, October 17 and 31, 1922; WCC, *Bulletin* (July-August, 1922, January 1923, and October 1927); and Bukowski, *Big Bill Thompson*, 185 and 188 for Fitzpatrick and Olander (heads of the CFL and IFL, respectively) and the

Wage Earners' League, which was composed of union men. Olander also wanted jobs at the health department.

85. See WCC, *Bulletin* (December 1928) for disagreements about supporting school superintendent McAndrew.

86. *Tribune*, March 1, 1928, and WCC, *Bulletin* (February 1928).

87. For 1930, see *Tribune*, March 11, 13, and 14, 1930; for IWA, see chapter 2; for 1915, see *Tribune*, March 14, 1915.

88. See David J. Hogan, *Class and Reform: School and Society in Chicago, 1880–1930* (Philadelphia, 1985), chapter 6. See also 218 for the rapaciousness of businessmen on the board over the years. The CTF had not opposed the Otis Law because it also provided for teacher tenure after three years of service. The bill had been sponsored by the Public Education Association, which had been formed in response to the Loeb rule by Addams, Grace Abbott, Merriam, and CFL leader John Fitzpatrick. See 210–11 and 219 for PEA and Otis Bill. Once merit protections were achieved, along with a strong superintendent, male activists turned their attention to other areas of municipal-decision making. See also City Club, *Bulletin* (Jan 8, 1923).

89. "Minutes," *Council and Executive Committee of Council for the Cook County League* (1927–32), ILWV Collection, Box 6, folder 41.

90. ILWV Collection, Box 6, folder 52, has the transcription of an interview with Sikes.

91. See the arguments made in this regard in the work of Carole Pateman, *The Disorder of Women: Democracy, Feminism and Political Theory* (Stanford, 1989), and Anne Phillips, *Engendering Democracy* (University Park, PA, 1991).

92. Merriam, *Chicago: A More Intimate View of Urban Politics*, 156. The examples to refute Merriam's contention are numerous. In addition to ones already mentioned in the text, the Woman's Party of Cook County in 1911 had called for a new state constitution to give cities the home rule right to "control living conditions within their own boundaries," and in 1913 had petitioned the Chicago city council to adopt a plan for the municipal ownership of a comprehensive municipal subway system. Even a neighborhood club, the Rogers Park Woman's Club discussed the issue of municipal ownership of public utilities. See, respectively, Chicago *Record-Herald*, August 12, 1911; City Council of Chicago, *Proceedings*, v. 1 (1913–1914), 2301 with follow-up mention in v. 2, 2404; and *Tribune*, March 7, 1915.

93. Andersen, *After Suffrage*, 169.

94. See Bukowski, *Big Bill Thompson*; Barrett, *The Automobile and Urban Transit*; Hogan, *Class and Reform*; Philpott, *The Slum and the Ghetto*; and Stradling, *Smokestacks and Progressives*. One of the few exceptions is Harold Platt, "Invisible Gases: Smoke, Gender and the Redefinition of Environmental Policy in Chicago, 1900–1920," *Planning Perspectives* (January 1995): 67–97, and "Jane Addams and the Ward Boss Revisited: Class, Politics and Public Health in Chicago, 1890–1930," *Environmental History* 5 (April 2000): 194–220.

95. WCC, *Bulletin* (November 1919, March 1920 and March 1930); WCC, typescript dated October 1926 in WCC Collection, folder 1, and *Bulletin* (November 1926); *Bulletin* (April 1928); and ILWV Collection, Box 5, folder 35 and Box 4, folder 31.

96. Typescript (October 1926), in WCC Collection, folder 1, and WCC, *Year-book* (1929–1930). See also the 1928 legislative program of the ILWV, Box 5, folder 35, for its similar agenda.

97. *Tribune*, April 4, 1928.

98. Barrett, *The Automobile and Urban Transit*, 145–46 and 151–53, points out that groups of Chicago men who sought such money for streets had opposed using public money for mass transit, that the Chicago bureau of public efficiency supported twelve million dollar bond issues for downtown street improvements, and that as the city plunged into economic depression when "business and clean-government reformers" opposed new bond issues it was because of technical quibbles, "not as opposition to spending *per se* or to spending for roads."

99. Bukowski, *Big Bill Thompson*, 6, 228, and 252. The quotations are from Merriam, *Chicago: A More Intimate View of Urban Politics*, 71–72 and 301–302. According to Philpott, *The Slum and the Ghetto*, 245, the Chicago Plan Commission in the 1920s "made no little plans, and regarding housing it continued to make no plans at all."

100. Curry, *Modern Mothers in the Heartland*, 19, 22, 129, and 152. The quotations are from *Illinois Medical Journal* in Curry, *Modern Mothers in the Heartland*, 146–47.

101. See "Principal Items on Legislative Program," November 1928, ILWV Collection, Box 5, folder 35, and "Meeting of October 17, 1932," in Ibid., Box 3, Ledger Book 1931–34.

102. Philpott, *The Slum and the Ghetto*, 251 and 252–54.

Chapter Eight
"I Am the Only Woman on Their Entire Ticket"

1. Kevin Mattson, *Creating a Democratic Public: The Struggle for Urban Participatory Democracy During the Progressive Era* (University Park, PA, 1998), examines the ideas and work of a handful of individual progressives—men and women—trying to bring more participatory democracy into the urban context and reminds us not to forget this important element of the politics of the Progressive Era. His study, however, does not include the contestations among differing groups of urban residents over this issue, investigate their gender dimension, or bring in the political parties. See also, Robert D. Johnston, "Re-democratizing the Progressive Era," *Journal of the Gilded Age and Progressive Era* 1 (January 2002): 68–92.

2. No book that investigates Chicago politics in this era mentions the Nestor campaign.

3. The *Federation News*, February 25, 1928, clipping in Agnes Nestor MS Collection and letter from Nestor to Margaret Dreier Robins, February 22, 1928, Box 6, folder 2, Chicago Historical Society.

4. For Mary and Anna Wilmarth, see Maureen A. Flanagan, "Anna Wilmarth Ickes: A Staunch Woman Republican," in Melanie Gustafson, Kristie Miller, and Elisabeth Israels Perry, eds., *We Have Come to Stay: American Women and Political Parties, 1880–1960*, (Albuquerque, 1999), 141–51

5. Kristie Miller, *Ruth Hanna McCormick: A Life in Politics, 1880–1944* (Albuquerque, 1992), 185.

6. Miller, *Ruth Hanna McCormick*, 190–92, 196 for quotation. Voter registration totals from *Tribune*, November 5, 1928. Male registration had increased 21 percent in that same time. McCormick received 405,338 votes in Cook County from a total of 805,338 statewide. *Daily News, Almanac* (1929).

7. For the WCC see, *Bulletin*, (March 1928) and *Tribune*, April 1, 1928. Other materials from Nestor MS Collection. Clipping from Chicago *Journal*, March (date unreadable) about Nestor speaking to the immigrant women at Christopher House Settlement; letter of Nestor to Mrs. B. Frank Brown (CWC), March 22, 1928, Box 6, folder 2; letters to Nestor from Andresen, March 24, 1928, and from Nestor to Berolzheimer, March 16, 1928, Box 6, folder 2; letter from Elsie Lofgren, March 29, 1928, and copy of Haley's letter, March 31, 1928, Box 6, folder 3. Box 6, folders 2, 3 and 4 contain additional information, including typescripts of February 13 and March 10, 1928 organizational meetings. A partial list of campaign contributors is in Box 3.

8. Quoted in Miller, *Ruth Hanna McCormick*, 186.

9. List of Ruth Hanna McCormick Volunteers, Hanna-McCormick Family MS Collection, Box 127, Precinct Committee Book, 1928–1930, Library of Congress, Manuscript Division, Washington, DC. The overwhelming majority of the more than 300 women listed here were Chicago residents. See also letter from McCormick to Agnes Nestor, February 23, 1928, Nestor Collection, Box 6, folder 2, in which McCormick wrote that friends have told her that she had the Democrat Nestor's support.

10. The massive Harold Ickes MS Collection contains one folder in Box 571 marked "Anna Wilmarth Ickes," which holds a few newspaper clippings and campaign speeches. Linda Lear, *Harold L. Ickes, The Aggressive Progressive, 1874–1933* (New York, 1981), 406, says that "what correspondence there might have been between Ickes and Anna Wilmarth Thompson or about their relationship has been removed." Thompson was the name of her first husband. Comment about the Robins from T. H. Watkins, *Righteous Pilgrim: The Life and Times of Harold L. Ickes, 1874–1952* (New York, 1990), 216.

11. The first two quotations are from Miller, *Ruth Hanna McCormick*, 189. Letter of Nestor to Robins, March 17, 1928, in Nestor Collection, Box 6, folder 2.

12. WCC, *Bulletin* (March 1928). In the presidential contest that year, Mrs. Glenn Plumb (who would run for Cook County commissioner in 1930) expressed a similar sentiment when she defended the Democratic nominee Alfred Smith: "Governor Smith may mispronounce 'radio,' but he does not mispronounce the more important words—justice, tolerance, humanity." *Tribune*, November 3, 1928.

13. WCC, *Bulletin* (March 1928) and unidentified newspaper clipping, April 28, 1928, in Harold L. Ickes Scrapbooks, v. 1 (1905–1933), in Ickes MS Collection, Container #465.

14. Miller, *Ruth Hanna McCormick*, 192.

15. See letter of Nestor to Mary Anderson, March 16, 1928, in Nestor Collection, Box 6, folder 2 and Catharine Waugh McCulloch to Nestor, April 16, 1928, Box 6, folder 4.

16. Miller, *Ruth Hanna McCormick*, provides the best assessment of the 1930 campaign.

17. *Tribune*, March 16, April 4 and 10, and November 5, 1930.

18. Ibid., November 3, 1930, for lack of *Tribune* endorsements. Josephine Perry had secured a Republican nomination for the state house from the 5th district. Mollie Baruch had finished fourth in the primary race in the 6th district. Anna Wilmarth Ickes was re-elected, but Flora Cheney had died while in office. Ibid., November 7, 1930.

19. Patricia A. Schechter, *Ida B. Wells-Barnett and American Reform, 1880–1930* (Chapel Hill, 2001), 241–43. Jones-Ellis came in fourth in the Republican primary. Vote totals for the April 1930 primary from *Tribune*, April 10, 1930.

20. Two women ran in the aldermanic primaries in 1931. In the 29th ward, Mary O'Connell garnered 1,341 votes to finish a distant third of seven candidates; in the 40th, Paula Milgrom received 2,323 votes to the winner's 22,363 votes in a two-person contest. The aldermanic primaries were now technically non-partisan, but both parties widely advertised their choices. *Daily News, Almanac* (1932). The *Almanac*, lists the salaries of all the heads of municipal departments and offices.

21. See Lynne Curry, *Modern Mothers in the Heartland: Gender, Health, and Progress in Illinois, 1900–1930* (Columbus, OH, 1999), 146, for Thompson's actions, and *Tribune*, November 2, 1928 for the CTF's unanimous endorsement of Bundeson as Democratic candidate for the office of coroner.

22. There were still none in 1932 on either the Cook County or state level central committees in 1932. Only the Socialist Party had one woman, Mary Reilly, on its State Committee in 1929 and 1930. *Daily News, Almanac* (1928–33). For Wells-Barnett, see *Tribune*, April 5 and 1, 1928.

23. See Kristi Andersen, *After Suffrage: Women in Partisan and Electoral Politics before the New Deal* (Chicago, 1996), 91, and *Tribune*, February 17, 1928.

24. *Tribune*, November 3, 1928.

25. Nestor Collection, Box 6, folder 4.

26. "Statement of Principles,"(October 1926) WCC MS Collection, Box 1, folder 1. See also WCC, *Bulletin* (November 1926). In 1914, for example, no women's civic organizations had signed a call for organizing a permanent campaign to close saloons. See *Tribune*, April 6, 1914.

27. See Miller, *Ruth Hanna McCormick*, 213–14, 224, and 229–31. But also see how Douglas Bukowski, *Big Bill Thompson, Chicago, and the Politics of Image* (Urbana, 1998), 229, assumes that she was a strict prohibitionist and that this was the "big" issue of the campaign. See also, John R. Schmidt, *"The Mayor Who Cleaned Up Chicago": A Political Biography of William E. Dever* (DeKalb, IL, 1989), for his assessment of the various factors in the 1927 campaign.

28. Typescript marked with heading "Notes for campaign speech to be given to women's clubs—1930," in Harold L. Ickes MS Collection, Box 571, folder labeled "Anna Wilmarth Ickes."

29. Ibid.

30. Letter of Anna Wilmarth Ickes to Mrs. Ralph B. Treadway, President ILWV, May 31, 1930, ILWV Collection, Box 4, folder 31.

31. WCC, *Bulletin* (March and December 1930). Speaking to the WCC, Sears had told the women that unemployment was inherent in the "present industrial organization."

32. *Tribune*, February 17, 1932. See David Beito, *Taxpayers in Revolt: Tax Resistance during the Great Depression* (Chapel Hill, 1989), 70.

33. Ester R. Fuchs, *Mayors and Money: Fiscal Policy in New York and Chicago* (Chicago, 1992), 51 and 55.

34. Beito, *Taxpayers in Revolt*, 38–41.

35. See Marjorie Murphy, *Blackboard Unions: The AFT and the NEA, 1900–1980* (Ithaca, 1990), 133–40. Beito, *Taxpayers in Revolt*, 37. The funds to pay male municipal employees such as police and firefighters were allocated from the municipal budget within which available revenues could be transferred from one budget line to another. See Marjorie Murphy, "Taxation and Social Conflict: Teacher Unionism and Public School Finances, 1898–1914," *Illinois State Historical Journal* (Winter 1981): 243.

36. Beito, *Taxpayers in Revolt*, 66–68. The small Men's Federation of Teachers supported the women teachers. After having been forced by the Loeb rule to drop its affiliation with the CFL, organized labor had not consistently supported the female teachers.

37. The split of the women teachers from the men of the CFL at this point was rooted in the circumstance identified earlier in this book: even when male workers and women activists may have supported an urban reform, they did so for different reasons. See Leidenberger, "Working-Class Progressivism and the Politics of Transportation in Chicago, 1895–1907" (Ph.D. Dissertation, University of North Carolina, 1995).

38. ILWV MS Collection, Box 4, folder 31 for both 1930 and 1931.

39. *Tribune*, November 7, 1932. The one assessment that I have ever found of this campaign, Alex Gottfried, *Boss Cermak of Chicago: A Study of Political Leadership* (Seattle, 1962), attributes Courtney's overwhelming majority to the strength of Cermak's democratic organization and to ethnic solidarity, with no consideration given to the possibility of women's votes as a factor in his election.

40. Murphy, *Blackboard Unions*, 141. Sikes wrote this in an editorial piece published in the *Daily News*, February 13, 1933, clipping in Wallin-Sikes MS Collection, Box 7, folder "Educational Reform," Chicago Historical Society.

41. See Bukowski, *Big Bill Thompson* and Alex Gottfried, *Boss Cermak of Chicago* for brief accounts of Horner and Cermak.

42. See chapter 3, for Lathrop addressing the Lakeview Woman's Club and urging them to become municipal activists. Sarah Tunnicliff, who for years had headed the WCC Clean Air Committee, went from being a member of Chicago Health Commission Advisory staff to director of education and of domestic heating in the Conservation Department of the U.S. Fuel Administration in Illinois. Adade Mitchell Wheeler and Marlene Stein Wortman, *The Roads They Made: Women in Illinois History* (Chicago, 1977), 123.

43. Robyn Muncy, *Creating a Female Dominion in American Reform, 1890–1935* (New York, 1991).

44. See also, Curry, *Modern Mothers in the Heartland*, chapter 5.

45. For the collapse of the public health movement in general and the loss of control by the Children's Bureau over certain welfare measures, see Muncy, *Creating a Female Dominion in American Reform*.

46. "Meeting of October 7, 1932," LWV MS Collection, Box 3, 1931–34 ledger book.

47. Joanne Goodwin, *Gender and the Politics of Welfare Reform: Mothers' Pensions in Chicago, 1911–1929* (Chicago, 1997).

48. For examples of how the Democratic party worked to secure African American and male working-class voters, see Roger Biles, *Big City in Depression and War: Mayor Edward J. Kelly of Chicago* (DeKalb, 1984), and Robert A. Slayton, "Labor and Urban Politics: District 31, Steel Workers Organizing Committee, and the Chicago Machine," *Journal of Urban History* 23 (November 1996): 29–65. See also Lizabeth Cohen, *Making a New Deal: Industrial Workers in Chicago, 1919–1939* (New York, 1990) for union organizing among Chicago workers in the 1930s.

49. Slayton, "Labor and Urban Politics," 35. Slayton says "prevailing wage rates for all city workers," but this did not include female teachers.

50. ILWV membership fell to a low of three thousand by the end of the decade.

51. Slayton, "Labor and Urban Politics," 60.

52. Nestor MS Collection, Box 3, folder 5 and *Daily News, Almanac* (1933).

Conclusion
Chicago Remains the City of Big Shoulders

1. For housing and racism especially, see Arnold Hirsch, *Making the Second Ghetto: Race and Housing in Chicago, 1940–1960* (New York, 1993).

2. See Ester R. Fuchs, *Mayors and Money: Fiscal Policy in New York and Chicago* (Chicago, 1992), 100–101 and 120–24. Between 1929 and 1975, the percentage of the municipal budget targeted for public welfare spending increased by 3.1 percent while that for safety increased by 17 percent. Fuchs, 119.

3. Organization for Economic Cooperation and Development Conference on Women in the City, *Women in the City: Housing, Services and the Urban Environment*, 4–6 October 1994 (Paris, 1995), 15–16, 28, and 55–56. See also speech of Anna Allen to University of Chicago Settlement Woman's Club, February 1914, in Wallin-Sikes MS Collection, folder Social Settlements, at Chicago Historical Society.

4. For early development of this split, see Maureen A. Flanagan, "The City Profitable, the City Livable: Environmental Policy, Gender and Power in Chicago in the 1910s," *The Journal of Urban History* 22 (February 1996): 163–90; for an examination of the economic, growth-oriented vision of the city promoted by Chicago's businessmen and Mayor Daley that characterized the city's development later in the century, see Roger Biles, *Richard J. Daley: Politics, Race and the Governing of Chicago* (DeKalb, IL, 1995).

5. Fuchs, *Mayors and Money,* 258; Biles, *Richard J. Daley,* 47 and 215.

6. Woman's City Club, *Bulletin* (October 1927 and March 1928). Women's Worlds Fair, *Souvenir* (1927), Chicago Historical Society. *Tribune,* March 16, 1930.

7. Kristi Andersen, *After Suffrage: Women in Partisan and Electoral Politics before the New Deal* (Chicago, 1996). See also Kevin Mattson, *Creating a Democratic*

Public: The Struggle for Urban Participatory Democracy During the Progressive Era (University Park, PA, 1998).

8. Sandra Haarsager, *Bertha Knight Landes of Seattle: Big-City Mayor* (Norman, OK, 1994), 85, 130–38, 142, 148–49, 152, 167–73, 221–27, and 258.

9. Charles Merriam, *Chicago*, 301–302, and Louise de Koven Bowen, *Growing Up with a City* (New York, 1926), 224–26.

10. Sidney H. Bremer, "Lost Continuities: Alternative Urban Visions in Chicago Novels, 1890–1915," *Soundings: An Interdisciplinary Journal* 64 (Spring 1981): 43, 31, 36, and 39.

11. See Lynne Curry, *Modern Mothers in the Heartland: Gender, Health, and Progress in Illinois, 1900–1930* (Columbus, OH, 1999), 25, for milk pasteurization.

12. "Women's Worlds Fair Marks Epoch," in *Women's Worlds Fair, 1925, Scrapbook*, at Chicago Historical Society, and *Souvenir* (1927). For African American women, see Patricia Schechter, *Ida B. Wells-Barnett and American Reform, 1880–1930* (Chapel Hill, 2001), 226 and 313n.55. For the Sisters of the Good Shepherd and their work for Chicago's women and children, see Suellen Hoy, "Caring for Chicago's Women and Girls: The Sisters of the Good Shepherd, 1859–1911," *Journal of Urban History* 23 (March 1997): 260–94.

Bibliography

At Chicago Historical Society—Manuscript Collections

Woman's City Club of Chicago
Chicago Woman's Club
Chicago Teachers' Federation
American Association of University Women—Chicago Branch
Illinois League of Women Voters
Chicago Federation of Labor
Chicago Fire—Personal Narratives
Chicago Relief and Aid Society/United Charities
Chicago Trades and Labor Assembly
Chicago Typographical Union #16
City Club of Chicago
Commercial Club of Chicago
Citizens' Association of Chicago
Civic Federation of Chicago
Agnes Nestor
Lucy Flower
Annie McClure Hitchcock
Katherine E. Tuley
Irene McCoy Gaines
Emily Washburn Dean
Mary McDowell
George and Madeleine Wallin-Sikes
Crane-Lillie Family
Pullman Family

At Chicago Historical Society—Printed Collections

Chicago Political Equality League *Yearbooks and Annual Reports*
Woman's City Club *Bulletin*
Good Samaritan Society *Pamphlets and Annual Reports*
Chicago Hospital for Women and Children *Annual Reports*
Bureau of Justice *Annual Reports*
Protective Agency for Women and Children *Annual Reports*
Women's Worlds Fairs *Souvenirs and Scrapbooks*
Louise Hadduck de Koven Bowen *Scrapbooks*
Chicago Women's Trade Union League *Annual Reports*
Women's Baptist Home Mission Society *Pamphlets*
Citizens' Association *Manual, Reports, Scrapbook*

Chicago Relief and Aid Society *Reports*
Chicago Association of Commerce *Pamphlets*
City Club *Bulletin*

At University of Illinois Chicago, Special Collections

Woman's City Club of Chicago
Chicago Women's Trade Union League *Manuscript Collection and Scrapbooks*
Chicago Woman's Aid
Harriet Vittum
Hilda Satt Polacheck
Caroline Huling

At University of Chicago, Special Collections

Grace and Edith Abbott
Julius Rosenwald
Sophonisba Breckinridge
Charles Merriam

At Northwestern University Library

Northwestern University Settlement—Harriet E. Vittum Election Bid Materials

At Newberry Library

Woman's City Club *Its Book*

At Radcliffe College Arthur and Elizabeth Schlesinger Library

Ethel Sturgis Dummer
Catharine Waugh McCulloch
Ellen M. Henrotin

At Smith College Library, Sophia Smith Collection

Ellen Gates Starr
Nancy Cox-Cushman

At University of Illinois Urbana, Illinois Historical Survey

Thomas and Elizabeth Morgan Collection

At Library of Congress, Manuscript Division

Walter L. Fisher
Louis F. Post

Harold L. Ickes
Breckinridge Family
Hanna-McCormick Family

At State Historical Society of Wisconsin

Raymond Robins

Primary Source Materials

Newspapers, Proceedings, Manuals and Almanacs

Chicago Tribune
Chicago Daily News
Chicago Record-Herald
Chicago Inter-Ocean
Chicago Republican
Chicago American
Chicago Examiner / Chicago Herald and Examiner
Chicago Evening Post
Broad-Ax
Chicago Defender
Daily Socialist
Lakeside Monthly, "The Anniversary Fire Number"
The Record (Chicago Trades and Labor Assembly)
Life and Labor (Women's Trade Union League)
Union Labor Advocate
Bulletin of Chicago Teachers' Federation
The Crisis (NAACP)
Chicago Daily News, Almanac
The Woman's Blue Book (Chicago)
Chicago City Manual
Chicago Charter Convention, 1906–07 *Proceedings*
Chicago City Council, *Journal of the Proceedings of the Chicago Common (City) Council*
Memorial: Corinne Stubbs Brown. 1914

Memoirs and Autobiographies

Addams, Jane. *Twenty Years at Hull House.* New York, 1910
Bowen, Louise de Koven. *Growing Up with a City.* New York, 1926 (reissued Urbana, 2002)
Haley, Margaret. *Battleground: The Autobiography of Margaret Haley.* Robert L. Reid, ed. Urbana, 1982
Merriam, Charles. *Chicago: A More Intimate View of Urban Politics.* New York, 1929
Nestor, Agnes. *Woman's Labor Leader: An Autobiography.* Rockford, IL, 1954
Polacheck, Hilda Satt. *I Came a Stranger: The Story of a Hull-House Girl.* Dena Polacheck Epstein, ed. Urbana, 1991

Wells, Ida B. *Crusader for Justice: The Autobiography of Ida B. Wells*. Alfreda M. Duster, ed. Chicago, 1970

Articles and Books, Primary

Abbott, Edith. "Are Women a Force for Good Government?" *National Municipal Review* 4 (1915): 437–47

Adams, Mildred. "What Are Women Mayors Doing?" *The American City* 26 (June 1922): 543–44

Addams, Jane. *Democracy and Social Ethics*. New York, 1902

———. "Woman's Work for Chicago." *Municipal Affairs* (September 1898): 507–508

Andreas, A.T. *The History of Chicago*, 2 volumes. Chicago, 1884–86

Bowen, Louise de Koven. *Speeches, Addresses and Letters*. Ann Arbor, MI, 1937

Breckinridge, Sophonisba. "The Color Line in the Housing Problem." *The Survey* 29 (February 1, 1913): 575–76

Bross, William J. *History of Chicago, Historical and Commercial Statistics, Sketches, Facts and Figures*. Chicago, 1876

Brown, Hallie Q. *Homespun Heroines and Other Women of Distinction*. Xenia, OH, 1926

Chicago Association of Commerce. "The Housing Problem in Chicago." Unpublished pamphlet. 1912

City Club of Chicago. "The Philadelphia Housing Conference." *Bulletin* 5 (December 20, 1912): 409–17

———. "Harbor Development and the Proposed Bond Issue." *Bulletin* 5 (March 29, 1912): 79–90

———. "Chicago's Garbage Problem." *Bulletin* 6 (December 20, 1913): 329–38

———. "The Third National Conference on Housing." *Bulletin* 7 (January 12, 1914): 2–12

———. "The Henrici Strike." *Bulletin* 7 (June 13, 1914): 189–204

———. "The Garment Workers' Strike." *Bulletin* 9 (January 10, 1916): 1–11

City Council of Chicago. "Report of the City Council Subcommittee on Harbor Development." *Journal of the Proceedings of the Chicago City Council* (October, 1911): 8–28

———. "Report of City Council Committee on Schools, Fire, Police and Civil Service to the Council." *Journal of the Proceedings of the Chicago City Council* (October 25, 1915): 1789–92

Cleveland, Lucy. "The Public Baths of Chicago." *Modern Sanitation* 5 (October 1908): 5–17

Free Bath and Sanitary League. "Souvenir of Dedication of the South Side Beach." 1897

Goodspeed, Rev. E.J. *History of the Great Fires in Chicago and the West*. Chicago, 1871

Hitchcock, Annie McClure. *Some Recollections of Early Life in Illinois*. Chicago, n.d

Howe Frederick C. *The City: The Hope of Democracy*. New York, 1905

———. *Confessions of a Reformer*. New York, 1925

———. *Wisconsin: An Experiment in Democracy*. New York, 1912

Hunter, Robert. *Tenement Conditions in Chicago: A Report by the Investigating Committee of the City Homes Association*. Chicago, 1901

Kaneko, Josephine. "What a Socialist Alderman Would Do." *Coming Nation* (March 1914)

Lowell, Josephine Shaw. *Public Relief and Private Charity*. 1884

Martin, Anne. "Women's Inferiority Complex." *New Republic* (July 20, 1921)

National American Woman Suffrage Association and First National Congress of the League of Women Voters. *Program*. February 12–18, 1920

Nicholes, Anna. "How Women Can Help in the Administration of a City." *The Woman's Citizen Library*, vol. 9. New York, 1913

Sandburg, Carl. *Chicago Poems*. New York, 1916

———. *Slabs of the Sunburnt West*. New York, 1922.

———. *Smoke and Steel*. New York, 1920.

Sheahan, James W. and Upton, George P. *The Great Conflagration: Chicago, Its Past, Present and Future*. Chicago, 1872

Statements, briefs etc. "The People of the State of Illinois...upon the relation of Ida L. Fursman...vs. The City of Chicago, the Board of Education of the City of Chicago, et.al." Further Abstract of Records, by Appellees. 1916

Stead, William T. *If Christ Came to Chicago*. Chicago, 1894

Steffens, Lincoln. *The Shame of the Cities*. New York, 1904

Steghagen, Emma. "Report on the Chicago Strike." *Life and Labor* (July 13, 1913)

Wald, Sadie T. "1900—Housing Conditions—1905. *Charities and the Commons* (December 30, 1905): 455–61

Williams, Fannie Barrier. "The Club Movement Among Colored Women of America." In J.E. MacBrady, ed. *A New Negro for a New Century*. Chicago, n.d

Woodruff, Clinton R, ed. *City Government by Commission*. New York, 1919

Wyatt, Edith. "The Chicago Clothing Strike." *Harper's Bazaar* (December 11, 1915): 556–8

Yeomans, Alfred B. *City Residential Land Development: Studies in Planning, Competitive Plans for Subdividing a Typical Quarter Section of Land in the Outskirts of Chicago*. Chicago, 1916

Secondary Source Materials

Books and Essays

Addams, Jane. *The Excellent Becomes the Permanent*. New York, 1932

Alpern, Sara and Baum, Dale. "Female Ballots: The Impact of the Nineteenth Amendment." *Journal of Interdisciplinary History* 15 (Summer 1985): 43–67

Alter, Sharon. "A Woman for Mayor?" *Chicago History* (Autumn 1986): 53–68

Andersen, Kristi. *After Suffrage: Women in Partisan and Electoral Politics before the New Deal*. Chicago, 1996

———. "Women and Citizenship in the 1920s." In Patricia Gurin and Louise Tilly, eds. *Women, Politics, and Change*. New York, 1990

———. "Women and the Vote in the 1920s: What Happened in Oregon?" *Women and Politics* (1994): 43–56

Angle, Paul M, ed. *Prairie State: Impressions of Illinois, 1673–1967.* Chicago, 1968

Avrich, Paul. *The Haymarket Tragedy.* Princeton, 1984

Ayer, Margaret Hubbard and Taves, Isabella. *The Three Lives of Harriet Hubbard Ayer.* Philadelphia, 1957

Baker, Paula. *The Moral Frameworks of Public Life: Gender, Politics, and the State in Rural New York, 1780–1930.* New York, 1991

———. "The Domestication of Politics: Women and American Political Society, 1780–1920." *American Historical Review* 89 (June 1984): 620–47

Barrett, James R. *Work and Community in the Jungle: Chicago's Packinghouse Workers, 1894–1922.* Urbana, 1987

Barrett, Paul. *The Automobile and Urban Transit: The Formation of Public Policy in Chicago, 1900–1930.* Philadelphia, 1983

Beck, Paul Allen. "A Socialization Theory of Partisan Realignment." In Richard Niemi and Herbert Weisberg, eds. *Controversies in American Voting Behavior.* San Francisco, 1976

Beckwith, Karen. "Comparative Research and Electoral Systems: Lessons from France and Italy." *Women and Politics* 12 (1992): 1–33

Beito, David L. *Taxpayers in Revolt: Tax Resistance during the Great Depression.* Chapel Hill, 1989

Berg, Barbara J. *The Remembered Gate: Origins of American Feminism, the Woman and the City 1800–1860.* New York, 1978

Biles, Roger. *Big City Boss in Depression and War: Mayor Edward J. Kelly of Chicago.* DeKalb, IL, 1984

———. *Richard J. Daley: Politics, Race and the Governing of Chicago.* DeKalb, IL, 1995

Blair, Karen J. *The Clubwoman As Feminist: True Womanhood Redefined, 1868–1914.* New York, 1980

Blumin, Stuart. *The Emergence of the Middle-Class: Social Experience in the American City, 1760–1900.* New York, 1989

Bordin, Ruth. *Woman and Temperance: The Quest for Power and Liberty, 1873–1900.* New Brunswick, NJ, 1990

Boris, Eileen. *Home to Work: Motherhood and the Politics of Industrial Homework in the United States.* Cambridge, UK, 1994

———. "The Power of Motherhood: Black and White Activist Women Redefine the 'Political.' " In Seth Koven and Sonya Michel, eds. *Mothers of a New World: Maternalist Politics and the Origins of Welfare States.* New York, 1993

Branham, Charles. "Black Chicago: Accommodationist Politics before the Great Migration." In Melvin G. Holli and Peter d'A Jones, eds. *The Ethnic Frontier: Group Survival in Chicago and the Midwest.* Grand Rapids, MI, 1977

Bremer, Sidney H. "Lost Continuities: Alternative Urban Visions in Chicago Novels, 1890–1915." *Soundings: an Interdisciplinary Journal* 64 (Spring 1981): 29–51

Bridges, Amy. *Morning Glories: Municipal Reform in the Southwest.* Princeton, 1997

Buder, Stanley. *Pullman: An Experiment in Industrial Order and Community Planning, 1880–1930.* Chicago, 1967

Buechler, Steven M. *The Transformation of the Woman Suffrage Movement: The Case of Illinois, 1850–1920.* New Brunswick, NJ, 1986

Buenker, John. *Urban Liberalism and Progressive Reform.* New York, 1973

——. "Sovereign Individuals and Organic Networks: Political Cultures in Conflict in the Progressive Era." *American Quarterly* 40 (June 1988): 187–204

Buhle, Mari Jo. *Women and American Socialism, 1870–1920.* Urbana, 1983

Bukowski, Douglas. *Big Bill Thompson, Chicago, and the Politics of Image.* Urbana, 1998

Campbell, Ballard. *The Growth of American Government: Governance from the Cleveland Era to the Present.* Bloomington, IN, 1995

Chafe, William. "Women's History and Political History." In Nancy Hewitt and Suzanne Lebsock, eds. *Visible Women: New Essays on American Activism.* Urbana, 1993

Chudacoff, Howard. *The Evolution of American Urban Society.* Englewood Cliffs, NJ, 1981

Clemens, Elisabeth. "Organizational Repertoires and Institutional Change: Women's Groups and the Transformation of U.S. Politics, 1890–1920." *American Journal of Sociology* 98 (January 1993): 755–98

Cobble, Dorothy Sue. *Dishing It Out: Waitresses and their Unions in the Twentieth Century.* Urbana, 1991

Cohen, Lizabeth. *Making a New Deal: Industrial Workers in Chicago, 1919–1939.* New York, 1990

Connolly, James J. *The Triumph of Ethnic Progressivism: Urban Political Culture in Boston, 1900–1925.* Cambridge, MA, 1998

Costain, Anne N. *Inviting Women's Rebellion: A Political Process Interpretation of the Women's Movement.* Baltimore, 1992

Costin, Lela B. *Two Sisters for Social Justice: A Biography of Grace and Edith Abbott.* Urbana, 1983

Cott, Nancy. *The Grounding of Modern Feminism.* New Haven, 1987

——. "Across the Great Divide: Women in Politics before and after 1920." In Patricia Gurin and Louise Tilly, eds. *Women, Politics, and Change.* New York, 1990

Crocker, Ruth H. *Social Work and Social Order: The Settlement Movement in Two Industrial Cities, 1889–1930.* Urbana, 1991

Cronon, William. *Nature's Metropolis: Chicago and the Great West.* New York, 1991

Crunden, Robert. *Ministers of Reform: The Progressives' Achievement in American Civilization, 1889–1920.* Urbana, 1984

Curry, Lynne. *Modern Mothers in the Heartland: Gender, Health, and Progress in Illinois, 1900–1930.* Columbus, 1999

Davis, Allen F. *Spearheads for Reform: The Social Settlements and the Progressive Movement, 1890–1914.* New York, 1967

Davis, Elizabeth Lindsay. *The Story of the Illinois Federation of Colored Women's Clubs.* Des Moines, IA, 1925

Dawley, Alan. *Struggles for Justice: Social Responsibility and the Liberal State.* Cambridge, MA, 1991

Deutsch, Sarah. *Women and the City: Gender, Space and Power in Boston, 1870–1940*. New York, 2000

———. "Learning to Talk More Like a Man: Boston Women's Class-Bridging Organizations, 1870–1940." *American Historical Review* 93 (April 1992): 379–404

Downs, Laura Lee. "If 'Woman' Is Just an Empty Category, Then Why Am I Afraid to Walk Alone at Night? Identity Politics Meets the Postmodern Subject." *Comparative Study of Society and History* (1993): 414–51

DuBois, Ellen Carol. *Harriot Stanton Blatch and the Winning of Woman Suffrage*. New Haven, 1996

———. "Working Women, Class Relations, and Suffrage Militance: Harriot Stanton Blatch and the New York Woman Suffrage Movement, 1894–1909." *Journal of American History* 84 (June 1987): 34–58

Ebner, Michael H. *Creating Chicago's North Shore*. Chicago, 1988

Edwards, Rebecca. *Angels in the Machinery: Gender in American Party Politics from the Civil War to the Progressive Era*. New York, 1997

Einhorn. Robin L. *Property Rules: Political Economy in Chicago, 1833–1872*. Chicago, 1991

Ethington, Philip J. *The Public City: The Political Construction of Urban Life in San Francisco, 1850–1900*. Cambridge, UK, 1994

———. "Recasting Urban Political History: Gender, the Public, the Household and Political Participation in Boston and San Francisco during the Progressive Era." *Social Science History* 16 (Summer 1992): 301–33

Evans, Sara. "Women's History and Political Theory: Toward a Feminist Approach to Public Life." In Nancy Hewitt and Suzanne Lebsock, eds. *Visible Women: New Essays on American Activism*. Urbana, 1993

Fairbanks, Robert B. *Housing Reform and the Community Development Strategy in Cincinnati, 1890–1960*. Urbana, 1988

———. "Rethinking Urban Problems: Planning, Zoning, and City Government in Dallas, 1900–1930," *Journal of Urban History* 25 (September 1999): 809–37

Finegold, Kenneth. *Experts and Politicians: Reform Challenges to Machine Power in New York, Cleveland, and Chicago*. Princeton, 1995

Fink, Leon. *Workingmen's Democracy: The Knights of Labor in American Politics*. Urbana, 1983

Fitzpatrick, Ellen F. *Endless Crusade: Women Social Scientists and Progressive Reform*. New York, 1990

Flanagan, Maureen A. *Charter Reform in Chicago*. Carbondale, IL, 1987

———. "Gender and Urban Political Reform: the City Club and the Woman's City Club of Chicago in the Progressive Era." *American Historical Review* 95 (October 1990): 1032–50

———. "Charter Reform in Chicago: Political Culture and Urban Progressive Reform." *Journal of Urban History* 12 (February 1986): 109–30

———. "The Predicament of New Rights: Suffrage and Women's Political Power from a Local Perspective." *Social Politics: International Studies in Gender, State and Society* 2 (Fall 1995): 305–30

———. "The City Profitable, the City Livable: Environmental Policy, Gender, and Power in Chicago in the 1910s." *Journal of Urban History* 22 (January 1996): 163–90

———. "Women in the City, Women of the City: Where Do Women Fit in Urban History?" *Journal of Urban History* 23 (March 1997): 251–59

———. "Anna Wilmarth Ickes: A Staunch Woman Republican." In Melanie Gustafson, Kristie Miller, and Elisabeth Israels Perry, eds. *We Have Come to Stay: American Women and Political Parties, 1880–1960.* Albuquerque, 1999

———. "Mayor Fred A. Busse: A Silent Mayor in Turbulent Times." In Paul Green and Melvin Holli, eds. *The Mayors: A Chicago Political Tradition.* Carbondale, IL, 1987

Foner, Eric. *Politics and Ideology in the Age of the Civil War.* New York, 1980

Frank, Henriette Greenebaum and Jerome, Amalie Hofer. *Annals of the Chicago Woman's Club for the First Forty Years of its Organization, 1876–1916.* Chicago, 1916

Frankel, Noralee and Dye, Nancy S., eds. *Gender, Class, Race and Reform in the Progressive Era.* Lexington, KY, 1991

Fraser, Nancy. *Unruly Practices: Power, Discourse, and Gender in Contemporary Social Theory.* Minneapolis, 1989

Freeman, Jo. *A Room at a Time: How Women Entered Party Politics.* Lanham, MD, 2000

Fuchs, Ester R. *Mayors and Money: Fiscal Policy in New York and Chicago.* Chicago, 1992

Getis, Victoria. *The Juvenile Court and the Progressives.* Urbana, 2000

Giesberg, Judith A. *Civil War Sisterhood: The U.S. Sanitary Commission and Women's Politics in Transition.* Boston, 2000

Gillette, Howard. *Between Justice and Beauty: Race, Planning and the Failure of Urban Policy in Washington, D.C.* Baltimore, 1995

Ginger, Ray. *Altgeld's America: The Lincoln Ideal Versus Changing Realities.* New York, 1958

Ginzberg, Lori D. *Women and the Work of Benevolence: Morality, Politics, and Class in the 19th-Century United States.* New Haven, 1990

Goldstein, Joel. *The Effects of the Adoption of Woman Suffrage: Sex Differences and Voting Behavior—Illinois, 1914–21.* New York, 1984

Goodwin, Joanne L. *Gender and the Politics of Welfare Reform: Mothers' Pensions in Chicago, 1911–1929.* Chicago, 1997

———. "An American Experiment in Paid Motherhood: The Implementation of Mothers' Pensions in Early Twentieth Century Chicago." *Gender and History* 4 (1992): 323–42

Gordon, Linda. *Pitied but Not Entitled: Single Mothers and the History of Welfare, 1890–1935.* New York, 1994

Gordon, Felice D. *After Winning: The Legacy of the New Jersey Suffragists, 1920–1947.* New Brunswick, NJ, 1986

Gottfried, Alex. *Boss Cermak of Chicago: A Study of Political Leadership.* Seattle, 1962

Graham, Sara Hunter. *Woman Suffrage and the New Democracy.* New Haven, 1996

Green, Paul and Holli, Melvin, eds. *The Mayors: A Chicago Political Tradition.* Carbondale, IL, 1987

Grinder, R. Dale. "The Battle for Clean Air: The Smoke Problem in Post-Civil War America." In Martin V. Melosi, ed. *Pollution and Reform in American Cities, 1870–1930.* Austin, TX, 1980

Gugliotta, Angela. "Class, Gender, and Coal Smoke: Gender Ideology and Environmental Injustice in Pittsburgh, 1868–1914." *Environmental History* 5 (April 2000): 165–93

Gullett, Gayle. *Becoming Citizens: The Emergence and Development of the California Women's Movement, 1880–1911.* Urbana, 2000

Gurin, Patricia and Tilly, Louise, eds. *Women, Politics, and Change.* New York, 1990

Gustafson, Melanie, Miller, Kristie, and Perry, Elisabeth Israels, eds. *We Have Come to Stay: American Women and Political Parties, 1880–1960.* Albuquerque, 1999

Haarsager, Sandra. *Bertha Knight Landes of Seattle: Big City Mayor.* Norman, OK, 1994

———. *Organized Womanhood: Cultural Politics in the Pacific Northwest: 1840–1920.* Norman, OK, 1997

Halpern, Rick. *Down on the Killing Floor: Black and White Workers in Chicago's Packinghouses, 1904–54.* Urbana, 1997

Hammack, David. *Power and Society: Greater New York at the Turn of the Century.* New York, 1987

Hancock, John. " 'Smokestacks and Geraniums': Planning and Politics in San Diego." In Mary Corbin Sies and Christopher Silver, eds. *Planning the Twentieth-Century American City.* Baltimore, 1996

Harrison, Cynthia. *On Account of Sex: The Politics of Women's Issues, 1945–1968.* Berkeley, 1988

Hays, Samuel P. *Conservation and the Gospel of Efficiency: The Progressive Conservation Movement, 1890–1920.* Cambridge, MA, 1959

———. *The Response to Industrialism, 1885–1914.* Chicago, 1957

———. "The Politics of Reform in Municipal Government in the Progressive Era." *Pacific Northwest Quarterly* 55 (1964): 157–69

Henderson, A. Scott. *Housing and the Democratic Ideal: The Life and Thought of Charles Abrams.* New York, 2000

Hendricks, Wanda A. *Gender, Race, and Politics in the Midwest: Black Club Women in Illinois.* Bloomington, IN, 1998

Hewitt, Nancy. *Women's Activism and Social Change: Rochester, New York, 1822–1872.* Ithaca, 1984

———. "Politicizing Domesticity: Anglo, Black, and Latin Women in Tampa's Progressive Movements." In Noralee Frankel and Nancy S. Dye, eds. *Gender, Class, Race and Reform in the Progressive Era.* Lexington, KY, 1991

Hewitt, Nancy and Lebsock, Suzanne, eds. *Visible Women: New Essays on American Activism.* Urbana, 1993

Higgenbotham, Evelyn Brooks. *Righteous Discontent: The Women's Movement in the Black Baptist Church, 1880–1920.* Cambridge, MA, 1993

Hine, Darlene Clark. "The Housewives' League of Detroit: Black Women and Economic Nationalism." In Nancy Hewitt and Suzanne Lebsock, eds. *Visible Women: New Essays on American Activism.* Urbana, 1993

———. *Black Women in White: Racial Conflict and Cooperation in the Nursing Profession, 1890–1950.* Bloomington, IN, 1989

Hines, Thomas S. *Burnham of Chicago: Architect and Planner.* Chicago, 1979

Hirsch, Arnold. *Making the Second Ghetto: Race and Housing in Chicago, 1940–1960.* New York, 1963

Hofstadter, Richard. *The Age of Reform: From Bryan to F.D.R.* New York, 1955

Hogan, David John. *Class and Reform: School and Society in Chicago, 1880–1930.* Philadelphia, 1985

Holli, Melvin G. and Jones, Peter d'A, eds. *The Ethnic Frontier: Group Survival in Chicago and the Midwest.* Grand Rapids, MI, 1977

Horowitz, Helen Lefkowitz. *Culture and the City: Cultural Philanthropy in Chicago from the 1880s to 1917.* Chicago, 1976

Hoy, Suellen. "Caring for Chicago's Women and Girls: The Sisters of the Good Shepherd, 1859–1911." *Journal of Urban History* 23 (March 1997): 260–94

———. "Municipal Housekeeping: The Role of Women in Improving Urban Sanitation Practices, 1880–1917." In Martin V. Melosi, ed. *Pollution and Reform in American Cities, 1870–1930.* Austin, TX, 1980

Huthmacher, J. Joseph. "Urban Liberalism and the Age of Reform." *Mississippi Historical Review* 44 (1962): 231–41

Issel, William. "Class and Ethnic Conflict in San Francisco Political History." *Labor History* 18 (1977): 341–59

Jaher, Frederic Cople. *The Urban Establishment: Upper Strata in Boston, New York, Charleston, Chicago, and Los Angeles.* Urbana, 1982

Jentz, John. "Class and Politics in an Emerging Industrial City: Chicago in the 1860s and 1870s." *Journal of Urban History* 17 (May 1991): 227–63

Johnston, Robert D. "Re-Democratizing the Progressive Era: The Politics of Progressive Era Political Historiography." *Journal of the Gilded Age and Progressive Era* 1 (January 2002): 68–92.

Kantowicz, Edward. *Polish-American Politics in Chicago, 1888–1940.* Chicago, 1975

Katz, Sherry J. "Redefining 'The Political': Socialist Women and Party Politics in California, 1900–1920." In Melanie Gustafson, Kristie Miller, and Elisabeth Israels Perry, eds. *We Have Come to Stay: American Women and Political Parties, 1880–1960.* Albuquerque, 1999

Katznelson, Ira and Zolberg, Aristide R., eds. *Working-Class Formation: Nineteenth-Century Patterns in Western Europe and the United States.* Princeton, 1986

Keating, Ann Durkin. *Building Chicago: Suburban Developers and the Creation of a Divided Metropolis.* Columbus, OH, 1988

Kerber, Linda. *No Constitutional Right to Be Ladies: Women and the Obligation of Citizenship.* New York, 1998

Kerber, Linda, Kessler-Harris, Alice and Sklar, Kathryn Kish, eds. *U.S. History As Women's History: New Feminist Essays.* Chapel Hill, 1995

Kleppner, Paul. "Were Women to Blame? Female Suffrage and Voter Turnout." *Journal of Interdisciplinary History* 12 (Spring 1982): 621–43

Kloppenberg, James. *Uncertain Victory: Social Democracy and Progressivism in European and American Thought, 1870–1920.* New York, 1986

Knupfer, Anne Meis. *Toward a Tenderer Humanity and a Nobler Womanhood: African-American Women's Clubs in Turn-of-the-Century Chicago.* New York, 1996

Kornbluh, Andrea T. *Lighting the Way...The Women's City Club of Cincinnati, 1915–1965*. Cincinnati, 1986

Kousser, J. Morgan. "Are Political Acts Unnatural?" *Journal of Interdisciplinary History* 15 (Winter 1985): 467–80

———. "Restoring Politics to Political History." *Journal of Interdisciplinary History* 12 (Spring 1982): 569–95

Koven, Seth and Michel, Sonya, eds. *Mothers of a New World: Maternalist Politics and the Origins of Welfare States*. New York, 1993

Ladd-Taylor, Molly. *Mother-Work: Women, Child Welfare, and the State, 1890–1930*. Urbana, 1994

Lasch-Quinn, Elisabeth. *Black Neighbors: Race and the Limits of Reform in the American Settlement House Movement, 1890–1945*. Chapel Hill, 1993

Lear, Linda. *Harold L. Ickes, The Aggressive Progressive, 1874–1933*. New York, 1981

Leiby, James. *A History of Social Welfare and Social Work in the United States*. New York, 1978

Lessoff, Alan. *The Nation and Its City: Politics, "Corruption," and Progress in Washington, D.C., 1861–1902*. Baltimore, 1994

Lindenmeyer, Kriste. *"A Right to Childhood": The U.S. Children's Bureau and Child Welfare, 1912–46*. Urbana, 1997

Love, Nancy. "Ideal Speech and Feminist Discourse: Habermas Re-Visioned." *Women and Politics* 11 (1991): 101–22

Lynn, Susan. *Progressive Women in Conservative Times: Racial Justice, Peace and Feminism, 1945 to the 1960s*. New Brunswick, NJ, 1992

Massa, Ann. "Black Women in the 'White City.' " *Journal of American Studies* 8 (December 1974): 319–37

Mattson, Kevin. *Creating a Democratic Public: The Struggle for Urban Participatory Democracy During the Progressive Era*. New Brunswick, NJ, 1998

Matthews, Glenna. *The Rise of Public Woman: Woman's Power and Woman's Place in the United States, 1630–1970*. New York, 1992

Mayer, Harold M. and Wade, Richard C. *Chicago: Growth of a Metropolis*. Chicago, 1969

McArthur, Judith N. *Creating the New Woman: The Rise of Southern Women's Progressive Culture in Texas, 1893–1918*. Urbana, 1998

McCarthy, Kathleen D. *Noblesse Oblige: Charity and Cultural Philanthropy in Chicago, 1849–1929*. Chicago, 1982

McCarthy, Michael P. "Chicago Businessmen and the Burnham Plan." *Illinois State Historical Journal* (Autumn 1970): 228–56

McCormick, Richard L. *From Realignment to Reform: Political Change in New York State, 1893–1910*. Ithaca, 1981

McDonald, Terrence J. *The Parameters of Urban Fiscal Policy: Socioeconomic Change and Political Culture in San Francisco, 1860–1906*. Berkeley, 1986

———. "The Burdens of Urban History: The Development of the State in Recent American Social History." *Studies in American Political Development* 3 (1989): 3–29

McGerr, Michael. *The Decline of Popular Politics: The American North, 1865–1928*. New York, 1986

———. "Political Style and Women's Power, 1830–1930." *Journal of American History* 87 (December 1990): 864–85

Melosi, Martin V. *The Sanitary City: Urban Infrastructure in America from Colonial Times to the Present.* Baltimore, 2000

———, ed. *Pollution and Reform in American Cities, 1870–1930.* Austin, TX, 1980

Meyerowitz, Joanne. *Women Adrift: Independent Wage Earners in Chicago, 1880–1930.* Chicago, 1988

Miller, Donald L. *City of the Century: The Epic of Chicago and the Making of America.* New York, 1996

Miller, Kristie. *Ruth Hanna McCormick: A Life in Politics.* Albuquerque, NM, 1992

Miller, Sally, ed. *Race, Ethnicity, and Gender in Early Twentieth-Century American Socialism.* New York, 1996

Monkkonen, Eric. *America Becomes Urban: The Development of U.S. Cities and Towns, 1780–1980.* Berkeley, 1988

Monoson, S. Sara. "The Lady and the Tiger: Women's Electoral Activism in New York City before Suffrage." *Journal of Women's History* 2 (Fall 1990): 100–35

Mowry, George. *The California Progressives.* Berkeley, 1951

Muncy, Robyn. *Creating a Female Dominion in American Reform, 1890–1935.* New York, 1991

———. "Gender and Professionalization in the Origins of the U.S. Welfare State: The Careers of Sophonisba Breckinridge and Edith Abbott, 1890–1935." *Journal of Policy History* 2 (1990): 290–315

Murphy, Mary. *Mining Cultures: Men, Women, and Leisure in Butte, 1914–41.* Urbana, 1997

Murphy, Marjorie. *Blackboard Unions: The AFT and the NEA, 1900–1980.* Ithaca, 1990

———. "Taxation and Social Conflict: Teacher Unionism and Public School Finance, 1898–1914." *Illinois State Historical Journal* (Winter 1981): 242–60

———. "The Pioneer Work of Women in Building the Teacher Union Movement in Chicago." *American Teacher*, Changing Education Section (n.d.): 3–4

Murolo, Priscilla. *The Common Ground of Womanhood: Class, Gender, and Working Girls' Clubs, 1884–1928.* Urbana, 1997

Naylor, Timothy. "Responding to the Fire: The Work of the Chicago Relief and Aid Society." *Science and Society* 39 (1975–76): 450–65

Nelli, Humbert. *Italians in Chicago: 1880–1930: A Study in Ethnic Mobility.* New York, 1970

Nelson, Otto. "The Relief and Aid Society, 1850–1874." *Journal of the Illinois State Historical Society* 59 (1966): 48–66

Oestreicher, Richard. "Urban Working-Class Political Behavior and Theories of American Electoral Politics, 1870–1949." *Journal of American History* 74 (March 1988): 1257–86

Organization for Economic Cooperation and Development Conference on Women in the City. *Women in the City: Housing, Services and the Urban Environment*, 4–6 October 1994. Paris, 1995

Pateman, Carole. *The Disorder of Women: Democracy, Feminism and Political The-ory.* Stanford, 1989

Payne, Elizabeth Anne. *Reform, Labor, and Feminism: Margaret Dreier Robins and the Women's Trade Union League.* Urbana, 1988

Perry, Elisabeth Israels. "Women's Political Choices After Suffrage: The Women's City Club of New York, 1915–1990." *New York History* (October 1990): 417–34

———. "Defying the Party Whip: Mary Garrett Hay and the Republican Party, 1917–1920." In Melanie Gustafson, Kristie Miller, and Elisabeth Israels Perry, eds. *We Have Come to Say: American Women and Political Parties, 1880–1960.* Albuquerque, 1999

Phillips, Anne. *Engendering Democracy.* University Park, PA, 1991

Philpott, Thomas. *The Slum and the Ghetto: Neighborhood Deterioration and Mid-dle-Class Reform, Chicago, 1880–1930.* New York, 1978

Pierce, Bessie. *A History of Chicago,* Vols 2 and 3. Chicago, 1940 and 1957

———. *As Others See Chicago: Impressions of Visitors, 1673–1933.* Chicago, 1933

Pinderhughes, Dianne M. *Race and Ethnicity in Chicago Politics: A Reexamination of Pluralist Theory.* Urbana, 1987

Platt, Harold L. *City Building in the New South: The Growth of Public Services in Houston, 1830–1915.* Philadelphia, 1983

———. *The Electric City: Energy and the Growth of the Chicago Area, 1880–1930.* Chicago, 1991

———. "Jane Addams and the Ward Boss Revisited: Class, Politics, and Public Health in Chicago, 1890–1930." *Environmental History* 5 (April 2000): 194–222

———. "Invisible Gases: Smoke, Science, and the Redefinition of Environmental Policy in Chicago, 1900–1920." *Planning Perspectives* 10 (1995): 67–97

Radford, Gail. *Modern Housing for America: Policy Struggles in the New Deal Era.* Chicago, 1996

Ray, P. Orman. *An Introduction to Political Parties and Practical Politics.* New York, 1917

Reiff, Janice L. "A Modern Lear and His Daughters: Gender in the Model Town of Pullman." *Journal of Urban History* 23 (March 1997): 316–41

Rodgers, Daniel T. *Atlantic Crossings: Social Politics in a Progressive Age.* Cam-bridge, MA, 1998

Rosen, Christine Meisner. *The Limits of Power: Great Fires and the Process of City Growth.* Berkeley, 1986

Ryan, Mary P. *Civic Wars: Democracy and Public Life in the American City during the Nineteenth Century.* Berkeley, 1997

———. *Women in Public: Between Banners and Ballots, 1825–1880.* Baltimore, 1990

Salem, Dorothy. *To Better Our World: Black Women in Organized Reform. 1890–1920.* Brooklyn, NY, 1990

Sapiro, Virginia. "Women, Citizenship, and Nationality: Immigration and Natu-ralization Policies in the United States." *Politics and Society* 13 (1984): 1–26

Sawislak, Karen. *Smoldering City: Chicagoans and the Great Fire, 1871–1874.* Chi-cago, 1995

———. "Relief, Aid, and Order: Class, Gender and the Definition of Community in the Aftermath of Chicago's Great Fire." *Journal of Urban History* 19 (November 1993): 3–18

———. "Smoldering City." *Chicago History* (Fall and Winter 1988–89): 70–101

Schackel, Sandra. *Social Housekeepers: Women Shaping Public Policy in New Mexico, 1920–1940.* Albuquerque, NM, 1992

Scharnau, Ralph. "Elizabeth Morgan, Crusader for Labor Reform." *Labor History* 14 (1973): 340–51

Schechter, Patricia A. *Ida B. Wells-Barnett and American Reform, 1880–1930.* Chapel Hill, 2001

Schiesl, Martin. *The Politics of Efficiency: Municipal Administration and Reform in America, 1880–1920.* Berkeley, 1977

Schmidt, John R. *"The Mayor Who Cleaned Up Chicago": A Political Biography of William E. Dever.* DeKalb, IL, 1989

Schneirov, Richard. *Labor and Urban Politics: Class Conflict and the Origins of Modern Liberalism in Chicago, 1864–1897.* Urbana, 1998

———. "Political Cultures and the Role of the State in Labor's Republic: The View from Chicago, 1848–1877." *Labor History* 32 (Summer 1991): 376–400

Schultz, Rima Lunin and Hast, Adele, eds. *Women Building Chicago, 1790–1990: A Biographical Dictionary.* Bloomington, IN, 2001

Schultz, Stanley. *Constructing Urban Culture: American Cities and City Planning, 1800–1920.* Philadelphia, 1989

Scott, Anne Firor. *Natural Allies: Women's Associations in American History.* Urbana, 1991

Shaw, Stephanie J. "Black Club Women and the Creation of the National Association of Colored Women." *Journal of Women's History* 3 (Fall 1991): 10–25

Shefter, Martin. "Trade Unions and Political Machines: The Organization and Disorganization of American Working Class Life in the Late Nineteenth Century." In Ira Katznelson and Aristide R. Zolberg, eds. *Working-Class Formation: Nineteenth-Century Patterns in Western Europe and the United States.* Princeton, 1986

Sims, Anastatia. *The Power of Femininity in the New South: Women's Organizations in North Carolina, 1880–1930.* Columbia, SC, 1997

Sklar, Kathryn Kish. *Florence Kelley and the Nation's Work: The Rise of Women's Political Culture, 1830–1900.* New Haven, 1995

———. "Two Political Cultures in the Progressive Era: The National Consumers' League and the American Association for Labor Legislation." In Linda Kerber, Alice Kessler-Harris, Kathryn Kish Sklar, eds. *U.S. History As Women's History: New Feminist Essays.* Chapel Hill, 1995

———. "The Historical Foundations of Women's Power in the Creation of the American Welfare State, 1830–1930." In Seth Koven and Sonya Michel, eds. *Mothers of a New World: Maternalist Politics and the Origins of Welfare States.* New York, 1993

———. "Hull House in the 1890s: A Community of Women Reformers." *Signs: Journal of Women in Culture and Society* 10 (Summer 1985): 658–77

Skocpol, Theda. *Protecting Soldiers and Mothers: The Political Origins of Social Policy in the United States.* Cambridge, MA, 1992

Slayton, Robert A. "Labor and Urban Politics: District 31, Steel Workers Organizing Committee, and the Chicago Machine." *Journal of Urban History* 23 (November 1996): 29–66

Smith, Carl. *Urban Disorder and the Shape of Belief: The Great Chicago Fire, the
Haymarket Bomb, and the Model Town of Pullman.* Chicago, 1995

Smith, Joan L. "Progressive School Administration: Ella Flagg Young and the
Chicago Schools, 1905–1915." *Illinois State Historical Journal* 73 (Spring
1980): 27–44

Spain, Daphne. *How Women Saved the City.* Minneapolis, 2001

Spear, Allan. *Black Chicago: The Making of a Negro Ghetto, 1890–1920.* Chicago,
1967

Spinney, Robert G. *City of Big Shoulders: A History of Chicago.* DeKalb, IL, 2000

Sterling, Dorothy. *Black Foremothers.* New York, 1979

Storrs, Landon R.Y. *Civilizing Capitalism: The National Consumers' League,
Women's Activism, and Labor Standards in the New Deal Era.* Chapel Hill, 2000

Stradling, David. *Smokestacks and Progressives: Environmentalists, Engineers, and
Air Quality in America, 1881–1951.* Baltimore, 1999

Stromquist, Shelton. "The Crucible of Class: Cleveland Politics and the Origins of
Municipal Reform in the Progressive Era." *Journal of Urban History* 23 (January
1997): 192–220

Tax, Meredith. *The Rising of the Women: Feminist Solidarity and Class Conflict,
1880–1917.* New York, 1980

Teaford, Jon. *The Unheralded Triumph: City Government in America, 1870–1900.*
Baltimore, 1984

———. "*Finis* for Tweed and Steffens: Rewriting the History of Urban Rule."
Reviews in American History 10 (1982): 133–49

Terborg-Penn, Rosalyn. "African American Women and the Vote: An Overview."
In Ann D. Gordon, ed. *African American Women and the Vote, 1837–1965.*
Amherst, MA, 1997

Thelen, David. "Urban Politics Beyond Bosses and Reformers." *Reviews in American History* 7 (1979): 406–12

Thompson, Mildred I. *Ida B. Wells-Barnett: An Exploratory Study of an American
Black Woman, 1893–1930.* Volume 15 in Darlene Clark Hine, ed. *Black Women
in U.S. History.* Brooklyn, NY, 1990

Tilly, Louise. "Gender, Women's History, and Social History." *Social Science History* 13 (Winter 1989): 439–62

Tingley, Donald F. *The Structuring of a State: The History of Illinois, 1899–1928.*
Urbana, 1980

Trattner, Walter. *From Poor Laws to Welfare State.* New York, 1979

Tuttle, William. *Race Riot: Chicago in the Red Summer of 1919.* New York, 1970

Tyler, Pamela. *Silk Stockings and Ballot Boxes: Women and Politics in New Orleans,
1920–1963.* Athens, GA, 1996

Vale, Lawrence J. *From the Puritans to the Projects: Public Housing and Public
Neighbors.* Cambridge, MA, 2000

Ware, Susan. *Beyond Suffrage: Women in the New Deal.* Cambridge, MA, 1981

Watkins, T. H. *Righteous Pilgrim: The Life and Times of Harold L. Ickes, 1874–1952.* New York, 1990

Wedell, Marsha. *Elite Women and the Reform Impulse in Memphis, 1875–1915.* Knoxville, TN, 1991

Wermiel, Sara E. *The Fireproof Building: Technology and Public Safety in the Nineteenth-Century American City.* Baltimore, 2000

Wheeler, Adade Mitchell. "Conflict in the Illinois Woman Suffrage Movement of 1913." *Illinois State Historical Journal* (Summer 1983): 95–114

Wheeler, Adade Mitchell and Wortman, Marlene Stein. *The Roads They Made: Women in Illinois History.* Chicago, 1977

White, Deborah Gray. *Too Heavy a Load: Black Women in Defense of Themselves, 1894–1994.* New York, 1999

———. "The Cost of Club Work: The Price of Black Feminism." In Nancy Hewitt and Suzanne Lebsock, eds. *Visible Women: New Essays on American Activism.* Urbana, 1993

Wiebe, Robert. *Businessmen and Reform: A Study of the Progressive Movement.* Cambridge, MA, 1962

———. *The Search for Order, 1877–1920.* New York, 1967

Wille, Lois. *Forever Open, Clear, and Free: The Struggle for Chicago's Lakefront.* 2nd edition. Chicago, 1991

Williams, Marilyn Thornton. *Washing "The Great Unwashed": Public Baths in Urban America, 1840–1920.* Columbus, OH, 1991

Wright, Gwendolyn. *Moralism and the Model Home: Domestic Architecture and Cultural Conflict in Chicago, 1873–1913.* Chicago, 1980

Theses, Dissertations, Unpublished Papers

Flanagan, Maureen A. "Men, Women and the Housing Problem: Chicago Activists, 1900–1920." Paper Presented at Social Science History Association. Baltimore, 1993

———. "Women and the Urban Environment: Crossing Borders and Boundaries to Investigate a Gender Perspective." Paper presented at "The City in North America: Historical and Comparative Perspectives on Public Works and Urban Services, the Environment, and Political Culture." Mexico City, Mexico, October 2001

Hendricks, Wanda A. "The Politics of Race: Black Women in Illinois, 1890–1920." Ph.D. Dissertation, Purdue University, 1990

Jenkins, Maude. "The History of the Black Women's Club Movement in America." Ed.D. Dissertation, Columbia University, 1984

Leidenberger, Georg. "Working-Class Progressivism and the Politics of Transportation in Chicago, 1895–1907." Ph.D. Dissertation, University of North Carolina, 1995

Mason, Karen M. "Testing the Boundaries: Women, Politics, and Gender Roles in Chicago, 1890–1930." Ph.D. Dissertation, University of Michigan, 1991

Mayer, John A. "Private Charities in Chicago from 1871–1915." Ph.D. Dissertation, University of Minnesota, 1978

McCarthy, Michael. "Businessmen and Professionals in Municipal Reform: The Chicago Experience, 1887–1920." Ph.D. Dissertation, Northwestern University, 1970

Murphy, Marjorie. "From Artisan to Semi-Professional: White Collar Unionism among Chicago Public School Teachers, 1870–1930." Ph.D. Dissertation, University of California, Davis, 1981

Perry, Elisabeth Israels. "Negotiating Political Space after Suffrage: Republican Women in New York, 1917." Paper presented to the Organization of American Historians, April 1994

Ruegamer, Lana. "The Paradise of Exceptional Women: Chicago Women Reformers, 1863–1893." Ph.D. Dissertation, Indiana University, 1982

Index

DATE DUE
